THE SYSTEM IN BLACK AND WHITE

Exploring the Connections between Race, Crime, and Justice

Edited by
Michael W. Markowitz
and Delores D. Jones-Brown

PRAEGER

Westport, Connecticut
London

Library of Congress Cataloging-in-Publication Data

The system in black and white : exploring the connections between
  race, crime, and justice / edited by Michael W. Markowitz, Delores
  D. Jones-Brown.
       p.   cm.
    Includes bibliographical references and index.
    ISBN 0–275–95974–0 (alk. paper)
    1. Crime and race—United States.   2. Discrimination in criminal
justice administration—United States.   I. Markowitz, Michael W.,
1959–   .   II. Jones-Brown, Delores D.
HV6197.U5S97 2000
364′.089′00973—dc21   98–53399

British Library Cataloguing in Publication Data is available.

Library of Congress Catalog Card Number: 98–53399
ISBN: 0–275–95974–0

First published in 2000

Praeger Publishers, 88 Post Road West, Westport, CT 06881
An imprint of Greenwood Publishing Group, Inc.
www.praeger.com

Printed in the United States of America

The paper used in this book complies with the
Permanent Paper Standard issued by the National
Information Standards Organization (Z39.48–1984).

10 9 8 7 6 5 4

Copyright Acknowledgments

"The Impact of Racial Demography on Jury Verdicts in Routine Adjudication," by James P. Levine (*Criminal Law Bulletin*, Volume 33, Number 6) copyright 1998 by West Group, 375 Hudson Street, New York, NY 10014, 1-800-328-4880, reprinted by permission of West Group, from the Criminal Law Bulletin.

"A Test of the Black Subculture of Violence Thesis: A Research Note," by Liqun Cao, Anthony Adams, and Vickie J. Jensen (*Criminology*, Volume 35, Number 2, pages 367–376) reprinted by permission from the American Society of Criminology and the authors.

This book is dedicated to
our ancestors and all the people
of color
who overcame the odds.

Contents

PART IV: Racial Dimensions of Punishment and Delinquency   197

Foreword

Historian James M. McPherson tells us that in the generation before the Civil War, the American South was providing three-fourths of the world's supply of cotton (1988:39) Almost all of this cotton came into the world market as a product of slave labor. This abundant harvest from slaves was quite a trick for Southern plantations, since the importation of slaves into the United States had been outlawed since 1807. In order to sustain a productive slave economy, the internal trade in slaves developed into a vibrant industry, as was chronicled at the time by such classics as Harriet Beecher Stowe's *Uncle Tom's Cabin*, and Theodore Weld's *American Slavery as It Is*. This industry had as a central requirement the breeing of young Negroes, not only for replacement of aging stock, but also for eventual sale to newly established plantations requiring cheap labor. Of course,this meant that breeders had a special value as a commodity, and that slave families had regularly to be broken apart in order to maintain a successful slave economy. This industry was so effective that at a time when slaves in other new world economies were actually on the decrease, slave populations in the United States doubled every 26 years (Curtin, 1969; cited in McPherson, 1988: 37).

Why begin the foreword to a book about contemporary race and justice with a few facts about U.S. life 150-200 years ago? There are two reasons. The first is so obvious that it barely requires mention: the role of race in the United States cannot be understood without a recognition of the impact of the history of slavery. Today we might bemoan the prevalence of "broken families" in the African-american community, but we are dishonest if we do not also accept that the genesis of this pattern lies in the convenient practices of our nation's slave trade. A second reason is more subtle. The socio-political workings of race have always had profound implications for broader social facts of American life.For example, slave labor enabled the South to sustain a vibrant, economically impractical, plantation economy at a time when the rest of the country was experiencing social change of modernization and industrialization. In the first half of the 1800s, the Northern labor force shifted momentously from 70 percent in agricultural work to 40 percent, as the economy shifted from farms to factories, and as families shifted from production units to consumption units. The South, bolstered by slave labor, remained fettered to its agricultural moorings, with a stable 80 percent working in agriculture throughout these years, when the North went through its bracing change (McPherson: 40). It is only today, more than a century later, that the South has caught the North in its productive efficiency.

We can analyze crime and justice with these same two lenses: the obvious and the subtle. We can understand how the trading of slaves has been a force reverberating through history into today's world of race and politics. As the essays in this book show, past images of the slave and realities of slave law are still of obvious importance in understanding crime, punishment, and crime control policy in today's world.

On a more subtle note, we can also consider how the burgeoning prisonindustrial complex affects the social life of the races. Studies now show that 7% of all African-american males aged 20-40 are now incarcerated (BJS, 1997) and that an astounding 28% of this group will be sentenced to prison during their lifetimes (Bonczar and Beck, 1997); in some cities' neighborhoods up to 25% of this group is incarcerated at any given time (Lynch and Sabol, 1997). It is not hard to speculate about the collateral consequences of this unprecedented concentration of imprisonment among a small percentage of our society.

Thus we study race in order to understand ourselves, our history, and our current circumstances. The authors in this volume convince us, in their various essays, that if we want to understand our crime and justice of the present, we must comprehend race as a defining force within it. This is an impressive collection of arguments, coming together to make the point that race, crime, and justice are inextricably linked in today's world. The knowledgeable scholar in justice must seek to understand in all its fullness, that link. This volume goes a great distance in assisting scholars in achieving that understanding.

Todd R. Clear
Associate Dean and Professor
School of Criminology and Criminal Justice
Florida State University

REFERENCES

Bonczar, Thomas P. and Allen J. Beck. *Lifetime Likelihood of Going to State or Federal Prison.* Bureau of Justice Statistics, U.S. Department of Justice (March, 1997).

Bureau of Justice Statistics Prisoners in 1996. Washington, DC: U.S.Department of Justice (1997).

Curtin, Philip D. *"The Atlantic Slave Trade."* (Madison, 1969).

Crime Policy Report, The Urban Institute State Policy Center, Washington,DC (August,1997).

Lynch, James P. and William J. Sabol. Did Getting Tougher on Crime Pay?

McPherson, James M. *The Battle Cry of Freedom: The Civil War Era.* NY: Oxford (1988).

Preface

The American landscape has been shaped throughout our history by a number of factors and forces. Two of the most significant have involved our reactions to both the recognition of "difference" and the proliferation of deviance. Both have come to the forefront of public attention and scrutiny in this century, particularly in the decade of the 1960s. The focus on the need for racial equality became a national goal through the efforts of those involved in the Civil Rights movement. Likewise, President Johnson's efforts to build a "Great Society" led to the conceptualization of crime as a pervasive anomaly in an otherwise successful social experiment. What is less easily explained, however, is how these two seemingly unrelated phenomena came to be linked in our national consciousness. Inherently, nothing about race or crime suggests any connection or causal relationship. Yet, for many, the assumption that the two are somehow associated has become a destructive part of "common sense."

This book is dedicated to the scientific analysis of the nexus between race and crime in America, not to support erroneous assumptions but rather to eliminate them. While the contributions to this volume are diverse in emphasis and approach, they all share certain qualities that can be viewed as foundational assumptions of the text. First, each chapter subscribes to the belief that race, as a singular biological factor, does not predispose any group toward certain types of behavior. Thus seen as a socially or culturally created phenomenon, the issue of race is described as a factor that affects how the actions of certain groups in America come to be defined as "crime" and how the collective society reacts to such definitions. From this critical perspective, each chapter presents scientific research designed to both challenge long-held assumptions and pose new questions regarding diversity and crime in the American context. Second, the volume deals almost exclusively with issues related to African Americans and criminal justice.

This emphasis is intentional, not to exclude or diminish the experiences of other minority groups in America but rather to highlight the justice challenges that still exist for African Americans in a society that claims to have solved its racist problems long ago. A final assumption of all contributions to this text is the recognition of the need for meaningful discourse and social change. The problems discussed herein are complex, having strong and deep roots in our national heritage. They will not be easily solved. However, the contributors to this volume share a commitment to the development of insight and understanding that can begin real progress toward changing the face of crime and the system it generates.

The book itself is divided into four parts, each addressing a compelling area of study and research in the field. Part I deals with the role of "theory" in defining the problem of crime in racial terms. In Chapter 1 Michael W. Markowitz presents an argument for the development of criminological theory that recognizes the significance of race as a factor that shapes both individual understandings of action as well as society's collective response to crime. This is followed by Paul Knepper's insightful analysis into the weaknesses inherent in our current methods of defining race for research purposes. Chapter 3 presents Becky L. Tatum's research into the significance of skin color, even among blacks, as a factor affecting definitions of, and reactions to, crime and is followed by Liqun Cao, Anthony Troy Adams, and Vicki J. Jensen's thorough critique of the long-assumed existence of a "black" subculture of violence in America.

Part II of the book presents six chapters analyzing various aspects of the role of race in shaping law enforcement responses to crime. Steven R. Cureton's review presents a compelling argument for an integrated approach to understanding the theoretical underpinnings of police action toward blacks. This is followed by Helen Taylor Greene's analysis of the various factors that contribute to race-based differences in the use of police violence. Chapter 7 presents H. Bruce Pierce's research on the potential of the Rodney King/Reginald Denney videotapes as a vehicle for police training in the use of violence. The controversial practice of police "profiling" of minorities is the subject of Scott L. Johnson's chapter, which is followed by Ramona Brockett's insightful analysis of the evolution of the police role in America following the passage of the Thirteenth Amendment. Daniel Kolodziejski, John Stilwell, Kimberly Torchiana, and Michael W. Markowitz in the final chapter in this section present an empirical analysis of racial differences in perceptions of the appropriateness of police conduct.

Part III of the text focuses on the American court system and the extent to which its function is shaped by racial issues. Delores D. Jones-Brown presents her research in Chapter 11 on the evolution of race as a legal construct and its impact on processes of justice in America. The two O. J. Simpson trials serve as the backdrop for James P. Levine's analysis of the nexus between the racial composition of juries and their verdicts and is followed by Darren E. Warner's review of research on the impact of race and ethnicity on criminal sentencing.

The final chapter in this section is Norma Manatu-Rupert's compelling assessmentof the link between media images of black women in America and prosecutions for crimes against them.

The last section of the book presents five unique contributions addressing the issues of punishment and delinquency in racial terms. In Chapter 15, Evelyn Gilbert uses the sanction of restitution to illustrate the racial disparity that often exists in the disposition of punishments. This is followed by Annette M. Girondi and Michael W. Markowitz's finding that jails, like America's prisons, experience significant workforce divisions based on race, divisions that impede both the function and the productivity of correctional institutions. In Chapter 17, Janice Joseph presents a thorough analysis questioning the "color blindness" of the juvenile justice enterprise in America, followed by Philip W. Harris, Peter R. Jones, and Jamie J. Fader's timely research on drug abuse and race in a delinquent population. The book concludes with Zelma Weston-Henriques and Delores Jones-Brown's unique assessment of America's prisons as "safehavens" for women of color.

For the readers of this text, it is our hope that the concepts and conclusions it presents will challenge long-held assumptions and spark new debates on these significant issues. For the student, these readings can serve as a tool for broadening understanding of the complex interplay of justice and race in the American landscape. For the scholar, this research can and should generate further study of relevant issues, thus expanding our knowledge of the social significance of race and the system of justice it affects. For our discipline, this work is intended to represent a clear statement of the need for meaningful acknowledgment and change of the inequities race creates in our system. Until this occurs, the debate will go on.

Part I

Race and the Study of Crime

Chapter 1

Theoretical Explanations of the Nexus between Race and Crime

Michael W. Markowitz

INTRODUCTION

The problem of crime has captured the attention of American society in a manner unlike few other issues. While the overall numbers have dropped during the last few years, Americans still remain fearful of the disintegrating effects of this phenomenon on our collective sense of stability and safety. Nowhere are these effects more vividly displayed than in those urban communities inhabited predominantly by African Americans. "Black-on-black" crime (as it has been labeled) remains an oppressive social problem, while homicide has become the leading cause of death among young black males in America. Despite the plaguing nature of these social facts, only recently have mainstream criminologists undertaken a thorough effort aimed at dealing with this phenomenon. Sadly, in this era of an emphasis on crime control, this effort has taken the form of punitive punishments aimed at long-term incapacitation. While the short-term returns of this endeavor seem pleasing to its supporters, the burdens it places on the criminal justice system are enormous. In addition, criminologists and demographers alike are suggesting that these returns will be short-lived.

The challenge this dilemma places before those who study the nexus of race and crime is compelling. While the social impact of any criminal justice policy or procedure must be assessed along a variety of relevant dimensions, a central component of such an assessment must be a critique of the theoretical assumptions that underlie the phenomenon in question. A seemingly elementary, yet significant, observation in this regard is that the success or failure of our social interventions rests, to a considerable extent, on the quality of scientific knowledge from which such interventions proceed. To clearly understand the phenomenon of crime committed by African Americans, the theoretical scientist must ask two significant questions: first, why, until very recently, has the singular significance of race been ignored as a relevant explanatory factor in the domain of criminological theory;

and second, what ontological foundations must be recognized for a useful theory of crime committed by blacks to be developed?

This chapter proposes answers to these questions by addressing them as interrelated phenomena. The first of these phenomena relates to the fundamental assumptions about crime that characterized the development of American criminology for much of this century. The impact of these assumptions upon the development of scientific knowledge is shown to have created a theoretical mindset that obscured the significance of race as a singular factor in the genesis of crime. Once these misinterpretations have been identified, the focus shifts to the proposal of a theoretical model that acknowledges the role of race in the complex interplay of the social structure. Affecting both the individual and the environment, criminal behavior is defined as the product of a series of dynamic interactions, with race serving as a central defining factor in these processes. The chapter concludes with a discussion of the potential of such a model for continued development of criminological theory along such integrative and socially realistic lines. I thus begin with a discussion of the selective focus of mainstream criminology.

CRIMINOLOGICAL THEORY AND ITS RECOGNITION OF RACE

The evolution of modern criminological theory has displayed a clear path toward the recognition of certain factors as relevant to an understanding of the genesis of criminality. Individual "free will," and the more structural elements of one's social class position have been heavily explored by criminologists. Only recently, however, has research into crime causation expanded to include study of the singular significance of race as a factor relevant to a comprehensive explanation of crime. Our path to this revelation, however, has been a long one. For example, early classical scholars saw crime to be the result of rational choices made by individuals who perceived deviance to be the more beneficial behavioral choice (viz., Bentham [1789] 1994). By the nineteenth century, scientific research in this area had shifted to the biological organism and the extent to which criminality was predetermined by one's physiology (Lombroso 1876). As the century drew to a close, the main thrust of criminological research was shifting to a focus on the role played by society in the shaping of criminal behavior (viz., Durkheim [1893] 1984).

While diverse in their perspectives, European scholars shared an implicit assumption with regard to deviance. This assumption portrayed the structures of society as inherently positive, working toward the goal of the survival and progress of the social collective. Crime, then, was seen as the product of deviant socialization within an environment designed to promote the contrary, and the responsibility for such deviance was laid squarely, albeit implicitly, at the feet of the individual. This "structural functional" view of the social order became a popular foundation for American criminologists as well, who embraced this assumption as they engaged in research aimed at explaining our own burgeoning social problems.

The changes occurring in American society as a result of industrialization and massive waves of immigration led twentieth-century sociologists to adopt the same "structural-functional" perspective as their European predecessors (Taylor, Walton & Young 1973). This focus led American criminologists to draw important conclusions with regard to the inherent causes of such change. In particular, two themes seemed to dominate mainstream research on crime for most of the century. The first maintained that a perceived loss of cultural homogeneity lay at the root of urban, social problems (Park, Burgess & McKenzie 1925). Emanating primarily from work conducted at the University of Chicago, this perspective suggested that deviance (and, by implication, crime) resulted from the clash of divergent systems of values and that behavioral choices made in such situations would reflect such conflict (Sutherland 1939; Shaw & McKay 1931, 1942). The solution to the problem therefore seemed simple to those criminologists who extended theory into social policy. By "Americanizing" immigrant groups, the cultural divergence that fostered the deviance in the first place would be assimilated into a melting pot of conformity. The massive "Chicago Area Project" stemmed from the work of Shaw and McKay and sought to instill much-needed conformist values into diverse immigrant groups settled in urban areas (Snodgrass 1976).

The second dominant theme of this century emphasized the significance of social opportunities in the development of individual behavior. As a principal architect of this perspective, Robert K. Merton (1938) suggested that the inordinate emphasis in American society on the attainment of desired symbols of "success" could induce an individual to venture beyond the boundaries of conformity when access to such symbols is blocked. Building upon the Durkheimian ([1897] 1951) concept of "anomie", Merton identified the effects of "societal strain": a pressure toward deviance resulting from goal frustration. Subsequent adherents to this perspective have suggested that such frustration begins in the classroom and stems from the denial of socially approved forms of status (Cohen 1955), as well as the notion that the processes of socialization among such disaffected youth create illegitimate as well as legitimate social structures (Cloward & Ohlin 1960). A prolific research tradition, this perspective has prompted the development of social improvement initiatives (e.g., the massive "Mobilization for Youth" program in New York [viz., Helfgot 1981]), as well as recent theories that have extended the effects of societal "strain" beyond the boundaries of the disadvantaged (Messner & Rosenfeld 1994).

While competing in their respective assumptions about the nature of social structure, both traditions maintained a simplistic view of the complexity of the social environment. The concept of *behavioral stratification* is assumed to be dichotomous in nature, that is, having two possible manifestations—that of the conformist to traditional American values versus that of the deviant. Likewise, both perspectives assume a similar dichotomy with regard to *group stratification*. Here, the distinction is between the values and socially desired trappings of the middleclass, as opposed to the socially devalued milieus of the lower classes. The biases inherent in this latter assumption are clearly established by contributors to both perspectives, whether it be Albert Cohen's recognition of the dominance of middle-class values in American schools (1955: 119) or Walter Miller's (1958) identification of the lower-class culture as the breeding ground for gang delinquency.

The negative impact of these assumptions on diverse groups becomes apparent when we consider the evolution of social policy that has proceeded from their foundation. Programs like the "Chicago Area Project" and "Mobilization for Youth" assumed a generic formula for assimilation and advance into American society. This formula centered on the simplistic notion of uniformity with regard to the immigrant experience, as well as the eradication of poverty as the sole impediment to the advance of disfranchised groups (Snodgrass 1976; Helfgot 1981). When the programs failed to push all groups up the status ladder, the blame was placed on those groups that failed, rather than on the faulty assumptions undergirding the programs themselves. This fact is particularly compelling with regard to African Americans. LaFree and Russell (1993: 275) note that early criminologists perpetuated widespread discrimination and stereotype against African Americans by attributing black crime to a perceived biological inferiority in the race as a whole. As mainstream criminology proliferated, disproportionate rates of offending among blacks still did not prompt researchers to thoroughly explore the uniqueness of race in the development of theory and its application to practice (276). Notable as an exception to this trend, however, was the work of Thorsten Sellin ([1930] 1988), who identified discriminatory treatment in the criminal justice system as a possible factor explaining the observed differences in question.

By the 1970s, a more eclectic trend in criminology paved the way for researchers to recognize the role played by a variety of social factors in the shaping of crime. Included in this diversity was the observation by a group of notable scholars that the study of race consciousness held significant potential for enhancing our understanding of criminal deviance. LaFree and Russell (1993: 279) note that, despite the call by some social scientists for the abandonment of a racial focus in criminological studies (viz., Wilson 1984), the compelling need for such analysis becomes evident when we consider official data on the reality of crime and victimization. For example, the U.S. Centers for Disease Control (1990) has reported that homicide has become the leading cause of death for black males between the ages of 15 and 24. Likewise, the Bureau of Justice Statistics reports that a likely scenario for the future (if current trends continue) will involve 1 in every 21 African American young men dying as a result of homicide, many at the hands of an assailant who is also black (1985: 8). Recent studies have also found that the disproportionate number of blacks who are imprisoned or otherwise involved with the correctional end of the criminal justice system is an ongoing (and increasing) social problem (viz., Langan 1991).

The observation of these trends in crime and punishment led criminologists to call for a *race-conscious* approach to the study of these social dynamics. LaFree, Drass & O'Day (1992) have noted that the failure to address the singularity of race in criminological studies has the potential to add further obscurity to an understanding of the root causes of crime. Likewise, Georges-Abeyie (1989) has observed that such failure can be found in the very theories that seek to explain the phenomenon as a whole. These conclusions and others like them support Russell's (1992) call for the development of a "black criminology." More than just research that focuses on race, a black criminology is seen as a paradigmatic approach to the study of crime, that explores concepts and variables that depart from the traditional domain of criminological research (1992: 673).

As an elaboration of Russell's proposal, the first logical step in the construction of this paradigm would seem to involve the development of social/behavioral theory that accurately and comprehensively recognizes the significance of race in relation to the phenomenon of crime. Avoiding the mistakes and simplifications of the past will require the specification of a theoretical model that operates on a number of analytical levels. Such a model must define the ontological parameters that encompass the varied dimensions of criminality among the racially diverse, and it must then endeavor to describe and explain those dimensions in a logical and scientifically useful manner. The remainder of this chapter represents a first step in this direction and begins with a discussion of the metatheoretical ground rules for such discourse.

THE THEORETICAL NEXUS BETWEEN RACE AND CRIME

To elaborate a comprehensive theory connecting race and crime, it is first necessary to specify the grand assumptions that define our domain of analysis and inquiry. To do so, we must begin at the level of metatheory by defining the environmental principles that shape the phenomenon under study. First among these is the recognition that an adequate theoretical model in this regard must emphasize the social nature of human behavior. While the psychological component of any action is essential to its explanation, when our subject matter is the more macrosocial concepts of race, racism, and crime, our level of analysis must be framed within the confines of the social context. Moreover, it must be clearly established what assumptions are to guide our understanding of the nature of human social relations. Here, we must choose between the competing assumptions of *harmony* and *discord* as explanatory frameworks for society. While a rich tradition exists in social theory emanating from the functionalist perspective (Parsons 1951), critical criminologists have argued that crime, like most other social phenomena, is the result of conflict between those who possess valued resources and commodities and those who struggle for them (Taylor et al. 1973). With nearly a century of criminological research to serve as a guidepost, useful theory regarding race and crime must acknowledge the struggle for survival that characterizes the lives of most criminals and the conflict that sustains that strugle.

Meaningful theory must also clearly define the levels of analysis to which its principles are to be directed. Here I refer to the distinction between macro-and microlevels of social interaction that occupy distinct domains within the realm of theory. The model to be proposed here must strive toward the ambitious goal of embracing both, as the connections between race and crime can be thoroughly explained only through such a comprehensive approach. The evolution of criminology is replete with examples of theories that have emphasized the preeminence of social structures in the determination of behavior (viz., Miller 1958; Hirschi 1969; Gottfredson & Hirschi 1990). The weakness in explanatory power of these models is shared by those perspectives that have adopted a more radically relativist view of interaction and crime (viz., Lemert 1951; Goffman 1963).

The approach to be undertaken here must be one of comprehensive elaboration and application. If the dynamics of social behavior are to be adequately explained in all their complexity, then the model that explains them must be similarly complex. While this stance flies in the face of the traditional emphasis in theory building on "parsimony," researchers have suggested that continued adherence to such unrealistic guidelines is threatening to the meaningful progress of social theory (Manicas & Secord 1983; Rigsby 1993).

For the theoretical task at hand, I refer to an earlier work (Markowitz 1996) in which an explanatory   model of criminal behavior was proposed that characterized such behavior as the product of multiple levels of social structure and interaction. Beginning with an emphasis on *contextualization*, this ecological model stresses the importance of defining behavior within the framework of an existing sociocultural setting (59). Context, in turn, is determined by analyzing the relevant levels of the social system in which individual interactions occur. Encompassing *micro-level* phenomena (those most immediate and influential domains of interaction, e.g., the family, the classroom, the peer group, etc.), *intermediate* structures (broader social networks that involve the individual by uniting more relative environments e.g., the school, the community, etc.), and *macroenvironments* (complex social structures that represent an overarching societal framework, i.e., the domain in which collective definitions of criminal deviance are maintained and enforced), the social context also reflects the effects of history by recognizing the evolution of all forms of social interaction and phenomena (59–60).

A second and equally significant level of focus for this model emphasizes the role of the individual in the production of social action. Unlike the "passive" portrayal of the actor in most criminological theory (viz., Shaw & McKay 1942; Cohen 1955), the individual here is seen as an active agent who both produces and reproduces behavior within an interactive environment of social development. Similarly affected by both systemlevel and history, the individual is the creative force within the social environment whose synergistic action within a framework of context establishes, changes, and/or perpetuates behavior as well as its social ramifications (Markowitz 1996: 61). This reflexive relationship with structure can be seen to create patterns of conduct, as well as to juxtapose such patterns against a broader framework with contrasting qualitative dimensions. When the aforementioned portrayal of social interaction as conflictual and power-based is applied, an explanation of criminal behavior can take shape from an application of these principles.

In light of these dynamics of both individual action and social structure, the social processes by which an act comes to be viewed as criminal deviance can be more clearly outlined. As mentioned, both the individual and his or her social network are interactively linked in dynamic processes of evolution. In traditional sociological terms, "norms" and "values" evolve at all levels of structure as collective representations of what is considered acceptable and unacceptable behavior in that context. Such definitions can be seen to evolve over time and to impact on the individuals and structures contained within (61).

As the level of social structure grows increasingly more complex, so norms of conduct come to reflect a more formalized array of interests and social concerns. In line with a synergistic portrayal of social interaction, individual behavior within these interrelated levels of context will evoke a reverberating series of social responses that impact not only the individual but also the social structure itself. At the most complex structural level (i.e., that of "society") the formalization of normative standards will create the strongest social response. In this context, we refer to "laws" and the formal responses to their violation that take their form in the criminal justice system.

At the individual level, social action is seen to occur within settings of social context that grow ever more complex. For the developing person, individual understanding of "right" and "wrong" develops through processes of interaction within these levels of context. The influence of context is seen to be the greatest (i.e., have the strongest impact upon the individual) at the "microstructural" level, as it is here that individual norms and values are communicated and internalized over time. Likewise, at this level the impact of such norms is reflected in the quality of behavior manifested by the individual and responded to by others in various social settings. If the normative quality of the microstructure is such that it influences the individual to act in a contrasting way with those values maintained at more complex social levels, then it is likely that the structural reverberation created by such action will result in its definition at the more complex level as some form of deviance. If the behavior in question is such that it is formally proscribed by law, then it will come to be defined as "crime" or criminal deviance (62).

For the individual, such action will evoke responses from the social environment. At the most immediate social level, these responses will serve to either reinforce or amend the behavior in question, setting the stage for further social action by the individual. Thus, as such processes occur repeatedly over time, stable patterns of behavior emerge as the phenomena of action, reaction, internalization, and further action serve to shape the developing person's sense of "self" and the behaviors associated with it.

In light of the fact that macrostructural responses to actions formally defined as deviance often take the shape of formalized punishment, negative social reactions of this kind can be seen to follow the same patterns described before, namely, feeding back to the individual for internalization. Recognizing that the most immediate contextual level of interaction will have the strongest impact upon the quality of individual behavior, negative reactions at more complex social levels will thus be counterbalanced by the "reception" of such behavior in the more relative social environments. Thus, criminal deviance can occur (and be legitimated) as individual action, despite its proscription at broader contextual levels of society.

The phenomenon of crime is therefore portrayed as individual action that has been defined as deviance at the broadest social levels. Such definitions can reflect collective norms and values or can represent the interests of those with the social power to define conduct as right or wrong. For the individual actor, this process of definition sets the broader contextual stage for a social reception of his or her behavior. The extent to which such action stands in contrast with macrosocietal standards determines how such conduct is defined (i.e., as conformity or crime) and how society responds to it. Despite such preexisting standards, individual behavior remains the product of interactions between the individual and his or her immediate social context. The normative quality of this context (itself evolving through interactions with the broader social levels that encompass it) is therefore an equal partner with the individual in the production of social action and in establishing stable patterns of behavior (62).

Applying this perspective to the phenomenon of race and crime in America requires a consideration of certain social and historical facts that have shaped the quality of the context of American culture. At the structural level, race is a significant defining factor in the nature of social relations, due, in part, to the negative impact of centuries of slavery on the evolution of African Americans, both collectively and individually (Rodriguez 1998). Surviving a heritage of involuntary immigration has been attributed to the development of a collective social identity among people of color that opposes the assumptions and institutions perceived as responsible for pervasive subjugation and exclusion (Fordham & Ogbu 1986). By the same token, the dominant culture of American society has done little in the last three decades to dispel the specter of racial disharmony. As part of what they define as the "racial state," Omi and Winant (1986) argue that the neoconservative revolution of the 1980s has served to reinstitutionalize racist practices through more covert forms of political and legal social policy, thus using the gains of the Civil Rights movement to neutralize any effective efforts at bridging the racial divide in America.

Within this broad social framework of racial disharmony and institutionalized divisions, crime can therefore be portrayed as, first, a structural occurrence, historically defined as a racial phenomenon through the effects of such macrocontextual factors. Crime must therefore not be analyzed in color-blind terms, as its character in this society has been clearly defined in terms of race. Consider the reactions of the public and the police to Susan Smith's contention that a black man had stolen her car and kidnapped her children. After dozens of African American men had been rousted by police, it was learned that her story was nothing more than a cover-up of her own acts of infanticide. In the aftermath, few focused on the willingness of society to accept her version of events, but the fact of its acceptance indicates the overall normative framework within which blacks and whites have come to understand criminal deviance.

At the more relative levels of behavioral development, insight can be drawn from perspectives that have described the criminal act as the result of interactions between individuals and sectors of society (Matthews & Young 1992). Here, it is useful to suggest that criminality ultimately proceeds from an individual identity shaped in *socioracial* terms and can be described as a behavioral transaction situated in a social context characterized by racially defined values, actions, and reactions.

The first component of this construct has already been described, namely, the broader social environment in which the quality and interpretation of behavior have taken on racial meaning. In such a climate, criminality must be seen as individual behavior that has been defined in similar racial terms. The perpetrator in such transactions is therefore both the author and the product of socialization experiences that have attached racial meaning to the actions involved. The victim's role in the construction of this transaction has been shaped through racialized socialization as well, with subsequent structural reverberations to the criminal act varying with regard to the characteristics of the victim (and the perpetrator) involved. The patterns of behavior that result from interactions within a racially defined context will therefore contribute to the development of a *socioracial identity* for the individuals involved, as well as the social groups they represent. Such an identity encompasses not only motivations for the initial criminal action but also collective responses to various levels of societal reaction. Understanding the race of the principals involved in a crime can therefore serve as a guidepost for exploring the extent to which an identity shaped through racialized socialization contributes to both the criminal act and society's responses to it.

This concept has significant heuristic value in that it portrays race as a central, yet not a determining, factor in the genesis of crime. Rather than a mistaken focus on the power of race to direct individual behavior, this approach suggests that the very context in which social behavior occurs comprises of qualitative assumptions about skin color. These assumptions are seen to affect the interpretations of social behavior in relation to the race of those involved. When these processes are situated within the context of American society (an environment characterized by power relations and racially defined group evolution), the roles and motivations of the perpetrator and victim of crime can be seen to evoke significantly different responses from society based on their respective races. This assumption allows for the theoretical exploration of race as a dynamic factor shaping the individual's identity through actions that both create and reinforce structural perceptions and responses to the actors involved.

THE SOCIORACIAL IDENTITY: POTENTIAL AND PITFALLS

The general theoretical outline just presented paves the way for the development of a useful research tradition that explores the significance of race in criminality in a unique fashion. Rather than seeing race as a deterministic factor that predisposes individuals to one type of behavior or another, the model proposed here portrays its relevance in dynamic terms, shaping both the individual and his or her environment. From this perspective, the phenomenon of criminal behavior can be understood as a developmental product of socialization, the nature of which is affected by institutionalized assumptions regarding skin color. The outline of this model presented here is necessarily vague, as the task of specific definition and operationalization must follow one study at a time. By developing a clear research agenda based on these principles, criminologists can direct specific theoretical and empirical efforts toward the myriad of factors involved. More than simply attempting to define the motivation of the individual offender, research in this effort can center on the interplay between individual and community and the extent to which such interactions are affected by race and produce criminality in various contexts. Likewise, the more macrodimensions of social context and justice administration can be explored to assess their role in the development and perpetuation of crime defined in racial terms. The key here is to focus on a dynamic portrayal of the processes involved, thus avoiding the static tendency that has dominated much of the research on race and crime.

Accomplishing such efforts will require a change in the research orientation of those who study crime. The long-held commitment of social scientists to quantitative methodologies, while useful, assembles only part of the puzzle related to the complexities of human action. If we are to understand the role of race in crime in a unique way, then we must commit the time and energies necessary to measure this phenomenon in all its complexity. Ethnographic studies, participant analyses, and longitudinal designs must be incorporated into this research tradition to answer the questions of why and how not addressed through surveys and crime data. Only through such a committed effort will the subtle dimensions of the social impact of race on crime be explored and understood.

A final concern centers on the nature of the political environment of the late twentieth-century academy. The commitment to a comprehensive understanding of race relevance has waned in recent years. While a new generation of scholars is effectively arguing for a renewal of interest in the topic (viz., Russell 1992), meaningful advance in our state of knowledge will come only when the political climate of research supports it. Nowhere is this more compelling than with regard to the study of the nexus between race and crime. For a theoretical perspective of this kind to be pursued thoroughly, considerable support must come from those agencies and institutions with the capacity to fund such efforts. Only then can thorough research proposals take form, and the knowledge they produce provide meaningful understanding and insight. The challenge is clear; accomplishing the goal awaits us.

REFERENCES

Bentham, J. [(1789) 1994]. "An Introduction to the Principles of Morals and Legislation." In J. Jacoby (ed.), *Classics of Criminology* 80–83. Prospect Heights, IL: Waveland Press.

Bureau of Justice Statistics. (1985). *The Risk of Violent Crime: Department of Justice Special Report*. Washington, DC: U.S. Government Printing Office.

Cloward, R. A. and L. E. Ohlin. (1960). *Delinquency and Opportunity: A Theory of Delinquent Gangs*. New York: Free Press.

Cohen, A. K. (1955). *Delinquent Boys*. New York: Free Press.

Durkheim, E. (1897 [1951]). *Suicide: A Study in Sociology.* New York: Free Press.

———. (1893 [1984]). *The Division of Labor in Society.* New York: Free Press.

Fordham, S. and J. U. Ogbu (1986). "Black Students' School Success: Coping with the Burden of 'Acting White.'" *Urban Review* 18(3): 176–206.

Georges-Abeyie, D. (1989). "Race, Ethnicity, and the Spatial Dynamic: Toward a Realistic Study of Black Crime, Crime Victimization, and Criminal Justice Processing." *Social Justice* 16: 35–54.

Goffman, E. (1963). *Stigma: Notes on the Management of Spoiled Identity.* Englewood Cliffs, NJ: Prentice-Hall.

Gottfredson, M. and T. Hirschi (1990). *A General Theory of Crime.* Stanford, CA: Stanford University Press.

Helfgot, J. H. (1981). *Professional Reforming.* Lexington, MA: Lexington Books.

Hirschi, T. (1969). *Causes of Delinquency.* Berkeley, CA: University of California Press.

LaFree, G., K. Drass, and P. O'Day (1992). "Race and Crime in Post-War America: Determinants of African American and White Rates, 1957–1988." *Criminology* 30: 157–188.

——— and K. K. Russell. (1993). "The Argument for Studying Race and Crime." *Journal of Criminal Justice Education* 4(2): 273–289.

Langan, P. A. (1991). *Race and Prisoners Admitted to State and Federal Institutions, 1926–1986.* Washington, DC: U.S. Government Printing Office.

Lemert, E. M. (1951). *Social Pathology.* New York: McGraw-Hill.

Lombroso, C. (1876). *L'Uomo Delinquente.* Milan: Hoepli.

Manicas, P. and P. F. Secord (1983). "Implications for Psychology of the New Philosophy of Science." *American Psychologist* 6: 399–413.

Markowitz, M. W. (1996). "Synthesizing Modernist and Post-Modernist Criminology: Toward the Development of an 'Ecological Theory of Criminal Deviance." *National Social Science Perspectives Journal* 10(1): 51–66.

Matthews, R. and J. Young. (1992). "Reflections on Realism." In J. Young and R. Matthews (eds.), *Rethinking Criminology: The Realist Debate* 1–23. London: Sage.

Merton, R. K. (1938). "Social Structure and Anomie." *American Sociological Review* 3: 672–682.

Messner, S. F. and R. Rosenfeld (1994). *Crime and the American Dream.* Belmont, CA: Wadsworth.

Miller, W. B. (1958). "Lower Class Culture as a Generating Milieu for Gang Delinquency." *Journal of Social Issues* 14: 5–19.

Omi, M. and H. Winant. (1986). *Racial Formation in the United States: From the 1960's to the 1980's.* New York: Routledge.

Park, R. E., E. Burgess, and R. D. McKenzie. (1925). *The City.* Chicago: University of Chicago Press.

Parsons, T. (1951). *The Social System.* Glencoe, IL: Free Press.

Rigsby, L. C. (1993). "Toward an Articulation of Research Traditions in the Sociology of Education." Unpublished manuscript.

Rodriguez, L. J. (1998). "The Color of Skin Is the Color of Crime" In C. R. Mann and M. S. Zatz (eds.), *Images of Color, Images of Crime* 130–133. Los Angeles, CA: Roxbury.

Russell, K. K. (1992). "Development of a Black Criminology and the Role of the Black Criminologist." *Justice Quarterly* 9(4): 667–683.

Sellin, T. ([1930] 1988). "The Negro and the Problem of Law Observance and Administration in the Light of Social Research." In S. Meyers and M. Simms (eds.), *The Economics of Race and Crime* 71–80. New Brunswick, NJ: Transaction.

Shaw, C. R. and H. D. McKay (1942). *Juvenile Delinquency and Urban Areas: A Study of Delinquents in Relation to Differential Characteristics of Local Communities in American Cities.* Chicago: University of Chicago Press.

———. (1931). *Social Factors in Juvenile Delinquency: Report of the Causes of Crime.* National Commission on Law Observance and Enforcement, Report No. 13. Washington, DC: U.S. Government Printing Office.

Snodgrass, J. (1976). "Clifford R. Shaw and Henry D. McKay: Chicago Criminologists." *British Journal of Criminology* 16(1): 1–19.

Sutherland, E. H. (1939). *Principles of Criminology.* Philadelphia: Lippincott.

Taylor, I., P. Walton, and J. Young (1973). *The New Criminology: For a Social Theory of Deviance.* London: Routledge and Kegan Paul.

U.S. Centers for Disease Control. (1990). "Homicide among Young Black Males—United States, 1978–1987." *Morbidity and Mortality Weekly Report* 39: 869–873.

Wilson, W. J. (1984). "The Urban Underclass." In L. W. Dunbar (ed.), *Minority Report* 75–117. New York: Pantheon.

Chapter 2

The Alchemy of Race and Crime Research

Paul Knepper

Race and crime research is founded on a paradox. Researchers have studied race and crime in search of objective social science knowledge about race and criminality and race discrimination. Yet researchers who study race and crime have noted the lack of an objective definition of race (LaFree 1995; LaFree & Russell 1993; Hawkins 1995; Mann 1993; Walker, Spohn & DeLone 1996).[1]

At the heart of the matter are the nation's crime statistics, particularly, the official system of racial classification used in crime statistics. While the inability to operationalize a key theoretical concept would ordinarily thwart the intended research activity, use of official race-crime statistics allows researchers to conduct analyses without clearly specifying the meaning of race. The races identified within national crime statistics and local court records allow researchers to look for varying levels of criminality across races and for the presence of discrimination against racial minorities. The questions of whether African Americans display a higher level of criminality, and if so, whether this is due to some characteristic of the black race or to discrimination against persons with brown skin have remained the central questions in criminology for many decades (Hawkins 1995). But do racial categories in official statistics provide an adequate basis for race and crime research?

Two views on racial classification within crime statistics have emerged. In one view, official statistics are, despite the problems of racial categorization, better than nothing. Objective data should not be suppressed because they are politically sensitive. Official race-crime statistics are needed in order to make objective social scientific statements about race and crime and to counter the uniformed speculation and fears of hate groups and others. The statistics are needed to document discrimination by the police and courts against minority populations and represent a necessary first step in the formulation of social policy designed to address inequalities (Gabor 1994; LaFree & Russell 1993; LaFree 1995). The other view charges that race-crime statistics contradict the principle of equality under law by scapegoating immigrants and reinforcing misconceptions about a genetic basis for race. The statistics do not furnish a useful basis for research because the data collection procedures render the figures unreliable and distort analyses based on them (Johnston 1994; Knepper in press).

This chapter extends the latter view of race-crime statistics to race and crime research. Official statistics do not furnish information suitable for making social scientific statements about race and crime. This is because the categories are politically contrived and not based on social science theory. This chapter describes the government's racial categorization scheme, and then identifies two primary types of research that have been derived from it. It then discusses four problem areas related to the use of official race-coded crime statistics: measurement, operationalization, objectivity, and morality.

Rather than relying on official statistics, researchers ought to create their own categories of race according to the theory to be tested and collect their own data. Only in this way can social science knowledge about race and crime be advanced. There is no statistical alchemy whereby data collected according to politically contrived categories of race can be made to yield findings suitable for making objective social scientific statements about race and crime. Research conducted with misspecified variables yields inconsistent and contradictory results that become part of the argument against inclusion and diversity.

THE OFFICIAL RACIAL CLASSIFICATION SCHEME

The primary classification scheme used in crime statistics is the scheme promulgated by the Office of Federal Statistical Policy and Standards (OFSPS), U.S. Department of Commerce. There are four official races: White, black, American Indian/Alaskan Native, and Asian and Pacific Islander and two official ethnic groups: Hispanic origin and not of Hispanic origin. OFSPS issued the scheme in 1977 as Directive No. 15, "Race and Ethnic Standards for Federal Statistics and Administrative Reporting," following a revision of the old guidelines, "Race and Color Designations in Federal Statistics," which had been issued by the Office of Management and Budget in 1952 (OFSPS 1978: 37).[2]

All federal data-collection agencies, as well as state agencies that must comply with federal record-keeping requirements, use this classification scheme. Designations based on these categories appear on birth certificates, school records, hospital records, and court records. They are used in computer databases maintained by local, state, and federal agencies and are the basis for collection and presentation of official statistics concerning education, health, and child welfare, as well as crime. The Federal Bureau of Investigation (FBI) presently uses this scheme in the nation's premier set of national crime statistics, the Uniform Crime Reports (UCR). Race data first appeared in the UCR in 1933 following the bureau's fingerprint initiative. The bureau began collecting fingerprint cards in 1932 that included age, sex, and race of arrestees along with other information. Although the categories changed several times, the UCR has followed the OFSPS scheme since 1980 (Knepper 1994).

While the categories mirror the popular division of humanity into five mutually exclusive, discrete races of white, black, red, yellow, and brown, OFSPS insists that the categories "should not be interpreted as being scientific or anthropological in nature" (OFSPS 1978: 37). There are no pure races of humankind. In fact, the majority of American Indians and African Americans and virtually all Latinos are descended from documentable multiracial genealogies (Root 1992). What criteria were used, then, to create the official categories? OFSPS category definitions include references to geography for all five groups but include cultural criteria for two (American Indian and Hispanic) and "racial" characteristics for one (black is defined as "black racial groups of Africa"). The original peoples of the Western Hemisphere included South American Indians as well as North American Indians, yet they are placed in separate categories. Mexicans, Puerto Ricans, Cubans, and persons from Central and South America, as well as Spain, are placed into a single category despite the fact that members of these groups do not identify as Hispanic but rather as Mexican, Puerto Rican, Cuban, and so on. Egyptians are placed in the white category, and Ethiopians in the black category, despite their origination on the continent of Africa (see Wright 1994: 50).

It may be that the categories mirror the way social groups have decided to define themselves. The Census Bureau insists that its categories merely reflect prevailing social definitions, not science (Usdansky 1992). But this argument ignores the reality that many Americans resist racial classification and seek to be defined in groups other than the official categories. The 1990 census included 43 racial categories and subcategories, yet the fastest growing category in the past two censuses was "other" (Spickard, Fong, & Ewalt 1995: 581).

Census categories have changed over the years in response to political pressure from various organizations. During the 1940s, for example, a protest by the Mexican government led the Census Bureau to eliminate Mexican as a separate racial category and count Mexican Americans as white (Usdansky 1992). Congress created the Hispanic category in 1976 (PL 94-311, 90 Stat. 688) and reclassified Mexican Americans in this new category along with "Americans of Spanish origin or descent." Recently, the House Committee on Census, Statistics and Postal Personnel concluded hearings on racial categories to be used for the 2000 census. The committee heard from various groups that argued that they had been misclassified. Senator Daniel K. Akaha of Hawaii, for example, argued that native Hawaiians belong to the American Indian category and not the Asian/Pacific Islander category. The Arab American Institute asked that persons of the Middle East, now categorized as white, be recognized as a separate category for Arabic peoples. The National Council of La Raza suggested that Hispanic be regarded as a race rather than an ethnic group (Wright 1994).

Race classification is the most volatile civil rights issue since de jure segregation because the categories make the policies possible. Organizations such as the Association of Multi-Ethnic Americans and Project Race have been carrying out campaigns to create a multi-or mixed-race category or allow persons to check more than one box. Leaders of African American and civil rights organizations have resisted creation of a multiracial category because it would dilute the political strength of the African Americans (Frisby 1996). Between 75 and 90 percent of those who check the "black" box on government forms could, for instance, check a "multiracial" box if available. Political conservatives have seized on the idea of a multiracial category because of its potential to undermine civil rights monitoring and affirmative action. But as the number of multiracial organizations and the number of persons who identify with the terms "mixed" continue to grow, the debate over recognition as an official category will likely increase (Gilanshah 1993).

RACE AND CRIME RESEARCH

Whether or not crime statistics ought to be broken down by race has been a major debate in Canada (Roberts 1994). In 1990, the Center for Justice Statistics released a policy statement announcing collection of race-based data as a part of the revised UCR program. In response to the furor that erupted in Toronto and elsewhere, the Justice Information Council issued a moratorium on the release of national race-crime statistics. The controversy among academic researchers, public officials, and policymakers over the usefulness of race-based crime statistics has continued.

No such debate has occurred in the United States, where race-crime information collected by federal agencies has been available to researchers for decades. Researchers looking for varying levels of criminality across racial groups have used the FBI's UCR statistics. The statistics have been used to support the idea that the black race displays a high prevalence of violent, predatory crime. The first quarterly UCR for 1933, for example, contains this statement: "Negroes constituted 23 percent of all persons whose records were received," and it says that 34 percent of those charged with homicide "were colored, and this race contributed to a correspondingly high proportion of individuals" arrested for assault, weapons charges, and gambling (UCR 1933).[3] More recently, Hindelang (1978) used national crime survey statistics to argue that overrepresentation of blacks in UCR statistics reflected their "disproportionate involvement in criminal offenses" and not "criminal justice system selection biases" (93). Hindelang contended that the question "whether and to what extent, race is related to involvement in common law personal crimes" represented "one of the most important theoretical questions facing criminology" and answered by concluding that blacks were overrepresented as offenders/arrestees for violent crimes of rape, robbery, and assault (103).

UCR statistics compare crime across races, which invites theoretical explanations based on differences between races. Yet Mann (1993) has shown that when crime rates for violent and property crime are analyzed within races, a comparably small percentage of individuals, *regardless of race*, are arrested for violent crime. When the percentage of black Americans arrested for violent crimes is compared with the percentage of blacks arrested for nonviolent crimes, the statistics suggest a different picture of violent crime. Only 7.7 percent of all blacks arrested are arrested for violent crimes. This compares with 3.3 percent of whites arrested, 3.2 percent of American Indians, and 3.8 percent of Asian Americans.

To make differences between races the focus of inquiry is to assume that races constitute distinct groups, but, in reality, the races of Americans are not monolithic. The designation "black" comprises a diverse mixture of persons of Caribbean, African, and Central and South American origin. There are black Puerto Ricans, Cubans, Virgin Islanders, Jamaicans, Haitians, Dominicans, Nigerians, Cameroonians, and South Africans.   Within each of these are populations   distinguished by culture, language, hair, and hue.   Nigerian Americans, for example, identify according to lineage as Ibo, Housa, or Yoraba (Georges-Abeyie 1989). The "black" category simply does not capture the most significant aspects of what it means to be black in the United States. "Is it not conceivable," asks Georges-Abeyie (39), "that different Black ethnic groups are more involved in extralegal and illegal activity than others, and that certain Black ethnics dominate certain criminal activities (or are believed to) and are thus more threatening than are other Black ethnics?" This question cannot be researched using official statistical categories of black and white.

Researchers interested in understanding the impact of discrimination on criminal defendants have relied on court records and other official sources. Zatz (1987) reviews five decades of research devoted to analyses of racial/ethnic bias in sentencing.   Access to databases and analytical techniques improved throughout this period.   In the 1930s, researchers plowed through "dusty piles of court records to unearth what happened to a given defendant," but beginning in the 1960s, researchers gained access to computer-based data sets that made tracking easier.   Researchers also developed new awareness of statistical limitations, including selection bias, specification error, and indirect effects, and developed new statistical models to account for cumulative disadvantage and devaluation of nonwhite victims.

Despite advances in computer-aided databases and statistical techniques, fundamental problems remain with coding and categories.   Coding of races within official records is unclear and inconsistent.   "Typically," Zatz (82) explains, "it [race/ethnicity] is coded white versus nonwhite (with all nonwhites arbitrarily lumped together) or white versus black (with all others excluded from analyses)."   In his analysis of Hispanic defendants in the Southwest, LaFree (1985) also refers to this problem. Because court records identify individuals by race according to official categories, they do not distinguish individuals of Spanish ancestry from Mexican Americans, or from Mexican nationals.   "As defined by official records," LaFree (228) explains, "Hispanics in El Paso include everyone from prominent Hispanic families, who may go back many generations in the Southwest, to recently migrated, unemployed or underemployed Mexican nationals."

In 1987, Wilbanks published his Myth of a Racist Criminal Justice System. Wilbanks' argument concerning the criminal justice system was based on a faulty premise. Wilbanks imagined a world in which a few white people discriminate consistently and uniformly against black people. Racism is far more pervasive in American society (Bell 1992). Yet Wilbanks did raise a technical challenge to discrimination researchers by calling attention to the large residual or unexplained variation in the multivariate analyses (Wilbanks 1987: 121). Wilbanks argued that the statistical models of discrimination did not fit the data, and therefore, there was no concrete evidence of discrimination. He was half right. The statistical models do leave large residual variation, but this results from misspecification of the race variable, not the absence of discrimination. One would expect a poor fit between the statistical model and the data when the data are based on categories so ambiguous in their construction that they yield meaningless and uninterpretable information.

PROBLEMS FOR RESEARCHERS

Measurement

What the official race categories actually measure is impossible to say. While the division of persons into the same categories across data sets suggests that racial groups are discrete, mutually exclusive categories, race is an elastic, fluid concept. Skin color, facial features, hair type, financial standing, way of speaking, and other aspects combine to create the races people recognize as black, white, red, yellow, and brown. Race is a matter of self-identity (what group a person chooses to identify with), social identity (what group others think a person belongs to), and legal identity (what group name appears on a person's birth certificate). Individuals, particularly members of minority populations, possess multiple racial identities. The same person may choose to identify as Dominican, be thought to be black American, and be legally identified as Hispanic.

Official racial identity, the race designated on school, health, court, and other public records, reflects some combination of self, social, and legal identity. "It seems clear," LaFree (1995: 187) explains, "that racial distinctions in most official data are probably based on a combination of common sense informed haphazardly and inconsistently by respondent self-identification." Official records contain an uncertain mixture of self-description and social identity. Sometimes the defendant is asked for his or her race; sometimes race is assigned based on language, surname, or appearance (Zatz 1987: 82).

Social identity is not a reliable basis for assignment to a category. What a person looks like or sounds like is not a reliable means of determining what race appears on the person's birth certificate or what race the person would say he or she belonged to if asked. Even those who believe in distinct races cannot determine a person's race by appearance. During the Jim Crow period, confusion over racial identity presented considerable problems for segregationists. Whites, having been mistaken for blacks, brought considerable litigation against railway carriers required by the law to seat them in separate cars (Bell 1980: 84). Even the proponents of separate but equal admitted that it was difficult to distinguish black from white. In the notorious *Plessy* case, Homer Plessy, who who was seven-eighths white, agreed to test Louisiana's Railway Accommodations Act because he appeared white. While the Court affirmed separate but equal, the U.S. Supreme Court offered its sympathy for railway employees required to assign passengers to separate cars based on their appearance. "We are not prepared to say," wrote Justice Henry Billings Brown, "that the conductor, in assigning passengers to the coaches according to their race, does not act at his peril" (*Plessy v. Ferguson* [1896]: 163 U.S. at 548–549).

Yet official crime statistics contain an unknown number of persons assigned to a category based on what category the record keeper thought the person belonged to based on the person's appearance. In the Bureau of Justice Statistics' (BJS) National Crime Victimization Survey (NCVS), the offender's race is determined by what race the victim believed to be the offender's race. Since its inception in 1973, NCVS used categories of "white," "black," and "not known/not available." This scheme is a practical necessity since victims seldom use racial descriptors other than white and black Law Enforcement Assistance Administration, [LEAA] 1976: 36). Although Hindelang noted that victims' descriptions of the racial characteristics of offenders may be affected by popular stereotypes, he asserted that "it is unlikely that biases in the victimization surveys linked to the race of the offender would be of such magnitude that the substantial overrepresentation of blacks in the offender population would disappear" (Hindelang 1978: 105). BJS statisticians, however, recognized this problem and addressed it in some detail in the first report (LEAA 1976: 35). Research has also affirmed the bureau's concerns. Schneider (1981) matched survey data with police records and found that victims overestimated the number of incidents involving black suspects in comparison with police estimates of whether the suspect was white or black.

Self-description should be the only basis for racial categorization, but it does not necessarily produce consistent assignment necessary for meaningful interpretation by researchers. LaFree (1995: 187) points out that even assuming that individuals know their ancestry and will accurately report it, there are different criteria for membership in various racial groups. Black persons with Spanish ancestry may identify as black or as Hispanic. There are also regional variations that change over time (LaFree 1995: 187).

The issue of what portion a person's ancestry must be to qualify for membership in a particular race has a long history in the United States. Unlike other slave societies, the United States has followed the "one-drop rule"—one drop of African blood qualifies a person as black. However, in some areas of South Carolina and Louisiana, persons of mixed ancestry occupied a third, intermediate class or, depending on financial status, were judged qualified for assimilation into the white class. Others "passed" as white to avoid the degradation of Jim Crow (Russell, et al. 1992). Currently, many blacks believe themselves not to be "pure" African but claim mixed ancestry. Many African Americans who identify themselves as black politically also identify as mixed, Hispanic, or Indian socially (Frisby 1996). Correspondence between self-description and official racial identity cannot be assumed.

Operationalization

Racial categories in official statistics do not provide data to explore criminality and race or racial discrimination. This is because there is a lack of fit between the theory and the data. Ideally, data collection should be theory-driven.That is, the information collected by the researchers should be collected according to specific requirements of the theory to be tested. In this way, theoretical concepts are formulated into measurable terms.

Government statistics allow researchers who find correlations between race and crime to offer an explanation for the correlation without first theorizing why race might be related to crime. Or, more specifically, researchers look for correlations between race and crime without first specifying what is meant by race. What is meant by race should be part of the theory, and the racial categories should reflect the operationalization of that theory. A researcher who presumed a biological basis for race would need to explain exactly what biological characteristic— genes, blood type, melanin—leads to differential rates of crime. Comparison groups would then need to be based on persons who differed according to the theorized biological difference—genes, blood type, melanin—and only in this way could a race effect be researched. Researchers who use government categories fail to properly operationalize the theory of race and crime; what theory emerges amounts to post hoc explanation for statistical correlations.

A similar problem plagues discrimination research. Discrimination hinges on perceived racial characteristics, not the race listed on a person's birth certificate. Official statistics permit analyses of differential outcomes based only on a person's official race, not skin color, demeanor, manner of speaking, or other characteristics that trigger biased responses. Only when the characteristics of a person's racial identity are identified can theories of discrimination be adequately tested. Researchers interested in the impact of skin color, on legal decision making would need to specify a theory of discrimination based on skin color, and then compare legal outcomes for categories of lighter- and darker-skinned persons. As it is, theories guiding discrimination research rightly postulate that skin color makes a difference in American society but then fail to investigate exactly what difference skin color makes. The result of using discrimination models with government categories produces contradictory and inconsistent findings.

Government categories simply do not allow for more realistic models of discrimination to be tested. More realistic models of discrimination are derived from the recognition of "unaware racism" or "unconscious motivation." Lawrence (1987) has developed a theory of "unconscious racial motivation." Lawrence argues that because Americans share a common historical and cultural legacy, all Americans are, to some extent, likely to attach significance to a person's race. In addition, most Americans are, unaware of their feelings and opinions about nonwhites. We do not always recognize the ways in which our cultural experience has influenced our beliefs about race or the occasions on which those beliefs affect our actions. Lawrence would apply a "cultural meaning" test to allegations of discrimination; allegedly discriminatory conduct would be examined to determine whether or not it conveys a symbolic message to which the culture attaches significance.

Lawrence's approach provides a theoretical framework for investigating institutional racism. Institutional racism or organizational discrimination can be under-

stood as discriminatory conduct that is reinforced by "well-established rules, policies, and practices of organizations" and regarded by the individuals who carry
them out as "simply part of the organization's way of doing business." The organizational environment makes possible "hidden and sometimes unintentional"
discriminatory actions "taken by persons who may not believe themselves to be
prejudiced but whose decisions continue to be guided by deeply ingrained discriminatory customs" (U.S. Commission on Civil Rights 1995). Lawrence's
approach also provides a framework for investigating "intraracial color discrimination" or "the color complex." The color complex refers to "a psychological fix-
ation about color and features that leads Blacks to discriminate against each
other." Harassment of darker-skinned blacks by lighter-skinned blacks stems
from the legacy of colonialism and the value white racism places on fair skin,
straight hair, and protruding noses. Historically, African Americans who looked
the least black and acted the most white received less harsh treatment from whites
and achieved positions of leadership within black communities (Russell, Wilson
& Hall 1992).[4]

The black and white categories within official statistics do not provide the data
necessary for testing such theories. "Since sentencing researchers rely almost
exclusively on court data, data collection and coding decisions will inevitably
shape research findings by determining the range of questions that can be
addressed" (Zatz 1987: 82). Future research on race must begin to consider such
differences (LaFree 1985: 230).

Objectivity

More than one researcher has emphasized the need for objective research into
race, criminality, and discrimination. Regrettably, no objective social scientific
statements can be made on the basis of the government's race categories. This is
because the categories are not objective anthropological, scientific, or social definitions of races but are, rather, political creations.

The concept of racial classification in place today has resulted from a legal ideology of distinct races built up over 200 years. Classification of race by the government descended directly from frameworks used during the time of slavery. The
legal concept of distinct races developed because no system of oppression based
on ancestry can operate in a social environment in which people recognize their
multiple heritages. Racial classification is a creation of government and has been
maintained by government. Both states and the federal government have coun-
tered pressures toward blurring racial distinctions with greater delineation of
racial lines.

The legal ideology of distinct races began during the slavery period. Slavery
required that diverse peoples taken from Africa's western coast lose their cultural, ethnic, and linguistic differences. Guinean and Dahomian, Ibo and Ashanti,
along with many others, became "negro," an English word derived from the
Spanish negro and the Latin niger, meaning black. According to Bennett (1993),
The first white colonists had no concept of themselves as white men, but displayed no color consciousness. White men identified themselves on legal

documents of the period as "Englishmen" or "Christians."

Bennett (1993) points out that blacks and whites had to be taught the meaning of blackness and whiteness. The institution of slavery required separation between black and white, between the category of people to be enslaved and the category of people to do the enslaving. The legal doctrine of distinct races began to take shape during the colonial period when lawmakers delineated the black and white races with attempts to prohibit miscegenation through legislation and to categorize the status of mixed offspring (Knepper 1994: 15; Diamond & Cottrol 1983: 259–266). The "two-category" pattern of race relations laid down in the eighteenth century provided the foundation for more rigid framework dividing black and white enacted in the late nineteenth and early twentieth centuries.

During the Jim Crow era, when white supremacists enacted a bewildering variety of laws requiring separation in public life, racial categories acquired their modern rigidity. State legislatures attempted to create rigid distinctions between races. In constitutions, separate school laws, antimiscegenation statutes, and other discriminatory legislation, lawmakers institutionalized the one-drop rule. State courts met challenges to these statutes by expanding the definition of blackness. The Supreme Court of Mississippi, for example, decided that "colored," as used in the separate-school provision of the state constitution, included "not only Negroes but persons of mixed blood having any appreciable amount of Negro blood" (*Moreau v. Gandich* 114 Miss.560 [1917]; Knepper 1994: 17–18).

Congress and the federal judiciary supported the state's elastic definition of race, enforcing a narrow definition of "white" to restrict immigration. During the early decades of the twentieth century, Congress enacted immigration laws designed to restrict immigration of 'inferior races" from Asia, the Pacific Islands, and Southern and Northern Europe. When challenged, federal courts responded with a narrow and exclusive definition of "white." "White person" has been construed to exclude Afghans, Arabs, Filipinos, Hawaiians, Asian Indians, and others. In Ozawa v. United States (1922), the U.S. Supreme Court ruled that a 20-year resident of California who had been born in Japan was not a "free white person" within naturalization law because state and federal courts had historically limited "white person" to "what is popularly known as the Caucasian race" (*Ozawa v. United States* 260 U.S. 178[1922]). That same year, in the case of *United States v. Bhagat Singh Thind*, the Supreme Court ruled that although the Asian Indian petitioner was a member of the "Caucasian or Aryan race" based on scientific terminology, he was not entitled to citizenship because he was not a "white person" according to the "understanding of the common man" (*United States v. Bhagat Singh Thind* 261 U.S. 404 [1922].

The slavery-based system of racial classification remains in place today because it serves a political purpose, the same purpose for which whites created it. Racial classification within crime statistics is one means of enforcing the government's classification scheme. While crime statistics broken down by race in government publications ostensibly provide objective statistics for use by discrimination researchers and others, what appears to be done for the benefit of minority populations is actually done to solidify the white majority. As Bell (1987) explains, the contradiction in constitutional law, which enshrined liberty, on one hand, and preserved slavery, on the other, is necessarily part of the American democracy. The founders realized that securing unity among northern and southern colonies meant preserving slavery; realizing the rights of Englishmen could be accomplished only by destroying the rights of Africans.

The "black" category used in official crime statistics represents African Americans as a monolithic group and begins the search for that something about the black race that leads to differential crime rates. Official statistics become a means of justifying particular crime control strategies, which have, in turn, had an adverse impact on African Americans. Tonry observes that the "justification" for "harsh drug and crime control policies," which differentially impact blacks, is "entirely political. Crime is an emotional subject and visceral appeals by politicians to people's fears and resentments are hard to counter" (Tonry 1996: 151).

Morality

Aside from arguments about the value of government racial classification as a means of furnishing data suitable for social science research, there is a separate question about whether the government ought to be classifying people by race at all. Given that the races of humankind are, as King (1981) puts it, "make-believe" to begin with, the most important questions to be answered do not have to do with explaining racial differences in crime rates but, rather, have to do with how and why race entered into crime statistics to begin with.

The first time crime statistics appear by race in government publications was in the census of 1850. A Massachusetts statistician consulted by the census board prepared a schedule for social statistics that gathered information on the nativity and color of convicted criminals in prison on June 1, 1850. The table shows the number of "foreign" and "native" criminals, along with the number of "whites" and "free colored," and the "free colored" category is subdivided into "black" and "mulatto." Census reports during the last half of the nineteenth century, however, contain very little information about the race of criminals. The few pages of figures that appear in the 1860, 1870, 1880, and 1890 censuses use categories framed around immigration: native- and foreign-born. The most extensive racial categories to appear during this period are in the 1880 and 1890 censuses. These reports contain more extensive criminal statistics due to the involvement of Frederick Wines, a prominent member of the National Prison Association, who produced a special volume for the 1890 census. But Wines did not expand racial delineations. He used the "native," "white," and "colored" categories and simply included Indians, Chinese, and Japanese as "colored" (Knepper 1994; in press).

The statistics for the early decades of the twentieth century display a new preoccupation with race. Special enumerations made in 1904, 1910, and 1923 drew sharp distinctions between prisoners according to color, race, nativity, and country of birth. A typical table produced from the 1900 census, for example, provides statistics for "white" and "colored" persons. The "white" category is divided into "native," "foreign-born," and "nativity unknown" subcategories. The "native" category is further subdivided into "native parentage," "foreign parentage," "mixed parentage," and "parentage unknown." The "colored" category is divided into Negro, Mongolian, and Indian subcategories. Commentary in the 1910 publication describes an attempt to distinguish "between 'black,' defined as covering full-blooded Negroes, and 'mulatto' defined as covering all persons not full-blooded Negroes but having some proportion or trace of Negro blood and regarded as Negroes in the community in which they live" (Knepper in press).

The categories and subcategories of race that appear in the census volumes of the early twentieth century coincided with the rise of criminal anthropology and the American eugenics movement. Casare Lombroso's *The Criminal Man*, first published in the United States in 1911, attempted to identify a criminal race according to physical characteristics that Bram Stoker later borrowed for his description of the evil Count Dracula. Lombroso wrote of the existence of "whole tribes and races more or less given to crime" and cited Africans, Orientals, Gypsies, and Jews as examples (Knepper 1994; in press). Lombroso's scientific racism was advanced in the United States by Havelock Ellis, Henry M. Boies, and August Drahms, among others. Eastern State Penitentiary in Philadelphia began publishing case studies to show that criminals constituted a distinct race in society as early as 1907 (Jenkins 1984); Indiana passed the first sterilization bill that year, and between 1911 and 1930, 33 states followed suit. Eugenicists carried out more than 60,000 sterilizations (Beckwith 1985).

Collection of statistics and the identification of "social defectives" were an essential part of the movement for institutionalization and sterilization. In 1902, there was a congressional attempt to establish a federal "laboratory for the study of criminal, pauper and defective classes." In 1907, the Harrimans, Kellogs, and Carnegies financed a Eugenics Record Office at Cold Spring Harbor, Long Island (Beckwith 1985). In 1927, the Census Bureau issued a detailed manual for compiling criminal statistics for local jails, prisons, police, courts, prosecutor, probation and parole agencies. The manual instructed the statistics to be broken down for "white," "negro," and "other" races (Knepper 1994; in press).

As criminal anthropology and eugenicist social policies gained currency in the early twentieth century, race found its way into the nation's crime statistics. Race became relevant to crime because the scientific racism of Lombroso and others said it was relevant. Contemporary race-crime statistics descended from an ancestry of scientific racism. Whatever social science knowledge can be gained from their use must be weighed against the harm to people caused by eugenicist programs.

CONCLUSION

There is no statistical alchemy in which the government's crime statistics broken down by race can be made to yield meaningful, social scientific information about the criminality of races or racial discrimination. The categorization scheme used in crime statistics has no anthropological or scientific basis; there are no races of humankind. Researchers who desire objective data must confront issues of measurement, operationalization, objectivity, and morality in their use of official crime statistics.

Exactly what the categories measure is difficult to say. The categories do not furnish reliable data for socially defined racial groups, because they reflect an uncertain mixture of self-description and social identity. Using the official racial categorization scheme is not an adequate substitute for operationalizing race according to the researcher's theory. Using the official categories amounts to post hoc explanation for correlations. Official categories do not provide objective data about race and criminality because the categories themselves are politically contrived. The categories reflect a political process by which race distinctions were created by government to enfranchise some and disfranchise others, not a benign accounting scheme useful for developing social policy. Race specifically entered into national crime statistics due to the influence of eugenicist thought. Race-coded crime statistics are descended from a legacy of scientific racism. It would be useful if objective data were readily available for use in conducting social science research, but no objective social scientific statements can be made on the basis of official statistics because race cannot be objectively defined. Rather than reliance on official statistics, researchers should construct their own categories and collect their own data, consistent with the theory specified. Only in this way can social science knowledge be advanced. Not to do so risks production of inconsistent and contradictory findings and the creation of material useful to those who would argue that racism is a myth. As Pope and McNeely (1981: 44) advised, the methodological issues with official statistics "must be carefully considered in order that future research dealing with race and crime does not unintentionally become part of the bibliographic arsenal of forces arguing in favor of retrenchment and racial repression in this country." The official scheme of race classification does not provide an adequate basis for social science research into race and crime. The categories are so sloppily designed, so inconsistently measured, and so burdened by legacies of political exclusion and scientific racism that they ought not be used.

NOTES

1. Some researchers have drawn a distinction between race and ethnicity. Generally, distinctions between "races" are based on biological differences, while distinctions between "ethnic groups" are based on differences of culture, language, and national origin. When the government's categories of race are used, this distinction is not meaningful because the government's definition of race, not the researcher's definition of ethnicity, generates the data. As one commentator put it: "A lot of behavioral scientists use the term 'ethnicity' but I don't really think they have an understanding of how it differs from 'race.' They have just substituted 'ethnicity' for 'race' and moved on" (Wheeler 1995: A15).

2. There are variations in state and local court records. In Kentucky, for example, a database maintained by the Cabinet for Human Resources, Department for Social Services, identifies six races: white, Hispanic, black, Asian/pacific islander, American Indian/Alaskan Native, and biracial and not reported.

3. The bureau printed this statement despite the fact that its own statisticians later admitted the information on which it was based was of dubious value. "This source of information [fingerprint cards]," the report for 1953 states, "it has always been recognized, was incomplete since the information was necessarily limited to cases in which persons taken into custody were fingerprinted and the fingerprint cards forwarded to Washington." In other words, the percentages indicate the portion of suspects fingerprinted, not the portion of offenses committed by black Americans.

4. My point here is not that discrimination occurs within the black community and that therefore discrimination by whites against blacks is somehow less significant or that discrimination within the black community as a topic of study is more or as worthy as that of whites against blacks. My point is that discrimination occurs within a racist culture and that discrimination cannot be understood without examining the cultural meaning of racial identity. The difference that hue has made historically in power and privilege within the African American community as a result of slavery and segregation testifies to the complex cultural legacy of white racism.

REFERENCES

Beckwith, J. (1985). "Social and Political Uses of Genetics in the United States: Past and Present." In Frank H. Marsh and Janet Katz (eds.), *Biology, Crime and Ethics.* Cincinnati, OH: Anderson.

Bell, D. (1992). Faces at the Bottom of the Well: *The Permanence of Racism.* New York: Basic Books.

———. (1987). *And We Are Not Saved: The Elusive Quest for Racial Justice.* New York: Basic Books.

———. (1980). *Race, Racism and American Law.* Boston: Little, Brown.

Bennett, L. (1993). *The Shaping of Black America.* New York: Penguin Books.

Diamond, R. and R. Cottrol (1983). "Codifying Caste: Lousiana's Racial Classification Scheme and the Fourteenth Amendment." *Loyola Law Review* 29: 255–285.

Federal Bureau of Investigation. (1933). Uniform Crime Reports. Washington, DC: U.S. Government Printing Office.

Frisby, M. (1996). "Black or Other." *Emerge* 7(December/January): 48–54.

Gabor, T. (1994). "The Suppression of Crime Statistics on Race and Ethnicity: The Price of Political Correctness." *Canadian Journal of Criminology* 36: 153–163.

Georges-Abeyie, D. (1989). "Race, Ethnicity, and the Spatial Dynamic: Toward a Realistic Study of Black Crime, Crime Victimization, and Criminal Justice Processing of Blacks." *Social Justice* 16: 35–54.

Gilanshah, B. (1993). "Multiracial Minorities: Erasing the Color Line." *Law and Inequality* 12: 183–204.

Hawkins, D. (1995). "Ethnicity, Race and Crime: A Review of Selected Studies." In D. F. Hawkins (ed.), *Ethnicity, Race and Crime: Perspectives across Time and Place,* 11- 45. Albany: State University of New York Press.

Hindelang, M. (1978). "Race and Involvement in Common Law Personal Crimes." *American Sociological Review* 43: 93–109.

Jenkins, P. (1984). "Eugenics, Crime and Ideology: The Case of Progressive Pennsylvania." *Pennsylvania History* 51: 64–78.

Johnston, J. P. (1994). "Academic Approaches to Race-Crime Statistics Do Not Justify Their Collection." *Canadian Journal of Criminology* 36: 166–174.

King, J. C. (1981). *The Biology of Race.* New York: Harcourt Brace Jovanovich.

Knepper, P. (in press). "Race, Racism and Crime Statistics." *Southern University Law Review*.

———. (1994). "The Prohibition of Biracial Legal Identity in the States and the Nation: Historic Overview." *State Constitutional Commentaries and Notes* 5: 14–20.

LaFree, G. (1995). "Race and Crime Trends in the United States, 1946-1990." In D. F. Hawkins (ed.), *Ethnicity, Race and Crime: Perspectives across Place and Time*. Albany: State University of New York Press.

———. (1985). "Official Reactions to Hispanic Defendants in the Southwest." *Journal of Research in Crime and Deliquency* 22: 213–237.

——— and K. Russell (1993). "The Argument for Studying Race and Crime." *Journal of Criminal Justice Education* 4: 273–290.

Law Enforcement Assistance Administration. (1976). *Criminal Victimization in the United States 1973*. Washington, DC: U.S. Government Printing Office.

Lawrence, C. (1987). "The Id, the Ego, and Equal Protection: Reckoning with Unconscious Racism." *Stanford Law Review* 39: 317–388.

Mann, C. R. (1993). *Unequal Justice: A Question of Color*. Bloomington: Indiana University Press.

Office of Federal Statistical Policy and Standards. (1978). *Statistical Policy Handbook*. Washington, DC: U.S. Government Printing Office.

Pope, C. and R. L. McNeeley. (1981). "Race, Crime and Criminal Justice: An Overview." In R. L. McNeeley and C. Pope (eds.), *Race, Crime and Criminal Justice*. Beverly Hills, CA: Sage.

Roberts, J. (1994). "Crime and Race Statistics: Introduction." *Canadian Journal of Criminology* 36: 149–151.

Root, M. P. (1992). "Within, Between and Beyond Race." In M. P. Root (ed.), *Racially Mixed People in America*. Newbury Park, CA: Sage.

Russell, K., M. Wilson, and R. Hall. (1992). *The Color Complex: The Politics of Skin Color among African Americans*. New York: Anchor Books.

Schneider, A. (1981). "Differences between Survey and Police Information about Crime." In R. Lehnen and W. Skogan (eds.), *The National Crime Survey: Working Papers*. Volume One. Washington, DC: U.S. Government Printing Office.

Spickard, P., R. Fong and P. Ewalt. (1995). "Undermining the Very Basis of Racism—Its Categories." *Social Work* 40: 581–584.

Tonry, M. (1996). "Racial Politics, Racial Disparities, and the War on Crime." In J. Inciardi (ed.), *Examining the Justice Process: A Reader*. Forth Worth, TX: Harcourt Brace.

Usdansky, M. (1992). "California's Mix Offers a Look at the Future." *USA Today* (December 4), 8A.

U.S. Commission on Civil Rights. (1995). "The Problem: Discrimination." In P. Rothenberg (ed.), *Race, Class and Gender in the United States*. New York: St. Martin's Press.

Walker, Samuel, Cassia Spohn, and Miriam DeLone. (1996). *The Color of Justice: Race, Ethnicity and Crime in America*. Belmont, CA: Wadsworth.

Wheeler, David L. (1995). "A Growing Number of Scientists Reject the Concept of Race." *Chronicle of Higher Education* (February 17): A15.

Wilbanks, William. (1987). *The Myth of a Racist Criminal Justice System*. Monterey, CA: Brooks/Cole.

Wright, Lawrence. (1994). "One Drop of Blood." *New Yorker* (July 25): 46–55.

Zatz, Marjorie. (1987). "The Changing Forms of Racial/Ethnic Biases in Sentencing." *Journal of Research in Crime and Delinquency* 24: 69–92.

Chapter 3

Deconstructing the Association of Race and Crime: The Salience of Skin Color

Becky L. Tatum

The relationship between race and crime is one of the most controversial issues in the field of criminology. Academic scholars have actively debated whether high minority crime rates can be explained by discriminatory criminal justice practices, the adequacy of crime data, and/or the criminogenic effects of racial inequality. Despite this scholarly discourse, our understanding of the phenomenon remains fairly superficial. The explosiveness of the issue of race and the potential misuse of research that suggests linkages with crime have dissuaded many criminologists from fully analyzing race-specific dynamics (Donziger 1996; Hawkins 1995; Lafree, Drass & O'Day 1992; MacLean & Milovanovic 1990; Russell 1994; Sampson & Wilson 1995; Silberman 1972). Widening racial differences in rates of criminal arrest, victimization, and incarceration, however, force the issue to center stage and call for more comprehensive theorizing and research investigations.

Generally, minority crime and victimization are theorized from a structural or conflict perspective. In particular, criminologists have examined how factors such as racial bias, underclass status, and community characteristics shape opportunities, attitudes, and behaviors. Although criminologists have largely ignored the effects of skin color on crime, an association between the variables has been suggested by several scholars (Georges-Abeyie 1989; Frazier 1957; Myrdal 1944; Poussaint 1983; Silberman 1972). In this chapter, we assess the value of skin color as a criminological concept. Specifically, we address four issues. First, we describe the interrelations of race and skin color and their roles as independent and interacting variables. Second, we review the extant literature that has addressed the effects of skin color on the social experiences of African Americans. In addition to summarizing the studies' findings, we examine the strengths and weaknesses of their methodological designs. Third, drawing on this research, we identify and discuss ways in which skin color may theoretically affect the race-crime relationship. Finally, we discuss the directions for future criminological studies examining race and skin color.

RACE AND SKIN COLOR

As a biological concept, race has little value (Davis 1991; Georges-Abeyie 1989; Vander Zanden 1972). Who is black or white (or any other race) cannot be scientifically determined by biological factors. Race is most useful when it is conceptualized as a social construct that is, how a racial group is socially defined and the perceptions, privileges, and opportunities that accompany this characterization. Based on this perspective, Feagin and Feagin (1996: 9) offer the following definition of race: "Race identifies a social group that persons inside and outside the group have decided is important to single out as inferior or superior, typically on the basis of real or alleged physical characteristics subjectively selected."

Race and its social consequences are commonly offered as explanations for the disproportionate number of racial minorities in the criminal justice system as both offenders and victims (Georges-Abeyie 1990, Mann 1993; Walker, Spohn and DeLone 1996). Some researchers argue that high minority crime rates are the results of greater exposure to criminogenic factors (Gibbons 1994; Russell 1994; Walker, et al. 1996). Others posit that minority individuals, in particular African Americans, are more likely to be perceived as criminal (Anderson 1995; Hall 1996) and, as a result, have a higher probability of being processed by the criminal justice system (Donziger 1996). Mann (1993) argues that the more severe treatment of African Americans in the criminal justice system is correlated with their higher level of racial visibility. Because of their darker skin color, African Americans are more "racially" different from Euro-Americans than the other minority subgroups (110). All racial minorities, however, are subjected to criminal stereotyping based on skin color. According to Mann, white Americans view the classic rapist as a "black man," the typical opium user as a "yellow man," the archetypal knife wielder as a "brown man," the "red man" as a drunken Indian, and people of color as collectively constituting the "crime problem" (viii).

Although Mann's conceptualization of skin color is synonymous with race, it is important to note that the two variables can represent separate phenomena. Skin color (or skin tone) can refer to the prejudicial or preferential treatment of in-group members based on the lightness or darkness of their skin. Like race, skin color is also a measure of the racial similarity or dissimilarity that in-group members share with the dominant group. Light skin has ascribed worth and brings more social privileges and opportunities. For example, the more white-skinned a person is, the greater his or her perceived level of morality, intelligence, and productivity. Dark skin, on the other hand, is devalued and carries several negative images and connotations. Consciously or unconsciously, black skin is frequently associated with dangerousness, criminality, ignorance, and untrustworthiness (Harvey 1995; Myrdal 1944).

When the two variables are used independently, race reflects a system of intergroup stratification. The racial grading system in American society divides people of color into several categories, with each successive layer from the top experiencing greater exclusion than the one above (Forbes 1990; Marger 1994). Skin color or skin tone is a system of intragroup stratification in which in-group members experience different degrees of exclusion based on an internal color-caste hierarchy. In short, skin color is a secondary stratification system that overlays the primary stratification of race.

Georges-Abeyie (1989: 38) provides a framework for understanding the differential treatment of nonwhite individuals that incorporates the significance of both race/ethnicity and skin color. In particular, he advances the theoretical perspective of "social distance." Social distance refers to the degree of closeness or remoteness that the majority group desires in its interactions with members of a particular group. Social distance may be influenced by six factors:

1. The extent of physiognomic, phrenologic, and anatomic differences;
2. Perceived extent of "contributions" to the national development;
3. Perceived extent of cultural and social network differences between minority/out-groups versus majority/in-group;
4. Perceived threat to the social order;
5. Perceived criminality; and
6. Perceived "intrinsic worth."

African Americans tend to rank more negatively on these factors than other racial minorities (Aguirre & Turner 1995; Feagin & Feagin 1996; Marger 1994). These rankings are the combined result of greater physical differences, a more devalued culture, and the consequences of the vestiges of slavery. Some support for the greater social distance of African Americans can be drawn from Baker's (1983) comparison of black slaves and American Indians. Baker found that white colonists viewed American Indians in less denigrative terms than black slaves. Although both were classified as being inferior to white men, American Indians were viewed as being "uncivilized" while blacks were viewed as being "subhuman." In fact, at one time, American Indians were considered to be assimilable if they gave up their culture (68). The higher levels of racial segregation of African Americans regardless of income from non-Hispanic whites provide additional support for the greater social distance of African Americans (Denton & Massey, 1988).

In-group members also rank differently on these six factors. Because of the devaluation of dark skin and its negative connotations, dark-skinned individuals experience greater social distance from the majority group than light-skinned individuals. Dark-skinned African Americans, for example, rank more negatively on the six factors and, consequently, have greater social distance from the majority group than African Americans with light skin.

The interactive effects of race and skin color also play a salient role in determining social distance. Take, for example, the social distance of dark-skinned African and Hispanic Americans. Because of skin color (or intragroup stratification), their degree of desired closeness to the majority group is similar in that it is less than that of their lighter-skinned counterparts. However, as we noted earlier, skin color stratification overlays racial stratification. The racial hierarchy in American society (or intergroup stratification) places dark-skinned Hispanics above dark-skinned African Americans, resulting in less social distance from the majority group and very different social experiences. As for the social status of African Americans, this further implies that those with dark skin represent the bottom of the hierarchical systems in terms of social value (Featherston 1994).

A conceptual diagram illustrating the independent and interacting effects of race and skin color on social distance is presented in Figure 3.1. which shows that social distance from the dominant group varies among racial minorities. Stated differently, there are degrees of minority status. Racial group members are further stratified by skin color. Dark-skinned individuals experience greater social distance from the dominant group than individuals who are light-skinned. Because of the interactive effects of race and skin color, social distance is highest for dark-skinned African Americans.

Figure 3.1
Association of Race and Skin Color

Race

Low Social Distance	RG1		RG2		RG3		RG4		High Social Distance
	L	D	L	D	L	D	L	D	

Skin Color

RG = racial group
L = light-skinned
D = dark-skinned

Georges-Abeyie (1989: 40) suggests that social distance from the dominant group as a result of race and skin color affects the criminal involvement and criminal justice processing of minority individuals. Before discussing the role of skin color in the race-crime relationship, it is important to review the literature that has examined the effects of skin color on racial minorities.

SKIN COLOR: EFFECTS ON RACIAL MINORITIES

Literature examining the issue of skin color in American society has primarily assessed how the variable affects African Americans. Because of this, the literature in this section consists only of research that has examined skin color effects for these individuals.[1] The literature is presented in two parts: research that has analyzed the structural effects of skin color and research that addresses the sociopsychological effects of the variable.

Structural Effects of Skin Color

The effects of skin color on the social and economic status of African

Americans are grounded in the legacy of slavery. Slaves were divided into two groups—house servants and field hands. House servants, who were usually light-skinned mulatto offspring, represented one part of the Negro upper class.[2] These individuals were trained in some skill and were socialized into the cultural mandates and lifestyles of the white ruling class (Blackwell 1991; Russell, Wilson & Hall 1992), factors that often enabled them to purchase their freedom or to be manumitted (Franklin 1980).[3] Field hands, who were largely dark-skinned, represented the bottom of the Negro social structure. Untrained and unskilled, this group of slaves worked with their hands and engaged in menial tasks (Blackwell 1991). Slave masters believed that because of their darker skin color, field hands were stronger and were better able to tolerate the heat of the sun (Russell, et al. 1992). The second part of the Negro upper class was comprised a small, free, mostly light-skinned Negro population.[4]

Because of the greater social opportunities and privileges that were afforded to light-complexioned Negro slaves, skin color played a major role in determining Negro social mobility. A disproportionate number of early Negro leaders, academics, and professionals were mulattos or very light-skinned (Crawford 1979; Davis 1991; Russell, et al. 1992). Some of these individuals included Robert Purvis (cofounder of the American Anti-Slavery Society), W.E.B. Du Bois (educator, activist, and founder of the National Association for the Advancement of Colored People [NAACP]), Walter White (NAACP president, 1931–1955), and A. Phillip Randolph (prominent New York city editor and activist) (Davis 1991). All of these men were college-educated. Du Bois, who was of African, French, and Dutch lineage, received a Ph.D. in history from Harvard University and studied at the University of Berlin.

The disproportionate number of mulattoes and light-skinned Negroes in influential positions was associated with the admission criteria and curricula of historically black colleges and universities. During the nineteenth century, several black colleges and universities, including Howard University, Morgan State University, and Hampton University, based applicants' admission on their ability to pass a color test (Russell, et al. 1992). Providing a liberal arts education, the mission of these schools was to groom mulatto students into the culture of the black middle class. Dark-skinned students, who were provided an industrial education, attended Tuskegee Institute or Bethune-Cookman College, which was founded expressly for "Black girls." The separate educational paths further divided the black community and channeled dark-skinned blacks into low-paying menial work (29).

In their qualitative analysis, Drake and Cayton (1945) and Frazier (1957) described the effects of skin color on the residence and employment opportunities of Chicago Negroes in the 1940s. Frazier found that darker-skinned Negro families with few economic resources and female-headed households were heavily concentrated at the core of the ghetto. These factors became less evident, and the percentages of mulattoes increased as one moved closer to the white residential areas. In their treatise *The Black Metropolis*, Drake and Cayton argued that dark skin color was an economic handicap for Negro women seeking positions as stenographers, physicians attendants, and waitresses (498–500).   Employers believed that clients, both black and white, preferred to interact with female workers who were light-skinned, a feature that they associated with attractiveness and intelligence.

The measurement of skin color, however, in these early qualitative studies was rather imprecise, with important differentials being made only among dark-skinned individuals and individuals with all other skin tones. Although Drake and Cayton hypothesized that the importance of skin color was lessening due to higher education, racial pride, and the accumulation of money by dark people, research conducted since their work has shown that light-skinned African Americans still fare better economically, vocationally, and educationally than their darker-skinned counterparts. For example, Ransford (1970), in an interview of 312 light-, medium-, and dark-skinned black males from middle- and lower-class neighborhoods, found that light-skinned blacks held higher-status occupations than those who were dark-skinned for all levels of education less than college graduation. Moreover, dark-skinned black males were three times as likely to be unemployed and were less likely to be employed in white-collar jobs. Medium-complexioned black males held an intermediate status between the light- and dark-skinned black males.

These findings were supported and extended by Harburg et al. (1973), who analyzed the structural effects of skin color on a sample of black and white males and females residing in racially segregated low- and high stress- areas.[5] Measuring skin color in categories of very light/fair, somewhat light/somewhat fair, somewhat dark, (brown)/somewhat dark and very dark/dark (the right side of the descriptive phrase represented color-coding scheme for whites), they discovered a negative correlation between skin color and levels of occupation, education, and income. Regardless of race or gender, occupational, educational, and income status decreased as skin tones darkened. Thus, even among whites, dark skin color appeared to negatively impact structural status.

Hughes and Hertel (1990) and Keith and Herring (1991) provide strong evidence of the continuing effects of skin color on African American structural status. Also measuring skin tones that ranged from very dark to very light,[6] these researchers advance the methodological design of past studies by (1) using the National Survey of Black Americans, a national probability sample representative of the black population in the United States (2) using data collected after the social and cultural changes of the 1960s and (3) using advanced statistical analysis to more clearly identify the effects of skin color in comparison to other demographic variables on socioeconomic status. While both studies reaffirm the findings of earlier empirical research—that is, as skin tone darkens, social status decrease—they make several additional contributions to the literature. Hughes and Hertel discovered that the impact of skin color on socioeconomic status among black Americans was as great as the impact of race (black-white) and that in studies conducted between 1950 and 1980, the effects of skin color on socioeconomic status did not appreciably change. Regressing skin color and other demographic and contemporaneous factors (e.g., age, gender, region) on education, occupation, personal income, and family income (separate equations), Keith and Herring found that skin color was a significant determinant of all stratification outcomes and was the best predictor of occupation, and personal and family income.[7]

In sum, the research suggests an inverse association between skin color and the structural status of African Americans that started in slavery and that has continued into the twentieth century. Both qualitative and quantitative studies point to the greater social and economic advantages of light-skinned African Americans despite positive cultural, political, and economic changes that have affected the African American community. Most importantly, the research shows that skin color is an addition to, rather than a replacement of, racial stratification. In short, dark-skinned African Americans have a harder time getting ahead. As stated by Keith and Herring (1991: 777), it appears that "the effects of skin color are not only historical curiosities from a legacy of slavery and racism, but present-day mechanisms that influence who gets what in America."

Sociopsychological Effects of Skin Color

Research on the sociopsychological effects of skin color is largely based on the symbolic interactionist perspective. These studies have attempted to examine how skin color bias impacts the personalities and self-identities of minority and majority individuals. Early studies (Morland 1969) revealed the devaluation of dark skin and the positive value of white skin by black and white children. It has been argued that the most serious injury to a Negro child was injury to his self-worth, which was related to skin color. These studies, however, were based on interracial (black-white) rather than intraracial (black-black) skin color differences. Although the methodological designs of the doll studies have been criticized for their forced-choice methodologies (see Morgan 1991),[8] recent research continues to show that preschool children are aware of society's preferences for light skin (Hopson & Hopson 1992).

The methodological designs of research examining the sociopsychological effects of intraracial skin color differences vary widely from the design of the classic doll studies. Intraracial studies of skin color bias, which are generally quantitative, measure several dimensions of black skin color and employ fairly sophisticated research and statistical methods that include multivariate analysis and complex experimental designs (e.g., Bond & Cash 1992; Holtzman 1973; Kennedy 1993; Robinson & Ward, 1995; Urdy, Bauman & Chase. 1971; Wade 1996). Bond and Cash (1992), who measured nine black skin color, specially argue that the common practice of using two or three black skin colors is adequate. Skin color in these studies is based on respondents' perceptions of their skin color or interviewers' ratings. The inadequacies of these studies lie in their small sample sizes and a general overreliance on college and high school students.

The findings of this research, however, provide important insights as to the effects of intraracial skin color bias on African American self-esteem and self-concept. The research reveals that the most positive perceptions of self are not necessarily exhibited by individuals who are fair-skinned (Holtzman 1973; Robinson & Ward 1995). While dark-skinned college students express the lowest levels of personal competence and efficacy, the highest levels are exhibited by students with medium skin tones, followed by light-skinned students.

The higher self-concept of medium-skin-tone students is most likely associated with the black community's stigmatization of light-skinned blacks because of their white ancestry (Davis 1991; Drake & Cayton 1945). Davis (1991) notes that in the Jim Crow era, blacks widely shared the beliefs that black-white sexual contacts occurred mainly between the biologically and morally weaker members of both groups. Since light mulatto girls were preferred as prostitutes, chorus girls, and singers, light skin color became associated with sin and degradation and, unless one could prove respectable parentage, was viewed suspiciously everywhere in the black community (Davis 1991: 57). However, when only light-and dark-complexioned subjects are compared, light-skinned African American teens have been found to exhibit more favorable academic self-concept and higher educational experiences than dark-skinned African American teens (Crawford 1979).

Skin tone has historically been a point of reference for attractiveness among African Americans, with light-skinned individuals being more physically appealing to the eye (Hall 1995; Neal & Wilson 1989). Neal and Wilson suggest that skin color has different psychological effects on women because physical appearance is more important in their lives (in terms of dating and marriage) than in the lives of men. It is further theorized that since women are not judged on their spouses' or partners' characteristics, dark-skinned females, unlike their male counterparts, cannot augment perceptions of themselves by marrying or associating with a fair-skinned male (Wade 1996: 360). Providing indirect support for these premises, research indicates that skin color plays a greater role in dating and mate selection of males who are likely to select light-skinned partners (Bond & Cash, 1992; Robinson and Ward 1995; Urdy, et al. 1971). Examining the impact of skin color on perceptions of sexual attractiveness among a sample of African American college students and alumni, Wade (1996) found (1) that dark-skinned males' self-ratings of sexual attractiveness were higher than those of fair-skinned African American males and (2) that self-ratings among females did not differ. Wade attributed the male ratings to the internalization of stereotypes of African American men as "sexual animals"; dark-skinned African American men, because of the derogatory characteristics associated with their skin tone, more closely fit this stereotype.

Intraracial skin color bias has been further shown to affect black and white perceptions of an individual's job suitability. Kennedy (1993), who investigated the perceptions of black and white community college students toward job applicants' fitness for white-and blue-collar occupations, found that white students perceived that light-skinned blacks were more suitable for white-collar occupations, and that dark-skinned blacks were more suitable for blue-collar positions.[9] Black students, however, rated the applicants in the opposite manner. Black students perceived that dark-skinned blacks were more suitable for white-collar occupations, and that light-skinned blacks were more suitable for blue-collar positions. Kennedy suggested that the findings were the result of racial bias: white subjects were possibly more biased against black subjects, while black subjects were more racially biased against whites, which was transformed to light-skinned individuals since they were similar to whites in appearance.[10]

A number of analytical studies have suggested that skin color bias exhibited by parents and teachers in their relations with children results in a self-fulfilling prophecy. Because fair-skinned children are often considered to be more intelligent, well mannered, and hygienic (Harvey 1995), parents and teachers may treat them in a more favorable manner than those children who have darker skin (Delgado 1995; Poussaint 1972). For some children, such prejudices may become incorporated into the psyche and be manifested as dysfunctional behavior. Poussaint (1972: 104-105) gives the following example of a government official who favored her light-skinned son over his darker brother:

When angry, the mother often would say to the darker brother, you act like a nigger, while comparing the favored light-skinned brother's behavior with that of white youngsters of friends or colleagues. Whites were consistently glorified; blacks were uniformly condemned. Normal rivalry between the brothers turned into a bitter exchange of derogatory, racial name-calling. The boy soon began to identify bad behavior with black behavior, and consequently, to see himself as being bad because he was black. Partly to hurt his mother, the youngster played what he considered "the dirty nigger role." this led to difficulties with teachers, troubles with schoolmates and petty larceny before he received help through psychiatric treatment.

Poussaint (1983) goes on to theoretically link skin color bias with high rates of black-on-black homicide. He hypothesizes that the effects of skin color bias on the self-esteem and self-worth of blacks may predispose them to become ready victims or perpetrators of violent attacks. According to Poussaint, the premium that society places on light skin causes racial self-hatred that affects how blacks feel about themselves and other blacks. When racial self-hatred and low self-esteem are combined with feelings of powerlessness, hopelessness, and frustration that arise from the social environments of blacks, they become highly sensitive to slights and threats to self-respect. Thus, any derogatory comments about skin color may be sufficient to produce a reaction that leads to an argument that escalates into physical assault and homicide (164).

The lower social acceptance of dark-skinned African Americans may also result in these individuals' directing their hostility toward members of the dominant group. Ransford (1970), whose research revealed higher social status for light-skinned blacks, also showed that dark-skinned individuals were more hostile toward whites, more willing to use violence to improve their social position, and more separatist in their outlook than light-skinned Negroes. More recent research provides support for this finding, indicating that darker-skinned blacks have higher levels of antiwhite feelings (Freeman, Armor & Pettigrew 1964) and stronger black identities and black separatist attitudes (Hughes & Hertel 1990).

To summarize, the literature shows that skin color plays a salient role in shaping the identities and personalities of African Americans. Differential treatment on the basis of skin color affects perceptions of self and others and, as illustrated by the literature, can impact both inter- and intragroup relations. The sociopsychological literature further suggests that the devaluation of darker-skinned individuals can lead to psychological impairment that may be played out in terms of crime and interpersonal violence. In the next section, we discuss the role of skin color in the race-crime relationship.

RACE, SKIN COLOR, AND CRIME

At least one study has attempted to empirically examine the link between skin color and crime. In her dissertation research, Peterson-Lewis (1983) analyzed the effects of socioeconomic status, academic achievement, and skin color on perceived personality and criminal traits of black offenders. She hypothesized that offenders with high socioeconomic status, high levels of achievement, and light complexions would be assigned more positive attributes than offenders who had the opposite characteristics. A sample of white undergraduate students was shown bogus crime reports with attached photographs of black offenders who were either light-or-dark complexioned with high or low levels of socioeconomic status (SES) and achievement.[11] Study results showed that high achievers were perceived as having lower criminal motivations and higher personal virtues than low achievers. However, light-complexioned offenders who were high achievers were perceived to have less internal criminal motivation and higher personal virtues than dark-complexioned high achievers. The findings illustrated the social value that American society, in this case white Americans, attribute to light skin and raised the question of the possibility of differential treatment of criminal offenders based on skin color.

Based on the review of the literature examining the structural and sociopsychological effects of skin color bias, we can draw at least three possible theoretical links between race, skin color, and crime. First, skin color biases may affect the processing of minority offenders by criminal justice agencies (Free 1996). As discussed previously, skin color is a salient factor in determining perceived social worth. The association of dark skin with negative attributes such as dangerousness, criminality, and untrustworthiness (among other traits) may result in dark-skinned African Americans, especially dark-skinned African American males, being perceived to be more criminally dangerous. This, in turn, may lead to more adverse reactions by criminal justice officials and a greater likelihood of discriminatory decision making at points of arrest, sentencing, and other stages of the criminal justice process.

Second, the effects of skin color on structural opportunities may lead to differential rates of criminal involvement and victimization. This assumption is consistent with strain theory, which posits that blocked opportunities lead to frustration, which, in turn, leads to crime. As was noted in the review of the literature, skin color, apart from social class and/or race, can also affect one's ability to achieve conventional goals. The higher probability of unemployment, lower occupational status, income, and residence in high-stress areas experienced by dark-skinned African Americans theoretically suggests that these individuals have higher levels of frustration and a higher probability of criminal offending. Moreover, the characteristics of high-stress residence areas (e.g., poverty, ineffective social institutions) may also lead to higher rates of crime and victimization.

Third, the literature suggests that the effects of skin color bias on personality and self-identity can have criminogenic consequences. We previously pointed out that much of the research examining the sociopsychological effects of skin color is grounded in the interactionist perspective that posits that how one is perceived by others affects behavior. The premium that society places on light skin and the differential reactions that accompany this bias may lead to lower self-concept and self-esteem and, in turn, higher involvement in crime, violence, and substance abuse by dark-skinned individuals. In short, dark-skinned individuals may internalize the negative definitions of self and either act out these labels in terms of criminal and deviant behavior or seek to escape this stigmatization through alcohol and/or drug abuse or suicide.

Skin color, however, is presented as a secondary variable that provides insights into the race–crime relationship. In short, it describes how intragroup stratification in addition to intergroup stratification can have criminogenic effects. It is still argued that racial or intergroup stratification is the primary factor in understanding the dynamics of the race–crime phenomenon. The primacy of race is illustrated in the implied interaction effect between race and skin color. Social distance from the dominant group results in dark-skinned racial minorities' facing similar, but, because of their racial status, different, social experiences. As a result, for the three theoretical premises discussed earlier, there should be a race effect, a skin color effect, and an interaction effect of race and skin color on crime and the differential treatment of minority offenders.

CONCLUSION

In this chapter, we examined the salience of skin color in the relationship between race and crime. Specifically, we attempted to show how the structural and sociopsychological effects of skin color bias can lead to violent and criminal behavior and how it may impact the treatment of minority offenders in the criminal justice system. Because such bias is proposed as a secondary system of stratification, the criminogenic effects of skin color overlay those of race. Thus, the addition of skin color as a theoretical variable in the race–crime relationship allows us to examine the significance of intragroup stratification and intra- and intergroup differences that may exist among racial minorities as well as the dominant group.

Because criminologists have failed to incorporate skin color measures into their research designs, at the present time we can make only assumptions about its role in crime and criminal justice processing. As we have argued in this chapter, this issue warrants further investigation. Using the extant literature as a foundation, future criminological studies examining skin color should be structured along the following lines. First, the research must be historically grounded. In other words,

criminologists must integrate a historical approach into their research methodologies. This will enable them to examine the origins and historical processes
involved in skin color bias for a particular racial group and to more fully explain
its contemporary effects on these individuals.

A historical approach will directly impact the types of theoretical frameworks
that should guide these studies. Traditional criminological theories are, for the
most part, ahistorical. Critical criminology (e.g., Marxist, postmodern perspectives), which more directly addresses issues of social stratification and suggest
that inequality of power is connected to crime (Vold, et al. 1998), also fails to provide a historical approach. Thus, the incorporation of a historical analysis into
skin color research will also require the modification of extant theories.

Second, because of the social complexities of skin color bias, criminological
studies of the phenomenon must make use of both qualitative and quantitative
methods. Important features of quantitative studies include national probability
samples and sophisticated statistical techniques that allow researchers to separate
the causal effects of skin color from those of other variables and contemporaneous factors. As for qualitative research, community studies such as those initiated by Drake and Cayton (1945) and Frazier (1957) can provide firsthand experience of the complex interconnection between race, skin color, and perceptual and
behavioral outcomes in contemporary minority
communities. Qualitative research should also be conducted from a standpoint
perspective; that is, the research should provide an account of skin color biases
through the eyes of racial minorities.

Third, criminological studies of skin color bias must extend their analysis to
include measures of other racial features. In addition to skin color, intragroup and
intergroup biases are based on the preference for European racial features (e.g.,
lips, nose, hair texture) (Bond & Cash 1992; Taylor 1993). In short, we must be
able to identify the separate and combined effects of these phenomena and their
effects on the perceptions, attitudes, and behaviors of both minority and majority
individuals.

Finally, criminological studies of skin color bias must pursue comparative lines
of inquiry. In addition to the internal group comparisons, external comparisons
that exemplify similarities and differences between comparable skin color categories of Euro-American samples and samples of other racial groups are needed.

NOTES

1. Although skin color bias is generally attributed to African Americans, it is a world-
wide phenomenon. Similar biases have been found among Mexican Americans (Telles &
Murguia 1990), among Ethiopian Jews (Henik, Munitz & Priel, 1985), in Jamaica (Tedrick
1973), in India (Banerjee 1985), and in Japan (Harris 1994).

2. Throughout this chapter we use the terms Negro, black, and African American inter-
changeably.

3. For the sake of clarity, we provide definitions of the mulatto and manumitted terms.
We use the term "mulatto" to refer to children of unions between one Negro parent and one
white parent or one white parent and one racially mixed (usually black and white) Negro
parent. According to Davis (1991: 57), the rapid decline in the proportion of unmixed

blacks in the decades prior to 1920 was primarily the result of mulatto-African black mis-cegenation. The term "manumitted" in this chapter refers to the release of a mulatto individual from slavery.

4. Davis (1991: 33) notes that part of the free Negro population consisted of mulattoes who were the offspring of the early unions of slaves or free blacks and white indentured servants. Although these mulattoes were free, especially those born to white mothers, they were generally despised and treated as blacks. The light skin tone of the free Negro population was also due to the ability of mulatto house servants to purchase their freedom or the manumission of these individuals.

5. High-stress areas were characterized by rates of low socioeconomic status, high crime, high density, high residential mobility, and high rates of marital breakup. Low-stress areas showed the converse conditions.

6. The specific skin color categories for the National Survey for Black Americans are very dark brown, dark brown, medium dark brown, light brown (light-skinned), and very light.

7. In June 1995, *USA Today* reported the findings of the Multi-City Study of Urban Inequality, which assessed the effects of skin color on the employment opportunities of 2,000 men in Los Angeles. This study found that being black and dark-skinned reduced the odds of working by 52 percent after excluding other factors. More specifically, the study indicated that 8.6 percent of white men in Los Angeles were unemployed, compared with 23.1 percent of blacks, 27 percent of dark-skinned men and 20percent of light-skinned black men.

8. Forced-choice methodologies refer to those study designs in which participants select from a set of specified responses. For example, researchers have placed a black doll and a white doll in the presence of white and black children and asked, Give me the doll that: (1) is the nice doll; (2) is the nice color; (3) looks bad; (4) you like to play with or you like the best; (5) looks like a white child; (6) looks like a colored child; (7) looks like a Negro child; (8) looks like you.

9. In this study, students reviewed fictional job applications that contained color photos of the applicants, personal/biographical information, educational history, work history, and references. The applications were approximately equal in terms of qualifications.

10. The federal case of *Morrow v. Internal Revenue Service* (1990) provides some support for Kennedy's conclusions. In this case, Tracy Morrow, a light-skinned African American female, filed a color discrimination suit against Ruby Lewis, a dark-skinned African American female. Although Morrow lost her suit, Moye, the federal judge who tried the case, conceded that color prejudice between black coworkers can and often does exist.

11. SES was based on parents' occupation; achievement was based on grade point average (GPA). For high SES, the offender's parents were both employed; the father was an attorney, and the mother was a primary school art teacher. For low SES, the father was a short-order cook; the mother was a maid in a private home. High GPA was 3.8 out of 4.0; low GPA was 1.8 out of 4.0.

REFERENCES

Aguirre, A. and J. Turner (1995). *American Ethnicity: The Dynamics and Consequences of Racism.* New York: McGraw-Hill.

Anderson, E. (1995) "The Police and the Black Male." In Margaret Andersen and Patricia Hill Collins (eds.), *Race, Class and Gender* 456–461. Belmont: Wadsworth Publishing Company.

Baker, D. (1983). *Race, Ethnicity and Power: A Comparative Study*. London: Routledge and Kegan Paul.

Banerjee, S. (1985) "Assortive Mating for Colour in Indian Population." *Journal of Biosocial Science* 17: 205–209.

Blackwell, J. (1991). *The Black Community: Diversity and Unity*. Third ed. New York: Harper and Row.

Bond, S. and T. Cash (1992). "Black Beauty: Skin Color and Body Images Among African American College Women." *Journal of Applied Social Psychology* 22(11): 874–888.

Crawford, Z. (1979). *Skin Color, Race, and Self Image: An Exploratory Study of a Group of High School Youths*. Palo Alto, CA: Reed and Eterovich.

Davis, F. J. (1991). *Who Is Black? One Nation's Definition*. University Park, University of Pennsylvania Press.

Delgado, R. (1995). "Words That Wound: A Tort Action for Racial Insults, Epithets, and Name-Calling." In Richard Delgado (ed.), *Critical Race Theory*. Philadelphia: Temple University Press.

Denton, N. and D. Massey. (1988). "Residential Segregation of Blacks, Hispanics, and Asians by Socioeconomic Status and Generation." *Social Science Quarterly* 69(4): 797–817.

Donziger, S. (1996). *The Real War on Crime: The Report of the National Criminal Justice Commission*. New York: HarperPerennial.

Drake, St. C. and H. Cayton. (1945). *Black Metropolis*. New York: Harcourt, Brace.

Feagin, J. and C. Feagin. (1996). *Racial and Ethnic Relations*. Englewood Cliffs, NJ: Prentice-Hall.

Featherston, E. (1994). *Skin Deep: Women Writing on Color, Culture, and Identity*. Freedom: CA: Crossing Press.

Forbes, J. (1990). "The Manipulation of Race, Caste and Identity: Classifying Afro Americans, Native Americans and Red-Black People." *The Journal of Ethnic Studies* 17(4): 1–51.

Franklin, J. (1980). *From Slavery to Freedom*. New York: Knopf.

Frazier, E. F. (1957). *The Negro in the United States*. New York: Macmillan.

Free, M. (1996). *African Americans and the Criminal Justice System*. New York: Garland.

Freeman, H., D. Armor, J. M. Ross, and T. Pettigrew. (1964). "Color Gradation and Attitudes among Middle-Income Negroes." *American Sociological Review* 31: 365–374.

Georges-Abeyie, D. (1990). "Studying Black Crime: A Realistic Approach." In Paul Brantingham and Patricia Brantingham (eds.), *Environmental Criminology* 97–109. Newbury, CA: Sage.

———. (1989). "Race, Ethnicity, and the Spatial Dynamic: Toward a Realistic Study of Black Crime, Crime Victimization, and Criminal Justice Processing of Blacks." *Social Justice* 16(4): 35–54.

Gibbons, D. (1994). *Talking about Crime and Criminals: Problems and Issues in Theory Development in Criminology*. Englewood Cliffs, NJ: Prentice-Hall.

Hall, R. (1996). "Impact of Skin Color upon Occupational Projection: A Case for Black Male Affirmative Action." *Journal of African American Men* 1(4): 87–94.

———. (1995). "The Bleaching Syndrome: African Americans' Response to Cultural Domination vis-a-vis Skin Color." *Journal of Black Studies* 26(2): 172–184.

Harburg, E., J. Erfurt, L. Hauenstein, C. Chape, W. Schull, and M. Schork. (1973). "Socio-Ecological Stress, Suppressed Hostility, Skin Color, and Black-White Male Blood

Pressure." *Psychosomatic Medicine* 35(4): 276–296.

Harris, V. (1994) "Prison of Color." In Elena Featherston (ed.), *Skin Deep: Women Writing on Color, Culture and Identity*. Freedom, CA: Crossing Press.

Harvey, Aminfu. (1995). "The Issue of Skin Color in Psychotherapy with African Americans." *Families and Society* 76(1): 3–10.

Hawkins, D. (1995). *Ethnicity, Race, and Crime: Perspectives across Time and Place*. Albany: State University of New York Press.

Henik, A., S. Munitz, and B. Priel. (1985). "Color, Skin Color Preferences and Self Color Identification among Ethiopian and Israeli Born Children." *Israeli Social Science Research*: 374–384.

Holtzman, J. (1973). "Color Caste Changes among Black College Students." *Journal of Black Studies* 4(1): 92–101.

Hopson, D. and D. Hopson. (1992). "Implications of Doll Color Preferences among Black Preschool Children and White Preschool Children." In A. Kathleen Hoard Burlew, W. Curtis Banks, Harriette Pipes McAdoo, and Daudi Azibo (eds.), *African American Psychology: Theory, Research, and Practice*, 183-189. Newbury, CA: Sage.

Hughes, M. and B. Hertel. (1990). "The Significance of Color Remains: A Study of Life Chances, Mate Selection, and Ethnic Consciousness among Black Americans." *Social Forces* 68(4): 1105–1120.

Keith, V. and C. Herring. (1991). "Skin Tone and Stratification in the Black Community." *American Journal of Sociology* 3: 760–778.

Kennedy, A. (1993). "The Darker the Berry . . . An Investigation of Skin Color Effects on Perceptions of Job Suitability." Thesis, Rice University.

LaFree, G., K. Drass, and P. O'Day. (1992). "Race and Crime in Postwar America: Determinants of African American and White Rates, 1957–1988." *Criminology* 30(2): 147–185.

MacLean, B. and D. Milovanovic. (1990). *Racism, Empiricism, and Criminal Justice*. Vancouver, Canada: Collective Press.

Mann, C. (1993). *Unequal Justice: A Question of Color*. Bloomington: Indiana University Press.

Marger, M. (1994). *Race and Ethnic Relations; American and Global Perspectives*. Belmont, CA: Wadsworth.

Morgan, H. (1991). "Race Preference Studies: A Critique of Methodology." *Western Journal of Black Studies* 15(4): 248–253.

Morland, J. (1969). "Race Awareness among American and Hong Kong Chinese Children." *American Journal of Sociology* 75: 360–374.

Myrdal, G. (1944). *An American Dilemma*. New York: Harper and Row.

Neal, A. and M. Wilson. (1989). "The Role of Skin Color and Features in the Black Community. Implications for Black Women and Therapy." Clinical Psychology Review 9: 323–333.

Peterson-Lewis, S. (1983). "Evaluating the Criminal Offender: The Effects of Offenders' Socio-Economic Status, Academic Achievement and Color on Personality." University of Florida.

Poussaint, A. (1983). "Black-on-Black Homicide: A Psychological-Political Perspective." *Victimology* 8: 161–169.

———. (1972). *Why Blacks Kill Blacks*. New York: Emerson Hall.

Ransford, E. (1970). "Skin Color, Life Chances and Anti-White Attitudes." *Social Problems* 18: 164–78.

Robinson, T. and J. Ward. (1995). "African American Adolescents and Skin Color." *Journal of Black Psychology* 21(3):256–274.

Russell, K. (1994) "The Racial Inequality Hypothesis: A Critical Look at the Research and an Alternative Theoretical Analysis." *Law and Human Behavior* 18(3): 305–317.

Russell, K., M. Wilson, and R. Hall. (1992). *The Color Complex: The Politics of Skin Color Among African Americans.* New York: Harcourt Brace Jovanovich.

Sampson, R. and W. J. Wilson. (1995). "Toward a Theory of Race, Crime, and Urban Inequality." In John Hagan and Ruth Peterson (eds.), *Crime and Urban Inequality* 37–54. Stanford, CA: Stanford University Press.

Silberman, C. (1972). *Criminal Violence, Criminal Justice.* New York: Vintage Books.

Taylor, J. (1993). "Reaction to Penn et al.'s: On the Desirability of Own Group Preference." *Journal of Black Studies* 19(3): 333–335.

Tedrick, K. (1973). "Skin Shade and the Need for Achievement in a Multiracial Society: Jamaica, West Indies." *Journal of Social Psychology* 89(1): 25–33.

Telles, E. and E. Murguia. (1990). "Phenotypic Discrimination and Income Differences among Mexican Americans." *Social Science Quarterly* 71(4): 682–696.

Urdy, J., K. Bauman, and C. Chase. (1971). "Skin Color, Status and Mate Selection." *American Journal of Sociology* 76: 722–733.

Vander Zanden, J. (1972). *American Minority Relations.* New York: McGraw-Hill.

Vold, G., T. Bernard, and J. Snipes. (1998). *Theoretical Criminology.* 4th ed. New York: Oxford University Press.

Wade, T. J. (1996). "The Relationships Between Skin Color and Self-Perceived Global, Physical, and Sexual Attractiveness, and Self-Esteem for African Americans." *Journal of Black Psychology* 22(3): 358–373.

Walker, S., C. Spohn, and M. DeLone. (1996). *The Color of Justice: Race, Ethnicity, and Crime in America.* Belmont, CA: Wadsworth..

Chapter 4

The Empirical Status of the Black-Subculture-of-Violence Thesis

Liqun Cao, Anthony Troy Adams, and Vickie J. Jensen

There is a paradox in the sociological and criminological literature: the black subculture of violence is perhaps one of the most cited, but one of the least tested, theses. On one hand, the black- subculture-of-violence thesis is widely cited in introductory sociology and criminology textbooks (Adler et al. 1994; Barlow 1996; Coser et al. 1990; Siegel 1992). On the other hand, the past three decades have seen a dearth of empirical studies testing the thesis. The preponderance of empirical studies has examined its equally famous thesis—the *southern* subculture of violence (see Hawley & Messner 1989)—while neglecting the *black*-subculture-of-violence thesis. The sparse attention given to the latter thesis has resulted in an imprecise use of the race–violence association.

The black-subculture-of-violence thesis has been most fully developed by Wolfgang and Ferracuti (1967). Based on research conducted in inner-city Philadelphia in the mid-1950s (Wolfgang 1958), Wolfgang and Ferracuti (161) attempt to bring together "psychological and sociological constructs to aid in the explanation of the concentration of violence in specific socio-economic groups and ecological areas." They argue that certain segments of society have adopted distinctively violent subcultural values. This value system provides its members with normative support for their violent behavior, thereby increasing the likelihood that hostile impulses will lead to violent action. Further, relying on official data on violent crime, Wolfgang and Ferracuti speculate that there are a *black* subculture of violence and a *southern* subculture of violence. With specific regard to the black subculture of violence, they write, "Our subculture-of-violence thesis would, therefore, expect to find a large spread to the learning of, resort to, and criminal display of the violence value among minority groups such as Negroes" (264).

This speculation was later incorporated into the literature as the black-subculture-of-violence thesis. In addition, Wolfgang and Ferracuti (1967) argued that the subculture of violence varies according to gender, age, social class, employment status, region, and urban environment. The research reported in this chapter tests their black-subculture-of-violence thesis.

The most unique aspect of Wolfgang and Ferracuti's thesis is that subculture is a value system among its group members (blacks, in our case) that can transcend geographic places and social locations in a society. Wolfgang and Ferracuti are not alone in arguing that the subculture of violence is a value system (Erlanger 1976). Reed (1972), for example, proposed his argument in a similar fashion. He is more explicit, however, that the existence of such a subculture of violence can be established with attitudinal data measuring beliefs in violence.

Thus far, most empirical studies have focused on testing the subculture-of-violence thesis predictions about southern violence (see Hawley & Messner 1989 for a summary report). Race has entered these analyses mainly as a control variable. At the macrolevel, a number of studies claiming to have invested in a black-subculture-of-violence thesis have used the variable of percentage of blacks in an area (Messner 1983; Parker 1989; Williams & Flewelling 1988) as a substitute for the black subculture of violence. While these studies have found a relationship between percentage of blacks and violence, it is difficult to tell if a subculture of violence among blacks is responsible. Thus, an association between the subculture of violence among blacks and violence remains largely inconclusive.

The subculture-of-violence thesis has also been tested using attitudinal measures of approval of violence at the individual level. We argue that these efforts are more appropriate than using aggregate group membership in testing the original thesis advanced by Wolfgang and Ferracuti (1967), who suggested that the subculture of violence is a value system. In this regard, a number of studies that have tested the subculture of violence as a value and belief system have helped to inform the present study. Using cross-tabular techniques to analyze a national probability sample of American males over 21 years of age and a group of 363 inmates from a Michigan prison, Ball-Rokeach (1973) tested the hypothesis that violent behavior results from a commitment to a subcultural value. She found little evidence in support of the subculture-of-violence thesis. Her analyses, however, were limited to the effects of gender, education, and income; the effect of race was not examined. In a similar fashion, Poland (1978), using the same Rokeach Value Survey but limiting his sample to youths aged 14 to 22, confirmed the findings of Ball-Rokeach: the value systems of violent and nonviolent youths do not differ.

Erlanger (1974) provided the only direct test of Wolfgang and Ferracuti's contention that there is a subculture of violence among blacks. Reanalyzing data collected for the President's Commission on the Causes and Prevention of Violence, Erlanger (283) found that there is "an absence of major difference by race" in approval of interpersonal violence. Further, using his own data on peer esteem and social-psychological correlates of fighting among males aged 21–64 who resided in Milwaukee, Wisconsin, Erlanger (285) reported that "poor whites are more likely to fight than poor blacks," again contrary to the expectation from the black-subculture-of-violence thesis. In another study, Erlanger (1976) tested the southern-subculture-of-violence thesis, but race was controlled for in the analyses. He found that Milwaukee blacks born in the south are actually *less* likely than those born in other regions to report having engaged in fights.

Based on interview data by the Roper Public Opinion Research Center, Doerner (1978) developed a multiple regression model to assess the southern subculture of violence. In addition to the findings of no divergent value system among southerners, the data indicated that whites are significantly more likely to approve of assaultive behavior. Using self-reported measures of violent behavior among junior and senior high school students and developing a multivariate model, Hartnagel (1980) also tested the southern-subculture-of-violence thesis. Although he had race in his model as a control variable, he did not report or discuss the effect of race on the subculture of violence. A careful reading of the tables, however, reveals either that race is insignificant in predicting violent behavior or that black students are *less* likely to approve violent behavior than their white counterparts. The data were limited to high school students, and only four demographic variables are included in the model. Austin's (1980) research provided some support for the subcultural explanation of violence as measured by beliefs. He, however, failed to control race in his models.

The most sophisticated study of the subculture of violence is that done by Dixon and Lizotte (1987), who examined gun ownership and its relationship to the southern subculture of violence using two direct index measures of subcultural values and beliefs. Relying on data from the General Social Survey, their analyses revealed that white males are significantly more supportive of the use of violence in both hypothetical defensive and offensive situations. While Dixon and Lizotte directly measured individuals' beliefs in violence, they did not control all of the independent variables proposed by Wolfgang and Ferracuti, such as employment and violent history. Their focus was the test of the association between the southern subculture of violence and gun ownership.

More recently, relying on the data from the 1983 General Social Survey but limiting the analysis to only one of the measures developed by Dixon and Lizotte—the defensive subculture of violence—Ellison (1991) tested the effect of religion and a series of interactional effects on the southern subculture of violence values. His work confirmed Dixon and Lizotte's (1987) finding that whites are more likely than nonwhites to condone interpersonal violence in retaliatory situations.

In short, this review of existing studies on the subculture of violence indicates that none of the previous studies have attempted to directly test Wolfgang and Ferracuti's black-subculture-of- violence thesis. In addition to the limitations of samples and techniques of statistical analyses and insufficient control variables, these studies typically downplay the salience of race in the subculture of violence by either briefly mentioning its effect or ignoring it completely. Further, when race has been addressed, whites are often contrasted with nonwhites, which is imprecise. Given the sustained usage of the thesis, our study attempts to fill this void in the literature. Limiting ourselves to a test of Wolfgang and Ferracuti's hypothesis that the subculture-of-violence thesis would expect to find a large spread of violent values among African Americans, our analysis hopes to advance the research testing the black-subculture-of-violence thesis in several ways.

First, most of the previous studies testing the subculture-of-violence thesis have focused on its southern version; they have ignored the importance of race originally laid out as part of the theory. In contrast, race and its association with the subculture-of-violence thesis are central in our study.

Second, Wolfgang and Ferracuti (1967) stated clearly in their argument that the subculture of violence is a value system. As a result, macrolevel studies that use proxy measures for the black subculture of violence risk mismeasuring the concept, and their results may provide misinformed knowledge about the association between race and the subculture of violence. Instead, we adopt the direct measures of the subculture of violence, which represents a more truthful reflection of Wolfgang and Ferracuti's original scheme. Third, many of the previous studies that tested the thesis at the individual level have relied on local samples, while we use a nationwide, representative sample to test the thesis.

Finally, Wolfgang and Ferracuti (1967) have identified a number of important determinants of the subculture of violence, but previous studies have not attempted to control for all of these factors in their models. Our model includes all the major variables identified by Wolfgang and Ferracuti and thus potentially offers the most complete examination to date of the factors affecting beliefs in violence.

METHODS

Sample

The data for this study were drawn from the General Social Survey (GSS). We include the years from 1983 to 1991, although 1985 data were not included because of yearly item rotation. People who were not born in this country or who identify themselves neither as whites nor as blacks were eliminated from our analysis. Further, only males and people under the age of 65 are selected for this analysis. There are several reasons for these decisions. Since the black subculture of violence is seen as flowing from the unique experiences of African Americans in the United States, inclusion of people who were not born and who did not grow up in this country may contaminate results. Also, the subculture of violence refers specifically to a particular minority group—blacks—with reference to the majority group whites, and, thus, inclusion of people who belong to neither racial group may blur the difference. Finally, statistically and physically, the old and females are less threatening to the public in their behavior. Wolfgang and Ferracuti (1967: 258) claimed, "Almost universally it can be asserted that the highest incidence of assaultive crimes such as homicide is found among young offenders, most of whom are in their twenties, many of whom are in their late teens or early thirties. Males predominate everywhere." A narrower designation by exclusion of the old and females has produced more distinct and relevant evidence of the hypothesized racial cultural difference.

The total number of cases in our analysis is 3,218, with 395 or 12.3 percent of the sample being African Americans. Some of the sample characteristics are presented in Table 4.1. On average, whites in our sample are slightly older, receive more than one year of education, have higher family income, and are more likely to be employed than blacks. Blacks are more likely than whites to be found in the census in the South[1] and in cities with more than 50,000 residents.

Table 4.1
Selected Sample Characteristics

Characteristics	Mean	Standard Deviation	Cases
A. Age			
Blacks	38.17	13.59	395
Whites	38.69	12.61	2,823
B. Education			
Blacks	11.94	3.05	395
Whites	13.24	3.00	2,823
C. Income			
Blacks	3.55	1.39	395
Whites	4.12	1.18	2,823
D. Cities greater than 50,000			
Blacks	0.58	0.50	395
Whites	0.22	0.42	2,823
E. Region			
Blacks	0.47	0.50	395
Whites	0.32	0.47	2,823
F. Employment			
Blacks	0.61	0.49	395
Whites	0.75	0.43	2,823

Dependent Variables

The dependent variable in this study—black subculture of violence—is operationalized using three measures. They are an index of violent defensive values and two items of violent offensive values. The index of violent defensive values taps support for violence in defense of women, children, and property. Although this is not a direct measure of Wolfgang and Ferracuti's subculture of violence (Dixon & Lizotte 1987), it is considered part of normative support for violence in interpersonal relations (see Ellison & McCall 1989, Corzine & Huff-Corzine 1988, and Dixon & Lizotte 1987 for details). The second and third measures are the direct measurement of Wolfgang and Ferracuti's subculture of violence: they measure support for violent response to situations that provide little or no justification for violence.

Dixon and Lizotte's (1987) index of violent defensive values taps approval for violence undertaken to protect children, women, and property from an assailant. It is composed of three situations in the General Social Survey. The respondents were asked, "Would you approve of a man punching a stranger who had hit the man's child after the child accidentally damaged the stranger's car?" "... was beating up a woman and the man saw it?" "... had broken into the man's house?" We coded the answers to each item according to Dixon and Lizotte's (1987) scale: 0 = no, 1 = don't know and not sure, 2 = yes. The final index variable varies from 0 = do not approve of punching in any of these situations to 6 = approve of punching in all of these situations. The reliability of our measure is .553.

As for the violent offensive values, we selected two items from the General Social Survey. These two items asked, "Would you approve of a man punching a stranger if the stranger was in a protest march showing opposition to the other man's view?" and "... was drunk and bumped into the man and his wife on the street?" These questions attempted to capture support for violent responses to nonphysical threat or unintentional conduct. Because these two items cannot be formed as an index variable, we coded them into two binary variables with 1 = yes and 0 = no. The logistic regression technique was used to analyze each item separately.

We did not use Dixon and Lizotte's four-item scale of offensive subculture of violence. The major weakness of their scale is that it suffers from confounding two types of items within their scale. In two of the items (as shown in the previous paragraph), the subject is *the generalized others* striking another man, while in the other two items the subject is the more specific others—*a policeman*—striking another male civilian.[2] Many empirical studies have shown that blacks in general have a significantly lower evaluation of the police than whites do (Peek et al. 1981; but also see Cao et al. 1996). Thus, the word "policeman" might cause a reaction that is different from the reaction to the word "man," which would confuse the racial difference toward the acceptance of violence. The subculture of violence is a rebellion against civil behavior or conventional culture, not necessarily against state power, which the *police* represent. For these reasons, we eliminated the two items containing *the police* as the subject of evaluation and used only two items as our measures of violent offensive subculture.

Independent Variables

Wolfgang and Ferracuti (1967) have specifically implied that the demographic groups with the "most intense" subculture of violence would be among young, black, and southern males and from the lower and working classes. We include all of these characteristics in our analysis.

The major independent variable of race treats whites as the reference group and codes blacks as 1 and whites as 0. The black-subculture-of-violence thesis hypothesizes that race is positively related to both violent defensive values and violent offensive values, and it is these predictions we wish to test.

The other major demographic variables are coded as follows. Age is coded as the respondent's age at the year interviewed. Because of aforementioned exclusions, it contains respondents between 18 and 65. Education is coded as years of formal schooling that respondents reported. In our sample, it ranges between 0 (no formal education) and 20 years of schooling. Family income[3] is coded as an ordinal variable. The categories are as follows: 1 = $3,999 and below, 2 = $4,000 to 6,999, 3 = $7,000 to $14,999, 4 = $15,000 to $24,999, and 5 = $25,000 and above. Wolfgang and Ferracuti (1967: 261) claimed that "the overwhelming majority of homicides and other assaultive crimes are committed by persons from the lowest stratum of a social organization." All three variables—age, education, and family income—are expected to have a negative effect on our dependent variables.

We also have two groups of control variables. The first group includes cities with more than 50,000 residents, region, employment status, and drinking habit. The second group consists of two variables of early socialization—family income at age 16 and violent history.[4]

Cities code those who reside in central cities larger than 50,000 people as 1 and those living outside them as 0. Wolfgang and Ferracuti (1967: 298) maintain that "the contemporary American city has the accoutrements not only for the genesis but also for the highly accelerated development of this subculture." Region codes the census South as 1 and the other regions as 0. Employment status is a dummy variable with 1=employment, and 0=other employment status. The last variable of this group, drinking, codes those who do not drink as 0, those who drink alcoholic beverages as 1, and those who sometimes drink more than they think they should as 2. Erlanger (1974: 289) proposed that "the use of liquor may be part of a broader social configuration which generates situations conducive to violence." It is expected that living in central cities, in the South, and drinking are positively related to holding violent subculture values while employment is negatively related to holding these values.

Finally, the first of two early socialization variables—family income when the respondent was 16 years old—is coded as 1=far below average, to 5 = far above average. The second, violent experiences, is a combined variable, composed of three items, that taps a respondent's experiences of being hit as a child, as an adult, and both and being threatened with a gun as a child, as an adult, and both. It varies from 0 = no such experiences, to 8 = both being hit and being threatened with a gun in both childhood and adulthood. It is expected that one's violent history is positively related to one's attitude condoning violence, while childhood family income is negatively related to it. These socialization variables are important because Wolfgang (1958) argues that subcultures of violence are characterized by social values that are transmitted during socialization and govern behavior in a variety of structurally induced situations.

RESULTS

To test the Wolfgang and Ferracuti's black-subculture-of-violence thesis, we ran an ordinary least squares regression on the index of defensive values and logistic regression on the two items of offensive violent beliefs. In addition, we computed descriptive statistics and zero-order correlations for the variables in the model. Since none of the correlations are above .5, multicollinearity is not a potential problem for our analysis.

Table 4.2 presents the results of ordinary least squares regression analysis of the impact of race on the defensive violent subculture. Whites are found to be significantly more vocal than blacks in expressing their support for the use of violence in defensive situations, with the effects of other factors held constant. This result contradicts the expectation from the black-subculture-of-violence thesis set forth by Wolfgang and Ferracuti. It is consistent, however, with previous findings using a similar measure (Dixon & Lizotte 1987; Ellison 1991).

Table 4.2
The Impact of Race on Defensive Subculture

Variables	b coefficients	B coefficients
Race (Black=1)	- .4465***	-.0891
Age	- .0116***	-.0900
Education	.0182	.0335
Income	.1110***	.0823
Cities	- .3073***	-.0825
Region (south=1)	.1085	.0311
Employment	.1519*	.0408
Drinking	.1212**	.0558
Income at 16	.1178***	.0605
Violent History	.0519***	.0751
(Constant)	3.9996***	

R-square =   .0664
F =   22.7902
Significance .0000

* $0.01 < p < 0.05$; ** $0.001 < p < 0.01$; *** $p < 0.001$

Consistent with our prediction, support for interpersonal violence in defensive situations declines with age. In addition, the control variables of drinking and violent history significantly increase such support. Contradictory to our expectations, support for interpersonal violence increases with family income, employment, and family income at age 16 but decreases for those residing in large cities. Other variables, notably, residence in the South, in our model are not statistically significant.

In short, when holding all other factors constant, a typical person with a defensive violent subculture is white, young, with good income, currently employed, and not living in central cities, likes alcohol, and is more likely to be the one who grew up in a well-to-do family at age 16 and who had some personal experiences with violence.

The results of the logistic regressions of the impact of race on violent reaction to nonthreatening situations are presented in Table 4.3. They show that there is no significant race effect in support of interpersonal violence in either of the offensive situations when the effects of other factors are controlled for. Again, the findings are inconsistent with the black-subculture-of-violence thesis but are consistent with previous findings on the subject (Doerner 1978; Erlanger 1974; Hartnagel 1980; Felson et al. 1994). Our results dispute the existence of such a unique subculture among African Americans, in particular, the violent subculture expressed in their attitudes that may be captured by our measures.

Other results from Table 4.3 are consistent with our predictions: a person's education, family income, and drinking decrease the support of interpersonal violence in offensive situations, while being in the South increases such support. However, contradictory to our expectation, residents in large cities seem to be less supportive of violence than others. The rest of the independent variables in our model are not statistically significant in their effects.

In short, when everything else is equal, a typical person with an offensive violent subculture is a less well educated person who currently lives in the South. Depending on the situation,[5] he is also more likely to be poor, not living in central cities, nonalcoholic, and with personal violent experiences.

DISCUSSION

Fischer (1975) calls ethnic subculture "the most difficult test case for subculture theory." We took up this challenge and tested Wolfgang and Ferracuti's thesis of the black subculture of violence. With a number of control variables, we explored whether there is a difference between whites and blacks in their values on defensive and offensive situations. Our results indicate that white males express significantly more violent beliefs in defensive or retaliatory situations than blacks. Furthermore, contrary to the expectations from the black-subculture-of-violence thesis, it is found that there is no significant difference between white and black males in offensive situations. These results, however, are quite consistent with a number of previous findings on the issue (Dixon & Lizotte 1987; Doerner 1978; Ellison 1991; Erlanger 1974; Felson et al. 1994; Hartnagel 1980). Ellison (1991: 1229), for example, concluded, that "With the effects of other factors held constant, whites are substantially more likely than nonwhites to endorse interpersonal violence in defensive situations." A few years earlier, Dixon and Lizotte (1987: 399) stated "Defensive attitudes, like violent attitudes, are more prevalent for white males than black males."

Table 4.3
The Logistic Regression of the Impact of Race on Violent Reaction to Opposing Protesters and Unintentional Bumps

Variables	Unintentional Bumps Logit coefficients	Reaction to Protestors Logit coefficients
Race (Black=1)	-.1100	.0347
	(.1876)	(.2467)
Age	.0043	.0057
	(.0047)	(.0069)
Education	-.0533**	-.1129***
	(.0204)	(.0289)
Income	-.1006	-.2068**
	(.0523)	(.0733)
Cities	-.3412*	-.1290
	(.1511)	(.2101)
Region (South=1)	.7025***	.4634**
	(.1208)	(.1769)
Employment	-.2028	.0927
	(.1398)	(.2039)
Drinking	-.1565*	-.1458
	(.0781)	(.1123)
Income at 16	-.0537	-.2381*
	(.0728)	(.1037)
Violent History	.0037	.0915**
	(.0248)	(.0351)
Constant	-.9788*	-.7485
	(.4184)	(.5976)
-2 Log Likelihood	2058.230	1133.905

* $0.01 < p < 0.05$; ** $0.001 < p < 0.01$; *** $p < 0.001$
* Standard error is in the parentheses.

In addition to the primary finding of race, other independent variables have yielded mixed results. Support for interpersonal defensive violence declines with age, and age is not significant in predicting interpersonal offensive violence. Social class, measured by family income at the time of interview and family income at the age of 16, is positively related to the defensive violent values but negatively related to the offensive values, although only one of them is significant. When it is measured by education, it does not affect defensive tendency but reduces both offensive tendencies. Inner-city residents score significantly lower in defensive values than people in other areas and in one of the offensive values. Living in the South predicts holding offensive violent values but not defensive violent values. Employment status increases tendencies of violence in defensive situations but not in the offensive situations. Drinking and violent history both increase the likelihood of possessing defensive violent values and the offensive violent values under one of the situations. Because the coefficients of these variables are small, and there is no consistent pattern, we do not draw any conclusion from them.

The major finding of this study warrants further discussion. Our data are limited to the general public, which may be inadequate to test subcultural theories (Matsueda et al. 1992). Specifically including criminals in our sample, however, would trigger a larger debate on the topic of whether criminals, as a group, regardless of race, have a different value system from that of law-abiding citizens (Agnew 1994; Sykes & Matza 1957). Another limitation of our data is that we were unable to locate the neighborhoods of our respondents. It is possible that a subculture of violence may involve belief systems that characterize a particular urban community (Cloward & Ohlin 1960; Fischer 1995). Inclusion of this ecological element, thus, would shift focus from subcultural beliefs in violence, which could transcend place, to a more complicated interaction between community and value system. This would change Wolfgang and Ferracuti's a priori presumption from the one that subculture is a value system to the one that subculture is a place, an opinion held by some subcultural theorists (Cloward & Ohlin 1960; Fischer 1995). Both of the issues are beyond the scope of this chapter.

It is possible that blacks have distinctive values that tolerate violence, but our measures fail to capture those values. We think that such a possibility is unlikely.[6] Our measures, taken from the General Social Surveys, are based on those used by Ball-Rokeach (1973) in an earlier test of the subculture-of-violence thesis. There is good reason to believe that these specific situations reflect the violent attitudes indicative of participation in a subculture of violence. Erlanger (1974: 283) argues that although acceptance of these items does not imply membership in a subculture of violence, "it seems reasonable to assume that persons who are in such a subculture would find it quite easy to support many of the items." In particular, the support for the use of aggression in situations that provide little or no justification for violence (our two offensive items) would be indicative of the violent attitudes expected of members of a subculture of violence. In sum, despite the previously mentioned limitations and concerns, our finding of no relationship between subcultural violent values and blacks in general is salient, is not a post hoc rationalization, does not reflect a response bias, and is unlikely to be a methodological artifact.

We do not claim that we have offered a complete test of Wolfgang and Ferracuti's theory. Our dependent variables measure only individuals' verbal approval of defensive and offensive assaults. We are not able to measure the connections of these beliefs to violent behavior, nor is it clear whether this support would be carried over to more lethal forms of violence, such as homicide. Wolfgang and Ferracuti's original development of the subculture-of-violence thesis was stimulated by an interest in both assault and lethal violence. Further, we found that Wolfgang and Ferracuti's theory is broad and has elements of a structural explanation of crime in addition to a cultural explanation of crime. For example, they (1967: 263–264) explain the black involvement with crime by arguing, "Restricted and isolated from the institutionalized means to achieve the goals of the dominant culture, many more Negroes than whites are caught in what Merton, Cloward and Ohlin, and others refer to as the differential opportunity structure, and are more likely to commit crime."   However, Wolfgang and Ferracuti (1967) do insist that the main component of a subculture of violence is a value system that can be separated from its structural carrier and that being African American should predict violent values. It is against this argument that we set up our test.

Based on our data and analyses, there is enough evidence to conclude that blacks in the general U.S. population are no more likely than whites to embrace values favorable to violence. Our findings thus repudiate the idea that the causes of black crime are rooted in unique aspects of black culture. Having stated this, one caveat about our conclusion is in order: it cannot be interpreted as a rejection of the subculture of violence as a useful concept to explain violent behavior. It simply means that being black does not imply a greater probability of embracing a subculture of violence as measured by individual's beliefs and attitudes.

Extending our findings beyond this chapter, we argue that within the sociology and criminology literature, the continuing usage of the black subculture of violence as an explanation of racial differences in violence is difficult to justify. It is clearly false to assume that all blacks in our society who live across all geographic places and across all stratification locations are homogeneous in values and lifestyles (Wilson 1978). Further, the concept of the black subculture of violence implicitly entails a pejorative indictment of all African Americans, which is unfair and potentially racist in nature (Parker 1989). To use this concept without sufficient empirical support lends legitimacy to politicians who use race-based stereotypes about crime as a means of stirring up racial enmity in our society. As Tonry (1995: 6) noted, the text may be crime (or violence, in our case), but "the subtext is race." Sociologists and criminologists cannot afford to shy away from race as a topic of serious scholarly attention (Wilson & Aponte 1985).

Finally, a more fruitful search for the root causes of black violence may lie, as Sampson (1987), Parker (1989), and Shihadeh and Steffensmeier (1994) have suggested, in the structurally disadvantaged position of blacks in U.S. society. At the same time that inner-city blacks have few legitimate opportunities for advancement in our social structure (Wilson 1986, 1996), they have ample opportunities to act violently. Thus, differential opportunities in conjunction with racial inequality may be the key to understanding black violence (Cloward & Ohlin 1960; Cullen 1983). Violent behavior may constitute "the normal reaction of normal people to abnormal conditions" (Plant 1937: 248)

NOTES

A shorter version of this article appeared in *Criminology* 35, (2): 367–379. We wish to thank Francis T. Cullen for helpful comments on the previous draft of this chapter. Direct all correspondence to Liqun Cao, Department of Sociology, Anthropology, and Criminology, Eastern Michigan University, Ypsilanti, MI 48197.

1. The census South is slightly different from the more traditional confederal South. It includes Delaware, Maryland, West Virginia, Virginia, North Carolina, South Carolina, Georgia, Florida, District of Columbia, Kentucky, Tennessee, Alabama, Mississippi, Arkansas, Oklahoma, Louisiana, and Texas.

2. One asked, "Would you approve of a policeman striking an adult male citizen if the male citizen had said vulgar and obscene things to the policeman?" and the other asked, "Would you approve of a policeman striking an adult male citizen if the male citizen was being questioned as a suspect in a murder case?"

3. In earlier analysis, we also included the subjective evaluation of one's class, but we deleted it from our final model since it was insignificant and since it was a less objective measure than income.

4. We also had variables of anomie, marital status, happiness, native South (a combination of growing up in the South and currently living in the South), and television watching, but we dropped them in our final model because none of them are statistically significant in predicting the subculture of violence, because their theoretical implication is not strong (marital and residence), or because we do not have their information on every year (anomie, happiness, and television watching). Our results do not change with/without these variables.

5. All these variables are significant at the .05 level in at least one of the situations. Further, even if the variables are not significant in predicting violent reactions, their signs of prediction are the same.

6. In response to the criticisms of their measures of the subculture of violence, Dixon and Lizotte argue that until a measure of aspects other than Wolfgang and Ferracuti's (1967) is found, they are not persuaded of these criticisms of measurement errors. "The burden of proof is with those advocating alternative conceptualizations and measures" (1989: 187).

REFERENCES

Adler, Freda, Gerhard O.W. Mueller, and William S. Laufer (1994). *Criminal Justice.* New York: McGraw-Hill.

Agnew, Robert (1994). "The Techniques of Neutralization and Violence." *Criminology* 32: 555–580.

Austin, Roy L. (1980). "Adolescent Subcultures of Violence." *The Sociological Quarterly* 21: 545–561.

Ball-Rokeach, Sandra J. (1973). "Values and Violence: A Test of the Subculture of Violence Thesis." *American Sociological Review* 38: 736–749.

Barlow, Hugh D. (1996). *Criminology.* New York: HarperCollins College.

Cao, Liqun, James Frank, and Francis T. Cullen. (1996). "Race, Community Context, and Confidence in the Police." *American Journal of Police* 15: 3–22.

Cloward, Richard A. and Lloyd E. Ohlin. (1960). *Delinquency and Opportunity: A Theory of Delinquent Gangs.* New York: Free Press.

Corzine, Jay and Lin Huff-Corzine. (1989). "On Cultural Explanations of Southern

Homicide: Comment on Dixon and Lizotte." *American Journal of Sociology* 95: 178–182.

Coser, Lewis A., Steven L. Nock, Patricia A. Steffan, and Daphne Spain. (1990). *Introduction to Sociology.* San Diego: Harcourt Brace Jovanovich.

Cullen, Francis T. . (1983). *Rethinking Crime and Deviance Theory: The Emergence of a Structuring Tradition.* Totowa, NJ: Rowman & Allanheld.

Dixon, Jo and Alan J. Lizotte. (1987). "Gun Ownership and the Southern Subculture of Violence." *American Journal of Sociology* 93: 383–405.

———. (1989). "The Burden of Proof: Southern Subculture-of-Violence Explanations of the Relationship between Gun Ownership and Homicide." *American Journal of Sociology* 95: 182–187.

Doerner, William G. (1978). "The Index of Southernness Revisited: The Influence of Wherefrom upon Whodunnit." *Criminology* 16: 47–65.

Ellison, Christopher G. (1991). "An eye for an eye? A Note on the Southern Subculture of Violence Thesis." *Social Forces* 69: 1223–1239.

Ellison, Christopher G. and Patricia L. McCall. (1989). "Region and Violent Attitudes Reconsidered: Comment on Dixon and Lizotte." *American Journal of Sociology* 95: 174–178.

Erlanger, Howard S. (1974). "The Empirical Sstatus of the Sub-Cultures of Violence Thesis." *Social Problems* 22: 280–292.

———. (1976). "Is There a Subculture of Violence in the South?" *Journal of Criminal Law and Criminology* 66: 483–490.

Felson, Richard B., Allen E. Liska, Scott J. South, and Thomas L. McNulty. (1994). "The Subculture of Violence and Delinquency: Individual vs. School Context Effects." *Social Forces* 73: 155–173.

Fischer, Claude S. (1975). "Toward a Subcultural Theory of Urbanism." *American Journal of Sociology* 80: 1319–1341.

———. (1995). "The Subcultural Theory of Urbanism: A Twentieth-Year Assessment." *American Journal of Sociology* 101: 543–577.

Hartnagel, Timothy F. (1980). "Subculture of Violence: Further Evidence." *Pacific Sociological Review* 23: 217–242.

Hawley, F. Frederick and Steven F. Messner. (1989). "The Southern Violence Construct: A Review of Arguments, Evidence, and the Normative Context." *Justice Quarterly* 6: 481–511.

Matsueda, Ross L., Rosemary Gartner, Irving Piliavin, and Michael Polakowski. (1992). "The Prestige of Criminal and Conventional Occupations: A Subcultural Model of Criminal Activity." *American Sociological Review* 57: 752–770.

Messner, Steven F. (1983). "Regional and Racial Effects on the Urban Homicide Rate: The Subculture of Violence Revisited." *American Journal of Sociology* 88: 997–1007.

Parker, Robert Nash. (1989). "Poverty, Subculture of Violence, and Type of Homicide." *Social Forces* 67: 983–1007.

Peek, Charles W., George D. Lowe, and Jon P. Alston. (1981). "Race and Attitudes toward Local Police." *Journal of Black Studies* 11: 361–374.

Plant, James, Stuart. (1937). *Personality and the Cultural Pattern.* London: Oxford University Press.

Poland, James M. (1978). "Subculture of Violence: Youth Offender Value Systems." *Criminal Justice and Behavior* 5: 159–164.

Reed, John Shelton. (1972). *The Enduring South: Subcultural Persistence in Mass Society.* Lexington, MA: D.C. Heath/Lexington Books.

Sampson, Robert. (1987). "Urban Black Violence: The Effect of Male Joblessness and Family Disruption." *American Journal of Sociology* 93: 348–382.

Shihadeh, Edward S. and Darrell J. Steffensmeier. (1994). "Economic Inequality, Family Disruption, and Urban Black Violence: Cities as Units of Stratification and Social Control." *Social Forces* 73: 729–751.

Siegel, Larry J. (1992). *Criminology.* New York: West.

Sykes, Gresham M. and David Matza. (1957). "Techniques of Neutralization: A Theory of Delinquency." *American Sociological Review* 22: 664–670.

Tonry, Michael. (1995). *Malign Neglect: Race, Crime and Punishment in America.* New York: Oxford University Press.

Williams, Kirk and Robert Flewelling. (1988). "The Social Production of Criminal Homicide: A Comparative Study of Disaggregated Rates in American Cities." *American Sociological Review* 53: 421–431.

Wilson, William Julius. (1978). *The Declining Significance of Race.* Chicago: University of Chicago Press.

———. (1986). "The Urban Underclass in Advanced Industrial Society." In P. E. Peterson (ed.), *The New Urban Reality,* 129–60. Washington, DC: Brookings Institution.

———. (1996). *When Work Disappears: The World of the New Urban Poor.* New York: Random House.

Wilson, William J. and Robert Aponte. (1985). "Urban poverty." *Annual Review of Sociology* 11: 231–58.

Wolfgang, Marvin E. (1958). *Patterns of Criminal Homicide.* Philadelphia: University of Pennsylvania Press.

——— and Franco Ferracuti. (1967). *The Subculture of Violence: Towards an Integrated Theory in Criminology.* New York: Tavistock.

Part II

Policing, Race, and Justice

Chapter 5

Determinants of Black-to-White Arrest Differentials: A Review of the Literature

Steven R. Cureton

The disproportionately higher ratio of black-to-white offenders in the United States' penal system has initiated debate about possible discrimination or discretionary justice (Walker et al. 1996). Many scholars have studied the determinants and consequences of police discretion in making arrests (Smith, Visher & Davidson 1984), and various theories have been formulated to explain black-to-white arrest differentials. Thorsten Sellin (1928) was one of the first researchers to investigate racial discrimination in the United States' legal system. The practice of discretionary justice, particularly by police officers, has been explained by psychological theories (Tittle 1994; Tittle & Curran 1988; Pruitt & James 1983; Chambliss & Seidman 1982; Gibson 1978), the effects of labeling (Tittle 1975), and general theories of societal organization. From the perspective of the criminal justice system, two organizational models have been explored because of the contradictory postulates of each with regard to the initiation of individuals into the system.

Consensus theory contends that the law will be more or less equally imposed on minorities and majorities so that any differences in application will be in response to actual criminal behavior. Consensus theory implies that criminal justice decisions are nondiscriminatory because decisions will be based on offensive conduct and/or relevant legal variables. Alternatively, conflict theory posits that the law will be differentially enforced against minorities and that this differential enforcement will vary in magnitude with the degree of threat posed (or perceived to be posed) to the elite positions by minorities. Conflict theory suggests that criminal justice decisions will be discriminatory and designed to sanction offenders based on extralegal variables (e.g., subordinate group characteristics—race, class, age, and gender) (Akers 1997: 147).

The following review of the literature explores the issue of which of these perspectives is more applicable as an explanation of the determinants of police arrest decisions. This exploration also highlights the extent to which racial discrimination has been identified through research as a factor affecting law enforcement decision making and, by implication, the overrepresentation of minorities in the criminal justice system. Before examining the literature, a brief presentation of the fundamental assumptions made by consensus and conflict theory is necessary.

Consensus theory contends that social order is contingent upon a society of people functioning together to preserve a common, agreed upon value system, to enforce the norms that such a value system generates, and to promote survival, continuity, and wholeness (Bernard 1983; Parsons 1951). The purpose of social control is to discourage threats to the group (e.g., criminal behavior), its value system, and/or the "collective conscience" (Tittle 1994).

Consensus theory further postulates that when equality is a fundamental value, sanctions will be objectively imposed on individuals who engage in behavior that is contrary to the generally accepted norms of conduct (Tittle 1994; Chambliss & Seidman 1971). This perspective thus suggests that the disproportionate attention paid by the legal machinery of the United States toward minorities is due more to their frequency of engaging in socially proscribed behaviors than to any institutional discrimination (Akers 1997; Tittle 1994).

Alternatively, conflict theory postulates that societies are held together by constraint and the coercion of one group over another, not by consensus or universal agreement (Dahrendorf 1958). State organizations (i.e., police departments) depend on the owners of the means of production and its outputs; therefore, state organizations are value-laden with the interests of rulers, making these organizations primary vehicles for coercive control and suppression of subordinates (Chambliss 1976; Chambliss & Seidman 1971). Thus, the socially powerful use social sanctions to assign "criminal" status to subordinates who threaten the power, resources, and interests of rulers (Turk 1969). Actual or perceived threat may or may not be independent of actual behavior. Consequently, discriminant application of the law and disproportionate attention of the U.S. legal institutions to minorities are due largely to group characteristics and the degree of "threat" presented by subordinate classes (Akers 1997; Tittle 1994).

Essentially, conflict theory postulates that patterns of legal sanctioning are inherently discriminatory in their reflection of the interest of the powerful, while consensus theory implies a more democratic and nondiscriminatory social orientation toward patterns of legal sanctioning (Tittle 1994). These competing theoretical foundations have served as overarching paradigms for the evolution of policing research with regard to race. The following analysis explores the extent to which such research has provided support for their respective tenets.

EMPIRICAL VALIDITY OF CONSENSUS AND CONFLICT THEORY

The studies selected for this analysis fulfilled two significant criteria: did the research involve determination of arrest differentials by race, and were such differentials measured by legal and/or extralegal variables? In particular, determinants of arrest differentials were measured by legal and extralegal factors to identify each set of conclusions as either consensus- or conflict- based. Factors were required to be significantly related to racial arrest differentials.[1]

Consensus theory implies that legal agents sanction those behaviors that threaten the social order, social welfare, preservation, continuity, and collective conscience of society; thus, police officers will arrest only those suspects whose offensive behavior(s) threatens functioning members of society and/or is disruptive of the social order.[2] Therefore, studies indicating that black-to-white arrest differentials are significantly related to criminal conduct or police obligation to protect functioning members of society (i.e., victim preference or citizen requested that the offender be arrested) are considered evidence in support of consensus theory. For example, Visher's (1983) investigation of police encounters with male and female offenders in St. Louis, Missouri, Rochester, New York, and Tampa - St. Petersburg, Florida, revealed that black male and black female suspects were arrested more than white suspects because of victim's preference and testimony (15-17). Black and Reiss (1970) also found that encounters with black juveniles more than encounters with white juveniles involved the presence of citizens or black complainants who expressed a preference for black juveniles to be taken into custody (67-69).

Other researchers have found that blacks were arrested more than whites because of their significantly higher rate of involvement in criminal activity and/or seriousness of offense (Wilson 1968; Black & Reiss 1970; Black 1971; Hindelang 1978; Lundman, Sykes & Clark, 1978; Williams & Drake 1980; Liska & Chamlin 1984). In another significant piece of research supporting consensus theory, Skolnick (1966) found that police discretion depends on whether officers are assured that suspects are trustworthy and able to post bail at a later time, as well as the number of outstanding warrants and suspects' residential stability. He found that since blacks are generally less likely than whites to measure up to these criteria, they are more susceptible to being arrested (81-84). These findings support the consensus notion that initial arrests reflect law enforcement agents' obligation to fulfill their roles as front- line providers of public safety and social order (Smith & Visher 1981: 172-174).

Discriminatory, extraneous processes such as police attitudes, values, beliefs, and suspicion support conflict theory. Conflict theory implies that legal agents function to protect the interest of the elites at the expense of subordinates. Given that elites and subordinates are engaged in a constant struggle for power and that elites use legal agents to suppress subordinate efforts to obtain power, it follows that there will be social distance, strained relations, and/or lack of identification between police officers and subordinates. Therefore, officers perceive subordinates, particularly blacks, as antagonistic and less deserving of legal protection (Smith, Visher, and Davidson 1984). For example, Wilson (1968) found that disproportionately higher black arrest rates were significantly related to an officer's personal attitudes and perceptions, a conclusion supported through other research that focused on police prejudice and suspicion based on skin color (Piliavin & Briar 1964; Skolnick 1966; Johnson Peterson, and Wells, 1977).

Additionally, studies that link race-based arrest differentials with perceived threatening group characteristics (i.e., race, age, low socioeconomic status [SES], unemployment, etc.) support conflict theory's contention that formal legal agents sanction subordinates in an effort to suppress, regulate, and deter threats to elite control of resources and social power (Williams & Drake 1980; Smith & Visher 1981; Visher, 1983; Liska & Chamlin, 1984; Smith, et al.1984).

Still other researchers have found that black arrests were disproportionately associated with the racial composition of an area, particularly if that area was populated by a significant percentage of poor nonwhites (Green 1970; McCarthy 1991). Hepburn (1978) suggested that blacks represent a powerless group; thus, arbitrary police dispositions against blacks held very little consequence for the police, as the punishment for such mistakes was not harsh. Hence, the costs of legally unjustified arrests are low, particularly if a member of the powerless group was involved (60–66). Moreover, other researchers have suggested that geographically or organizationally concentrated populations of concentrated blacks represent a threat to elite status because such concentrations maximize chances of concerted action against envious, jealous, and suspicious elites (Chambliss & Seidman 1982; Turk 1969).

SUMMARY OF FINDINGS

Table 5.1 summarizes research concerning black-to-white arrest differentials since 1964. As mentioned, research supporting consensus theory finds criminal conduct/crime seriousness to be significantly related to racial arrest differentials. Conversely, in research supporting conflict theory, investigator(s) found higher black arrest rates relative to whites to be due to differential police concentration, control, and/or practices, independently of crime-related factors. It is worth noting that some studies with both legal and extralegal measures found support for both consensus and conflict theory.

Seven out of 16 studies showed that blacks were arrested more than whites because of both criminal conduct/crime seriousness (consensus) and subordinate group characteristics (conflict). Eight out of 16 studies showed that subordinate group status was a stronger predictor (compared to criminal conduct) of higher arrests for blacks than whites. Only one study indicated that criminal conduct and/or crime seriousness was a stronger determinant (compared to subordinate group status) of higher arrests for blacks than whites.

DISCUSSION

In all 16 studies examining black-to-white arrest differentials, the one constant factor that emerges is that blacks are arrested more than whites. Three themes emerge from the studies. First, even though research demonstrates that black arrests are higher than arrests for whites, the evidence does not definitively support either theoretical perspective as a "best" explanation for police decisions to arrest. Thus, based on previous research, we cannot conclusively accept or reject either consensus or conflict theory as the perspective better suited to explain police decisions to arrest. In addition, any generalizations concerning the pervasiveness of discrimination by police would be premature in light of the fact that the evidence reviewed reveals that black arrest disparities are significantly related to both their involvement in criminal behavior and/or their subordinate status. Finally, dichotomizing the nature of society using the consensus and conflict models may be misleading, as such "ideal types" fail to exist in the social reality of American society. The nature of social order may not be limited to a value-neutral state functioning for the benefit of everyone or value-laden with the interest of the elites at the expense of subordinates. The state could be an independent entity, that functions to protect itself from behaviors and people that contradict or threaten social continuity, social order, and economic capitalistic progression (Beirne & Quinney 1982; Quinney 1973).

Table 5.1
Research Examining the Determinants of Black-to-White Arrest Differentials

Investigator(s)	Race/ Ethnicity Test	Higher Arrests for Blacks	Consensus	Conflict
Piliavin/Briar 1964	yes	X		X
Skolnick 1966	yes	X	X	X
Wilson 1968	yes	X	X	X
Black/Reiss 1970	yes	X	X	
Green 1970	yes	X	X	
Black 1971	yes	X	X	X
Johnson et al. 1977	yes	X	X	
Hepburn 1978	yes	X	X	
Hindelang 1978	yes	X	X	X
Lundman et al. 1978	yes	X	X	
Williams/Drake 1980	yes	X	X	X
Smith/Visher 1981	yes	X	X	
Visher 1983	yes	X	X	X
Liska/Chamlin 1984	yes	X	X	X
Smith et al. 1984	yes	X	X	
McCarthy 1991	yes	X	X	
Totals	**16(100%)**	**16(100%)**	**15(94%)**	**8(50%)**

X=studies tested for and found a significant relationship between higher black arrests and consensus and/or conflict predictors

Recent research on the topic of racially based decision making by police has considered the microlevel effects of suspect demeanor and lack of deference, finding a significant relationship between disposition of the suspect and police decisions to arrest (Klinger 1994, 1996; Lundman 1994; Smith 1987; Black 1971; Black & Reiss 1970; Wilson 1968; Skolnick 1966; Piliavin & Briar 1964). Rather than focusing on social orientation alone, future research should consider the joint effects of both macrolevel structural predictors (posited by consensus and conflict theory) and microlevel process predictors such as intra/interracial crime, informal police organizational rules, socialization experiences, and the like. Theoretical integration of such factors across social levels, combined with thoughtful operationalization of concepts, would enable a more comprehensive and meaningful analysis of the problem, thus bringing us that much closer to understanding the relationship between race and arrest.

NOTES

1. Significant relationship = probability < .05.

2. Social order refers to behavior consistent with agreed upon informal values and norms and institutionalized, formal legal codes.

REFERENCES

Akers, R. (1997). *Criminological Theories: Introduction and Evaluation.* Los Angeles, CA: Roxbury.

Beirne, P. and R. Quinney. (1982). *Marxism and Law.* New York: John Wiley and Sons.

Bernard, T. J. (1983). *The Consensus-Conflict Debate: Form and Content In Social Theories.* New York: Columbia University Press.

Black, D. J. (1971). "The Social Organization of Arrest." *Stanford Law Review* 23: 1087-1111.

Black, D. J. and A. J. Reiss. (1970). "Police Control of Juveniles." *American Sociological Review* 23: 63-77.

Chambliss, W. J. (1976). "Functional and Conflict Theories of Crime: The Heritage of Emile Durkheim and Karl Marx." In W. J.Chambliss and M. Mankoff (eds.), *Whose Law? What Order?: A Conflict Approach to Criminology.* 1-28. New York: John Wiley and Sons.

Chambliss, W. J. and R. B. Seidman,. (1982). *Law, Order, and Power.* 2nd ed. Boston, MA: Addison-Wesley.

————. (1971). *Law, Order, and Power.* Boston, MA: Addison-Wesley.

Dahrendorf, R. (1958). "Out of Utopia: Toward a Reorientation of Sociological Analysis." *American Journal of Sociology* 64: 115-127.

Gibson, J. (1978). "Race as a Determinant of Criminal Sentences: A Methodological Critique and a Case Study." *Law and Society Review* 12: 455-478.

Green, E. (1970). "Race, Social Status and Criminal Arrest." *American Sociological Review* 35: 476-490.

Hepburn, J. R. (1978). "Race and the Decision to Arrest: An Analysis of Warrants Issued." *Journal of Research In Crime and Delinquency* 15: 54-73.

Hindelang, M. J. (1978). "Race and Involvement in Crimes." *American Sociological Review* 43: 267-271.

Johnson, W. T., R. E. Peterson, and L. E. Wells. (1977). "Arrest Probabilities for Marijuana Users as Indicators of Selective Law Enforcement." *American Journal of Sociology* 83: 681–699.

Klinger, D. (1996). "More on Demeanor and Arrest in Dade County." *Criminology* 34: 61-82.

————. (1994). "Demeanor or Crime? Why 'Hostile' Citizens are More Likely to Be Arrested." *Criminology* 32: 475-493.

Liska, A.E. and M. B. Chamlin. (1984). "Social Structure and Crime Control among Macro Social Units." *American Journal of Sociology* 90: 383–395.

Lundman, R. J. (1994). "Demeanor or Crime? The Midwest City Police–Citizen Encounters Study." *Criminology* 32: 631–656.

———, R. E. Sykes, and J. P. Clark. (1978). "Police Control of Juveniles: A Replication." *Journal of Research in Crime and Delinquency* 15: 74–91.

McCarthy, B. R. (1991). "Social Structure Crime and Social Control: An Examination of Actors Influencing Rates and Probabilities of Arrest." *Journal of Criminal Justice* 19: 19–29.

Parsons, T. (1951). *The Social System.* New York: Free Press.

Piliavin, I. and S. Briar. (1964). "Police Encounters with Juveniles." American Journal of Sociology 70: 206–214.

Pruitt, C. and W. James. (1983). "A Longitudinal Study of the Effect of Race on Sentencing." *Law and Society Review* 17: 613–635.

Quinney, R. (1973). *Critique of the Legal Order. Boston:* Little Brown.

Sellin, T. (1928). "The Negro Criminal: A Statistical Note." Annals of the American *Academy of Political and Social Science* 140: 52–64.

Skolnick, J. H. (1966). *Justice without Trial: Law Enforcement in Democratic Society.* New York: John Wiley and Sons.

Smith, D. A. (1987). "Equity and Discretionary Justice: The Influence of Race on Police Arrest Decision." *Journal of Criminal Law and Criminology* 75: 234–249.

——— and C. A. Visher. (1981). "Street-Level Justice: Situational Determinants of Police Arrest Decisions." Social Problems 29: 167–177.

———, C. A. Visher, and L. A. Davidson. (1984). "Equity and Discretionary Justice: The Influence of Race on Police Arrest Decisions." *Journal of Criminal Law and Criminology* 75: 234–249.

Tittle, C. R. (1994). "The Theoretical Bases for Inequality in Formal Social Control." In G. S. Bridges and M. A. Myers (eds.), *Inequality, Crime and Social Control.* Boulder, CO: Westview Press.

———. (1975). "Labeling and Crime: An Empirical Evaluation." In W. R. Gove (ed.), *The Labeling of Deviance: Evaluating a Perspective.* New York: John Wiley and Sons.

Tittle, C.R. and D. Curran. (1988). "Contingencies for Dispositional Disparities in Juvenile Justice." *Social Forces* 67: 23–58.

Turk, A. T. (1969). Criminality and Legal Order. Chicago: Rand-McNally.

Visher, C. A. (1983). "Gender, Police Arrest Decisions and Notions of Chivalry." *Criminology* 21: 5–28.

Walker, S., S. Cassoa, and M. Delone. (1996). *The Color of Justice: Race, Ethnicity, and Crime in America.* New York: Wadsworth.

Williams, K. R. and S. Drake. (1980). "Social Structure, Crimes and Criminalization: An Empirical Examination of the Conflict Perspective." *Sociological Quarterly* 21: 563–575.

Wilson, J. Q. (1968). "The Social Organization of Delinquency Control." In S. Wheeler and H. M. Hughes (eds.), *Controlling Delinquents* 9–30. New York: John Wiley and Sons.

Chapter 6

Understanding the Connections between Race and Police Violence

Helen Taylor Greene

INTRODUCTION

Unnecessary, excessive police violence, including both physical brutality and killings, continues to be a critical issue in the study of race, crime, and justice. Excessive use of force is prohibited by 421 USC 1983, 1985, and 1986 and other provisions of the U.S. Constitution, including the Fourteenth Amendment (Taylor Greene 1994). While there is agreement about the necessary use of force by the police, there is uncertainty about the continued abuse of this power, especially against black males. Additionally, we know very little about the extent of police violence since there are no readily available statistics.[1] We do know that the number of deadly -force incidents has decreased since the 1980s (Sherman & Cohn 1986; Blumberg 1993). This is attributed, at least in part, to the 1984 Supreme Court decision in *Tennessee v. Garner* (prohibiting the use of deadly force against unarmed fleeing felons), civil liability lawsuits against police departments (and taxpayers), and more restrictive departmental policies. In spite of efforts to control and prevent police violence, controversial killings and other brutal incidents by police continue to occur. As a result, many victims, their family members and friends, and many others believe that police accountability is lacking. Can you imagine Rodney King filing a brutality complaint at his local precinct and being taken seriously without the availability of a videotape of the incident?

Pinkney (1978) noted that police in the United States have historically used their positions to legitimate violence against ethnic minorities.[2] Whether we focus on the brutality of slave patrols, the 1962 police raid of the Nation of Islam Mosque in Los Angeles, the 1967 Algiers Motel incident during the riots in Detroit, the 1979 killing of Arthur McDuffie in Miami, the 1991 beating of Rodney King in Los Angeles, the 1992 killing of Malice Greene in Detroit, the death of Jonny Gammage following a police encounter in Pittsburgh in 1995, or the 1997 savage beating and torturing of Abner Louima in a New York City police station, it is clear that violence against black males transcends both time and place.

Within the black community knowledge of violent police–citizen encounters abounds. When rappers targeted injustices by the police, their antipolicing rhetoric was criticized, although their message was not entirely wrong. During hearings held by the National Association for the Advancement of Colored People (NAACP) in six cities during 1991 to investigate police conduct in minority communities, many citizens reported that police misconduct was an ongoing problem. Black officers who testified also acknowledged the reality of police brutality (NAACP 1995). Black scholars have studied police violence for decades, although few police practitioners, and researchers are aware of their contributions.

The purpose of this chapter is to present a multicomponent, theoretical framework for understanding police violence that includes black perspectives on the historical, political, sociological, and criminal justice contexts of police violence. Unlike other theories, it recognizes that

it is impossible to study the police in this country without studying race. It is impossible to understand the police conduct in the Rodney King beating—or the daily incidents of police "use of force"—without understanding the history of police–minority relations. (NAACP 1995; 10)

A brief overview of (1) the emergence of black perspectives in the study of criminology and (2) previous explanations of police violence are also included.

BLACK PERSPECTIVES IN THE STUDY OF CRIMINOLOGY

Taylor Greene (1979) originally used the term "black perspectives" to synthesize research identified during the first study of black contributions in criminology.[3] At the time, "black perspectives" was used to refer to recurring themes that appeared in both the historical and contemporary research by blacks on crime - and justice -related issues. These themes include social, economic, and political conditions confronting black Americans and focus on the effects of slavery, emancipation, segregation, racism, and oppression. Other themes, including (1) the use of statistical methods to present distorted views of blacks and crime and (2) the effects of social disorganization, have also appeared in research by blacks (Caldwell & Taylor Greene 1981; Young & Sulton 1991; Young & Taylor Greene 1995).[4]

Until recently, most research by black scholars on crime and justice appeared in both black journals and periodicals. Their exclusion from the criminology and criminal justice body of knowledge has contributed to misconceptions and misunderstandings about blacks, crime, and justice (Young & Sulton 1991).[5] Young and Taylor Greene (1995) called for pedagogical reconstruction to overcome these dilemmas in the discipline. They recommended that criminologists familiarize themselves with the contributions of blacks in the discipline and incorporate their research into the curriculum.

Taylor Greene (1994) specifically addressed the exclusion of black perspectives in the study of police brutality. She identified research by black scholars and provided a multicomponent analytical framework for understanding it. She argued that police brutality is best understood in historical, sociological, political, and criminal justice contexts. Here, the earlier framework is revised and applied to understanding police violence, including police brutality. First, traditional explanations of police violence are presented.

EXPLANATIONS OF POLICE VIOLENCE

Police violence is one type of deviant police behavior, a term used by Barker and Carter (1991) to describe activities by an officer that are inconsistent with the official and organizational authority, values, and standards of ethical conduct. One of the problems of explaining police violence is the absence of a standard definition (Klockars 1996). Available definitions include (1) justified and unjustified physical force (Sherman 1980) or (2) legitimate and illegitimate use of force that produces either physical or emotional harm (Friedrich 1980). Often, excessive force is used to describe the unnecessary use of police coercive power (Kania & Mackey 1977; Klockars 1996; Skolnick & Fyfe 1993).

Previous explanations of police violence and excessive force focus on the culture of policing, the existence of bad officers who are overly aggressive and/or harbor racist attitudes, the threatening actions of suspected offenders, the lack of deference or docility by offenders/victims during police–citizen encounters, and the lack of officer accountability and police skills, as well as sociological, psychological, and organizational theories (Klockars 1996; Skolnick &Fyfe 1993; Westley 1970; Worden 1996). Theories of police violence include explanations of excessive force, police brutality or police abuse of force (Geller and Toch, 1996; Klockars. 1996; and Worden, 1996).

Klockars (1996: 2) correctly notes that the range of legitimate authority of the police to use force exacerbates defining and controlling its excessive use. He identifies three mechanisms for controlling excessive force—criminal law, civil liability, and fear of scandal—that also embody definitions of excessive force. According to Klockars, the standard for defining excessive force should not be based on crime, civil damages, or public scandals. He presents a "highly skilled police officer" standard that defines excessive force as more force than a highly skilled officer would find necessary to use (8, 12). While this definition is helpful for controlling excessive force, it does not adequately explain police violence. Worden (1996) reviews sociological, psychological, and organizational theories of police brutality. Sociological theories focus on the nature of police–citizen encounters, and psychological theories focus on behavioral predispositions and authoritarian personalities of officers, while organizational theories emphasize formal and informal organizational factors. Although he presents sociological, psychological, and organizational theories of police behavior separately, Worden calls attention to the importance of combining several factors in understanding police violence.

Geller and Toch (1996) do not explain police abuse of force, although they do recommend that in light of its complexity, researchers should explore the interactions between variables, as opposed to studying them separately. They specifically note that various influences, parameters, and variables working together have implications for future research. They encourage researchers to consider interactions between variables and study relationships between microlevel and macrolevel variables (295).

Some researchers have included micro- and macrolevel variables in their analyses of police violence (Knight 1994; Locke 1996; Taylor Greene 1994; Skolnick & Fyfe 1993; Thierry Texiera 1995). As previously stated, Taylor Greene (1994) used a multicomponent approach that included several historical, sociological, political, and criminal justice factors to explain police brutality. Skolnick and Fyfe (1993: 24) viewed police brutality as "both historically and sociologically" related to lynching and other vigilante activities involving the police. They described the Rodney King beating as a "symbolic lynching" and cited several other similarly disturbing police–citizen encounters (23).

Most blacks study police violence within a multicomponent theoretical framework. Their writings include definitions of police violence, describe violent incidents, and offer strategies for its prevention and control (Taylor Greene 1994). Since research on police brutality by black scholars is described elsewhere (see Taylor Greene 1994), only a summary of their works is included here for informational purposes (see Table 6.1).[6] Recent research on police violence by black scholars also offers a multicomponent approach. Locke (1996) addressed the issues of race, politics, and individual and organizational factors in his discussion of police abuse of power. Thierry Texeira (1995) utilized the internal colonial model and conflict theory to explain institutional racism within police departments, a model that condones acts of racist animosities. Knight (1994) cited the historical tradition of violence against blacks, police brutality against the Nation of Islam, and racial politics in his analysis of the 1962 police shootings of members of the Nation of Islam in Los Angeles.

A general theory of police violence that includes several variables and addresses various types of police violence is not available. Here, a multicomponent theoretical framework is presented to further our understanding of excessive force, including physical brutality and, deadly and nondeadly police violence.

A MULTICOMPONENT THEORETICAL FRAMEWORK OF POLICE VIOLENCE

The study of American policing usually includes an overview of its historical, political, and sociological contexts. The historical context gives an overview of policing in ancient times, in Britain, and in the United States. The political context focuses on the relationships between police and other political figures at the federal, state, and local levels, as well as upon efforts to reform policing. The sociological context presents issues such as the police role, police organizations, police subcultures, and police–community relations. More recently, with the emergence of criminology and criminal justice studies, the role of the police in the criminal justice system has become an important focus in the study of police in American society. Within this context, emphasis is placed upon the police in relation to other components of the system, such as courts and corrections.

Table 6.1
Black Perspectives on Police Violence (1967–1996)

Author	Date	Focus
Black Scholar	1981	Special Issue on Police Violence
Conyers, J., Jr.	1981	Police Violence and Riots
Cray, C.	1987	The Great Muslim Temple Raid
Georges-Abeyie, D.	1992	Policing Bias in Florida
Harris, Syl	1989	Police Violence in Racine, Wisconsin
Haynes, Andrew, Jr.	1970	Black Panthers
Jones, Charles	1988	Black Panthers
Karenga, M.	1976	Black Panthers
Knight, Frederick	1994	Nation of Islam
Locke, Hubert	1995	Race and the Abuse of Power
Lumumba, Chokwe	1981	The RNA
Marable, Manning	1984	Political Repression of Black Militants
Palmer, Edward	1973	Role of Black Police
Pierce, H. Bruce	1986	Role of Blacks in Law Enforcement
Pinkney, Alphonso	1978	Black Nationalism
Pinkney, Alphonso	1972	Police Violence
Raine, Walter	1977	Perceptions of Police Brutality in South Central Los Angeles
Reaves, James N.	1991	Police Violence in Philadelphia, Pennsylvania
Smith, Damu	1981	Police Repression
Smith, Jr., J. C.	1988	An Annotated Bibliographic Index of the MOVE Bombing
Staples, Robert	1974	Violence in Black America
Taylor Greene	1994	Police Brutality
Thierry, Mary T.	1995	Policing the Internal Colony

Within these contextual frameworks, issues related to policing blacks are often absent. For example, Kelling and Moore (1988) presented a theoretical analysis of the evolving strategies of the police in which they identified the political, reform, and community problem-solving eras in the history of policing. Their analysis has become a part of the historical sections of many policing textbooks and readers (Greene & Mastrofski 1991; Kappeler 1995; Langworthy & Travis 1994; Miller & Hess 1994). Williams and Murphy (1990) criticized Kelling and Moore for ignoring how blacks were treated in the evolution of policing in their analysis. They specifically noted their omission of (1) information on slave patrols, black laws, and disfranchisement of blacks during the political era, (2) the lack of meaningful change in policing black communities during the reform era, and (3) a lack of recognition of the contributions of black police officers during the community problem-solving era.[7] Williams and Murphy's critique is also applicable to understanding police violence.

Here, a reconceptualization of police violence that includes the black experience and the four contexts of policing is presented. In this multicomponent theoretical framework, each context (historical, political, sociological, and criminal justice) provides different, though interrelated, themes for understanding police violence (see Figure 6.1).

Figure 6.1
A Multicomponent Theoretical Framework for Understanding Excessive Police Violence

Historical Context	Sociological Context	Political Context	Criminal Justice Context
Slavery	Race Relations	Disenfranchisement	Police Violence
Slave Codes	Social Control	Voter Registration	Unequal Treatment of Black Victims
Emancipation	Social Problems	Black Political Ascendancy	Black Police Ascendancy
Racist Ideology	Cultural Values & Norms	Judicial Decisions	Black Police Organizations
19th and 20th Cent. Race Riots	Social Change	Legislation	Covert Operations
Civil Rights Movement	Social Movements		Prevention & Control
Police Killings 1960s–1990s	Subculture of Policing		Situational Characteristics

Historical Context

Instead of focusing on just the most recent history of police violence (since the 1970s), its history dates back to the era of slavery, emancipation, Reconstruction, post-Reconstruction, and the early twentieth century (Smith 1981; Staples 1974; Thierry Texeira 1995).[8] During and after slavery, an overtly racist ideology prevailed that, along with slavery, was used to justify violence against blacks by the police and other Americans. Williams and Murphy (1990) noted that in the South, the earliest police forces were based not on the British model but rather on the "peculiar institution" of slavery. By the late 1700s, slave codes were enacted to both control the behavior of African slaves and police them in the southern colonies. Slave patrols were "authorized to stop, search, whip, maim, and even kill any African slave caught off the plantation without a pass, engaged in illegal activities, or running away" (Dulaney 1996; 2).

While it is generally accepted that the history of policing in the South was quite different from policing in the North, the experience in the South is often omitted. If there is anything that policing in the North and South had in common, it was the police repression of both free Negroes and slaves. In both regions, rebellious responses by blacks to their repression did not go unnoticed. Historians, both black and white, have described the widespread fear of slave uprisings prior to the Civil War. Although this issue receives no attention in the policing literature, there was certainly a police response to slave rebellions that fed into the prevailing ideology about the criminality and inferiority of blacks.

Hutchinson (1994) presents some of the history of "the Negro as Beast" ideology during the nineteenth and twentieth centuries. He notes the successful efforts of Carroll (1900) and Fitzhugh (1854), in creating an image of black males as "criminal, sex crazed, violent and degenerate" (Hutchinson 1994: 11). Hoffman, a German scholar of the day, summed up the racist thinking of the time by stating that the immorality and crime of black men were due to their "race traits and tendencies" (Hutchinson 1994: 11). These beliefs contributed to, and justified, the acceptance of violence against blacks by whites, including the police. The lynching era (1880s–1930s) represents the most heinous and barbaric brutality and violence against blacks, often condoned by those expected to uphold the law.

The continuation of lynchings and race riots during the early twentieth century and police actions during integration and the Civil Rights movement of the 1950s and 1960s are also important to understanding the historical context of police violence. These events are evidence of the overall failure of police to protect black citizens. An example of this is found in the classical work of Myrdal (1944: 541), who stated:

In many, but not all, Southern communities, Negroes complain indignantly about police brutality. It is part of the policeman's philosophy that Negro criminals or suspects, or any Negro who shows signs of insubordination, should be punished bodily, and that this is a device for preventing crime and for keeping the "Negro in his place" generally. It is apparent, however, that the beating of arrested Negroes—frequently in the wagon on the way to jail or later when they are already safely locked up—often serves as vengeance for the fears and perils the policemen are subjected to while pursuing their duties in the Negro community.

Myrdal's observations capture societal norms and values regarding blacks that are best understood in a sociological context.

Sociological Context

During the early 1900s policing was studied primarily by sociologists and historians since criminology had not yet emerged as a separate discipline in the United States. Sociological issues related to policing include the sociology of police organizations, institutional racism, social and economic conditions, and discrimination. Additionally, the sociological context of cultural norms and values, race relations, social change, social control, social movements, social problems, and the subculture of policing are important to understanding police violence. Since a discussion of each is beyond the scope of this chapter, race relations and social control, important for understanding police violence, are presented.

Some of the earliest sociological publications concerned with race relations offered justifications of slavery (Frazier 1947). Hughes (1854) and Fitzhugh (1854) were two early sociologists[9] who viewed slavery as morally good and capable of rescuing blacks from vice and crime. Although they are often either excluded or downplayed in the study of sociology, their rhetoric was accepted by influential southern planters and other power brokers of their time (Hutchinson 1994). Other, more prominent sociologists also viewed blacks as inferior and a social problem (Cooley 1919; Ellwood 1910; Odum 1910; Ross 1920). While race relations was an important topic to early sociologists, the more difficult issues, like lynchings and discrimination in the administration of justice, were usually ignored by white scholars.

Another common theme in the sociological context that helps understand police violence is social control. Frazier (1953), in an effort to understand extralegal social control that emerged on plantations, identified traditions and customs, as well as physical force and punishment, as elements of social control during slavery. More specific examples of police violence and social control during the twentieth century come from the Civil Rights movement of the 1960s. Officers frequently used clubs, dogs, and water hoses to savagely beat and arrest blacks for demonstrating, often peacefully, against segregation. In Mississippi, during efforts to register black voters, excessive police violence against blacks included bombings of homes and churches, false arrests, sadistic brutality, and murder (Taylor Greene 1994). These acts of police violence can also be understood in a political contextual framework.

Political Context

As previously stated, politics has played an important role in the evolution of policing. Most studies describe the influence of politics on police administration, operations, and how police served the interests of politicians, especially during elections. Dulaney (1996) describes the pattern of linking black police appointments to political patronage in several cities during the nineteenth and twentieth centuries. However, few scholars explore the political context of police violence.

According to Taylor Greene (1994), police brutality is better understood when (black) political powerlessness, political movements, and political ascendancy, as well as judicial decisions and legislation, are taken into consideration. More specifically, excessive police violence and efforts to prevent and control it are better understood in the context of the (historical) disfranchisement of blacks, the voter registration movement, and black political ascendancy at the federal, state, and local levels. While black political ascendancy during the last 25 years is impressive, the transition from disfranchisement to full political participation has taken over 100 years. Nevertheless, black politicians have profoundly affected police violence through legislation, the hiring of black police chiefs, and policy changes. Yet, the problem of police violence persists in spite of political gains by blacks.

Criminal Justice Context

The criminal justice context explores police violence in light of the police as part of the administration of justice process (Taylor Greene 1994). Within this context, police violence is better understood when the unequal treatment of blacks and counterintelligence operations are considered. The criminal justice context also allows us to focus on situational characteristics of violent incidents and explore the problem in other countries. It is also within this context that the ascent of black police and their role as change agents for preventing and controlling this problem within law enforcement are best understood.

CONCLUSION

In spite of more restrictive statutes and policies, police violence persists. Yet, according to Locke (1996: 146), research fails to support a systematic relationship between race and the police use of excessive force, although there is evidence of what he labels "racially linked outcomes in law enforcement." Of course, these outcomes include "disproportionately high numbers of persons of color who are shot at, injured, or killed by police." The disproportionate representation of blacks as victims of police violence is best understood in a multicomponent theoretical framework that includes historical, sociological, political, and criminal justice factors.

While the multicomponent framework helps to understand police violence, finding solutions to this problem is also necessary. The prevention and control of police violence are more closely related to understanding the racial attitudes of police officers, especially the so-called repeat offenders. In spite of human relations and diversity training, blacks are still viewed by many officers as criminal, inferior persons to be feared. Until the relationship between racist attitudes (as opposed to race) and police violence is better understood, the problem will persist.

NOTES

1. The Violent Crime Control and Law Enforcement Act of 1994 mandated the collection and publication of use of excessive force data (McEwen, 1996).

2. Pinkney also notes that legitimate violence is also used against other non-conformists.

3. See Julius Debro and Helen Taylor (1978).

4. While these themes also appear in the writings of white scholars, they are viewed as black perspectives since most whites ignore the significance of these themes and tend to focus more often on the criminality and inferiority of blacks in their research.

5. It is important to note that at least within the professional journals, progress has been made in the representation of black scholarship. However, there is no way of knowing the extent to which these materials are utilized within the study of criminology/criminal justice generally and police violence specifically.

6. See Taylor Greene (1994).

7. Interestingly, Williams and Murphy's analysis is rarely cited. One exception is Kappeler (1995).

8. Williams and Murphy (1990) can also be cited.

9. Sociological training was unavailable.

REFERENCES

Barker, Thomas and David L. Carter. (1991). Police Deviance. Cincinnati, OH: Anderson.

Black Scholar. (1981). Special Issue on Police Violence 12(1).

Blumberg, Mark. (1993). "Controlling Police Use of Deadly Force: Assessing Two Decades of Progress." In Roger G. Dunham and Geoffrey P. Alpert (eds.), *Critical Issues in Policing* 469–492. Prospect Heights, IL: Waveland Press.

Caldwell, Loretta and H. Taylor Greene. (1981). "Implementing a Black Perspective in Criminal Justice." In A. W. Cohn and B. Ward (eds.), *Improving Management in Criminal Justice* 143–156. Beverly Hills, CA: Sage.

Carroll, Charles. (1900). The Negro a Beast.

Conyers, J., Jr. (1981). "Police Violence and Riots." Black Scholar 12(1): 2–5.

Cooley, Charles. (1919). "Genius, Fame and Comparison of Races." *Annals of the American Academy of Political and Social Science* 9 (May): 1–42.

Cray, C. (1967). "The Great Muslim Temple Raid." In The Big Blue Line 128–152. New York: Coward-McCann.

Debro, Julius and Helen Taylor. (1978). "Study on the Status of Black Criminology in the United States." Washington, DC: National Institute of Mental Health (unpublished).

Dulaney, Marvin. (1996). *Black Police in America*. Bloomington, IN: Indiana University Press.

Ellwood, Charles A. (1910). *Sociology and Modern Social Problems*. New York: American Book.

Fitzhugh, George. (1854). *Sociology for the South: Or the Failure of Free Society*.

Frazier, E. Franklin. (1953). "Theoretical Structure of Sociology and Sociological Research." *British Journal of Sociology* 4: 292–311.

———. (1947). "Sociological Theory and Race Relations." American Sociological Review 12(3): 265–71.

Friedrich, J. J. (1980). "Police Use of Force: Individuals, Situations, and Organizations." *The Annals* (November): 67–82.

Geller, William A. and Hans Toch (eds.). (1996a). *Police Violence: Understanding and Controlling Police Abuse of Force*. New Haven, CT: Yale University Press.

————. (1996b). "Understanding and Controlling Police Abuse of Force." In William A. Geller and Hans Toch (eds.), *Police Violence: Understanding and Controlling Police Abuse of Force* 292–328). New Haven, CT: Yale University Press.

Georges-Abeyie, Daniel. (1992). "Law Enforcement and Racial and Ethnic Bias." *Florida State University Law Review* 19(3): 717–726.

Greene, Jack R., and Stephen D. Mastrofski (eds.). (1991). *Community Policing: Rhetoric or Reality?* New York: Praeger.

Harris, Syl. (1989). *A Reason for Being: The Syl Harris Story.* New York: Carlton Press.

Haynes, Andrew, Jr. (1970). Police Black Panther Conflict.

Hughes, Henry. (1854). Treatise on Sociology, Theoretical and Practical.

Hutchinson, Earl. (1994). *Assassination of the Black Male Image.* Los Angeles: Middle Passage Press.

Jones, Charles. (1988). "The Political Repression of the Black Panther Party 1966–1971, the Case of the Oakland Bay Area." *Journal of Black Studies* 18(4): 415–434.

Kania, R., and W. C. Mackey. (1977). "Police Violence as a Function of Community Characteristics." *Criminology* (May): 27–48.

Kappeler, Victor (ed.). (1995). *The Police and Society: Touchstone Readings.* Prospect Heights, IL: Waveland Press.

Karenga, M. (1976). *The Roots of the U.S.–Panther Conflict: The Perverse and Deadly Games Police Play.* San Diego, CA: Kawaida.

Kelling, George L., and Mark H. Moore,. (1988). "The Evolving Strategy of Policing." *Perspectives on Policing,* No. 4. Washington, DC: National Institute of Justice and Harvard University

Klockars, Carl B. (1996). "A Theory of Excessive Rorce and Its Control." In William A. Geller and Hans Toch (eds.), *Police Violence: Understanding and Controlling Police Abuse of Force* 1–22. New Haven, CT: Yale University Press.

Knight, Frederick. (1994). "Justifiable Homicide, Police Brutality, or Governmental Repression? The 1962 Los Angeles Police Shooting of Seven Members of the Nation of Islam." *The Journal of Negro History* 79(2): 182–197.

Langworthy, Robert H. and Lawrence F. Travis, III. (1994). *Policing in America: A Balance of Forces.* New York: Macmillan.

Locke, Hubert G. (1996). "The Color of Law and the Issue of Color: Race and the Abuse of Police Power." In William A. Geller and Hans Toch (eds.), *Police Violence: Understanding and Controlling Police Abuse of Force* 129–149). New Haven, CT: Yale University Press.

Lumumba, Chokwe. (1981). "Short History of the U.S. War on the R.N.A." *Black Scholar* 12(1): 72–81.

Marable, Manning. (1984). *Race, Reform, Rebellion: The Second Reconstruction in Black America.* Jackson: University Press of Mississippi.

McEwen, Tom. (1996). *National Data Collection on Police Use of Force.* Washington, DC: U.S. Department of Justice, National Institute of Justice.

Miller, Linda S., and Karen M. Hess. (1994). *Community Policing Theory and Practice.* Minneapolis/St. Paul, MN: West.

Moss, Larry. (1977). *Black Political Ascendancy in Urban Centers and Black Control of the Local Police Function: An Exploratory Analysis.* San Francisco: R and E Research Associates.

Myrdal, Gunnar. (1944). *An American Dilemma: The Negro Problem and American Democracy.* New York: Harper and Brothers.

NAACP. (1995). *Beyond the Rodney King Story: An Investigation of Police Conduct in Minority Communities.* Boston: Northeastern University Press.

Odum, Howard W. (1910). *Social and Mental Traits of the Negro.* New York: Columbia University Press.

Palmer, Edward. (1973). "Black Police in America." *Black Scholar* 5:19–27.

Pierce, H. Bruce. (1986). "Blacks and Law Enforcement: Towards Police Brutality Reduction." *Black Scholar* 17(3): 49–54.

Pinkney, Alphonso. (1978). *Red, Black and Green: Black Nationalism in the United States.* New York: Cambridge University Press.

Raine, Walter. (1977). *Perception of Police Brutality in South Central Los Angeles.* San Francisco: R and E Associates.

Reaves, James N. (1991). *Black Cops.* Philadelphia: Quantum Leap.

Ross, Edward A. (1920). *The Principles of Sociology.* New York: Century.

Sherman, Lawrence W. (1980). "Causes of Police Behavior: The Current State of Qualitative Research." *Journal of Research in Crime and Delinquency* (January): 69–96.

Sherman, Lawrence W., and Ellen G. Cohn. (1986). *Citizens Killed by Big City Police,* 1970–1984. Washington, DC: Crime Control Institute.

Skolnick, Jerome H., James J. Fyfe. (1993). *Above the Law.* New York: Free Press.

Smith, Damu. (1981). "The Upsurge of Police Repression: An Analysis." *Black Scholar* 12(1): 35–56.

Smith, J. C., Jr. (1988). "The MOVE Bombing: An Annotated Bibliographic Index." *Howard Law Journal* 31(1): 95–142.

Staples, Robert. (1974). "Violence in Black America: The Political Implications." *Black World.*

Taylor Greene, Helen. (1994). "Black Perspectives on Police Brutality." In Anne T. Sulton (ed.), *African American Perspectives on Crime Causation, Criminal Justice Administration and Crime Prevention.* Englewood, CO: Sulton Books.

———. (1979). *A Comprehensive Bibliography of Criminology and Criminal Justice Literature by Black Authors from 1895 to 1978.* Hyattsville, MD: Ummah.

Thierry Texeira, Mary. (1995). "Policing the Internally Colonized: Slavery, Rodney King, Mark Fuhrman and Beyond." *The Western Journal of Black Studies* 19(4): 235–243.

Westley, W. A. (1970). *Violence and the Police: A Sociological Study of Law, Custom, and Morality.* Cambridge: Massachusetts Institute of Technology Press.

Williams, Hubert and Patrick V. Murphy. (1990). "The Evolving Strategy of Policing: A Minority View." *Perspectives on Policing* 13(January): 1–16.

Worden, Robert E. (1996). "The Causes of Police Brutality: Theory and Evidence on Police Use of Force." In William A. Geller and Hans Toch (eds.), *Police Violence: Understanding and Controlling Police Abuse of Force* 23–51. New Haven, CT: Yale University Press.

Young, Vernetta, and Anne Sulton. (1991). "Excluded: The Current Status of African-American Scholars in the Field of Criminology and Criminal Justice." *Journal of Research in Crime and Delinquency* 28(1): 101–116.

Young, Vernetta, and Helen Taylor Greene. (1995). "Pedagogical Reconstruction: Incorporating African-American Perspectives into the Curriculum." *Journal of Criminal Justice Education* 6(1): 85–104.

Chapter 7

The King-Denney Tapes: Their Analysis and Implications for Police Use of Force Training

H. Bruce Pierce

INTRODUCTION

Historically, with the exception of the civil rights era, the concerns, both culturally and politically, of African American people were literally "out of sight and out of mind." With the advent and widespread lay and professional use of videotapes in the 1990s, African American concerns were reintroduced into the American consciousness as in no time since the Civil Rights struggles of the 1960s. In fact, that past era of exposure to African Americans is poignantly exemplified in the video documentary, *Eyes on the Prize*.

Our current 1990s African American imagery, often produced and directed by African Americans themselves, might best be called "Eyes on the Tragedy." Tragedy in this instance as defined by Aristotle says it best: "Everyone is wounded, some fatally."

Paradoxically, while 1960s African American civil rights victories were explored in *Eyes on the Prize*, sadly and regressively, the 1990s stories of Rodney King and Reginald Denney's taped attacks are the stories of "Eyes on the Failure," namely, the failure of America's race relations, its criminal justice system, and its police. This chapter is written from the perspective of an African American male, a professor of America's criminal justice system, and a former member of two New York City police forces, namely, the Transit and City Police Departments. My teachings, research, writings, and life experiences have contributed to the development of this chapter by addressing police use of force training through an application of several analytical principles I have developed: a common denominator survival hypothesis, an equity theory of intergroup relations, and a cyclical sequence of police–community conflict.

The criminal justice system is a 1967 invention of the Johnson era, where there was an arbitrary linkage applied to the then-separate and still separate five entities of police, courts, corrections, probation, and parole. While examined as an equivalent componential analysis of crime, the police, with their cyclical and perennial issues of corruption, brutality, urban unrest, and civil disobedience, remain the most visible of the five components. As background to the "visibility" of policing and its critical role in my proposed common denominator survival interaction hypothesis, the following observations are offered. The "revolution" in policing currently being fueled by community policing and its place in the future of our lives has been eloquently cited by Professor Herman Goldstein (1993) who writes that the very quality of life and the equilibrium of our cities depend on the way in which the police function is carried out. Nowhere is the police function more dramatically carried out than in the police use of force, both deadly and nonlethal.

Nowhere in recent American memory has the excessive use of nonlethal force "revolutionized" policing than in the Rodney King videotape. In fact, police history may now be measured as BK and AK, that is Before King and After King. The dilemma facing law enforcement in this AK era is where to begin to make the perennial issue of police use of force compatible with the hoped-for contributions of a cooperative and mutual interest-based community policing. The common denominator survival interaction hypothesis builds directly on the desire of the community in an AK use of force era and has to do with a concept of interactions between the police and citizens and especially African American citizens, a concept that attempts to postulate what behaviors between the two groups may lead to problem resolution or to injury or death.

Specifically, the common denominator survival interaction hypothesis states that if the police and community interact with mutually beneficial behaviors, then the police and community will both survive and achieve problem resolution. Conversely, if the police and community interact with mutually harmful behaviors, then the police and/or community may encounter injury or death.

The common denominator survival interaction hypothesis revolves around two key police parameters, namely, the police training function and the use of force. Relevant police training and use of force research includes the classic observational studies of force by Reiss (1980) and Bayley and Garafalo (1989), wherein three decision points in violent encounters were observed, specifically, the initial contact, the processing, and the exit stages. Given the premise of mutually beneficial versus mutually harmful behaviors between police and communities, it is possible to imagine the role of initial contact, processing, and exit on a positive or negative outcome in the interaction between police and the community.

Ironically, historically and now and well into the future, the "common denominator" in police and minority community interactions especially has been, is, and will be the paradoxically simple and complex act of "getting home safely," that is being alive following a potentially violent police interaction.

Research and hard-won practical evidence suggest that regular, "noncrisis" interaction (community policing), respect, and rapport built over time and learning to "humanize" one another have powerful positive interaction implications between police and communities.

The hypothesis naturally leads to training implications for both the police and the minority and other communities as to which behaviors lead to problem resolution or escalation. Historically and now, the police training function has been the place for both reactive and proactive policing issues. The challenge for training in a community policing, post-King era on the use of force issue is to overcome the idea that "real" police work is not learned in training and to advance, as Bayley and Bittner (1989) do, the idea that progress in police training will come by focusing on the particularities of police work, as it is experienced by serving officers and by analyzing that experience and making it available to (current) and future officers.

Goldstein (1993) goes even further for training advocacy in suggesting:

Training to support changes of the magnitude now being advocated in policing, requires more than a one-shot effort consisting of a few classroom lectures. It requires a substantial commitment of time in different settings spread over a long period, a special curriculum, the best facilitators, and the development of problems, case studies, and exercises that engage the participants. It requires the development of teamwork in which subordinates contribute as much as superiors. And it requires that the major dimension of the training take the form of conscious change in the day-to-day interaction (and performance) of personnel—not in (just) a training setting, but on the job.

Bayley and Bittner (1989) and Goldstein, (1993) clearly see the goal of policing, as I do, as more successfully handling its functions, especially its perennial and most troublesome function, the use of force.

The use of force issue is currently attached, as previously described, to the twin "revolutions" of community policing and the King videotape. Never before and perhaps never again will the day-to-day reality of policing be given this powerful and political forum for advancing its profession. That advancement will depend greatly on the innovation and excellence provided by police trainers, specifically, as they assist in the potentially mutually beneficial outcomes of police and community interactions, especially those involving the use of force.

Prior to a discussion of a proposed cyclical sequence of police-community conflict, which helps explain the common denominator survival interaction hypothesis, as well as the King and Denney beatings, an exploration of some selected theories of intergroup relations is in order.

A working assumption is the definition of intergroup relations advanced by Taylor and Moghaddam (1987) encompasses any aspect of human interaction that involves individuals perceiving themselves as members of a social category, or being perceived by others as belonging to a social category. Their definition places no limitation on the size or type of social category involved or any requirement for shared motivations or group cohesion. By this definition, police and individual citizens or whole communities are capable of intergroup relations.

The theories cited by Taylor and Moghaddam are advanced for having met the criteria of being broad in scope and able to attempt answers to these pervasive issues in intergroup relations: How do conflicts arise? What course do they take? How are they resolved? The theories advanced include realistic conflict theory, social identity theory, equity theory, relative deprivation theory and elite theory.

An analysis of these five theories revealed that equity theory had the greatest "explanatory power" for the King–Denney beatings and the cyclical sequence of police-community conflict.

Equity theory is presented with its scope, assumptions, and propositions and is then discussed for its relevance to the King–Denney beatings.

Scope: Equity theory deals mainly with relations between individuals but has implications for both advantaged and disadvantaged groups in the context of intergroup relations. Equity theory specifies the conditions associated with intergroup conflict (real or perceived injustice).

Assumptions: A fundamental assumption is that individuals strive to maximize rewards for themselves. However, in pursuit of this end, individuals learn that they must conform to certain norms of justice in their dealings with others.

Propositions: Equity theory proposes that people strive for justice in their relationships and feel distressed when they perceive injustice.

A relationship is judged to be just when the ratio of one group's inputs and outcomes is equal to that of the other involved in the relationship. When the ratios are unequal, psychological distress will be experienced by both groups, and steps will be taken to restore justice by actually or psychologically adjusting the inputs and outcomes of one or both groups in the relationship. Of special relevance for my cyclical sequence of police-community conflict is the equity theory proposition that "when group inputs and outcomes are unequal ...steps will be taken to restore justice."

Building on equity theory, I have proposed a five-step pattern to the cyclical sequence of police-community conflict, which includes the following:

1. Period(s) of relative quiescence: Law enforcement–citizenry exchanges, while not cordial, occur with minimal negative outcome.

2. Catalytic police incident: Law enforcement–citizenry exchanges are tensioned to the "breaking point" as the police agent(s) terminates the life or injures a minority comunity citizen.

3. Community/political outcry: The outraged community and its elected and appointed representatives, coupled with its "grassroots" people, organize around the latest victim of police brutality and issue various demands (for justice): officer imprisonment, police review boards, more minority officers, and policies regarding deadly and excessive use of force.

4. Police sensitvity training: The law enforcement agency institutes or increases "diversty" training and issues new use -of -force guidelines.

5. Return to relative quiescence: The cycle and sequence are complete when again law enforcement–citizenry exchanges, while not cordial, produce minimal negative oucome.

Building on this model, Helen Taylor Greene (1994) makes the following observations with direct implication for the King tape: throughout the 1970s, 1980s and continuing into the 1990s, police brutality incidents have occurred. Pierce (1986) suggests the preceding five-step systemic and cyclical sequence in the emergence of police brutality. Examples of Pierce's sequence can be found by examining incidents occurring in Florida. Two recent, controversial brutality incidents leading to community outcry and civil unrest are the LaFleur and McDuffie cases. In 1979, the home of Nathaniel LaFleur, a schoolteacher, mistakenly was raided by Dade County police officers. In December 1979, Arthur McDuffie was killed following a police chase. However, the catalytic incident that resulted in a community outcry in 1980 was the acquittal of officers involved in McDuffie's death.

Community outcry also occurred after the April 1992 acquittal of police who had beaten Rodney King in Los Angeles. This outcry proved to be the most devastating and deadly riot to occur in decades. In 1991, Rodney King had been brutally beaten by police officers after a high-speed chase. A resident of an apartment complex near the scene of the beating captured the incident on videotape. Citizens in Los Angeles and across the country were outraged by the incident. When officers involved were acquitted, there was an immediate, violent outbreak that further devastated already strained police–community relations. Dozens of people were killed, nearly 1000 injured, and thousands jailed. Arson, looting, and other destruction reportedly resulted in over $200 million worth of damage.

Unlike earlier civil unrest, property damage extended beyond the black community in Los Angeles. While south-central Los Angeles was the hardest hit, Beverly Hills also was affected. Schools were closed, mail service was discontinued, final examinations at area colleges and universities were canceled, and federal troops were requested by city officials. Disturbances also occurred in other cities, including Madison, Wisconsin; Las Vegas; Atlanta; San Francisco; Minneapolis; Seattle; and Eugene, Oregon. Peaceful demonstrations were held in Baton Rouge, Louisiana; Kansas City Missouri; Newark, New Jersey; and other cities.

The implications of the Los Angeles civil unrest forced many federal, state, and local officials to more closely scrutinize police brutality. Then Attorney General Richard Thornburgh, at the behest of Michigan congressman John Conyers, directed the Civil Rights Division of the U. S. Department of Justice to investigate 15,000 police brutality complaints since 1987.

Against this background I will analyze the King–Denney tapes and suggest their academic value in criminal justice education and their conflict resolution value between the police and African American and other minority communities.

THE KING–DENNEY TAPES: QUESTIONS AND APPLICATIONS

Using the King and Denney tapes as poignant examples of modern-day tragedy often seen in police–community interaction, five key questions and initial answers emerge. First, why was there no immediate riot following the original beating of Rodney King? A preliminary answer would appear to be that the tape raised especially high and ultimately unwarranted expectations that, since "pictures don't lie" the African-American community would finally have its successful "day in court" and that, paralleling equity theory, "justice would be served."

Next, did the postverdict riots really surprise anyone? Here, the early answer must be yes and no. While the majority community was surprised, the depth of disappointment and outrage in the African American community fully anticipated a revolt, consistent with equity theory's proposition on the injured group's taking "steps to restore justice."

Third, did the beating of Reginald Denney, an innocent, white truck driver caught in the "wrong" part of Los Angeles at the time of the revolt, surprise anyone? Again, the yes and no response applies, with the majority community possibly expecting demonstrations, but never a "King-like" beating of one of their own. As for the African American community, there were regrets at Denney's horrible attack but, again, an understanding of the explosive rage and equity theory-based "step for justice" that caused it.

Fourth is the critical criminal justice question, did the Denney assailants' acquittals surprise and shock? The answer speaks to the terror experienced by both majority and minority Los Angeles citizens and even a "sheltered" jury's knowledge and fear of such a recurrence as the 1992 riot, as well as the possibility of equity theory's being utilized by the jury as a "step for justice."

Fifth is the provocative question, did the calls for calm and "getting along" after the King and Denney incidents shock and surprise? This may be explained by the Native American proverb "to understand a man, walk a mile in his moccasins." Clearly, these two brutalized and damaged human beings wished that no one ever had to experience what they had gone through.

These preliminary questions and answers should, through further research and analysis, be deepened and enlarged to produce an evaluation tool of these tapes and convert them to use as adjunct instructional material for courses on such topics as ethics in criminal justice, African American responses to oppression, and police community conflict and resolution as well as police–community workshops on conflict prevention.

Specific instructional material to accompany this work would be an extensive and relevant tape library on pertinent demonstrations of police–community interactions, both positive and negative, an extensive bibliography of pertinent writings, and observations and interviews, as well as my proposals for a common denominator survival interaction hypothesis and the cyclical sequence of police–community conflict. In addition and most sadly, since these and similar incidents flood our avaricious television industry, I would expect that the tapes available for such analysis would increase.

CONCLUSION

Finally, most dangerously, and urgently lies the questions, what is the tolerance level between the police and African American and other minority communities, and can it in any meaningful way be positively altered by the work of a former police officer turned academic? As an African American and former police officer with respect and love for both groups, I pray the answer is yes.

My 33-year journey to academe has led me through subway tunnels, over ghetto roofs, and into prison classrooms and funeral parlors and has given me, at age 54, a genuine sense of urgency at finding a way to go beyond the classroom and focus on what I believe may be a major contribution to the criminal justice system's perennial dilemma of police and community conflict.

REFERENCES

Bayley, D. H. and E. Bittner. (1989). "Learning the Skills of Policing." In R. G. Dunham and G. P. Alpert (eds.), *Critical Issues in Policing* 88. Prospect Heights, IL: Waveland Press.

———— and J. Garofalo. (1989). "The Management of Violence by Police Patrol Officers." *Criminology* (27)1: 49–54.

Goldstein, H. (1993). "The New Policing: Confronting Complexity." *National Institute of Justice, Research in Brief* (December): 2.

Greene, H. T. (1994). "Black Perspectives on Police Brutality." In A. T. Sulton (ed.), *African-American Perspectives on Crime Causation, Criminal Justice Administration and Crime Prevention.* Englewood, CO: Sulton Books.

Pierce, H. B. (1986). "Blacks and Law Enforcement: Towards Police Brutality Reduction." *Black Scholar* 17: 49–54.

Reiss, A. J. (1980). "Controlling Police Use of Deadly Force." *Annals, AAPSS* 452(November): 122–134.

Taylor, D. M. and F. M. Moghaddam. (1987). *Theories of Intergroup Relations: International Social Psychological Perspectives.* New York: Praeger.

Chapter 8

The Self-Fulfilling Prophecy of Police Profiles

Scott L. Johnson

If men define situations as real, they are real in their consequences.
—Jerome Miller quoting W. I. Thomas

The War on Drugs has exacted tremendous costs on American society. People of color disproportionately bear these costs. For instance, although African Americans constitute only 12 percent of the population of the United States and only 13 percent of its monthly drug users, they constitute 35 percent of drug arrests, 55 percent of drug convictions, and 74 percent of state incarcerations for drug offenses (Mauer & Huling 1995). Criminal justice research has long sought an explanation for this distressing disproportionality.

One potential source of this disparity could be the drug courier profile, (see Table 8.1) which is one of several enforcement strategies in the War on Drugs. The profile is a list of characteristics and behaviors that supposedly reflect the traits and behaviors of drug couriers (Lyman & Potter 1996; MacDonald & Kennedy 1983). Law enforcement officials compile this list from the experience of the agency. Theoretically, when investigators see an individual matching some profile characteristics, in addition to engaging in other suspicious behaviors, officers have reasonable suspicion to approach the individual and briefly interrogate him or her. During this investigative detention, officers should either discover other factors that warrant further investigation, or the officers should allow the individual to go. Controversy surrounds the drug courier profile because of its questionable validity and its potential liability. For instance, disagreement exists about whether the profile accurately represents the behavior of drug couriers. Proponents and opponents also argue over whether the profile results in differential enforcement of the law against people of color. Since the profile is a police-initiated investigative strategy, the racist history of American law enforcement, the discriminatory social construction of the drug problem, and broad police legitimacy and discretion create a climate fraught with the potential for abuse. The primary focus of this inquiry is the possible effect of the drug courier profile on the African American community. If profiles are products of past police behavior, they should address the issues of the discrimination inherent in that past, because profiles currently serve as a tool used to legitimate investigation, detention, and sometimes arrest. Racism in the profile would create further racism. This chapter discusses the development of drug courier profiles, evaluates their accuracy, and assesses their impact in terms of the magnitude of the violations they currently allow.

Table 8.1
List of Profile Characteristics

Travel from a source city	Carries little luggage
Nervous appearance	Carries excessive luggage
Cash-paid ticket	Frequent travel to source cities
Use of an alias	Use of public ground transportation
Made several phone calls	Fast turn-around time
Left false information with airline	One-way ticket
Carries large amount of cash	Circuitous routes
Known courier or trafficker	

THE DEVELOPMENT OF DRUG COURIER PROFILES

Drug courier profiles first appeared in the early 1970s through the efforts of Special Agent Paul Markonni of the Drug Enforcement Agency. Having seen the success of hijacker profiles previously developed by the Federal Aviation Administration, Agent Markonni and his team believed that a similar tool could be useful in drug interdiction efforts in airports. By compiling a list of traits and behaviors from the experiences of veteran law enforcement professionals, officers would be better able to identify and intercept people trafficking in illegal narcotics. The popularity of the profile spread to use nationwide in airports and eventually in all commercial transportation centers such as bus and train stations. Toward the end of the decade, state police agencies had begun to use profiles on highways. Law enforcement agencies continue to use profiles in deciding whom to detain and question. The terminology may be different, but the basic idea remains the same.

Drug courier profiles have faced repeated legal challenges to their validity. Through a long line of cases, the U. S. Supreme Court has endorsed the use of drug courier profiles (*United States v. Sokolow*, 490 U.S. 1, 1989). The Court interprets profiles as a useful tool in helping to establish reasonable suspicion under the dictates of *Terry v. Ohio*, 392 U.S. 1, (1968). Under the *Terry* doctrine, police may approach a person when the officer has "reasonable suspicion" to believe crime may be afoot. This suspicion cannot rest on "inchoate [or] unparticularized suspicion or hunch"but rather must be"specific reasonable inferences which [the officer] is entitled to draw from his experience" (*Terry*, 392 U.S. 1). *Terry* gave officers the authority to approach and briefly   question a person regarding behavior the officer deems suspicious. The nature of this questioning should be brief and should not assume the custodial character of an arrest. In other words, individuals should not feel as if they are unable to leave. Profiles, according to the decisions of the U. S. Supreme Court, provide a partial basis for reasonable suspicion and, as such, an investigative detention. However, the Court has never demanded that enforcement agencies validate these profiles in terms of their usefulness as an enforcement strategy in the War on Drugs, nor has the Court required police to prove that they use profiles in a nondiscriminatory fashion. This section of this discussion reviews the four major U. S. Supreme Court cases involving profiles. This review shows that inadequate judicial review of drug courier profiles created an environment with an alarming potential for abuse.

The first case in which drug courier profiles were an issue is *United States v. Mendenhall*, 446 U.S. 544, (1980). Mendenhall was a 22 year -old African American woman. The accused in *Mendenhall* also exhibited the following characteristics:

(1) the respondent was arriving on a flight from Los Angeles, a city believed by the agents to be a place of origin for much of the heroin brought to Detroit; (2) the respondent was the last person to leave the plane, "appeared to be very nervous," and completely scanned the whole area where [the agents] were standing; (3) after leaving the plane the respondent proceeded past the baggage area without claiming any luggage; and (4) the respondent changed airlines for her flight out of Detroit. (*Mendenhall*, 446 U.S. 544, at 547, n.1)

During the investigative detention the agents learned that she was using an alias. The suspect consented to a search of her person and her handbag. The officers discovered two packages of heroin hidden in her underwear. The justices disagreed in their opinions of the circumstances in *Mendenhall*. Justice Stewart, authoring the opinion of the Court and joined by Justice Rehnquist, suggested that the suspect was not seized before her arrest. Therefore, the Fourth Amendment was not in question. Three concurring justices asserted that there was a *Terry*-type stop involved here but that the stop was valid because the officers had reasonable suspicion for the investigative detention. The concurring justices believed that the profile characteristics Mendenhall displayed were sufficient to provide reasonable suspicion. The dissenting justices argued that the defendant had been seized before her arrest and that her seizure had not been supported by reasonable suspicion. Although the Court validates and recognizes profiles in this case, it defines them as nothing more than "an informally compiled abstract of characteristics"(446 U.S. 547, n 1). This fluid and insubstantial definition of profiles is especially troublesome given their unquestioned acceptance by the majority. In the concurring opinion, Justice Powell argues that the use of profiles is a highly sophisticated and coordinated law enforcement strategy. However, this seems inconsistent with the definition of profiles provided by the majority opinion and with the priority placed upon them in the resolution of the issue in this case. Nevertheless, *Mendenhall* introduced the issue at the national level and permitted the continued use of drug courier profiles.

The second major Supreme Court case in which profiles were an issue was *Reid v. Georgia*, 448 U.S. 438, (1980). Here the Court directly confronted the question as to whether drug courier profiles constituted reasonable suspicion. Reid arrived from a source city and traveled during early morning hours, supposedly to take advantage of reduced law enforcement presence. Attempting to conceal the fact that they were travelling together, Reid and his carried only shoulder bags. The Court said that these characteristics did not justify a *Terry*-type investigative detention, saying that only one characteristic referred directly to the suspect. The Court thought the rest of the factors identified were so general that agents could stop virtually anyone in the airport based them, articulating the fundamental problem with the practice of profiling. In fact, the Court seems to diminish the importance and validity of profiles, calling them "a somewhat informal compilation of characteristics believed to be typical of persons unlawfully carrying narcotics" (*Reid* 448 U.S. 438, 440).   However, *Reid* did not prohibit the use of profiles, nor did it substantively resolve any of the major questions about their use. The Court still allows that some combination of profile characteristics should cause an officer to suspect criminal behavior and would substantially add to reasonable suspicion. However, the Court never asks what characteristics the police use, or why police include some characteristics as opposed to others. Furthermore, this case did not resolve the issue of the role of profile characteristics in establishing reasonable suspicion. In other words, the Court asserts that profiles can be a meaningful aspect of reasonable suspicion, but the Court did not explain to what degree they are an aspect. Furthermore, the Court presumes the equitable use of the profile in practice. In other words, officers approach and detain all people with profile characteristics, but the Court asks for no verification of this. Given the constitutional concerns inherent in the use of profiles, *Reid* represents another example of a failure of the Court to provide meaningful guidance to law enforcement or protection of individual liberties.

Florida v. Royer, 460 U.S. 491, (1983) is the next major case that involves the use of drug courier profiles. In *Royer* the following traits were considered indicative of criminality:

(a) Royer was carrying American Tourister luggage, which appeared to be heavy, (b) he was young, apparently between 25–35, (c) he was casually dressed, (d) appeared pale and nervous, (e) he paid for his ticket in cash with a large number of bills, and (f) rather than completing the airline identification tag to be attached to checked baggage which had space for name, address, and telephone number, he wrote only name and destination (406 U.S. 491, at 493 n. 2).

Officers approached Royer and asked if he had a moment to speak with them. After checking his identification, the officers found that Royer was traveling under an alias. In the officers' opinion, Royer became more nervous during this point in the conversation. The detectives told Royer that they were narcotics officers and suspected him of transporting narcotics. They asked if he would accompany them to their interrogation room. Without Royer's consent they obtained his checked baggage and asked if they could search it. The Supreme Court argued that the fact that the officers informed Royer that they suspected him of transporting narcotics and retained his ticket indicated that Royer was not free to go. Therefore, the encounter had progressed beyond an investigative detention to the custodial level. Custodial detentions require the higher standard of probable cause, not reasonable suspicion. Therefore, Royer's challenge succeeded. However, in this case the Court asserted that the initial profile characteristics upon which the officers stopped Royer were sufficient to warrant an investigative detention, further legitimating the use of drug courier profiles but failing to provide more effective guidelines for defining or applying them.

The most important case to date in the history of the drug courier profile is *United States v. Sokolow*, 490 U.S. 1, (1989). The legal understanding of reasonable suspicion is that an officer may not act on "inchoate and particularized suspicion or hunch" (*Terry*, as cited before). According to established Court jurisprudence, when deciding the legality of the investigative detention, the Court must consider the totality of the circumstances. Sokolow exhibited the profile characteristics of travel to a distant source city, payment for tickets in cash from a large roll of 20 bills, nervous actions, no checked baggage, and a return after only 48 hours while wearing the same clothing. As Sokolow and his traveling companion exited the airport, they were approached by four Drug Enforcement Administration (DEA) agents, one of whom grabbed Sokolow by the arm and moved him back onto the sidewalk. After failing to produce any identification, the agents took Sokolow and his traveling companion to the DEA office at the airport, where a dog sniffed their luggage. After the dog alerted agents to Sokolow's shoulder bag, they arrested him. Agents obtained a warrant to search the bag. They found no drugs during this search, but they discovered items that suggested involvement in illicit drug trafficking. The dog sniffed Sokolow's bags again and indicated that it smelled drugs in another piece of luggage. The agents kept this bag overnight because it was too late to obtain another search warrant. In the morning a second dog also alerted agents to the bag identified by the earlier dog, and the agents obtained a search warrant. This search produced a kilo of cocaine.

The majority in *Sokolow* reiterated the reasoning behind *Terry*-style investigative stops. They argued that totality of the circumstances allows the stop. Even totally legal behaviors when taken together could suggest criminal activity to the experienced police officer. The majority argued that behaviors exhibited by Sokolow justified a reasonable suspicion. Furthermore, "A court sitting to determine the existence of reasonable suspicion must require the agent to articulate the factors leading to that conclusion, but the fact that these factors may be set forth in a 'profile' does not somehow detract from their evidentiary significance as seen by a trained agent" (490 U.S. 1, 10). In other words, because the simultaneous occurrence of the characteristics leads to reasonable suspicion, the fact that the characteristics came from the profile is incidental. The indirect effect of this decision is the validation of the profiles themselves. The problem with the Court's ruling is that it, like the ones preceding it, offers no guidelines as to what constitutes reasonable suspicion or the role profiles play in establishing reasonable suspicion.

Thus, the conclusion of this and other reviews of major Supreme Court cases addressing the use of drug courier profiles is that the Court has failed to provide effective judicial review regarding the profiles (Guerra 1992; Cloud 1985; Johnson 1983). The Court has unquestionably accepted the validity of this practice through endorsing the continued use of profiles without demonstrating their usefulness or providing any guidelines as to their use. In other words, the cases discussed establish that profiles may contain only facts or conditions that are neutral and innocent on their face and that some combination of these charcteristics may contribute to establishing a level of suspicion justifying a *Terry*-style investigative detention. However, the existing case law does not examine the accuracy of these charcteristics in revealing potentially criminal conduct, nor does it specify the combination of the characteristics that constitutes legitimate suspicion. Moreover and most relevant for the purposes of this discussion, existing case law does not explore the fair application of this formula to all individuals possessing profile characteristics, meaning that the decision to detain someone possessing these charcteristics in some manner is left to the discretion of police officers. As discussed later, these issues open the door to a variety of racially biased practices. It appears from existing research that the use of profiles is biased against people of color in that police detain persons of color at a disproportionately higher rate than that for Caucasians. This would constitute institutional racism by the criminal justice system. A policy that is racially neutral on its face has a discriminatory effect in practice due to a biased application by law enforcement personnel.

THE ACCURACY OF DRUG COURIER PROFILES

In her discussion of drug courier profiles, Johnson (1983: 214) argues that "neither courts nor legal scholars have stressed the necessary first step of such a calculation [of criminality]: separating facts that contribute to the likelihood of criminal activity from those that do not." To establish the legitimacy of profiles, police could provide evidence that the characteristics they contain accurately indicate the behavior of drug couriers. Agents assert that the characteristics of the profile must be kept secret because drug couriers could then modify their behavior to escape detection. However, it is still logical to assume that agents could verify the accuracy of the profile, if not through empirical research, at least through anecdotal evidence. There is embarrassingly little evidence of any kind to support the accuracy of drug courier profiles. For instance, agents testifying in court to the validity of the profile do not provide overwhelming or convincing evidence of its usefulness as a drug interdiction tool. For example, in *Royer* (460 U.S. at 526 n.6), one DEA agent who testified suggested that approximately 60 percent of the people who matched profile characteristics had drugs. In one case involving a suspect detained because of a profile, the arresting officer states that "there is no true drug courier profile" (*United States v. Taylor*, 910 F. 2d. 1402, at 1408). In other cases agents suggest that as few as 3 to 5 percent of the people they stop according to the profile are carrying drugs. Most of these agent estimates range between 20 and 40 percent (Cloud 1985: 875, n. 135). There are bolder assertions. For instance, after the initiation of the profile at Detroit airport under Special Agent Markonni, the agents searched 141 people during 96 investigative detentions. During the 96 detentions, agents found drugs 77 times (*United States v. Van Lewis*, 556 F. 2d. 385, 6th Cir. 1977).

This small amount of data is unconvincing for a variety of reasons. First, the methodological validity of these evaluations is unknown. The formula for the application of these characteristics is not revealed. Second, if the profile is valid, meaning that these charcteristics are so strongly indicative of drug trafficking that they warrant inclusion in the profile, then disparate experiences of different agencies and officers should be explained. Law enforcement asserts that these charcteristics justify suspicion of the individuals who possess them, yet the outcomes of using these traits to detain people yield these widely varying results. This suggests either that the profile was inaccurate initially or that certain officers applied the profile incorrectly. If the latter is true, police should be able to articulate how the profile is supposed to work so that its officers could correct their mistake. If the former is true, then the police should abandon or alter the profile because it does not accomplish its only goal of revealing potentially criminal conduct. Third, the costs of the profile must also be considered. While some of these outcomes sound impressive, they do not discuss the inconvenience or character of the investigative stops of innocent people, nor do these assessments of profiles document how many persons with profile characteristics were not stopped for questioning. This inconsistency in application begs the question of the necessity of profiles. If the profile contains a list of behaviors that are innocent on their face, it seems unlikely that police stop all people engaged in these behaviors or having these traits. If they do, then the accuracy of profiles must be questioned because they produce, at best, widely inconsistent outcomes. However, as was previously discussed, the Supreme Court states that profiles alone do not justify reasonable suspicion (*Reid v. Georgia*, 448 U.S. 438). Therefore, there must be something else present in the circumstances that warrants the further investigation, but if it is the missing ingredient in addition to the presence of profile characteristics that warrants the investigation, then the relevance of the profile should be reconsidered. Therefore, this review concludes that evidence offered to support the claim that profiles accurately represent criminal conduct is weak. Moreover, the successful contribution of the drug courier profile as an interdiction strategy remains questionable. Since those who apply it offer such weak testimony to its value, it seems that it cannot be argued that its discontinuation would significantly affect law enforcement efforts.

Morgan Cloud (1985) empirically tested the validity of the original drug courier profile first developed by DEA special agent Paul Markonni as expressed in the appellate court cases of *United States v. Elmore*, 595 F.2d 1036, 5th Cir. (1979) and *United States v. Ballard*, 573 F.2d 913, 5th Cir. (1978). These cases outlined 15 characteristics contained in the drug courier profile, and many cases have since used these characteristics as indicative of drug traffickers. In a review of approximately 200 court opinions referring to the drug courier profile, Cloud tabulated the frequency with which certain profile characteristics appeared. Most of these characteristics were listed in the *Elmore* or *Ballard* profiles.

Of the 15 characteristics studied, only 3 characteristics were present in more than half of the cases, and only 6 were present in more than one-third of the cases. Of the 3 characteristics present in more than half of the cases, 2 of these are so poorly defined that they provide little substantive clues as to the actual characteristics of drug couriers. For instance, travel to or from a source city is the most frequently cited characteristic on the profile. However, there is no definition of those factors that designate a location a source city. Virtually every major metropolitan area can be classified as a source city. The list includes Boston, Chicago, New York, New Orleans, Washington, D.C., Seattle, and many others. Moreover, California and Florida should be designated source states since travel to or from anywhere within their borders seems to qualify in this regard. The Sixth Circuit addressed the vagueness of this criterion in *United States v. Andrews* (600 F. 2d. 563, 1979):

Travel from Los Angeles cannot be regarded as in any way suspicious. Los Angeles may indeed be a major narcotics distribution center, but the probablitity that any given airline passeneger from that city is a drug courier is infinitesimally small. Such a flimsy factor should not be allowed to justify—or help justify— the stopping of travelers from the nation's third largest city. Moreover, our experience with DEA agent testimony in other cases makes us wonder whether there exists any city in the country which a D.E.A. will not characterize as a major narcotics distribution center or a city through which drug couriers pass on their way to a major narcotics distribution center. (600 U.S. 563, at 567)

Therefore, since travel to almost anywhere seems to qualify, this aspect of the profile has been so broadly defined that it is, in essence, meaningless.

The second characteristic that appeared more than 50 percent of the time was suspect nervousness. Regarding this profile trait, officers assert that the nervousness exhibited by drug couriers is somehow distinguishable from that of other persons. Justice Marshall addressed this concern in his dissent in *Sokolow*: "With news accounts proliferating of plane crashes, near collisions and air terrorism, there are manifold and good reasons for being agitated while awaiting a flight, reasons that have nothing to do with one's involvement in criminal behavior" (490 U.S. 1, at 15). The Court has yet to ask officers to validate this claim. By accepting this claim without validation, the Court has substantially broadened police discretion regarding the profile. The third most frequently displayed characteristic is carrying little or no luggage. This characteristic is shared by 51.3 percent of the suspects. However, almost 40 percent of defendants carried both carry -on bags and suitcases that would burden the suspect. Furthermore, more than 45 percent of defendants checked their baggage, which contradicts the assumption underlying the inclusion of the absence of bags as a profile characteristic, that drug couriers wish to move easily and quickly through the airport to avoid detection. Beyond this, however, is the fact that in *Ballard* the carrying of many bags is viewed as suspicious, presumably because suspects could move larger quantities of contraband and abandon it at baggage claim if detected. In sum, Cloud's empirical analysis suggests that most of the characteristics documented in court cases as constituting the drug courier profile are not consistent throughout case law. Those characteristics that appear most frequently appear only in about half of the cases and either are so broadly defined that they are virtually meaningless or are directly contradicted by other data (Cloud 1985).

Cloud also discovered some characteristics present in the opinions that were not identified as part of the Elmore or Ballard characteristics. He included those six that appeared most frequently as part of his analysis. However, only one of these extraneous characteristics, eye contact with an agent, was present in more the half of the studied cases, but this characteristic was not present in a significant majority of cases. In fact, it was present in only 53 percent of the cases. Each of the remaining five characteristics— concealed traveling companions, early morning travel, style of dress, last to deplane, and age of suspect—present in fewer than 20 percent of the cases. This does not support the existence of a nationally accepted drug courier profile that contributes significantly in law enforcement efforts because it shows that different agencies use different characteristics. The wide number of items on the profile could broaden the profile so significantly that the profile has little or no meaning.

The conclusion of this attempt to validate the accuracy of drug courier profiles is that there is no indication that profiles actually represent the behavior of most drug couriers. Moreover, evidence suggests that because profiles include so many characteristics, there may be no profile at all. Some profile characteristics are so poorly defined that officers can interpret virtually any innocent behavior as indicative of criminality. Police agencies disagree as to how to prioritize profile characteristics or measure their worth in establishing reasonable suspicion for investigative detention. Most importantly, courts have been derelict regarding the phenomenon of drug courier profiles in that they never demanded evidence that profiles do, in fact, contain traits that represent the behavior of the aggregate of drug couriers. Courts accepted this claim without question and, as such, have given police the equivalent of a blank check to legitimate their detention and interrogation of anyone.

THE IMPACT OF DRUG COURIER PROFILES

The evidence examined to this point explores major questions surrounding the accuracy of profiles. This section focuses on issues concerning their application. The aforementioned observations are limited in that the research focuses on the use of profiles by agents at major transportation centers. However, a recent Supreme Court decision, *Whren v. United States*, 116 S. Ct. 1769, (1996), could significantly affect the disproportionate representation of African Americans and Latinos among drug offenders because of the expansion of this controversial practice of drug courier profiling to highways and streets. The *Whren* decision asserts that if a police officer makes a legitimate traffic stop, any other investigative inquiries conducted at such time are facially valid. Given the problems previously discussed regarding drug courier profiles, this decision becomes especially troublesome.

The facts in *Whren* are as follows: plainclothes vice detectives in an unmarked police unit observed two young, African American men driving an expensive, new sports utility vehicle with temporary license tags in an area known for drug activity. The vehicle stopped at a stop sign for what appeared to the officers to be an unusually long time. The vehicle turned suddenly and sped away in excess of the speed limit. The officers pursued and stopped the vehicle. When they approached, presumably to warn and cite the driver about his behavior, they observed the passenger holding bags of cocaine in each hand. The central issue was whether these officers were truthfully attempting to enforce the traffic codes or used the traffic codes to justify further investigation of individuals about whom they were suspicious. According to the Supreme Court, since the officers were there to address a violation of the law, any other subjective intent on behalf of the officers is irrelevant (*Whren v. United States*, 116 S. Ct. 1769, [1996]).

The problematic aspect of this decision is its broader implications. Law enforcement officers operating under the profile or another set of assumptions need now only observe the suspect committing some trivial traffic violation to justify a stop with broader investigatory parameters. This pattern sounds exactly like what the U. S. Supreme Court sought to prevent in cases like *United States v. Brignoni-Ponce*, 422 U.S. 873, (1975) and *Delaware v. Prouse*, 440 U.S. 648 (1979). In *Brignoni-Ponce*, the Court argues that roving checks of cars by the Border Patrol are, without reasonable suspicion, unconstitutional. Similarly, *in Prouse*, an officer makes a stop only to check license and registration, with no investigatory objective or suspicion, and the Court asserts that such a traffic stop cannot justify a search and seizure. With profiling, facially neutral and innocent charcteristics can warrant suspicion in the eyes of the police, and though insufficient to constitute reasonable suspicion themselves, the profile charcteristics contribute to reasonable suspicion. However, with *Whren*, reasonable suspicion is no longer required because the officer is there presumably to enforce the traffic laws. This is especially problematic because traffic codes are so broad and all-encompassing that people violate them frequently, knowingly and unknowingly. In practice, this means that things such as tinted windows, loud stereos, headlight covers, failing to use turn signals, driving too fast, driving too slowly, weaving in lanes, remaining too long at stop signs, or rolling through stop signs can allow a police officer to detain a suspect. Should profile charcteristics also be present, this can lead to longer detentions and further intrusions on individual liberty. Therefore, an officer following the characteristics outlined in a profile need only follow a suspected motorist until the officer observes a violation of the traffic codes. In other words, the profile dictates those people to treat with suspicion; *Whren* allows officers to detain them under the pretext of a traffic violation and investigate further.

History and recent experience demonstrate that police do not apply profiles uniformly throughout American society. David Harris (1997) documents some of the most notorious examples of these events. For instance, in Volusia County,

Florida, more than 70 percent of drivers stopped by the Sherriff's Selective Enforcement Team as part of the county's major drug interdiction effort were African American or Hispanic, although only 5 percent of drivers on the county's roads were of these races. Moreover, these officers stopped motorists of color for longer periods and subjected them to heightened inquiry. More than 80 percent of the cars searched belonged to people of color. More alarming in terms of the *Whren* decision is the fact that the deputies in Florida repeatedly argued that each of these stops was for a valid traffic violation (Harris 1997: 561-563). In another case lawyer from Washington, D.C., sued the Maryland State Police after he and his family were unjustifiably detained returning from a trip to Chicago. This suit uncovered a pattern of selective enforcement directed at persons of color. The police had recently issued a memorandum that told officers to watch for "dealers and couriers [who] are predominantly black males and black females. . . utilizing Interstate 68" (565). Following the settlement in this case the police had to maintain records on whom they stopped and under what conditions. Three years later the records show that 75 percent of people stopped were African Americans (566). Harris also documents similar patterns of racist law enforcement in other states.

Showing another example of bias in police action concerning people detained for investigatory stops, Justice Carol Berkman of the New York State Supreme Court struck down cocaine possession charges against a black woman arrested at the Port Authority Bus Terminal. Noting that all the defendants that the Port Authority Police had brought before her court were minorities, Justice Berkman stated: "The picture that emerges is one of discriminatory law enforcement which does incalculable damage to our civil liberties and which produces at best questionable results for the War on Drugs." Although denying any bias, Port Authority admitted that 65 to 75 percent of those arrested in its drug interdiction campaign were Hispanic or black (McCoy & Block 1992: 7-8). Furthermore, in *United States v. Taylor* (910 F 2d. 1402, at 1409) the arresting officer testified that approximately 75 percent of the individuals her task force followed were African American. In addition, Jerome Miller found in Jacksonville, Florida, that the largest single group of individuals brought to the jail were arrested for "driving with a suspended license." This violation is also almost exclusively police-initiated. Moreover, the most common charge for which African American men were arrested and jailed was "resisting without violence." He concludes that the facts surrounding this crime would involve an individual's objection to being stopped and searched for a relatively minor infraction. He adds, The practice of stopping 'suspicious' cars driven by black men who fit a 'profile' was also reflected in many of those arrests" (Miller, 1996: 108). In other words, police are stopping the vehicles of young men of color on the basis of profiles or trivial traffic violations, and when these young men object, police arrest them for their resistance to police authority.

Miller summarizes the effect of this discovery on criminal justice professionals in his area. This reaction reveals the important social implications of this problem for African Americans and other racial minorities in the United States:

I thought that these figures on race and the local criminal justice system would shock the local authorities. However, few seemed concerned. Far from being a badge of embarrassment, the depressing data was seen as a kind of badge of honor, demonstrating the fortitude of local law enforcement authorities in getting tough on crime. The figures on juveniles, for example, were quoted in a letter the state's attorney circulated to the county's secondary schools as a warning to would-be errant teenagers. The presumption—apparently shared by most of the nation—was that so many African American youths and young adults were being dragged off to jail because, as one judge commented to me, "they're the ones committing the violent crimes.". . . Although inner-city males committed a disproportionate share of violent crimes, particularly homicide and robbery, the absolute number of such crimes was insufficient to explain the thousands of young African Americans brought into the jail every day. (Miller 1996: 49)

In other words, the Caucasians in this jurisdiction assumed that African Americans are disproportionately involved in drugs and crime because either crime statistics prove this or this is common knowledge. So when African Americans continue to be disproportionately arrested, whether based on profiles or not, it confirms this presumption. Since people's racist presumptions are now justified, people do not have to consider questions concerning the legitimacy of the practice that supplied the justification. In other words, if many citizens assume criminal justice statistics to be objective representations of criminal behavior, they never have to contemplate that crime statistics are more the products of the behavior of criminal justice professionals than they are products of the behavior of criminals. Seeing their worst racist fears confirmed through such "objective" means as criminal justice statistics allows people erroneously to ascribe the blame for racial disproportions in the statistics to racial identity, making racism legitimate and socially acceptable.

However, these crime statistics do reflect the biases and attitudes of police, prosecutors, judges, and jurors, as well as criminal behavior. Police officers developing a profile should be sensitive to the fact that previous drug wars have been racist and myopic in their approach. For example, research shows that the first campaigns against opium in the late nineteenth century disproportionately focused upon Chinese Americans. Also in the 1880s the campaign against cocaine was triggered due to racist beliefs about African Americans, despite its widespread popularity among Caucasians. Chicanos have been traditionally the focus of marijuana interdiction efforts going back to myths in the 1930s that migrant workers caught smoking marijuana were more prone to violence. All these wars on drugs focused on people of color despite popular use among Caucasians. Moreover, these types of panics were rekindled during the late 1940s and 1960s with similar foci and results (Mann 1993; Johns 1992). Therefore, basing the profile on statistics or experiences generated by these events would have a disparate impact on persons of color. Despite the fact that the Supreme Court argues in *Whren* that the "Constitution prohibits selective enforcement of the law based on considerations such as race," it is illogical to assume that the profile in practice would not include racial suppositions if it is the product of the previous experience of society and applied through decisions of human beings who are also products of that experience (153 L Ed 2d 89, at 98).

Other criminal justice research also supports the assertion that profiles would be applied unfairly (Walker 1992: Walker et al. 1996; Mann 1993: Hacker 1992; Cose 1995). Michael Tonry (1995) argues that it is primarily the War on Drugs that dramatically worsened the racial disproportion in the criminal justice system. Under the false rubric of public safety and morality, the Reagan and Bush administrations declared a war fought against one group of American citizens as opposed to others. He suggests that frequency of outdoor behavior in poorer neighborhoods and lower levels of formal social organization in these neighborhoods create the differential levels of enforcement against African Americans for drug-related offenses. He cites the incompatible rises in the African American and European American percentages of drug arrestees in several jurisdictions in the late 1980s as proof of this. For example, the African American percentage of drug arrestees nationally rose 115 percent compared to a 27 percent increase for Europeans between 1985 and 1989. Furthermore, the easier location and documentation of urban drug dealing has made it inaccurately representative of all drug dealing in the minds of most Americans. The point is that these proactive police efforts in areas populated predominantly by persons of color produce the figures and experiences that agencies use to establish the profile. More importantly, in the minds of officers who seek to be proactive and empowered through tools such as profiles, it justifies stopping persons of color as opposed to Caucasians. However, these data imply that these numbers are the products of biased law enforcement. Therefore, profiles legitimate past bias in drug enforcement, which then generates more bias.

Christina Johns describes the extensive societal implications of this phenomenon. She argues that this practice allows the majority to further distance themselves from the critical social problems that underlie the War on Drugs. Though proponents of profiles produce data that suggest the overwhelming majority of people support practices like profiling and other aggressive, proactive police policies, Johns asserts that these respondents may be misperceiving the implications of their answers:

Even though large numbers of respondents in surveys indicate that they are willing to support an expansion of search and seizure, it is arguable that these people are responding to what they perceive as search and seizure policies that will affect others, not themselves. In the Washington Post/ABC News poll, respondents said that they were willing to have their homes searched without a court order even if houses of "people like you were sometimes searched by mistake." However, it is arguable that many people in responding to such polls do not perceive these policies as a direct threat to themselves personally. And this is not an unreasonable perception. As with other law enforcement tactics, expanded search and seizure [such as profiles] primarily affects the poor and minorities. (Johns 1992: 91)

In other words, the majority of Americans, including African Americans, endorse the use of practices like profiles because they mistakenly believe that only the right people will be subjected to them. The widespread civil rights violations and abuses that profiles permit, such as those previously described, will continue until this misperception is corrected.

This section of the chapter examines the impact of drug courier profiles on society. The conclusion of this discussion is that drug courier profiles have created an environment in which abuse is frequent and law enforcement is biased. Police use the profile to legitimate racist beliefs about crime and drugs. The preceding research shows some of the dramatic disparities in the numbers of African Americans detained and searched by police compared to Caucasians. Though only 12 percent of the population of the United States and 13 percent of its estimated monthly drug users, African Americans comprise 35 percent of those arrested, 55 percent of those convicted, and 74 percent of those incarcerated for drug use and possession in the United States (Mauer & Huling 1995). This dramatically disproportionate result is due, at least in part, to the effects of facially neutral practices like drug courier profiles, which officers often apply in a biased fashion to persons of color.

CONCLUSION

This review of the history, accuracy, and impact of the drug courier profile concludes that as a law enforcement tool it should be immediately abandoned unless law enforcement or acade can demonstrate its value as an interdiction tactic. Current research shows that there is, in fact, no single drug courier profile that law enforcement officers apply uniformly. Second, police define many characteristics of the drug courier profile so broadly or allow so much subjectivity in its application that these characteristics are virtually meaningless. Many aspects of the profile occur after the investigative detention has begun, such as discovering that the person is traveling under an alias; therefore, they cannot be used to justify the decision to detain the individual. Additionally, courts have inexplicably accepted the validity of profiles without question. Law enforcement has never established that profiles accurately represent the behavior of the aggregate of drug couriers, nor have they routinely demonstrated that the characteristics listed in the profiles accurately represent the behavior of the defendant at the time in question. Lastly, profiles legitimate the racism of police officers and the racist construction of the drug and crime problems. They represent past practices of the criminal justice system, either the experiences of individual officers or the statistical amalgamation of these experiences. However, criminal justice research shows that the history of policing in the American system of criminal justice regarding drug enforcement has been racist. The drugs preferred by members of minority groups draw the focus of police and the harshest criminal penalties. It appears from current research on the nation's highways that there is a presumption of guilt regarding minorities and that while the charcteristics contained in profiles are racially neutral, they create suspicion in the minds of police officers primarily when exhibited by members of minority groups.

The great irony in this is that police and society endorse profiles because they have led to the apprehension of some guilty offenders. However, discrimination in the application of profiles may allow several guilty offenders to escape capture because these people do not arouse suspicion in officers. This research discusses how profile characteristics are very broadly defined, innocent in nature, and facially race-neutral. But it appears that police officers apply these characteristics to a grossly disproportionate number of people of color as opposed to Caucasians, though race is not a spoken criterion of the profile. This begs the question that if two people of different races, both possessing profile characteristics, were passing in front of officers, who would be stopped? Does a Latino in a business suit arriving from a source city on a cash-paid ticket warrant more suspicion than a casually dressed Caucasian arriving from the same place with a cash-paid ticket? This vagueness surrounding the profile is its central problem. While there undoubtedly are other variables to consider in this situation, the decision to stop one of these persons would rest with the individual officer. The current research suggests that people of color get stopped much more often than Caucasians. Moreover, the impact of unwarranted investigative detention of innocent travelers who possess some profile characteristics should not be underestimated, especially if police stop a disproportionate number of people of color because of a presumption of guilt resulting from the institutionally racist nature of this practice.

When examining images of African Americans, Latinos, and other racial minorities in popular American culture, the continued use of drug courier profiles suggests that the image of young men of color is fraught with elements of criminality and dangerousness. In a society where citizens are presumed equal and presumed innocent until proven guilty, a discriminatory law enforcement practice violates these highly regarded ideological values. Profiles allow law enforcement officers to suspect people of complicity in one of the greatest social problems of this age. The zealous desire to overcome this problem creates an environment in which young people of color find themselves presumed guilty, hunted, and overly monitored. Moreover, the guilt of a small minority is used to justify continued suspicion and persecution of all, creating a self-fulfilling prophecy. The police suspect, detain, and catch more people of color, which is thought to justify continuing the policy.

REFERENCES

Cloud, M. (1985). "Search and Seizure by the Numbers: The Drug Courier Profile and Judicial Review of Investigative Formulas." *Boston University Law Review* 65(5): 843–921.

Cose, E. (1995). *The Rage of Privileged Class.* New York: HarperCollins.

Guerra, S. (1992). "Domestic Drug Interdiction Operations: Finding the Balance." *The Journal of Criminal Law and Criminology* 82(4),: 1109–1161.

Hacker, A. (1992). *Two Nations: Black and White, Separate, Hostile, and Unequal.* New York: Ballantine Books.

Harris, D. (1997). "'Driving While Black' and All Other Traffic Offenses: The Supreme Court and Pretextual Traffic Stops." *The Journal of Criminal Law and Criminology* 87(2): 544–585.

Johns, C. (1992). *Power, Ideology, and the War on Drugs: Nothing Succeeds Like Failure.* New York: Praeger.

Johnson, S. (1983). "Race and the Decision to Detain a Suspect." *Yale Law Journal* 93(2):

214–258.

Lyman, M. and G. Potter. (1996). *Drugs in Society: Causes, Concepts, and Control.* 2d ed. Cincinnati: Anderson.

MacDonald, J. and J. Kennedy. (1983). *Criminal Investigation of Drug Offenses.* Springfield, MA: Charles C. Thomas.

Mann, C. (1993). *Unequal Justice: A Question of Color.* Bloomington: Indiana University Press.

Mauer, M. and T. Huling. (1995). *Young Black Americans and the Criminal Justice System: Five Years Later.* Washington, DC: Sentencing Project.

McCoy, A. and A. Block (eds.). (1992). *War on Drugs: Studies in the Failure of U.S. Narcotics Policy.* Boulder, CO: Westview Press.

Miller. J. (1996). *Search and Destroy: African American Males in the Criminal Justice System.* Cambridge: Cambridge University Press.

Tonry, M. (1995). *Malign Neglect: Race, Crime, and Punishment in America.* New York: Oxford University Press.

Walker, S. (1992). *The Police in America: An Introduction.* 2d ed. New York: McGraw-Hill.

Walker, S., C. Spohn, and M. DeLone. (1996). *The Color of Justice: Race, Ethnicity, and Crime in America.* New York: Wadworth.

Chapter 9

Conceptual Incarceration: A Thirteenth-Amendment Look at African Americans and Policing

Ramona Brockett

Freedom for the African American was achieved during the later part of the nineteenth century with the ratification of the Thirteenth Amendment.[1] Upon ratification, the Thirteenth Amendment permits Africans who were enslaved in this country not only to have the benefit of being considered full humans but also to discard the slavery badge of "chattel" and give them the status of presumed equality with white men. This freedom, which permits America to consider the African human, was further secured by the implementation of the Fourteenth[2] and Fifteenth Amendments, which permitted, in part, rights of citizenship not to be abridged and, further, that race should not bar voting rights.[3] Ironically, the freedom that the Thirteenth Amendment boasts for the African slave also simultaneously reenslaves the African through the advent of punishment or, alternatively, incarceration. This chapter analyzes the impact of punishment and the Thirteenth Amendment upon the idea of conceptual incarceration.

The freedom given to the African by the Thirteenth Amendment is lodged within the main clause of the amendment, which abolishes slavery or involuntary servitude within the United States or any place subject to its jurisdiction. Conversely, the "punishment" clause, which is located within the commas, reads that slavery is abolished "except as a punishment for crime." The "punishment" to which the Thirteenth Amendment refers is incarceration. Therefore, the amendment proposes the abolishment of slavery, yet reinstates slavery upon incarceration. The amendment specifically differentiates slavery from involuntary servitude, which means its framers intended to distinguish varying states of servitude. In America, the Africans, who were transported on slave ships, were considered slaves. Indentured servants generally were European prisoners who were bound as servants for a period of seven years. Therefore, the conclusion that must be drawn from the wording of this amendment is that Africans in America, being considered slaves or "chattel", upon emancipation subsequently regain that status upon incarceration; thus begins the notion of conceptual incarceration.

For the purposes of this chapter, I propose that Africans in America, by law and varying forms of social control, are subject to a constant state of punishment. Further, in this constant state of punishment lies the concept of incarceration. A concept is defined as a general understanding or thought that is derived from particular instances or occurrences.[4] Social control theories focus on the strategies and techniques used to regulate human behavior so as to lead to obedience and conformity of society's rules.(Adler et al. 1995) This conceptual incarceration empowers those proponents of social control to exercise such controls through various forms of punishment. For instance, in the case of African Americans punishment becomes reenslavement, which is mandated and supported by the Thirteenth Amendment to the U.S. Constitution, U.S. Supreme Court decisions, and tough-on-crime control legislation. Conceptual incarceration, therefore, is the idea or thought that Africans in America, subject to the provisions of punishment lodged within the Thirteenth Amendment and through the exercise of social control, are cast into a perpetual state of slavery due to their status, which changes from human to chattel upon incarceration. This chapter further analyzes, identifies and determines the controls within the system of punishment that allow conceptual incarceration to exist.

Three controls promote the existence of conceptual incarceration: constitutional interpretation, the police, and, get-tough-on-crime legislation. Each one of these mechanisms supports the punishment, incarceration, and reenslavement of African Americans through various forms of social control. For instance, the Thirteenth, Fourteenth, and Fifteenth Amendments, while used to secure the freedoms of formerly enslaved Africans, have been subject to the interpretation of the meaning of the framers' original intent regarding freedom, equality, and fair treatment. The U.S. Supreme Court uses its decision-making authority to interpret the original framers' constitutional intent and apply its meaning to current social norms. Current trends in U.S. Supreme Court decision making as applied to constitutional interpretation also further the notion of conceptual incarceration by usurping civil liberties in support of governmental intrusion through the more restrictive interpretation of the Fourth Amendment. This not only ensured the reenslavement of the African in America through punishment, but also reinstated the Black Codes by taking property rights from the African American through violations of the Fourteenth Amendment's search and seizure protections. First, let us examine conceptual incarceration in terms of privileges, immunities, and equal protection for African Americans as guaranteed by the Thirteenth, Fourteenth, and Fifteenth Amendments.

After the Civil War, the Thirteenth Amendment, ratified in 1865, abolished slavery and involuntary servitude. The Fourteenth Amendment, ratified in 1868, both provided citizenship and guaranteed equal protection for former slaves. In addition to these two amendments, the Civil Rights Act of 1866 was enacted by Congress after the ratification of the Thirteenth Amendment (Mann 1993). This was the first civil rights act. It was enacted in response to the Black Codes, which sought to reduce the status of African Americans to semislavery (Allport

1979). The Black Codes limited rights of African Americans to own property, denied African Americans the right to testify against Euro-Americans, prevented African Americans from being in the streets after dark, provided imprisonment for any breach of employment contract, and provided an employment provision that mandated the allocation of menial jobs for African Americans (Allport 1979). Further, protection in terms of equality came with the ratification of the Fifteenth Amendment, enacted in 1870, which gave African Americans the right to vote. Following the ratification of the Fifteenth Amendment, the Civil Rights Act of 1875, which was enacted during the Reconstruction era, provided federal power to limit racial discrimination by redefining the titles of Americans as "citizens" instead of "blacks" or "whites."[5] Therefore, the promise of equality was delivered to the African American upon the ratification and enactment of these provisions; however, the U. S. Supreme Court in the 1880's interpreted the framers' intent, redefining equality for African Americans and ultimately denying their rights. The following analysis of Supreme Court intervention allows the reader to further understand the impact of the preceding amendments and civil rights acts in light of the insidious nature of the U. S. Supreme Court's power to determine the African American's right to citizenship, equality, and fairness.

First, prior to the Thirteenth Amendment and the Civil Rights Act of 1866, in the case of *Dred Scott v. Sanford*, 60 U.S. 393 (1857), the question being determined by the Court was whether a Negro whose ancestors were imported to this country as slaves could become a member of the political economy and community through the privileges and immunities clause guaranteed by the Constitution; and, further, whether that Negro could be considered a citizen of the United States. The U. S. Supreme Court unequivocally concluded no. Further, the Court concluded that only those who presently held the right to be citizens could grant that same right to Negroes, upon the grantor's discretion. There is a distinct irony lodged within the reasoning of this decision, because as equality is given to Africans by Euro-Americans, this exercise of power still inherently places the Euro-American in a position of superiority. The superiority lies in the Euro-American's authority to grant this right, which, in turn, also gives the Euro-American the distinct right to reenslave the African. Therefore, the Supreme Court permitted two outcomes from this decision. First, it established unequal citizenship. Hence, Euro-Americans, who were human, could be considered citizens, while Africans, who were subhuman, could be considered neither human nor citizens. Thus, there were two classes of citizenship. Second, the Court granted the oppressor the constitutional right to grant, at will, the oppressed person's freedom. This right always inherently allows the oppressor the right of superiority over the oppressed. Consequently, this act gives the oppressor the inherent right to reenslave the oppressed in the form of conceptual incarceration through imprisonment.

The Supreme Court continued its rampage of racist decision making in the late 1800s, which mirrors the rash of racist decision making currently, during the late 1900s. The first decision came in 1873 with the *Slaughter-House Cases*,[6] in which, after the Civil Rights Act of 1866 and the establishment of the Thirteenth,

Fourteenth, and Fifteenth Amendments, the Court restored the Dred Scott Doctrine. This decision threatened the privileges and immunities clause of the Fourteenth Amendment by reinstating the idea of two classes of citizenship, chiefly national and state. Further voting rights and the restoration of civil rights were given to the control of the states with the cases of *United States v. Cruishank* (1875)[7], and *United States v. Reese* (1875). These decisions radically usurped the power of the Fourteenth and Fifteenth Amendments by granting states the right to enforce these amendments as they pleased. The decision that ultimately abolished the power of the Thirteenth Amendment and reinstated the philosophy of Dred Scott came from the language of the decision in the case of *Plessy v. Ferguson* (1896). Supreme Court justice Brown describes the Negro as abject, ignorant, childlike, and unfit. These particular words describing the Negro in America have never been overturned. Further, these words used to describe the Negro justified the Court's decision to continue the dual classes of citizenship by constitutionally mandating separate, but equal, facilities for blacks and whites. This decision killed whatever remnants were left of the Act of 1875, which permitted people within the United States to be considered "citizens" instead of, "black" or "white."

Presently, this debate of dual citizenship still exists and furthers conceptual incarceration through the inequality of the African in America in terms of property ownership and the right to contract. First, in the late 1960s and mid-1970s the Court wrestled once again with the Thirteenth Amendment, the Black Codes, and the rights associated with citizenship in terms of property ownership, the right to contract, and the right to attend private school. In two separate cases, *Jones v. Alfred H. Mayer, Co.* (1968)[8] and *Runyon v. McCray* (1976),[9] the Court considered the Act of 1866 and 42 U.S.C. sect. 1981, which prohibits racial discrimination in the making and enforcement of private contracts.[10] In both cases the Court dealt with the right to contract privately. In both cases it was determined that a Negro should be allowed to contract to buy a home or go to private school and that that contract should not be prohibited by the badge of indicia lodged in the color of his skin. What becomes more important, however, in both of these cases are the dissenting opinions.

Justice Rehnquist, who presently is the chief justice of the Supreme Court, along with Justices Harlan and White, states in the dissents of both *Runyon* and *Jones* that the basic law of contracts promotes the notion of mutual assent. Mutual assent in the law is the agreeing of two parties to a contract. This agreement is the basic constitutional right of each party to enter unencumbered into a contract. These justices, sharing the same sentiment, conclude that in a contract, regardless of whether there is racial animus on the part of the white party, if the white person who is party to the contract does not want to contract with a black person, then no mutual assent exists. Without mutual assent, Rehnquist concludes, this supersedes the provision of 42 U.S.C. sect. 1981, which prohibits racial discrimination in the making of private contracts. Although this is part of the dissenting opinion, legal analysis has consistently revealed that dissenting opinions often have influence when similar issues are later reexamined by the

Supreme Court and become the basis for majority opinions in subsequent cases. Therefore, once again, the examination of private contractual agreements promotes the idea of reenslavement through the reinstatement of Black Codes that prohibit the Fourteenth Amendment's securities binding such actions. This type of legal reasoning opens the floodgates for the denial of rights for the African American, thus incorporating the idea of conceptual incarceration.

In our final consideration of constitutional interpretation as it relates to conceptual incarceration, the Fourth Amendment is reviewed.[11] The "Coca Cola Bottle Theory" (Brockett & Jones 1995) examines the liberal and conservative interpretation by the U.S. Supreme Court and the Fourth Amendment bar against unreasonable search and seizure. Throughout the twentieth century the Supreme Court has broadly and narrowly construed the breadth of Fourth Amendment guarantees in light of civil liberties. However, as the twentieth century ends, and the twenty first century begins, it is apparent that the Rehnquist Court is determined to abandon the protections guaranteed by the Fourth Amendment against unreasonable searches and seizures.

The Rehnquist Court has broadened the scope of exigency or emergency circumstances as a bar against providing a search warrant: *California v. Hodari D.* 499 U.S. 621 (1991); *Maryland v. Buie* 494 U.S. 325 (1990). Essentially, what the Court has condoned is the taking of a person's property at will if that government official or police person considers that person or the situation dangerous. The danger, then, is termed an emergency, which allows the government to take or seize property without a warrant. Thus, case law, reflects the Supreme Court, has condoned the aggressive actions of police invariably promulgated against African American suspects, by allowing cops to seize evidence that would otherwise be excluded as unconstitutional.

The Rehnquist Court has justified the seizure of this evidence through the notion that the exigency or emergency of the circumstances surrounding the arrest allows any search of any part of the home for the protection of potential, victims, calling this a protective sweep. Therefore, a person's property can be taken at any time and for any reason as long as the police suspect that person of wrongdoing. African Americans are arrested at a much higher rate than Euro Americans. Hence, the taking of property greatly affects African Americans.

Some criminologists have determined that this type of punishment is purposefully granted by the legal system of the United States through its laws and even its Constitution and, further, that it is not arbitrary. Once again, constitutional interpretation permits conceptual incarceration or slavery to be justified through the denial of civil liberties in light of governmental intervention. Even further, these liberties allow governmental takings at will, which is a denial of the right to property. This same denial of the right to property was originally contained in the Black Codes. Therefore, it is apparent that the Constitution's ratification of the Thirteenth, Fourteenth, and Fifteenth Amendments, along with several civil rights acts, has not served as a bar against the reinstatement of slavery or conceptual incarceration.

Next, this chapter analyzes how conceptual incarceration determines police action. In order to understand conceptual incarceration and its impact on the African American population within the system of policing, it is important to understand the police from a historical perspective. Historically, the uniformed police patrol as we know it today grew out of policing in London during the early nineteenth century (Klockars 1989). The establishment of the police patrol was adopted in this country by the middle to the end of the nineteenth century. Police patrols in America were unlike those in Britain. Their primary purpose was not to protect the aristocracy; the primary goal of policing was to promote the best interest of politics.

The political process and the employment of policemen were intertwined. This interest grew out of the basic practice that established jobs for police. For instance, if a person wanted to become a policeman in any of the major cities in the country, that person would not only have to see his alderman or ward leader but also pay him to become a practicing policeman. As such, this served only to promote the interests of the political structure, which, in turn, served the policing subculture. Further, this practice promoted elitism through class. This happened based on a political infrastructure that for the purpose of promotion, was in the best interest of both politics and economic gain.

The early fundamental principles of policing were based upon a military analogy (Fogel 1977). Many police administrators urged politicians and persuaded the public to view the police as a "domestic" army with a relationship toward local politicians analogous to that of military–political relations on the national level (Klockars 1989: 314). Ultimately, this philosophy allowed the local politicians to determine what strategies were important politically; and the police were left to administrate law and order based on the particular political agenda (Klockars 1989: 314). Critical theorists contend that this practice allowed the police to be an instrument used to promote the interests of the power elites (Harring 1981; Platt 1982; Reinman 1984; Spitzer 1975). This claim has validity when we consider that the first police departments, which were established in the northern industrial cities, helped to promote industrialization by policing the behaviors of the working class through criminalizing their actions. The policing of their actions was conducted through the breaking up of strikes as ordered by the managers and owners of the major corporations for which the working class were employed. This helped the police to promote the interests of capitalism in favor of the ruling class (Lynch 1984; Platt 1982). Not only were the working class employed by these power elites, but also the police were relied upon by the same power elites to govern social order in their, the power elites', best interest.

The introduction of capitalism influenced the sociopolitical agenda, which promoted not only a military form of policing but also nationalism. This type of socioeconomic, political agenda could promote notions of nationalism and elitism only in the interest of capitalism (Miller Bryant 1993). Nationalism was promoted through the fiction of social order; and elitism was promoted by the dictates of class.

Ultimately, these notions led to a distinct affinity toward the delineation and recognition of the class differential within the practice of policing, which promoted either reactive or proactive policing practices (Miller & Bryant 1993). More specifically, reactive policing was unprobing and reactionary, based on information of criminality given to the police; and proactive policing was probing and justice seeking as demonstrated through police reaction (145). Notably, police generally are proactive in poorer areas and reactive in more affluent areas. At the turn of the century police activated their proactive prowess upon the working class in favor of the elites. Therefore, policing historically represented the social, political, and economic interests of society within the distribution of power and authority (Miller & Bryant 1993). Consequently, the historical perspective upon which policing is based promotes four distinct features that preserve policing philosophy today: crime fighting and self-image; quasi-military administrative structure; the law as a basis for the legitimacy of police action; and the politics of police power (Klockars 1989: 315). Thus, this represents the basic philosophy and premise upon which policing in America is formed. Further, considering the history of police with respect to the power elite and those who retain authority, it is then understood why conceptual incarceration could exist well within the realm of policing. If the idea in America is that Africans in America are not considered citizens with authority, then those who are in authority who have the power to enslave them can use police as the social control mechanism to reenslave through conceptual incarceration.

Generally, the type of person who becomes a law enforcement officer is concerned with the moral and social meaning of rule-breaking behavior. Those who enforce the law must believe in its inherent good. Often, those who are able to fit within the paradigms of law enforcement come from the segment of the class structure for which legitimacy of social order is dictated by a strong sense of nationalism. From a Marxist perspective law enforcement lends legitimacy to the capitalist state within the class structure, ultimately benefiting the select few (Lynch & Graves 1986). It has been found that police generally come from the lower middle class, in which racial attitudes are firmly fixed because of the generally low level of education, and social and economic status (Johnson 1943). Generally, many of those who come from this segment of society strive to achieve society's goals legitimately, often seeing themselves as the protectors of the status quo. This attitude is reflects nationalism, which fosters social harmony through the maintenance of social peace at any cost, along with compliance to social dictates (Haas 1986). As such, the Marxist perspective regards policing as born out of the class struggle. This also implies an inherent hierarchy that mandates who in our society invariably deserves respect from the police and who does not.

The expectation in our society is that police will carry out any and all decisions that promote societal order. As such, the expectation is that law enforcement will be evenly distributed and that all perpetrators will be viewed the same way. Unfortunately, however, several distinct issues prevent this from happening within society. More specifically, with regard to conceptual incarceration, the Thirteenth Amendment mandates the distribution of law enforcement.

The distribution of law enforcement can be viewed from different perspectives that can explain why police treat different people differently. The first reason for the uneven distribution of law was discussed previously in terms of the constitutional mandate by the Thirteenth Amendment. The second reason for the uneven distribution of law enforcement lies in legitimacy in relation to the class structure (Lynch & Graves 1986). From a critical perspective, law enforcement is viewed as placating the upper class, which, in turn, is in charge of the redistribution of wealth (Chambliss 1976). Further, those Euro-Americans who represent the upper echelons of the class typology generally find police action to be legitimate. Further, the police in America have historically protected the capitalist class, which historically has been represented by Euro-Americans. Based on an understanding of the history of the African American within the framework of the American power and class structure, African Americans do not represent the class that police would have an interest in protecting. Even further, other notions of critical criminology contend that conceptual incarceration exists because in America the focus is on the street-level criminal instead of the white-collar criminal, which promotes an uneven perspective on fear and subsequent punishment since the street-level criminal usually is represented by the poor, uneducated black male. Therefore, conceptual incarceration and the historic role of the police would dictate the use of police authority to punish the African American, thus promoting social order.

The impact of police use of authority to promote conceptual incarceration in support of the capitalist agenda has far-reaching social implications for African Americans who are victims of police brutality. All too often, reports, that exemplify police as racist overseers looking for reasons to hurt, stop, maim, or kill perpetrators, especially those who are black, are received from African Americans. Interestingly, this attitude and perception did not begin with Rodney King or Malcolm X. In fact, its origins exist in the Thirteenth Amendment's license to equality that was given to the African in America by way of the Act of 1866 (Avins, 1970). Granville Cross notes in his article entitled "The Negro, Prejudice, and the Police" that passed the two amendments of the U. S. Civil Rights Code that, in 1866 and 1870, not only ratified the Civil War amendments but also were installed to deter the police who committed crimes against minorities (Cross:1964). Cross contends that the Supreme Court, at least in theory, proposed desegregation and accommodation laws; however, they became a fiction when, as he puts it, "the 'Negro' confronts the police officer who renders him powerless to enforce his rights" (407). Decker (1981: 80--87) reiterates this notion by stating that race, treatment from the police, age, and negative experiences predict and dictate police reaction.

For instance, in their study, Browning, et al. using a bivariate analysis with sociodemographic characteristics, including gender, age, education, and income, found a direct relationship between race and being hassled by the police. With an N of 103 blacks and 136 whites, they determined, using two dependent variables that included actually being "hassled" and being "vicariously hassled," that 46.6 percent of African Americans as opposed to 9.6 percent of whites were hassled by the police. Further, they determined that the act of harassing potential suspects causes a vicarious hassle effect. Sixty-six percent of African Americans in the sample felt vicariously hassled, while only 12.5 percent of the Euro-Americans experienced the same phenomenon. The meaning of "vicarious" in this sample was being "aware" of others of their same ethnic background, who had been hassled by police. The socioeconomic range encompassed the entire class structure. The mean education level for whites was 14 and for African Americans was 13.5 (6). Thus, police were hassling not only the poor, uneducated, homeless African Americans, but also the middle-and upper-class blacks. These types of studies indicate that conceptual incarceration is alive and well. Further, it indicates that police consider African Americans as suspects for reasons other than their having actually committed a criminal act. The idea of being considered a suspect is incarcerating. It is a form of punishment. This punishment, when acted upon by police, places African Americans in a state of conceptual incarceration.

Police autonomy has a greater effect on the punishment of African Americans and the idea of conceptual incarceration. The amount of police autonomy has a direct effect on the role of policing communities. The outgrowth of this concept from a Marxist perspective is that two types of police enforcement occur: coercive and deceptive (Marx 1988). Consequently, autonomy either promotes or usurps police discretion (Miller & Bryant 1993). For instance, a study done by Miller and Bryant (1993) shows the difference between policing that promotes autonomy and policing that does not. This autonomy is primarily based on the size of the administrative budget, which is dictated by the amount of money allotted to certain precincts, which, in turn, is dictated by local tax structures. The larger the budget the police are acting under, the less proactive they are. Conversely, the lower the police budget, the less reactive the police become. Further, class differences influence police decision making (Flowers 1988). Research has found that police discretion varies within the socioeconomic status of the neighborhoods where the incidents take place (Flowers 1988: 150). For instance, police tend to be more formal in lower-income neighborhoods and informal in upper-income neighborhoods (150). The Miller-Bryant study (1993: 143) found, in addition, that two social ecological variables are statistically significant in predicting proactive policing: families living below the poverty line and most nonwhite residents experience proactive policing. Interestingly, the study also found that police in poorly subsidized agencies, such as those in the inner cities, rely on in-house income-generated tactics such as asset seizure, hence, proactive policing. This suggests that proactive policing in low-income areas where the families live below the poverty line is to deter street-level drug enforcement; however, there might not be any explanation within the study for the existence of proactive policing in nonwhite jurisdictions. The study noted that police have more autonomy in jurisdictions where the fiscal economy dictates low government funding. In other words, police become more aggressive in lower-income areas where African Americans not only live but are gravely affected. This, then, allows police to exercise their authority to reenslave the African through punishment and incarceration. Conceptual incarceration becomes a reality when economic conditions dictate proactive policing, which generates jails filled with black bodies. Explanations for such actions may lie in a sociological aspect of criminology called impression formation discussed later (Vrij & Winkel 1992).

Conversely, reactive policing seems to take place in small, white communities where it is less likely that police will initiate drug enforcement operations. Further, in a study conducted by Richard Hollinger, (1984), he found that proactive policing occurred in drunk driving cases. The variables most influential in a policeman's proactive stance were race and occupational status of the subject. Although class structure typically predicts respect and compliance with authority, the influences of race, beliefs, and nonverbal communication often result in a negative assessment by police of certain types of citizens (Vrij & Winkel 1992: 1546). Therefore, it appears that police response is related not only to economics and class, as was indicated earlier, but also to ethnicity. Hollinger contends that occupational status was a statistically significant variable. However, since African Americans are not viewed as having high-status occupations, police would tend to negatively react to their presence when stopped. This is primarily due to their ethnic status more than their economic status.

In a more recent study examining demeanor and police behavior, Worden and Shephard (1996) looked at the correlation between disrespect and hostility and the likelihood of arrest. In their reproduction of Smith and Visher's (1991) work, where they measured demeanor as a dichotomous variable along with the severity of the offense, they found that persons who were characterized as hostile during the initial stages of the police–perpetrator encounter were most likely to be arrested (92). The importance of the correlation between the observed disrespect and hostile demeanor during the initial stages of the police–perpetrator encounter introduces yet another facet of this phenomenon that rebuts the premise of class and serves as an aid in the development of understanding conceptual incarceration as it relates to punishment: impression formation.

The sociological aspect of impression formation imparts the badge of indicia and promotes the negative attitude that results from its insidious application. The literature seems to indicate, specifically, that the cross-cultural police–citizen interaction and the influence of impression formation influence attitudes and perceptions (Vrij & Winkel 1992). Impression formation is the influence of race, beliefs, and nonverbal communication that results in a negative assessment of deviance by police during the process of interpreting the actions of "black" citizens. The framework of impression formation analyzes the physical actions of black citizens and predicts their potential criminality through nonverbal communication, which ultimately leads to police reaction. Treatment of African Americans by police and law enforcement officials, however, directly affects perception and attitude response by African Americans. For instance, excessive force is a tool that many African Americans view as used in violent attacks by police against citizens, especially minorities; so this force may be used based on a perception by police of deviance (Friedrich 1993). Differential enforcement of law and wide latitude, or police autonomy, are often issues that face police and plague the minority community, especially the African American. Discretion is generally based on the police officer's judgment in a given situation. However, if impression formation is the paramount   determinant within police discretion because of the nonverbal correspondence between police officers and black citizens, it would appear that this perception generally yields negative results. More specifically, the research has found that, despite class, indicators of observed "black" deviance by police include high-pitched voice, indirect answering, gaze aversion, frequent smiling, and excessive body language (1547). Interestingly, these types of reactions to authority figures by African Americans may not be a result of, or indication for, criminality as much as they may be indicative of a history of oppression and slavery. It is a well-known fact that slavery, which still today dictates treatment of African Americans, has had a great deal of influence on the way many African Americans act and react to those who police society. During slavery, it was not proper for a slave to stare his or her master in the eye. Further, to appear happy was a dictate of many European masters. A practice of gaze aversion, frequent smiling, or certain types of body language may be left over from lessons learned by generations past whose non adherence to such bodily actions may have resulted in lynching and/or death.

Whatever class, impression formation, which represents the reactions of white police to black citizens, promotes conceptual incarceration by criminalizing the actions of African Americans, thus placing them in peril, with authorities exercising social control ultimately leading to arrest and/or incarceration. Impression formation does not necessarily exclude the response of African American police to African American citizens (Flowers 1988). African American police trained by European standards all too often view the African American suspect as criminal.

A wide volume of literature states that African American police also view African American perpetrators in the same light as do white police. Although some black officers identify closely with the black community, there exists a large anti-black sentiment among black officers who proclaim that crime is out of control in minority communities due to the perceived lack of control exhibited by the minorities themselves (Walker 1983; Dulaney 1984). Walker found in his study that black officers view street demeanor, along with manners of dress and behavior, as threatening. This perception is due to their knowledge of the foundation from which these actions stem (27). Therefore, although Vrij drew these conclusions from nonverbal communication ascertained by white officers, it is apparent that this attitude is not endogenous to white officers only. In fact, this type of thinking implicates the criminal justice system. The training that the system implements compels officers to see the African American as the deceptive perpetrator. Further, that training, combined with the history of policing, promotes notions that teach officers to protect what they value in society. In American society, the African is not considered valuable.

Vrij & Winkel (1992: 1555–1556) made four distinct conclusions when conducting his impression formation study. First, negative assessments are made by police based on skin color. Second, although skin color played a role that promoted the negative assessment of citizens, once the interaction occurred, police assessed blacks more favorably than whites. The explanation was due to the inherent nature of the history of racism and the negative image the police generally have for harassing blacks; therefore, the police favored a less aggressive posture once they stopped the blacks. Third, initial negative assessments of blacks were due to the nonverbal behavior displayed by them. Fourth, campaigns designed to induce police not to perceive skin color as negative generally do not work because of the conditioning police have toward correlating skin color and criminality. More specifically, skin color was not necessarily a determining factor in negative responses by police to black citizens (31). However, one interesting observation of this study was the additional analysis that showed that when the black citizens conformed and exhibited "white" nonverbal behavior, police often treated them with more respect (31). This observation may be an indicator of the class differential that causes non-verbal behavior to be interpreted differently based on race. The literature on impression formation accentuates the nexus between police interaction, race, class, and conceptual incarceration.

The last aspect of this chapter that analyzes conceptual incarceration examines the get-tough-on-crime strategies, more specifically, the promotion of the "three-strikes-you-are in" philosophy. This initiative, which has swept the country, began with the 1994 election in California (Tyler & Boeckmann 1997). This initiative mandates life in prison upon the commission and conviction of three felonious crimes. Once a person is incarcerated, most of his or her rights are taken away as part of the punishment. Even further, if African Americans are incarcerated, the Thirteenth Amendment permits the system to enslave them.

Critical criminologists have stated that public support for supporting these types of initiatives are linked to judgments about social conditions and social values. Further, while crime prevention is a concern, and social conditions and values are important, it has been found that support for the crime problem and the get-tough-on-crime initiatives come from another social source. Tyler and Boeckmann (1997) in their study which sought to understand the reasons for public support of the "three- strikes-you-are-in" campaign, found the following results. Using a random sample of 166 adults living in the East Bay Area of northern California, 66 percent of whom were Euro-Americans, 20 percent African American, 7 percent Latino American, and 6 percent Asian American, the respondents overwhelmingly said two factors were key to the adoption of the initiative: the family and diversity. Although the initiative is punitive, the respondents concluded there was fear that minorities are dangerous and that ethnocentrism caused them to see those they feared as outsiders. In other words, fear for their families' safety caused them to condone the California initiative as a positive social control because of the lack of understanding and knowledge of different people and cultures.

In American history, the lack of understanding of other cultures has led the government to intern Asians, Haitians, and others in camps as a measure of social control. African Americans now occupy 75 percent of the jails in America. Even further, those who are in jail do not have the right to such personal effects as their own pillowcases or body cavities. (*Hudson v. Palmer* 468 U.S.517[1984]; *Bell v. Wolfish* 441 U.S. 520[1979]). The idea of enslavement goes back to Dred Scott and the Black Codes. America enslaved those who seemed to threaten its unity and norms. This is reflective of enslavement. Incarceration furthers that same notion. The promotion of the "three-strikes-you-are-in" campaign solidifies African reenslavement and codifies conceptual incarceration.

If Tyler and Boeckmann's study reflects current attitudes toward minorities and African Americans, then it says that putting people in jail for life is the answer to diversity. If people are different, then it justifies criminalizing their actions and their beliefs and punishing them for their badge of indicia—chiefly, their ethnicity. Punishment of this badge of indicia is what the Thirteenth, Fourteenth, and Fifteenth Amendments, along with the civil rights acts, were ratified and enacted to deter. However, it appears that the country has not progressed past the Dred Scott or Black Code initiative to have dual citizenship because of criminalizing the outsiders and conceptually incarcerating them.

CONCLUSION

Constitutional interpretation, policing strategies, and get-tough-on-crime initiatives have resulted in the reenslavement of the African American through the punitive measures of social control that are legally condoned by the Thirteenth Amendment. From the perspective of the African American and the police, punishment is both given and received. The African American's punishment is received due to the badge of indicia he or she has received due to the nature of his or her role in America.

African Americans are trapped by a Constitution that allows their existence to be plagued by the constant threat of punishment, incarceration, and subsequent reenslavement. This plague is allowed to exist virtually unaddressed due to years of oppression dealt by the hand of the slave master who, by virtue of the Thirteenth Amendment, was allowed to tell the oppressed a fiction that they were now set free. However, how can the oppressor truly tell the oppressed that he or she is set free without having the authority to still oppress?

The irony that lies within the Thirteenth Amendment is the struggle that the African American must face daily. This irony is that he or she is the suspect or the criminal because of his or her status as an outsider. This philosophy allows African Americans to constantly be in a state of conceptual incarceration. Likewise, the police, who are imbued with the distinct honor of enforcing the law, also are the ones promoting punishment. The constant administration of justice results in a strain between law enforcement and that segment of society against which it appears to continually exercise its prowess.

Analysis of these issues is necessary for the development of effective policing strategies not only in minority communities but in all communities where minorities may exist. Unfortunately, criminal justice seems to accept the fiction that problems between police and minorities exist only within certain socioeconomic strata. However, this chapter suggests that the Constitution, along with legislative interpretation, despite social or economic class, has stigmatized and enslaved the African in America yet again. Why policing strategies aimed to thwart deviance seem to perpetually address the criminality of Africans in America seems to be tied to the concept of conceptual incarceration. This chapter suggests a basis for offering restructuring policing policies that would incorporate a more utilitarian approach to policing; providing an altruistic solution to the problem of conceptual incarceration.   The remedy lies in the restructuring of the Thirteenth Amendment and the abolition of inequality.

NOTES

1. Proposed by Congress January 31, 1865; ratification completed December 18, 1865. The amendment was passed by the Senate, 38 to 6, on April 8, 1864; however, it was defeated in the House, 95 to 66, on June 15, 1864. The House reconsidered the amendment on January 31, 1865, and the resolution passed, 119 to 56. It was approved by President Lincoln on February 1, 1865. Section 1. of the amendment reads: "Neither Slavery nor involuntary servitude, except as a punishment for crime whereon the party duly convicted, shall exist within the United States, or any place subject to their jurisdiction." Section 2: "Congress shall have power to enforce this article by appropriate legislation."

2. The Fourteenth Amendment was proposed to the legislatures of several states by the 39th Congress, June 13, 1866, and ratified by the secretary of state, July 28, 1868. It reads in part: "Section 1. All persons born or naturalized in the United States, and subject to the jurisdiction thereof, are citizens of the United States and of the State wherein they reside. No state shall make or enforce any law which shall abridge the privileges or immunities of citizens of the United States; nor shall any State deprive any person of life, liberty, or property, without due process of law; nor deny to any person within its jurisdiction the equal protection of the laws."

3. The Fifteenth Amendment was proposed to the legislatures of the several states by the 40th Congress, February 26, 1869, and was declared to have been ratified in a proclamation by the secretary of state, March 30, 1870. "Section 1. The right of citizens of the United States to vote not be denied or abridged by the United States or by any state on account to race, color, or previous condition of servitude. Section 2. The Congress shall have the power to enforce this article by appropriate legislation."

4. Webster's II New Riverside University Dictionary defines concept as "n.1. A general understanding, esp. one derived from particular instances or occurrences. 2. A thought."

5. Congress passed the Civil Rights Act March 1, 1875, giving equal rights to blacks in public accommodations and jury duty. The act was invalidated in 1883 by the Supreme Court.

6. 83 U.S.(16 Wall.) 36 (1873).

7. 92 U.S. 542 (1875).

8. 392 U.S. 409, 1968.

9. 427 U.S. 160, 1976.

10. 42 U.S.C. sect. 1981. Equal rights under the law: "All persons within the jurisdiction of the United States shall have the same right in every State and Territory to make and enforce contracts to sue, be parties, give evidence, and to the full and equal benefit of all laws and proceedings for the security of persons and property as is enjoyed by white citizens, and shall be subject to like punishment, pains, penalties, taxes, licenses, and exactions of every kind and to no other."

11. Fourth Amendment: "No person shall be held to answer for a capital, or other infamous crime, unless on a presentment or indictment of a Grand Jury, except in cases arising in the land or naval forces, or in the militia, when the actual service is in time of war or public danger; nor shall any person be subject for the same offense to be twice put in jeopardy of life or limb; nor shall be compelled in any criminal case to be a witness against himself, nor be deprived of life, liberty, or property, without due process of law; nor shall private property be taken for public use without just compensation."

REFERENCES

Adler, Freda, G.O.W. Mueller, and William Laufer. (1995). *Criminology*. New York: McGraw-Hill.

Allport, Gordon W. (1979). *The Nature of Prejudice*. Reading, MA: Addison-Wesley.

Avins, Alfred. (1970). "Equal Protection against Unnecessary Police Violence and the Original Understanding of the Fourteenth Amendment: A Comment." *Buffalo Law Review* 19: 599–608.

Brockett, Ramona and Delores Jones (1995). "The Role of the J.D. in Criminal Justice Education." In Nikki Ali Jackson (ed.), *Contemporary Issues in Criminal Justice Shaping Tomorrow's System* 14-29. New York: McGraw-Hill.

Brown, Craig M. and Barbara D. Warner. (1995). "The Political Threat of Immigrant Groups and Police Aggressiveness in 1900." In Darnell F. Hawkins (ed.), *Ethnicity, Race and Crime: Perspectives across Time and Place* 82–98. Albany: State University of New York Press.

Browning, S.L., F.T. Cullen, L. Cao, R. Kopache, and T. J Stevenson. (1994). "Race and Getting Hassled by the Police: A Research Note." *Police Studies* 17(1): 1–19.

Centers, R. (1949). *The Psychology of Social Classes: A Study of Class Consciousness*. Princeton: Princeton Univerwsity Press.

Chambliss, William J. (1976). Whose Law? What Order? A Conflict Approach to *Criminology*. New York.

Cross, G. J. (1964). "The Negro, Prejudice, and the Police." *Journal of Criminal Law* 55: 405–411.

Decker, Scott H. (1981). "Citizen's Attitudes toward the Police: A Review of Past Findings and Suggestions for Future Policy." *Journal of Police Science and Administration* 9: 81–115.

Dulaney, William Marvin. (1984). *"Black Shields: A Historical and Comparative Survey of Blacks in American Police Forces."* Diss., Ohio State University. Ann Arbor, MI: University Microfilms International.

Flowers, R. B. (1988). *Minorities and Criminality*. Westport,CT: Greenwood Press.

Fogel, Robert William. (1977). "Cliometrics and Culture: Some Recent Developments in the Historiography of Slavery." *Journal of Social History* 11(1): 34–51.

Friedrich, Robert (1993). "Racial Prejudice and Police Treatment of Blacks' Evaluating Alternative Law Enforcement Policies."

Haas, E.B. (1986). "What Is Nationalism and Why Should We Study It?" *Internal Organization* 40(3)(Summer): 707–744.

Harring, S. (1981). *Policing in a Class Society: The Experience of American Cities, 1865–1915*. New Brunswick, NJ: Rutgers University Press.

Hollinger, Richard C. (1984). "Race, Occupational Status, and Pro-Active Police Arrest for Drinking and Driving." *Journal of Criminal Justice* 12: 173–183.

Klockars, Carl B. (1989). "Order Maintenance, the Quality of Urban Life, and Police: A Different Line of Argument." *Police Leadership in America* 309–321.

Lynch, M. L. (1984). *Class Based Justice: A History of the Origins of Policing in Albany*. New York: Hindlelang.

———. and W. B. Graves. (1986). *A Primer in Radical Criminology*. New York: Harrow and Heston.

Mann, Coramae Richey. (1993). *Unequal Justice: A Question of Color*. Indiana University Press.

Marx, G. (1988). *Undercover: Police Surveillance in America*. Los Angeles: Twentieth

Century Fund.

Miller, J. Mitchell and Kevin Bryant. (1993). "Predicting Police Behavior: Ecology, Class, and Autonomy." *American Journal of Criminal Justice* 18(1): 133–151.

Platt, A. (1982). *The Iron Fist and the Velvet Glove*. San Francisco: Synthesis Press.

Reinmann, J. (1984). *The Rich Get Richer and the Poor Get Prison*. New York: John Wiley & Sons.

Smith, Douglas A. and Christy A. Visher. (1981). "Street-Level Justice: Situational Determinants of Police Arrest Decisions." *Social Problems* 29: 167–177.

Spitzer, S. (1975). "Toward a Marxian Theory of Deviance." *Social Problems* 22: 638–665.

Trojanowicz, Robert C. and Mark H. Moore. (1988). *The Meaning of Community in Community Policing*. East Lansing, MI: National Neighborhood Foot Patrol Center.

Vrij, Aldert and Frans Willem Winkel. (1992). "Crosscultural Police–Citizen Interactions: The Influence of Race, Beliefs, and Nonverbal Communication on Impression Formation." *Journal of Applied Social Psychology* 22(19): 1546–1559.

Walker, Donald B. (1983). "Black Police Values and the Black Community." *Police Studies* 5: 20–28.

Worden, Robert E. and Robin L. Shephard. (1996). "Demeanor, Crime, and Police Behavior: A Reexamination of the Police Services Study Data." 34: 83–106.

CASES

Arizona v. Hicks (1987) 480 U.S. 321.

California v. Hodari D. (1991) 499 U.S. 621.

Dred Scott v. Sanford (1857) 60 U.S. 393.

Jones v. Alfred H. Mayer, Co. (1968) 392 U.S. 409.

Katz v. US (1967) 389 U.S. 347.

Mapp v. Ohio (1961) 367 U.S. 643.

Maryland v. Buie (1990) 494 U.S. 325.

Miranda v. Arizona (1966) 384 U.S. 436.

Oliver v. US (1984) 466 U.S. 170.

Plessy v. Ferguson (1896) 163 U.S. 537.

Runyon v. McCray (1976) 427 U.S. 160.

Slaughter-House Cases (1873. 83 U.S.(16 Wall.) 36.

United States v. Cruishank (1875) 92 U.S. 542.

United States v. Reese (1875) 92 U.S. 214.

United States v. Salerno (1987) 481 U.S. 739.

United States v. Ursery (1995) 116 S.Ct. 2135.

Wayte v. US (1985) 470 U.S. 598.

Wilson v. Arkansas (1995) 514 U.S. 927.

Chapter 10

Black and White Perceptions of the Appropriateness of Police Conduct

Daniel Kolodziejski, John Stilwell, Kimberly Torchiana, and Michael W. Markowitz

An important issue facing American criminal justice is the manner in which their constituents, namely, the public, perceive the conduct of the police. In a democratic society such as the United States, the exercise of police powers is assumed to occur within established parameters as stated in the Constitution (Arthur & Care, 1994: 167). When performing their duties of protecting and defending the citizens of their communities, the police are expected to adhere to standards of equal protection, the rule of law, and due process (167), an expectation that should not vary according to a citizen's color or place of residence. However, this is not always the case.

Police use of violence when dealing with minorities in America has reinforced the idea that police are discriminatory in their deployment practices and use of force (168). Thus, just as many believe that policing varies by context and group, it is also logical to assume that perceptions of the fairness and consistency with which police follow the rule of law vary as well. Well-known cases such as the Rodney King incident and, more recently, the savage attack against Abner Louima in New York City bring the potential for abuse of police power to the public's attention. However, research indicates that such practices, while perhaps not as extreme, occur regularly in urban settings and contribute to the perception among many in minority communities that police treatment of people of color is significantly harsher than that experienced by whites and those in the suburbs (168).

An overrepresentation of minorities in America's poor, urban communities has been shown to contribute to disproportionately higher arrest rates for blacks in these areas. Tonry (1994) suggests that such patterns emerge from patrol practices of the police and the ease with which arrests can be made in such socially disorganized areas. Seen as the basis for negative perceptions of police conduct, victimization has also been shown to have an impact on such perceptions. Decker and Wagner (1985) found that minorities are the most likely victims of crime, as well as the most likely to hold negative attitudes toward the police.

Discrimination against blacks by law enforcement officers has been well documented in the literature. For example, Kerstetter, Rasinski, & Heiert (1996), in their study of police brutality investigations, found that the race of the investigating officer and the race of the complainant were significantly related to decisions that claims of excessive force by police were unsustainable. Also, in his review of research on public support for the police, Weitzer (1996) found numerous examples of disproportionate use of force and formal treatment in situations involving minority citizens (viz., Piliavin & Briar 1964; Milton, et al. 1977; Smith 1986).

A consistent theme emerging from these studies is that police discriminate against minorities, especially blacks, in the discharge of their duties. The link between such activity and opinions of the police has also been established through research. In a nationwide survey of attitudes regarding the police, Arthur & Care (1994) found that members of groups with greater power, status, and wealth (including affluent white males) were more likely to favor police use of force (168). Similarly, Decker and Wagner (1985) found that minorities who are most often suspects and victims of crime are also the most likely to hold negative attitudes toward the police. Levin and Thomas (1997) conducted a similar study regarding the effects of racial identity of the police on perceptions of police brutality and found that black subjects were more likely to judge two white officers arresting a black male more harshly than if one of the officers was black.

What has not been thoroughly explored in the literature, however, is the issue of direct comparison between the attitudes of blacks and whites regarding the appropriateness of police conduct. In this era of "community policing" and efforts to reconnect the officer with the citizen, it is useful to determine the extent to which attitudes about the police differ by race. The substantial body of research that concludes that police officers frequently exhibit prejudice and discrimination against blacks in the discharge of their duties makes such an analysis all the more compelling. Thus, our specific research hypotheses are:

H1: African Americans evaluate police conduct less favorably than whites do.

H2: Males evaluate police conduct less favorably than females do.

H3: Participants from different areas of residence evaluate the appropriateness of police conduct differently.

H4: Respondents who have been previously victimized evaluate police conduct less favorably than respondents who were not victimized.

H5: Respondents who have committed a crime evaluate police conduct less favorably than respondents who have not.

METHODS

Subjects

A convenience sample of 110 white and 50 black students from a small university in a northeastern state constituted the group of participants for this study. The participants varied by year in school, place of residence, past victimization, and possible arrest. Data were collected in undergraduate classes, through distribution to members of the university's Black Student Union, and at various gathering places around campus.

Measurement Instrument

The questionnaire for this study was modeled after the instrument used by Durham, Elrod, and Kinkade (1996) in their study of public support for the death penalty. In an effort to measure participants' perceptions toward the appropriateness of black and white officers' conduct, 12 scenarios were constructed, four for each of the three operationally defined areas of police conduct: use of force, restraint, and intervention. Each category included scenarios that depicted a white officer with a black citizen, a white officer with a white citizen, a black officer with a black citizen, and a black officer with a white citizen. Additionally, the scenarios reflected behavior by those involved that ranged from appropriate to extreme.

A five-point Likert Scale was used to measure the responses of the participants. Each participant was asked to read the scenarios and report his or her level of support for the officer's conduct in each. The choices ranged from very appropriate to very inappropriate, with each receiving a numerical value ranging from one to five points. Composite scores of responses were then used as an indicator of support for the appropriateness of the police conduct. After responses to the scenarios were coded, participant scores ranged from a low of 12 (full support of the actions of the officer(s) involved) to a high of 60 (a complete lack of support for all police actions).

RESULTS

The composition of our sample consisted of 160 participants. The reliability of responses to the scenarios was calculated to be .6729, indicating a moderate level of consistency among sample participants (see Table 10.1).

Table 10.1
Reliability Analysis- Scale (Alpha)

Statistics for Scale	Mean	Variance	Std. Dev.	Number of Variables
	38.4268	42.4642	6.5165	12

Reliability Coefficients
Number of Cases = 160.0   Number of Items = 12
Alpha = .6729

Of the total, 110 of the subjects were white, and 50 were black, with mean scores of 36.59 and 42.80, respectively. There were 84 males with a mean of 36.62, and 76 females with a mean of 40.64. Also, 21 of the subjects reported having been arrested (mean = 37.42), compared with a mean of 38.71 for those who had not.

One hundred eleven of the participants had been or had known a crime victim (mean = 39.00), while 49 had not (mean = 37.51). In terms of residence, 59 were from urban areas with a mean of 40.22, 83 were from suburban areas with a mean of 37.63, and 18 were from rural areas with a mean of 37.22.

H1: African Americans evaluate police conduct less favorably than whites do.

The race of the subject was the first independent variable that was tested. The mean for the 110 white participants was 36.59, which suggests a certain level of ambiguity in their perceptions, while the mean for the 50 black participants was 42.80, which demonstrates their less favorable perceptions of police conduct. Using a t-test to determine if the two groups differed significantly, comparison of the means yielded a t value of -6.23, which indicates a significant difference between blacks and whites in their perceptions of police conduct at the .05 level, thus supporting our initial hypothesis (see Table 10.2).

Table 10.2
T-Tests for Independent Samples of Race of Respondent

Variable	Number of Cases	Mean	SD	SE of Mean
Total Score				
White	110	36.5963	5.344	.512
Black	50	42.8000	6.791	.960

Mean Difference = -6.2037
Levene's Test for Equality of Variances: F = 2.858   P = .093

Variances	T-Test for Equality of Means t-value	df	2-Tail Sig	SEof Diff	95% CI for Diff
Equal	-6.23	158	.000	.997	(-.8172, -4.235)
Unequal	-5.70	77.93	.000	1.088	(-8.370, -4.037)

H2: Males evaluate police conduct less favorably than females do.

The second independent variable tested was gender. The mean for the 84 males in the study was 36.62, which demonstrates a certain level of uncertainty with regard to the appropriateness of the police conduct described. For the 76 females, however, the mean of 40.64 indicates an overall dissatisfaction with the police involved. Statistical comparison of these means yielded a t value of -4.09, which was significant at the .05 level. Thus, while a significant difference was found, it was not in the direction predicted, and our second hypothesis was not supported (see Table 10.3).

Table 10. 3
T-Tests for Independent Samples of Gender of Respondents

Variable	Number of Cases	Mean	SD	SE of Mean
Total Score				
Male	84	36.6265	6.003	.659
Female	76	40.6447	6.395	.734

Mean Difference = -4.0182
Levene's Test for Equality of Variances: F = 1.054   P = .306

T-Test for Equality of Means					95%
Variances	t-value	df	2-Tail Sig	SE of Diff	CI for Diff
Equal	-4.09	158	.000	.983	(-5.961, -2.076)
Unequal	-4.07	153.47	.000	.986	(-5.966, -2.070)

H3: Participants from different areas of residence evaluate the appropriateness of police conduct differently.

The third independent variable, area of residence, was tested using analysis of variance. The 59 respondents living in urban areas evaluated police conduct the least favorably, with a mean score of 40.22. For the 83 respondents living in suburban areas the mean was 37.63, and for the 18 respondents living in rural areas the mean was 37.22. The F value for the comparison of these groups was 3.23, thus indicating a significant difference at the .05 level and supporting our third hypothesis. However, a post hoc test to determine which pairs of groups significantly differed did not yield notable results (see Table 10.4). This latter finding is explored in more detail later.

Table 10.4
One-Way Analysis of Variance

Variable by Variable	Total Score Residence	Place of Residence			

Analysis of Variance

Source	D.F.	Sum of Squares	Mean Squares	F Ratio	F Prob.
Between Groups	2	265.1251	132.5626	3.2321	.0421
Within Groups	157	6398.2711	41.0146		
Total	159	6663.3962			

Scheffe Test with Significance Level .05:
The difference between two means is significant if
  MEAN (J) -MEAN (I) >= .3768 * SQRT (1/N(I) + 1/N(J))
  with the following value(s) for RANGE: 3.49

No two groups are significantly different at the .05 level.

H4: Respondents who have been previously victimized evaluate police conduct less favorably than respondents who were not victimized.

The fourth independent variable that was tested was victimization. The mean for the 111 respondents who answered yes that they or a family member had been a victim of a crime was 39.00, while the mean for the 49 respondents answering no was 37.51. A statistical comparison of these means yielded a t value of 1.35, insignificant at the .05 level. Thus, our fourth hypothesis was not supported (see Table 10.5).

Table 10.5
T-Tests for Independent Samples of Victim
(Respondent or anyone in family)

Variable	Number of Cases	Mean	SD	SE of Mean
Total Score				
Yes	111	39.0091	6.621	.631
No	49	37.5102	6.138	.877

Mean Difference = 1.4989
Levene's Test for Equality of Variances: F = .535   P = .466

T-Test for Equality of Mean Variances	t-value	df	2-Tail Sig	SE of Diff	95% CI for Diff
Equal	1.35	158	.180	1.113	(-.699, 3.696)
Unequal	1.39	122.92	.168	1.080	(-.645, 3.643)

H5: Respondents who have committed a crime evaluate police conduct less favorably than respondents who have not.

The fifth and final independent variable that was studied was criminal status. The 21 respondents who answered yes to having been arrested for a crime had a mean of 37.42, while the 139 respondents who answered no had a mean of 38.71.

Comparison of the two groups yielded a t value of -.85, insignificant at the .05 level, thus rejecting our fourth hypothesis (see Table 10.6).

Table 10.6
T-Tests for Independent Samples of Crime
(Has respondent ever been arrested?)

Variable	Number of Cases	Mean	SD	SE of Mean
Total Score				
Yes	21	37.4286	7.639	1.667
No	139	38.7174	6.316	.538

Mean Difference = -1.2888
Levene's Test for Equality of Variances: F = 1.214   P = .272

Variances	t-valu	df	2-Tail Sig	SE of Diff	95% CI for Diff
Equal	-.85	158	.399	1.523	(-4.296, 1.718)
Unequal	-.74	24.34	.469	1.752	(-4.901, 2.324)

T-Test for Equality of Means

The results of these statistical analyses indicated a number of factors to be relevant in explaining differing perceptions of police conduct. To determine if these initial results indicated a more complex association of factors, our final analysis interactively compared differences in reported scores based on those variables that had shown significant singular relevance, namely, race, gender, and area of residence. Table 10.7 displays the results of the factorial ANOVA used to measure these variables and shows that, while race and gender retain significant main effects in the more complex model, area of residence loses its explanatory relevance. This may be explained by the fact that many American communities are racially homogeneous, and what was assumed to be the impact of "area" was, in fact, the strong effects of "race." This interpretation is further corroborated by the fact that post hoc testing did not find significant differences to exist between areas in the initial ANOVA model. Further testing indicated that while a significant, overall two-way interaction effect was observed, no two pairs of variables were significantly related. Also, the model failed to yield a significant three-way interaction.

DISCUSSION

The results of our analyses show that our primary hypothesis was supported. There is a significant difference in the perceptions of the appropriateness of police conduct between African Americans and whites. The black participants in our sample were less supportive of the actions taken by the police officers, a finding that supports conclusions in the literature that minorities view the police role and use of force to favor whites and those of high status (Arthur & Care 1994; Tonry 1994; Decker & Wagner 1985).

Table 10.7
Analysis of Variance

	Total Score	
By	Race	Race of Respondent
	Residence	Place of Residence
	Gender	Gender of Respondent
	Unique sums of squares	
	All effects entered simultaneously	

Source of Variation	Sum of Squares	DF	Mean Square	F	Sig of F
Main Effects	1110.059	4	277.515	9.161	.000
Race	739.046	1	739.046	24.397	.000
Residence	1.065	2	.532	.018	.983
Gender	150.464	1	150.464	4.967	.027
2-Way Interactions	372.114	5	74.423	2.457	.036
Race Residence	141.337	2	70.669	2.333	.101
Race Gender	45.671	1	45.671	1.508	.221
Residence Gender	113.558	2	56.779	1.874	.157
3-Way Interactions	112.731	2	56.365	1.861	.159
Race Residence Gender	112.731	2	56.365	1.861	.159
Explained	2210.424	11	200.948	6.634	.000
Residual	4452.973	148	30.292		
Total	6663.396	159	42.173		

160 cases were processed.
0 cases were missing.

In addition to race, gender and area of residence had a significant impact on perceptions of policing. The women in our sample were clearly less supportive of police conduct in the scenarios than men. The fact that this statistical significance was independent of any other factor lends further importance to the role of gender in assessing perceptions of the police and suggests an important area for future research. Also, while the initial significance of area of residence supported our third hypothesis, its relevance was subsequently shown to be an artifact of the effect of race.

Two of our hypotheses stated that people who had either been or known a crime victim and those who had been arrested would evaluate the conduct of police officers less favorably. We believed that contact with officers would create a negative perception toward them, in line with the findings of research by Tonry (1994) and Decker and Wagner (1994). However, our results did not support these hypotheses. We found no significant differences in their perceptions.

Although our primary hypothesis was supported, those who wish to extend this research in the future could improve our methodology. An important area of improvement would involve increasing the number of black participants, thus providing a more representative sample and increasing the validity of any observed differences. A second and related improvement would involve increasing the sample size of the study. While our research was limited to college students, similar studies could and should be conducted among diverse populations to determine if the trends observed here apply to other groups as well. A third improvement would involve the use of pretests to refine the research instrument used. While a moderate level of reliability was achieved in this study (see Table 10.1), future analyses could improve consistency by refining the instrument to minimize any ambiguity perceived by participants.

Despite these limitations and suggestions, the results of this study do indicate an important and troubling finding, namely, that perceptions of overall police conduct do differ significantly based on race. While not representative of the general population, the participants in this study do reflect the attitudes of typical young people who lack a sustained and negative relationship with the criminal justice system. Since the majority of this sample did not report criminal activity, their conclusions can be interpreted to reflect a more general consensus of attitudes on the police.

The importance of this finding suggests that efforts made by police agencies to improve their image among members of minority communities have been less than successful. Considerable public attention of late has been focused on the importance of police responsiveness to the needs of their communities. One such need is clearly the trust and support of all groups, regardless of race. The conclusions of this study indicate a significant direction for policing policy, namely, the implementation of strategies that foster trust and confidence, rather than separation and fear. The stability and safety of our urban communities may depend on their success in these efforts.

REFERENCES

Arthur, J. A. and C. E. Care. (1994). "Race, Class, and Support for the Police Use of Force." *Crime Law and Social Change* 21: 167–182.

Decker, S. H. and A. Wagner. (1985). "Black and White Complainants and the Police." *American Journal of Criminal Justice* 10: 105–116.

Durham, A., H. P. Elrod and P. T. Kincade. "Public Support for the Death Penatly: Beyond Gallup." *Justice Quarterly* 13(4): 705–735.

Kerstetter, W. A., K. A. Rasinski, and C. L. Heiert. (1996). "The Impact of Race on the Investigation of Excessive Force Allegations against Police." *Journal of Criminal Justice* 24: 1–15.

Levin, J. and A. R. Thomas. (1997). "Experimentally Manipulating Race: Perceptions of Police Brutality in an Arrest." *Justice Quarterly* 14: 577–586.

Milton, C., J. Halleck, J. Lardner, and G. Albrecht. (1977). *Police Use of Deadly Force.* Washington, DC: Police Foundation.

Piliavin, J. and S. Briar. (1964). "Police Encounters with Juveniles." *American Journal of Sociology* 70: 206–214.

Smith, D. (1986). "The Neighborhood Context of Police Behavior." In A.J. Reiss and M. Tonry (eds.), *Communities & Crime. Series in Crime and Justice, an Annual Review of Research,* (8):313–341. Chicago: University of Chicago Press.

Tonry, M. (1994). "Racial Politics, Racial Disparities, and the War on Crime." *Crime and Delinquency* 40: 475–491.

Weitzer, R. (1996). "Racial Discrimination in the Criminal Justice System: Findings and Problems in the Literature." *Journal of Criminal Justice* 24: 309–312.

Part III

Race, Courts, and the Law

Chapter 11

Race as a Legal Construct: The Implications for American Justice

Delores D. Jones-Brown

> If you can't be better than a nigger, who are you better than?
> — *Mississippi Burning*, 1988

> We should not expect a consensus on social and moral
> issues. . . [because] we frequently differ on what we
> feel are the facts.
> — *Andrew Hacker*, 1992

INTRODUCTION

While attending a Minority Student Program banquet given in honor of students graduating from the Rutgers Law School, it occurred to me that America, with its history of racial and ethnic oppression,[1] must, with each turn of the century, reaffirm its commitment to the oppression of some group of people. As the twentieth century comes to a close, legal scholars and legislators are locked in heated debates over issues related to the rights of immigrants.

In a similar vein, listening to the banquet's keynote address, given by the first African American male appointee to the New Jersey Supreme Court, reminded me that near the start of this century (1896), the *Plessy v. Ferguson* decision was handed down by the federal Supreme Court, establishing the ominous rule of law known as the "separate but equal doctrine." Plessy was ominous in that it foretold the violence that would be done to American jurisprudence in the effort to preserve racial harmony while attempting to disentangle the seemingly perpetual relationship between race and law. Here, it is argued that it is precisely because of the historical entanglement of race and law that America cannot resolve its race "problems," especially as those problems relate to issues of crime and the perception of justice.

Defining the Problem

Without question, race is a major factor in the administration of justice in America. Minorities, especially those of black racial identity, are disproportionately represented among persons being processed through the criminal justice system. In most regions of the country, blacks overwhelmingly constitute the population in secure correctional settings. Given the country's reputation for justice and fairness, there are continuous debates over the extent to which the current state of affairs reflects individual maladies or entrenched aspects of the prevailing social structure. Through an analysis of past legislation and judicial decisions, this chapter explores the reality of legal history. It argues that by using the courts to define who is black and enacting laws geared toward disadvantaging or "punishing" blackness, the lawmakers and judges of the past have ensured the current problem of the overrepresentation of blacks in the criminal justice system through both socioeconomic failure and delegitimization of law as a means of social control.

RACE AND LAW IN AMERICA

The Legal Creation of an Inferior Race

The opening quote from the film *Mississippi Burning* that appears at the beginning of this chapter, represents a mind-set that is as American as apple pie. It is a mind-set so deeply rooted within the American psyche that while some individuals spend countless hours denying that they have it, others are completely unaware, at the conscious level, that they possess such a state of mind. This mindset negatively affects both blacks and whites. In whites, it creates a false sense of entitlement that historically has led to lynchings and other atrocities. In contemporary society, it contributes to the formation of white hate groups and leads to acts of domestic terrorism.[2] For blacks, this mindset has led to feelings of powerlessness and mistrust,[3] resulting in riots, civil "disturbances," and general social mayhem.

While it is popular to blame the victims of an oppressive legal system for the outcomes that the system has produced, here it is argued that crime, criminality, and general social disorder are the natural by-product of the legal construction of race in America. By operating, simultaneously, a legal system dedicated to the uplifting of one group and the oppression of another, the founders of American democracy have ensured a divided perception of "justice" in America,[4] with the majority of those who have benefited from the system likely to see the system as just, while the majority of those who have suffered from the system's schizophrenia are likely to see it as unjust.

Hacker's statement about consensus, "feelings," and "facts" quoted at the start of this chapter is reflective of the paradox that is Anglo-American law. We are taught to think of facts as truisms, information that is neutral, not involving feelings. However, by using law to define race and to determine the rights to which members of a given racial group were entitled, the neutrality of facts has been lost. How else, absent the commission of some crime, could one human being be held captive and forced to provide unpaid labor to another in a land where the law provides,"We hold these truths to be self-evident, that *all* men are created equal, that they are endowed by their Creator with certain unalienable rights, that among these are life, *liberty*, and the pursuit of happiness"? (emphasis added).

How else but by a profoundly cunning, "legal sleight of hand"? With the swift stroke of a fountain pen, a human was turned into "chattel," a cow (or other piece of personal property) under man-made law. To seal the fate of those transformed, legislators and their constituents reinforced the transformation of Africans from human beings to beasts of burden by resorting to church law as the original legal doctrine authorizing the African's enslavement.

The interplay of man-made and church law thus created three conceptions of African people, each related and each more detrimental than the next. The first two, black-man-as-sinner and black-man-as-property, coalesced to support the third conception of black-man-as-inferior.[5] As sinner, the black man was morally inferior. As property, the black man's humanity was nonexistent. The irrationality of the man-made law condemned the African (and his or her offspring) to a fourth and final role—black-man-as-criminal (see Russell 1996, & 1998). Although these roles represent acts of legal fiction, they still exercise strong influence over how blacks see themselves and how they are seen by others.

THE HISTORY

Racialized Rights and the Creation of Black Man-as-Criminal

Through a process of racialized rights enforced by racialized justice, the rules of law surrounding race have sent a well-defined message of black racial inferiority (Crockett 1972; Mann 1993; Miller 1966). Among the significant consequences of racialized rights enforced by racialized justice was the creation of the race/crime nexus.

While many choose to believe and behave as if the connection between race and crime is a fairly recent phenomenon and one that is either purely accidental or the responsibility of minorities who disproportionately perpetrate criminal offenses, in actuality, the connection between race and crime in America is neither accidental nor of recent origin.

The connection between race and crime in America began with the importation of African slaves. While there were free blacks in the country at the time that the practice of slave importation began, there are no indications that those free blacks were any more criminal than other immigrant ethnic groups. In fact, members of various European subgroups were considered the "criminal class" before, and even shortly after, the importation of African slaves.

However, in order to institute and maintain the slave system, which itself, was, contrary to the professed moral and legal beliefs of the country's founders and in order to make slave labor more economically feasible, the states and (eventually) the federal government enacted laws that would secure the practice. The enactment and enforcement of these laws began the race/crime nexus in America.

Legal Contradictions

It is estimated that the first African slaves were brought to this country in 1619, and while the Declaration of Independence, the language of which is quoted previously in this chapter, was signed on July 4, 1776, the practice of slavery continued. In fact, the words in the Declaration of Independence were directly contradicted in 1856 by the following pronouncement from the U. S. Supreme Court: "The right of property in a slave is *distinctly* and *expressly affirmed* in the Constitution " (emphasis added). Of citizenship, Justice Tanney wrote:

The descendants of Africans who were imported into this country and sold as slaves, when they shall become emancipated, or who are born of parents who had become free before their birth, are not citizens of the state in the sense which the word "citizens" is used in the Constitution of the United States.

In declaring the Missouri Compromise unconstitutional and void, to the extent that it purported to confer free status upon Dred Scott and his children, the Supreme Court also created the following rules of law:

• the word "citizen" in the Constitution does not embrace one of the negro race . . .

• [a] negro cannot become a citizen . . .

• [a] slave [is] not made free by residence in a free state or territory . . .

• [The] Declaration of Independence does not include slaves as part of the people . . .

• [T]he rights and privileges conferred by the Constitution upon citizens do not apply to the negro race . . .

While the decision in *Dred Scott v. Sanford* was officially overturned by the enactment of the thirteenth, forteenth, and fifteenth Amendments, it and other governmental action shaped and/or enforced social relationships among groups of people the impact of which can still be felt today. The "separate but equal doctrine" represents but one example.

In 1787, these words were ratified in the Preamble to the U. S. Constitution:

We the People of the United States, in Order to form a more perfect Union, establish Justice, insure domestic Tranquility, provide for the common defense, promote the general Welfare, and secure the Blessings of *Liberty* to ourselves and our *Posterity*, do ordain and establish this Constitution for the United States of America. (emphasis added)

Yet in 1896, a man who was seven-eighths white, who certainly should have been included within the meaning of "our posterity," was told by the U. S. Supreme Court that:

The statute of Louisiana, acts of 1890 . . . requiring railway companies carrying passengers in their coaches . . . to provide equal, but separate, accommodations for the white and colored races, . . . and providing that no person shall be permitted to occupy seats in coaches other than the ones assigned to them, on account of the race they belong to; . . . and *imposing fines or imprisonment* upon passengers insisting on going into a coach or compartment other than the one set aside for the race to which he or she belongs; . . . are *not* in conflict with the provisions of either of the Thirteenth Amendment or of the Fourteenth Amendment of the Constitution of the United States. (emphasis added)

The Louisiana statute that the Supreme Court upheld also granted railroad employees the authority to refuse to transport any passenger who refused to occupy a compartment assigned to his or her race; and it exempted the railroad employee from any civil liability for refusing to transport the passenger.

Hence, while Homer Plessy was able to take advantage of the privilege of citizenship that had been granted in 1868 by the enactment of the fourteenth Amendment, his degree of "whiteness" did not permit him the degree of liberty that others of his complexion enjoyed. The prevailing legal definition of the period was that "one drop" of African blood made a person "negro" or "colored." Therefore, for refusing to occupy a "colored" compartment, Plessey was arrested, and bail was set at $500.

The arrest and conviction of Plessy, a New Orleans shoemaker, were upheld by the U.S. Supreme Court decision *Plessy v. Ferguson*. The decision gave birth to the "separate but equal" doctrine and branded Homer Plessy a criminal. The rule of law in the *Plessy* decision was not overturned for nearly 60 years (in the 1954 decision of *Brown v. Board of Education of Topeka Kansas*).

A Right to Some, Crime to Others

Dred Scott v. Sanford and *Plessy v. Ferguson* are two landmark decisions that highlight the significance of race in the American legal process. They are, however, latecomers to the American jurisprudential scenery.

In *Criminalizing a Race: Free Blacks during Slavery*, McIntyre (1993) documents various laws and legal practices that, singled out blacks for special "treatment" or, more accurately, mistreatment. While liberty was a concept bestowed upon whites by virtue of birth, it was a commodity that had to be purchased by black slaves through a process called manumission. While whites were accumulating wealth through the acquisition of property, blacks were denied this right and were instead permitted to buy back family members if they could be located within the slave system. For blacks, this reality destroyed the possibility of accumulating wealth via inheritance for at least four generations. Hence, the concept of "old money," a powerful means of defining economic well-being in America, is a relatively foreign concept to African Americans.

With reference to punishment for wrongdoing, Adamson (1983) writes:

The existence of slavery made two separate systems of punishment necessary. Through plantation justice, masters sought to impose an absolute system of authority on their bondsmen. Like monarchial law, the slave codes prescribed barbaric and public punishments. (5)

Adamson goes on to present an example: "The heads of 16 rebels in Louisiana were stuck upon poles along the Mississippi River as a grim warning to other slaves."[6] For a similar purpose, the state of South Carolina enacted a law" for burning alive slaves who murder their masters." [7] (But masters could kill slaves with impunity.)

The Slave Codes mentioned by Adamson were a set of laws enacted in 1690 designed specifically for the discipline and control of the slave. These codes "clearly delineated the social and legal relationship of the black man to the white man" (Owens & Bell 1977: 7).[8] They were generally designed to prevent slaves from carrying weapons, owning property, or having any legal rights or protections (Mann 1993; Owens & Bell 1977). They provided for punishment in the form of whipping, hanging, branding, castration or other forms of death, should a slave be found in violation of the codes (Mann 1993; Owens & Bell 1977).

The prohibition of slavery did little to improve the legal status of African Americans. Once slavery was outlawed, Black Codes were enacted in many southern states that imposed similar legal restrictions upon the "free" black as had been imposed upon the slaves. These codes limited the rights of African Americans to own *or* rent property; allowed for *imprisonment* for breach of employment contracts; and denied African Americans the right to bring charges or testify against whites in court (Mann 1993).

So complete was the control of African Americans under the Black Codes that in some towns, they could not be on the streets after dark, and they could hold only menial jobs (Mann 1993; Miller 1966; Todd 1979). The following are examples of statutes under the Slave and Black Codes.

An ordinance in Charleston, South Carolina, provided:

It shall be *lawful* to, and for any person or persons, to send his, her or their slave or slaves to the Work House to be there corrected by whipping: but the Master of the Work House shall not inflict or cause to suffer to be inflicted on any one slave more than twenty lashes at one and the same time, nor more than 2 corrections in a week, at intervals of at least 3 days between the 1st and 2nd corrections. (emphasis added; *Slavery and Catholicism*, as cited in Miller 1957)

The ordinance further lays out the fees for services by the Work House for "dieting, lodging, confining, delivering, putting irons on, and correcting of a slave." The fees ranged in cost from 18 3/4¢ to 25¢.

Section 2 of "An Act to Amend the Laws in Relation to Slaves and Free Persons of Color" provided in pertinent part:

If any person shall employ or keep as a clerk, any person of color, or shall permit any slave or *free person of color* to act as a clerk or salesman, in or about any shop, store or house used for trading, such person shall be liable to be indicted therefor and upon conviction thereof, shall be fined for each and every offense not exceeding one hundred dollars, *and* be imprisoned not exceeding six months; the informer to be a competent witness, and to be entitled to one half of the fine. (emphasis added; *Slavery and Catholicism*, as cited in Miller 1957)

An act such as this is legally significant for a number of reasons. It severely limits the kinds of gainful employment that may be engaged in by "free" blacks, and it encourages a paid informant system.

Recall that under the Slave and Black Codes, African Americans could neither bring charges against whites nor testify against whites. Statutes like the preceding one allowed individuals, including blacks, to testify in court and get paid for their testimony. The promise of pay, no doubt, served as an incentive to some to inform about such acts whether they were real or imaginary. The statute quoted took effect in 1834, 59 years after the birth of the new "free" nation.

Perhaps the greatest legal disadvantage to Africans was the ban on teaching and learning. As late as 1835, South Carolina maintained laws against teaching slaves and free persons of color to read or write. While the first section of the law applied to *any* person who would educate a slave, the penalties for the offense were designated as follows:

free white person—up to $100 fine, and up to 6 months imprisonment
free person of color—whipped up to 50 lashes, fined up to $50 if a slave—whipped up to 50 lashes

The second section of the statute provided that:

if any free person of color or slave shall keep a school or other place of instruction for teaching any slave or *free person of color* to read or write, such free person of color or slave shall be liable to the same fine, imprisonment, or corporal punishment as imposed and inflicted upon free persons of color and slaves for teaching *slaves* to read and write. (emphasis added: *Slavery and Catholicism* as cited in Miller 1957)

Like the ordinance forbidding persons of color from working as store clerks or salespersons, this statute provided that informers were entitled to one-half of the fine and were deemed competent witnesses.

While it is still hotly debated whether blacks are inherently less intellectually capable than their white counterparts, rarely is this lengthy legal ban on education mentioned during the debate. If there were any merit to a claim of genetic intellectual deficiency on the part of blacks, why bother to outlaw the education of blacks, both slave and free?

Lest the idea be given that only the southern states maintained a system of law that subordinated blacks to other Americans, the contributions of the first federal government cannot be overlooked. No doubt, in an effort to secure the support of the southern colonies in the ratification of the new Constitution, the authors of that document included three clauses that nationally confirmed the subordinate legal status of blacks:

- In Article 1, section 2: slaves were counted as three-fifths of a human being;
- In Article 4, section 2: the citizens of all states were required to "deliver up" any person accused of being a runaway slave;
- Article 1, section 9: allowed for the continued importation of slaves until the year 1808, 20 years beyond the ratification of the celebrated document.

Also, under Article 1, section 9, the new *federal* government could collect taxes in an amount up to $10 per head for each slave imported.

The inclusion of these sections in the federal Constitution has invoked strong comments. Mann (1993) states that "the United States Constitution and the laws following it continued to sustain racial inequality, compromise African American rights, and ensure white dominance and control."

Crockett (1972) expresses a similar view, stating that, "the false principle of the inferiority of black people because of their race or color, which over the years had become imbedded in our national consciousness, now became part of our country's fundamental law."[9]

Mann continues, quoting Miller (1966):

Once established by law and internalized in the national mind, the results of such legislation persisted, . . . "Americans simply have a double standard of judgement as to the rights of white persons as contrasted to those of Negroes. To them, white persons are born vested with that vast array of rights and privileges vaguely thought of as natural rights. Negroes, on the other hand, are regarded as entitled to such rights as the white majority grants them. It is commonly said that Negroes must 'earn' the rights they would enjoy. That attitude is deeply rooted in our history." (Miller 1966: 63).[10]

In addition to the fugitive slave clause included within the Constitution, two federal fugitive slave statutes were enacted, one in 1793 and an amended version in 1850. These laws imposed an obligation upon *all* Americans, whether pro-slavery or abolitionist, to report all runaway slaves and otherwise assist in their capture. The penalty for failure to abide by the statute was federal prosecution resulting in fine and/or imprisonment.

Consequently, the "slave patrol" became the precursor of the modern police force in America. Many of its "officers" were untrained citizens who—the Fugitive Slave Act of 1850 authorized slave owners ("their attorneys or assigns") to recruit for the purpose of assisting in the recovery of the owner's "property." The statute even "authorized and required" payment to those assisting in the capture and transport of the "criminals."

Finally, the northern states were not without fault in the creation and perpetuation of a dual legal system. The ports of northern colonies, such as Massachusetts and Rhode Island, were popular sites for the importation of slaves. After slavery, many of the blacks who fled to avoid lynching in the South discovered that prejudice and segregation were prevalent even "up north."

Race and the Rule of Law

Finckenauer (1995: 14) notes that the "rule of law" is a critical Western legal concept that "implies principally the absence of arbitrary power and the limitation of discretionary authority." The "rule of law" is frequently thought of as synonymous with notions of fairness and democracy. However, when the concept is examined within the context of the development of the American legal system and the intersection of race and crime in America, it is one of the most profound reminders that, rather than an abstract principle, law is a power relationship.

Marshall (as cited in Finckenauer 1995: 14) notes that "the values underlying the rule of law include fairness, impartiality, independence, equality, openness, rationality, certainty, and universality." Accordingly, "[I]mpartiality and independence require that the processes of justice be divorced from undue political influence and control" (Finckenauer 1995: 14). Hence, the importation of African slaves created a tremendous potential legal dilemma for a developing nation that would eventually adopt as its prevailing rule of law the notion that all men are created equal and born with a right to liberty.

In order to maintain slavery and subsequently be true to the concept of the "rule of law," it became necessary to dehumanize the African. As noted, with the stroke of a pen, persons of African ancestry were transformed from men and women into chattel (the French word for cattle). While this legal transformation resolved the immediate philosophical, political, and potentially jurisprudential problem, little or no attention appears to have been given to the long-term effects of such a decision.

One fairly immediate result of this decision was to divide the residents of the developing nation into two categories: (1) humans who were recognized as humans and therefore entitled to "human rights" and, (2) humans who were not recognized as humans and therefore not entitled to "human rights."

This dichotomous categorization created much work for the courts. "Freedom suits" for the purpose of obtaining at least some human rights were filed by individuals whose complexion evidenced African ancestry. McIntyre (1993: 46–47) notes that:

Most courts proved readily available for freedom suits, but the burden [of proof][11] shifted from place to place according to the complexion of the [alleged] slave. A general principle stood in all states where slavery persisted that every African American should be presumed a slave. But, the courts in North and South Carolina, Tennessee and New Jersey held this presumption only for those Black in color and not for those of apparent mixed ancestry, so-called "Mulatto and Mestizo."[12]

By contrast, within the Maryland courts, the rule was a simple one: all "negroes" within its borders were considered slaves (McIntyre 1993: 11).

Beyond the glut of court cases in various jurisdictions, the legal sanctioning of slavery presented a problematic national image. The maintenance of a slave system was a clear moral violation of the national proclamation of the "new world" as a place of freedom and equality. As noted, the long-term effect of this violation was to call into question the "justice" of the American legal system.

The legal philosopher John Rawls (1971: 236) argues that "other things being equal, one legal order is more justly administered than another if it more perfectly fulfills the precepts of the rule of law." In listing those precepts and discussing how they affect compliant behavior, Rawls notes the following:

1. The actions which the rules of law require or forbid should reasonably be actions which people would be expected to do or avoid anyway.

2. "Not only must the authorities act in good faith, but their good faith must be recognized by those subject to their enactments. Law and commands are accepted as law and commands only if it is generally believed that they can be obeyed and executed."

3. "Similar cases should be treated similarly." This precept limits discretion and forces the justification of distinctions made between persons "by reference to the relevant legal rules and principles";

4. "There is no offense without a law." "This precept demands that laws be known and expressly promulgated, that their meaning be clearly defined, that statutes be general both in statement and intent and *not be used as a way of harming particular individals.*" (emphasis added)

5. "[T]he rule of law requires some form of due process; that is, a process reasonably designed to ascertain the truth, in ways consistent with the other ends of the legal system, as to whether a violation has taken place and under what circumstances . . . judges must be independent and impartial . . . [t]rials must be fair and open" (Rawls 1971: 235–243, as cited in Finckenauer 1995: 15)

As noted previously, contrary to the fundamental values and precepts underpinning the notion of the "rule of law," with regard to race, the American legal process was highly influenced by the prevailing politics and consistent only in its efforts to single out blacks as the primary group to be subjected to control via the criminal law. The use of the law in this manner has had the greatest lasting negative effect upon social relations in America.

According to Perkins and Boyce (1982: 6), "[A]n incidental but very important function of the criminal law is to teach the difference between right and wrong". The extent to which this statement is accurate provides one explanation for the enduring significance of race within American human relations.

As the previous pages demonstrate, America has had a lengthy history of local, state, and federal laws that criminalized various forms of conduct if engaged in by blacks. So complete was the legal control of blacks that it could be argued that the status of being "black" was itself a crime. If we were to take the Perkins and Boyce statement as a given, what, then, was taught by a criminal legal system that imposed harsh punishments upon one group and denied that same group the "liberties" afforded others? A logical answer would be that the law taught that the group in question is deserving of punishment and is undeserving of basic human rights. Or, put another way, maltreatment of the group is "right," and individual liberties for members of the group are "wrong." The extent to which such "lessons" continue to permeate the conscious and subconscious thoughts of all Americans is the key to determining whether "color-blind" justice is an achievable goal.

Evidence of cause for pessimism in this regard emerges daily. The successful transmission of the message behind the old "rules of law" is reflected in the behavior of some white law students. During a recent incident at a prominent law school, white students called a black student "boy" and "nigger." Before affirmative action was done away with in the state of California, students at the UC–Berkeley Law School were known to leave hate messages in minority student mailboxes, blaming them for taking seats that "belong" to white students. The notes were written in such a way that it was clear that the author(s) equated being "white" with being "deserving" of law school attendance and being nonwhite as being undeserving and unqualified. The irony of this state of affairs is, that law schools were among the first places that the courts believed would benefit by integration.

In an effort to "un-teach" the lessons of the past, lawmakers have attempted to create new statutes that address some of the serious harm inflicted upon blacks (and other minorities) by past legislation. In the civil law area, there is the rapidly disappearing affirmative action legislation; and, in the area of criminal law, many jurisdictions have enacted bias statutes to punish individuals who harm others because of their race, ethnicity, religion, or sexual orientation.

It is interesting to note, however, that the remedies for past legal harm appear to be much shorter-lived than the disadvantaging statutes. While discriminatory legal practices were left unchallenged or declared constitutional for more than 300, after only approximately 30 years of alleged enforcement, affirmative action legislation is dying a slow legal death, and, bias statutes are consistently being subjected to constitutional challenges, primarily on First Amendment grounds [13]

The slow road to recognition and renunciation of discriminatory legal practices by a people who professed high moral standards is one reason that those who fell victim to that system of laws still lack confidence in the American system of justice (see Tyler 1990; Gibson 1989; Hagan & Albonetti 1982; and Davis 1974). The short and tumultuous life of those pieces of legislation that were designed to provide a remedy for past practices only serves to reinforce that mistrust.

RACE AND CRIMINAL JUSTICE

Racialized Justice: Blacks as Victims and Perpetrators

Ginzburg (1962: 174, 220, 240) documents 5000 reported lynchings in America during the period 1859 through 1918. Lynching was the summary "justice" administered to blacks accused of "crimes" ranging from murder, rape, and theft, to "insulting a white person" and "startling a white child. The lynching of blacks included hanging, dragging through the streets, multiple shooting, and burning, either after death or while the victim was still alive. Lynching events were particularly brutal. They were public, and, often no one was punished. The following account was reported in the *New York Herald,* June 9, 1903:

The crowd in the jail had broken into Wyatt's cell. He had fought fiercely for his life. A blow from a sledge hammer felled him. A rope was tied around his neck. He was dragged out into the corridor, down the stairs and into the jail yard, then into Spring Street, up to Main street and to the centre of the square. A man riding a white horse led the way to an electric light pole in the square. The end of the rope was thrown over it. The body was drawn up above the heads of the crowd, who cheered and waved hats. Men on the pole kicked Wyatt in the face. The swaying form was stabbed repeatedly. Mutilations followed. Kerosene was bought and poured over the body and it was set on fire, while the crowd cheered. The rope burned through and the body fell. More kerosene was poured on the body as the flames slowly consumed it. (Ginzburg 1962: 52)

Often, following a successful lynching, body parts were taken or distributed (even sold) as souvenirs (Ginzburg 1962).

The impact of lynching on African American citizens was, at least, two-fold. First, lynching taught blacks that despite their "free" status, the law *could not* or *would not* protect them from the same levels of violence to which they had been legally subjected under slavery. The fact that blacks could not testify in court against whites and the fact that whites would not testify helped to reinforce mistrust in American criminal procedure that endures among African Americans today.

Second, lynching helped to enforce a feeling of hopelessness among blacks. Often, following a lynching or attempted lynching, members of the agitated white mob would ride through the "black" section of town burning black homes and businesses and assaulting or otherwise terrorizing black residents and business owners. Rarely was anyone prosecuted for these episodes, and there was no civil remedy for regaining the funds necessary to rebuild what had been destroyed. Thus, blacks were left with an enduring sense of the transient nature of their newly gained rights of property ownership and personal freedom.

Blacks and the Bill of Rights

Much of American criminal procedure is governed by the language contained within the first ten amendments to the U. S. Constitution. The Bill of Rights and its common-law interpretation by the U. S. Supreme Court are considered the "supreme law of the land." Mann (1993) and Miller (1966) make these observations regarding blacks and the Bill of Rights:

It is commonly believed that the original Constitution and the Bill of Rights protected the rights and liberties of *all* Americans. However, "in truth, the equalitarian guarantees explicit and implicit in the Constitution and amplified in the Bill of Rights offered absolutely no protection to . . . persons held in slavery . . . [and] little more protection . . . [to] free Negroes of the South *and* the North." (Miller 1966: 64, emphasis added)[14]

Returning briefly to the discussion of lynching, while there is little doubt that some of the accused blacks were guilty of the crimes for which they were lynched, *there is* ample evidence also suggests that many of those lynched were, in fact, not guilty. The actions of the lynch mobs, however, deprived all "suspects" of a fair and impartial hearing during which evidence could be presented and evaluated. In at least one reported case, even after the suspect was acquitted by white jurors, the defendant who had been acquitted was promptly lynched nonetheless (Ginzburg 1962: 212). "Lynch justice" allowed the members of the mob to take on the role of judge, jury, and executioner.

Even when there were "trials" during and after slavery, blacks were deprived of the safeguards set forth in the fourth, fifth, and sixth amendments. As noted previously, many state statutes prohibited blacks from bringing charges against whites and from testifying against whites in the courts. In many locations, blacks were also legally barred from serving on juries.[15]

With the procedural stage set against them, many blacks found themselves convicted of crimes. Upon conviction, despite notions of due process and equal protection embodied in the fifth and fourteenth Amendments, states were permitted to designate different punishments for blacks and whites convicted of the same offense.

For example, during the slavery period, castration was a common penalty authorized for black men convicted of the rape or attempted rape of a white woman (Jordan 1974, as cited in Mann 1993: 119). After slavery, sentencing statutes permitted blacks to be put to death for offenses for which the same statutes authorized only imprisonment for whites. These capital offenses included not only homicide and rape but also burglary and theft.

Even blacks who were able to gain employment as law enforcement officers during the twentieth century were subject to legally sanctioned dual justice procedures. For example, in the early 1900s, the laws of Oklahoma prohibited black law enforcement officers from arresting whites.

The extent of dual "justice" procedures across the country is too involved to describe fully here. However, may it suffice to say that the procedures and the mind-set that created and perpetuated them still haunt both the reality and perception of "justice" in America today.

DISTINGUISHING RACE AND ETHNICITY

In Chapter 2, Knepper aptly explains the anthropological origins of the concept of race and distinguishes it from ethnicity. As noted by Knepper, in America, despite miscegenation laws that prohibited "race mixing," interracial sexual interaction has to a large extent, nearly obliterated the physical distinctions between the "races," leaving race to be viewed as "primarily a social construct" (Spickard 1992: 18, as cited in Walker et al. 1996: 6).

However, race as a legal construct has presented the greatest challenge to American "democracy," not only by requiring that clear distinctions be drawn between black and white but also by leaving some groups in a legal "limbo" land. For example, are Native Americans and dark- skinned Hispanics/Latinos, and Americans of East Indian descent black or white? Lest this chapter end having created the impression that blacks were the only persons to suffer under the American system of justice, the examples in note 1 clearly indicate otherwise. The determination of Blackness and the rights commensurate with that status has, however, likely encompassed more judicial and legislative time and energy than any other racial, ethnic, or other issues in the history of the country.

SUMMARY AND CONCLUSION

LaFree and Russell (1993: 273) acknowledge that "all roads in American criminology eventually lead to issues of race." What is not so readily acknowledged by those who dare to study race and crime in America is the intentional role that government has played in establishing the race/crime connection. This chapter ends with the proposition with which it began: by using the courts to define who is black and allowing legislators to enact laws geared toward disadvantaging or "punishing" blackness, the lawmakers and judges of the past have ensured the lasting significance of race within the American legal process. Short periods of legal gains for blacks (e.g., the Reconstruction period and the civil rights era) have been followed by long periods of retrenchment (e.g., the Jim Crow era and the post-Bakke decisions).

Those who would argue that the past has little or nothing to do with the present must consider the following:

- Numerous studies confirm that racial minorities, African Americans in particular, have a distinct mistrust of the American legal system.

- Violent lynchings in the South and racial segregation in the north forced African Americans to take up residence in densely populated, homogeneous communities. These very communities are the sites of a major portion of minority crime, especially crime involving violence.

- While various (voluntary) immigrant groups have been able to achieve economic prosperity in America through work, investment, and inheritance, a significant proportion of African Americans whose ancestors had to purchase freedom, who, under the law, were denied rights of property ownership, who were denied access to education, and who were not permitted to participate in various types of gainful employment are themselves currently over represented among the nation's poor.[16]

- Even African Americans who engage in work comparable to that of their white couterparts receive less pay for such work.

- African Americans who engage in offenses similar to those of their white counteparts tend (in many locations) to receive harsher penalties.

The last two points reinforce the notion that the use of criminal law to control African Americans has, in fact, taught other Americans that blacks, regardless of class or social status, are less deserving of human liberties and more deserving of punishment.

The investigation and attempts at explanation for current criminal justice problems, such as sentencing disparity and minority overrepresentation, cannot and should not be divorced from their historical context. While, ideally, the operation of law should mirror the following line from *The Mikado*—"The law is a perfect embodiment of everything that is excellent, it has no kind of fault or flaw"—the reality of American legal history is that the law has fallen far short of that ideal. In fact, for a substantial period of time, the law was used as a means of *depriving* some people of liberties and economic opportunities, while at the same time *supporting* the liberties and economic opportunities of others. To expect that these contradictions would not have serious lasting effects on American social and legal life is both foolish and naive.

NOTES

An earlier version of this chapter was presented at the 46th annual meeting of the American Society of Criminology in Miami, Florida.

1. This history includes, among other blights, the massacre of Native Americans,

exploitation of Chinese laborers, Japanese internment, and the chattel enslavement of people of African ancestry.

2. Now that recompense has been attempted through affirmative action, and economic opportunities have shrunk.

3. There is a clear sense that the law and its operatives are not to be trusted (viz., Browning et al. (1994).

4. Reactions to the Simi Valley and Simpson civil trial verdicts are just two examples of the evidence that Americans cannot reach consensus over what is "just."

5. A chicken-and-egg argument could be made here.

6. Stampp (1956: 135), as cited in Adamson (1983).

7. Carey (1831: 12), as cited in Adamson (1983).

8. As cited in Mann (1993).

9. As cited in Mann (1993: 120).

10. Ibid.

11. Of free or slave status.

12. McIntyre (1993: 47) points out that "in the North Carolina case of *Samuel Scott versus William* (1828), the judge instructed the jury that if a[n] [alleged] slave woman 'was of black African complexion, they might presume from that fact that she was a slave; it she was of a yellow complexion, no presumption of slavery arose from her color."

13. Another controversial legal reality surrounding bias statutes is that when they are used to prosecute minorities, such statutes are viewed as punishing the very people they were designed to protect.

14. Finckenauer (1995: 120),

15. Although the 1880 case of *Strauder v. West Virginia*, 100 U.S. 303, held that such statutes deny Black defendants equal protection of the law, it was not until the 1986 case of Batson v. Kentucky, 476 U.S. 79, that the Supreme Court expressly prohibited the use of peremptory challenges to exclude minorities from jury service.

16. Various theories support the notion that poverty is significantly related to crime.

REFERENCES

Adamson, C. R. (1983). "Punishment after Slavery: Southern State Penal Systems, 1865–1890." *Social Problems* 30(5): 555–569.

Browning, S., F. Cullen, L. Cao, R. Kopache and T. Stevenson. (1994)."Race and Getting Hassled by the Police: A Research Note." *Police Studies* 17(1): 1–11.

Carey, J. T. (1978). Introduction to Criminology. Englewood Cliffs, NJ: Prentice-Hall.

Crockett, G. W. (1972). "Racism in the Law." In L. E. Reasons and J. L. Kuykendall (eds.), *Race, Crime and Justice*. Pacific Palisades, CA: Goodyear.

Davis, J. (1974). "Justification of No Obligation: Views of Black Males toward Crime and the Criminal Law." *Issues in Criminology* 9(Fall): 69–87.

Finckenauer, J. O. (1995). *Russian Youth: Law, Deviance and the Pursuit of Freedom*. New Brunswick, NJ: Transaction Publishers.

Gibson, J. (1989). "Understandings of Justice: Institutional Legitimacy, Procedural Justice, and Political Tolerance." *Law and Society Review* 23(3): 631–635.

Ginzburg, R. (1962). *One Hundred Years of Lynchings*. Baltimore, MD: Black Classic Press.

Hacker, A. (1992). *Two Nations*. New York: Ballentine Books.

Hagan, J. and C. Albonetti. (1982). "Race, Class, and the Perception of Criminal Justice in America." *American Journal of Sociology* 88(2): 329–355.

Jordon, W. D. (1974). The White Man's Burden. New York: Oxford University Press.

LaFree, G. and K. Russell. (1993). "The Argument for Studying Race and Crime." *Journal* of Criminal Justice Education 4: 273–290.

Marshall, G. (1977). "Due Process in England." In J. Roland Pennock and J. Chapman (eds.), Due Process. New York: New York University Press.

Mann, C. (1993). Unequal Justice: A Question of Color. Bloomington: Indiana University Press.

McIntyre, C. (1993). Criminalizing a Race: Free Blacks during Slavery. Queens, NY: Kayode.

Miller, J. (1996). Search and Destroy: African-American Males in the Criminal Justice System. Cambridge, MA: Cambridge University Press.

Miller, K. S. (1966). "Race, Poverty and the Law." In J. tenBroek (ed.), The Law of the Poor. San Francisco, CA: Chandler Publishing Co.

Miller, R. R. (1957). Slavery and Catholicism. Durham, NC: North State Publishers.

Owens, C. E. and J. Bell. (1977). Blacks and Criminal Justice. Lexington, MA: D. C. Heath.

Perkins, R. and R. Boyce, (1982). Criminal Law. 3d ed. Mineola, NY: Foundation Press.

Rawls, J. (1971). A Theory of Justice. Cambridge, MA: Harvard University Press.

Russell, K. K. (1998). The Color of Crime. New York: New York University Press.

———. (1996). "The Racial Hoax as Crime: The Law as Affirmation." Indiana Law Journal 71: 593–621.

Schneider, A. (1981). "Differences between Survey and Police Information about Crime." In R. Lehnen and W. Skogan (eds.), The National Crime Survey: Working Papers 1. Washington, DC: U.S. Government Printing Office.

Spickard, P. R. (1992). "The Illogic of American Racial Categories." In M. P. Root (ed.), Racially Mixed People in America. Newbury Park, CA: Sage.

Todd, T. N. (1979). "From Dred Scott to Bakke and Beyond: The Evolution of a Circle." Dollar and Sense (June–July): 64–74.

Tyler, T. (1990). Why People Obey the Law. New Haven: Yale University Press.

Walker, S., C. Spohn, and M. Delone. (1996). The Color of Justice: Race, Ethnicity, and Crime in America. New York: Wadsworth.

CASES

Batson v. Kentucky
Brown v. Board of Education of Topeka Kansas
Dred Scott v. Sanford
Plessy v. Ferguson
Strauder v. West Virginia

Chapter 12

The Impact of Racial Demography on Jury Verdicts in Routine Adjudication

James P. Levine

INTRODUCTION

This chapter reports the results of empirical research dealing with the persisting quandary about the relationship between the racial composition of juries and the verdicts they render. The study tests the hypothesis that juries dominated by whites are more conviction-prone than those that are largely composed of people of color, especially when the defendants are nonwhite. By examining thousands of little-publicized verdicts rendered in jurisdictions that vary widely demographically, an attempt is made to better inform the raging debates about jurors' susceptibility to racial bias—debates brought to a head by the murder trials of O. J. Simpson.

Whether the charges against O. J. Simpson produced the "trials of the century" is for history to judge. But without doubt the trials brought to center stage significant issues regarding the relationship between the race of jurors and jury verdicts. Allegations about Simpson's exculpation in the criminal case abounded: black defense attorney Johnnie Cochran played "the race card" in his trial strategy; the predominantly black jury ignored the defendant's history of domestic violence, very incriminating forensic evidence, and the lack of a credible alibi out of empathy with a successful black man; black jurors denigrated white victim Nicole Brown for having "stolen" an attractive person of their own race; Marcia Clark, the white prosecuting attorney, antagonized the jury; the jury engaged in "racial nullification"—acquitting a man they knew was guilty of a double murder to punish the Los Angeles Police Department for its racism, most noticeably revealed in the bigotry of Detective Mark Fuhrman.

New York Times columnist Maureen Dowd minced no words: "Mr. Simpson's jury in the criminal trial had plenty of evidence, but made a decision based on race." [1] The jurors themselves disavowed such notions, claiming that the forensic evidence was inconclusive, most of the other evidence was circumstantial, no murder weapon was ever found, and "the glove didn't fit." [2] A watchful nation divided largely along racial lines, blacks overwhelmingly believing that the verdict was correct, and whites by and large believing that the acquittal was a gross miscarriage of justice. [3]

The seemingly incongruous verdict against Simpson in the civil wrongful death suit brought by the families of Nicole Brown and Ronald Goldman rendered by a largely white jury devoid of African Americans seemed to confirm widely held sentiments that the racial composition of the jury was decisive. As always, there were differences in the two cases aside from the jurors' race that could explain the divergent outcomes. The "cast of characters" in the two trials varied, resulting in quite dissimilar trials: Judge Hiroshi Fujisaki, who presided in the civil case, kept tight reins on the trial, in contrast to the much looser approach of Judge Lance Ito, who handled the criminal case; the lawyers on both sides of the civil case were lower-keyed and evidence-oriented in contrast to the often theatrical approach of the prosecution and the racially inflammatory strategies of the "Dream Team" defense in the criminal case; Simpson refused to testify in the criminal case (as was his constitutional right) but was forced to in the civil case, where his professions of innocence were said to lack credibility. Evidence, too, varied: testimony about police misconduct dominating the first case was disallowed in the second; photographs of Simpson wearing Bruno Magli shoes, the kind that left footprints at the murder scene, were presented in the second case but not the first; and the analysis of blood linking Simpson to the crime was not impugned in the second case to the extent it was in the first. But in the eyes of many, all of these differences between the two trials pale in comparison with the striking disparities in the racial makeup of the two juries.

We may never know with absolute certainty which jury got things right and whether Simpson was, in fact, a double murderer. The nation remained racially split after the civil verdict against Simpson, approved by three-fourths of whites and criticized by two-thirds of blacks. [4] The second-guessing goes on, replete with scores of books, one of which is a collection of essays appropriately entitled *Postmortem*. [5] Although much of the writing and the endless talk-show commentary have generated more heat than light, public debate about race-based jury behavior continues unabated.

The debates are important, but ultimately they will tell us *nothing* about everyday justice in the courts. The Simpson trial is the "celebrated case" [6] par excellence; it has little in common with the tens of thousands of felonies processed annually. It is to these cases that we must look for an adequate answer to the questions. Does the race of jurors routinely affect the outcomes of adjudication, and is "racial justice" embedded in the jury decision-making system? The research reported in this chapter seeks to answer these questions.

THE IMPACT OF RACIAL BIAS ON JURORS

The Simpson case is hardly the first to suggest that viewpoints about race affect verdicts. There are other notorious cases in which verdicts seemed to be more a product of racial considerations than the quantity or quality of the evidence. In years past, all-white juries would exonerate white defendants of crimes allegedly committed against blacks in the face of overwhelmingly incriminating evidence.[7] It took an all-white Mississippi jury little more than an hour in 1955 to acquit two white men clearly implicated in the killing of Emmett Till, a 14-year-old black visitor from Chicago who had talked "fresh" to a white woman who waited on him in a store.[8] Nearly 40 later, in 1992, came the first Rodney King trial, resulting in the riot- inducing acquittal of four police officers for excessive use of force, the acquittal handed down by a California jury lacking any black jurors, a verdict that seemed to fly in the face of videotapes that had graphically captured the officers' vicious beating of the helpless black motorist. An all-white Pittsburgh jury's acquittal in November 1996 of a white police officer of killing a black driver by the application of lethal force while pinning him to the ground in a scuffle following a traffic stop was dèja vú: protesters carried signs decrying the "kangaroo court," and Rev. Jesse Jackson called the victim's death "a lynching."[9] Many other verdicts have been tainted by claims that white racism in the jury room doomed innocent blacks or exonerated guilty white defendants; the cases of the "Scottsboro boys" and Medgar Evers are notable examples.

The tide is said to have turned in recent years: black jurors allegedly are *acquitting* guilty members of their own race in disregard of the evidence. Marion Barry, the popular black mayor of Washington, D.C., was acquitted of smoking crack cocaine by an overwhelmingly black jury, although law enforcement officials who had hired his former girlfriend to lure him into a hotel room had videotaped his criminal behavior. The Reginald Denney case involved a hapless white truck driver who was viciously kicked and assaulted with bricks to the point of near death when he found himself in the middle of the post–Rodney King riot in Los Angeles; his black assailants, who had also been videotaped in the act, were acquitted of most charges by a predominantly black jury.

Equally unsettling to many was the acquittal in 1992 of African American Lemrick Nelson for the murder of Yankel Rosenbaum, a killing occurring in the midst of anti-Semitic rioting pitting blacks against Jews in the Crown Heights section of Brooklyn. The killing was sparked by an automobile accident in which a car driven by a Hasidic Jew killed a black youth. Although Nelson confessed to the police, was found with the knife that apparently killed Rosenbaum, and was identified by the victim shortly before he died, he was acquitted by a jury of six blacks, four Hispanics, two whites, and no Jews.[10] Contentions that the skewed racial composition of the jury accounted for the verdict were bolstered when a federal jury including five whites and two Jews in February 1997 convicted Nelson of violating Rosenbaum s civil rights, having concluded on the basis of evidence very similar to that presented in the earlier state trial that Nelson was, in fact, the killer.[11]

A number of commentators have argued that these cases of racially tainted jury verdicts returned by black-controlled majorities are *not* aberrations. Attention is drawn to jury behavior en masse—the tendencies of juries in predominantly black jurisdictions to acquit more than average. Washington, D.C., where 95 percent of all defendants are black, and 70 percent of all jurors are also black, is said to produce a disproportionately high number of acquittals[12] as are places such as Detroit[13] and the borough of the Bronx in New York City. [14] Butler, in an influential article in the *Yale Law Journal*, maintains that some black jurors acquit black defendants on the basis of race alone.[15]

This contention is consistent with theories about jury behavior. Kalven and Zeisel, in their classic work on the American jury, developed the argument that the ambiguity of evidence in many cases liberates jurors to decide according to their own values.[16] These values can relate to their opinions about the law, their sense of the underlying equities of the case, concerns about the ethics of law enforcement officers, and their feelings about the parties to the case. Where doubt exists about what happened, the jury will stretch the evidence to achieve a morally satisfying verdict; and there is almost always *some* doubt. British jurist Patrick Devlin has made the point somewhat differently: jurors who want to acquit are usually able to take a "merciful view of the facts."[17]

The story model of jury behavior that has achieved considerable currency is consistent. Bennett and Feldman suggest that jurors sort through the welter of evidence presented to them at the trial by searching for a train of events that seems believable.[18] Since there are plenty of plausible stories to go around, which version a juror is willing to believe may well depend on the juror's predispositions and the preferred verdict. As Pennington and Hastie point out, once jurors are confident that they have the *real* story, they will often interpret subsequent evidence in a manner that corroborates that interpretation. [19]

Thus, personal predilections invariably affect a juror's decision-making process; "factfinding and value judgments are subtly intertwined."[20] Preferences or antagonisms can enter this complex mental process, including biases about the personal characteristics of defendants, victims, third parties, or attorneys. Whatever is of concern to people outside the courtroom may well drift into the deliberation process; the jury room is not impervious to social conflicts. Race is one of the great divides in American society, [21] and it defies common sense to imagine that jurors can totally ward off the personal biases and distinctive perceptions associated with race that bear upon people's judgments in the workplace, the school, and the ballot box. "Race matters," in the simple, but penetrating, words of Cornel West.[22]

But does race matter in a court of law where jurors take a solemn oath to base their judgment on the facts and where justice is supposed to be color-blind? Ford's review of mock jury research concludes that racial biases are more persuasively demonstrated in the literature than biases related to any other personal characteristic of the defendant.[23] A survey of other experimental research led Johnson to state that there is a tendency among white jurors to convict black defendants in situations where whites would have been acquitted.[24] The most thorough compilation of research findings to date is in accord: King asserts that the studies "demonstrate that jury discrimination can and does affect jury decisions." [25]

But the body of research on which such claims are primarily made must be received cautiously, because it suffers from two significant defects. First, very few studies have presented the same simulated trials to predominantly white and predominantly black juries, so we have yet to determine whether the racial composition of the jury as opposed to the race of the defendant has a decisive impact. Second, this entire genre of work suffers from serious external validity problems: not only do the unavoidably abbreviated and artificial accounts of cases presented to mock jurors sometimes lack verisimilitude, but the absence of real consequences makes it problematic to generalize to actual jury behavior.

The vast literature on jury selection, ably summarized by Fukarai, et al. clearly demonstrates how bias enters every stage of jury empanelment, from the creation of "master wheels," to the now impermissible, but nonetheless persisting, use of race-based peremptory challenges.[27] However, there is no evidence presented showing how this affects the jurors' decision processes apart from citation of a handful of cases where race *seemed* to play a role. The authors' conclusion that "race and the jury are inescapably interdependent"[28] is therefore unsubstantiated.

THE STUDY

The present study examines whether the racial composition of juries actually affects the verdicts they reach. It entails an analysis of the relationship between the racial makeup of counties within New York state and the jury acquittal rates in those counties over the 10-year period between 1986 and 1995. Although there are 62 counties within the state, only the 27 in which at least 100 criminal verdicts were rendered were included in the analysis. The reason for excluding counties with small numbers of jury trials is the concern that outcomes would be idiosyncratic rather than true indications of jury proclivities. What remained after eliminating the 35 counties with relatively few jury trials is a total of 35,595 verdicts, ranging from 110 in Sullivan County to 8,817 in New York County (Manhattan).

For the purposes of the present inquiry, the numbers of blacks and nonblack Hispanics in each county as indicated by the 1990 federal census were lumped together to obtain the percentage of blacks and Hispanics living in each county. Because Hispanics can be of any race, they were counted separately and added to the number of blacks who did *not* identify themselves as Hispanic. Double counting is thus avoided.

The rationale for merging a racial group with an ethnic group is that blacks and Hispanics have much in common regarding assessment of the criminal justice system and perceptions of those on trial. Both are minority groups that have suffered from discrimination and have had troubled relations with the criminal justice system. It is hypothesized that jurors from both groups are more likely to have negative affect toward law enforcement officials and are less likely to have hostility toward those on trial than white jurors, resulting in a lower inclination to convict.

The research design is built on the premise that there is a direct correlation between the minority population of a county and the numbers of such individuals actually serving on juries. Some time ago this assumption would have been unwarranted, but reform measures in the last few decades have broadened the jury rolls and increased the number of empaneled blacks and Hispanics.[29] Jurisdictions have gone beyond voting registration lists to secure jurors, and furthermore the underrepresentation of blacks and Hispanics within the electorate has abated. New York state in particular has long utilized multiple source lists—voter registration, driver's license, and state income tax mailing lists; public assistance and unemployment rolls were added in 1994.[30] But to the extent that the racial and ethnic composition of juries over the long run still does not accurately reflect the county's demography (a phenomenon not examined in the present study), the rationale for expecting differential acquittal rates is weakened.

The racial and ethnic characteristics of the defendants were not investigated because aggregate verdict data provide no information about individual case characteristics. But it reasonably can be assumed that higher concentrations of minority groups in counties result in an even higher percentage of people in such groups on trial, given the disproportionate involvement of blacks and Hispanics engaged in street crime and involved with the criminal justice system.[31] Such a correlation between numbers of minority jurors and numbers of minority defendants should foster more juror identification with defendants and therefore elevate the acquittal rate. But even if blacks and Hispanics are not overrepresented within the ranks of the accused, it is expected that juries with substantial contingents of jurors from minority groups will still be less inclined to convict because of their disdain for the legal system and their suspiciousness of law enforcement personnel.

A final methodological issue is the potential for misinterpreting correlations of aggregate data—the so-called ecological fallacy. There is a danger in making assertions about individuals based on relationships among aggregates of which they are a part. Thus, a showing that counties with more blacks and Hispanics have higher acquittal rates does not in itself imply that specific juries with greater minority representation are more inclined to acquit *specific* defendants. We may be able to reach tentative conclusions, but we must entertain alternative explanations of the correlations.[32]

FINDINGS

Table 12.1 demonstrates a close relationship between racial demography (the independent variable) and jury behavior (the dependent variable). The percentage of blacks and Hispanics in a county's population varies from a low of 2.4 percent (St. Lawrence County), to 74.1 percent (Bronx County). The range of acquittal rates runs from 12.3 percent in Ontario County, to 38.4 percent in the Bronx. The table reveals the association between the independent and dependent variables at the extremes: Bronx County is highest in acquittals and highest in minority population, while Ontario County is lowest in acquittals and second from the bottom in minority population. The statistical correlation (Pearson's) between percentage minority population and acquittal rate across all 27 counties is .55, significant at the .01 level.

Table 12.1
Racial Demography,[1] Jury Acquittal Rates,[2] and Trial Rates[3] in New York State, 1986–1995, by County

	Percent Black and Hispanic (x)	Jury Acquittal Rate (y)	Jury Trial Rate (z)	Number of Jury Verdicts
Albany	10.0 %	28.8 %	7.2 %	469
Bronx	74.1	38.4	5.3	4,893
Broome	3.1	20.0	4.2	259
Chemung	6.7	16.9	2.4	248
Dutchess	11.7	23.4	8.6	111
Erie	13.5	29.3	6.4	1,314
Jefferson	8.4	23.2	3.1	112
Kings	54.8	31.3	6.2	7,595
Monroe	15.3	25.0	8.7	1,623
Nassau	14.2	20.1	4.0	1,324
New York	43.5	23.7	5.7	8,817
Niagara	6.4	21.0	10.8	409
Onandaga	9.4	23.5	4.8	631
Oneida	7.4	20.0	3.5	260
Ontario	3.0	12.3	6.1	211
Orange	13.7	24.7	3.2	219
Queens	40.0	28.3	4.4	4,186
Rensselaer	4.5	29.4	5.0	153
Richmond	15.4	21.3	3.4	202
Rockland	15.8	16.6	4.1	169
Schenectady	5.8	26.7	3.5	131

Table 12.1 continues

Table 12.1 Continued

	Percent Black and Hispanic (x)	Jury Acquittal Rate (y)	Jury Trial Rate (z)	Number of Jury Verdicts
St. Lawrence	2.4	31.6	8.7	196
Suffolk	12.5	24.0	2.3	768
Sullivan	14.9	15.5	4.0	110
Tompkins	5.5	23.7	9.8	152
Ulster	8.5	21.7	3.8	115
Westchester	22.9	20.9	4.5	918

rxy = .55; p. < .01 (one-tailed);   rxyz = .57; p. < .01 (one-tailed)

1. Figures on race and ethnicity were obtained from the federal census as reported in Nelson A. Rockefeller Institute of Government, *1995 New York State Statistical Yearbook* 11 (1995).
2. Data on criminal court dispositions and jury verdicts were provided by the New York State Office of Court Administration.
3. Only counties having 100 or more jury verdicts during the years 1986–1995 are included.

In assessing this correlation, it must be asked whether the mix of strong and weak prosecutions is similar across jurisdictions, or are we comparing apples and oranges? Without data on individual cases, we cannot assay this issue definitively; but Table 12.1 presents an indirect control—the trial rate, that is, the percentage of all cases going to trial. We would expect counties with low trial rates to have more acquittals if juries were behaving uniformly, and jurors were unbiased, because we could assume that juries in such counties would be dealing with more cases entailing genuine uncertainty and fewer "dead-bang" prosecutions in which evidence was almost incontrovertible. If low trial rates are associated with high minority populations, the correlation between racial demography and jury behavior might be spurious.

This complicating possibility is disconfirmed by Table 12.1, which suggests a rather haphazard relationship between trial rates and our independent and dependent variables. The partial correlation between the percentage of black and Hispanic residents in counties and acquittal rates when controlling for trial rate goes up slightly to .57 (also significant at the .01 level). Whether the addition of more controls taking account of other differences in the mix of cases confronting juries in various counties (such as type of crime) or other differences in the nature of counties (such as their economic conditions) would depress the correlation is an open question, the answer to which is beyond the scope of the data available in the present study.

Table 12.2 confines our analysis to the New York City metropolitan area, defined as the five counties within the city itself and the city's two adjacent suburban counties. Scaling down the analysis in this fashion is useful for two reasons. First, the demographic variable is more normally distributed, diminishing the possibility that outliers have artificially magnified the correlation. Second, it seems more likely that the mix of cases across counties is similar in that all seven counties are marked by similar urban crime problems.

Table 12.2
Racial Demography,[1] Jury Acquittal Rates,[2] and Trial Rates[2] in the New York City Metropolitan Area, 1986–1995, by County

	Percent Black and Hispanic (x)	Jury Acquittal Rate (y)	Jury Trial Rate (z)	Number of Jury Trials
Bronx	74.1 %	38.4 %	5.3 %	4,893
Kings (Brooklyn)	54.8	31.3	6.2	7,595
Nassau (Long Island)	14.2	20.1	4.0	1,324
New York (Manhattan)	43.5	23.7	5.7	8,817
Queens	40.0	28.3	4.4	4,186
Richmond (Staten Island)	15.4	21.3	3.4	202
Westchester	22.9	20.9	4.5	918

$r_{xy} = .95$; p. < .005 (one-tailed); $r_{xyz} = .95$; p. < .005 (one-tailed)

1. Figures on race and ethnicity were obtained from the 1990 federal census as reported in Nelson A. Rockefeller Institute of Government, *1995 New York State Statistical Yearbook* 11 (1995).
2. Data on criminal court dispositions and jury verdicts were provided by the New York State Office of Court Administration.

As it turns out, the correlation is an extraordinary .95, significant at the .005 level. Bronx County is highest in both percentage of minority residents and its jury acquittal rate, while Nassau County on Long Island is lowest on both variables. The partial correlation between racial demography and jury verdicts, controlling for trial rates, remains .95.

This validates what pundits and legal practitioners have long claimed: Bronx juries are, indeed, very different. Their unusual willingness to acquit confirms the aptness of a headline some years ago atop a *New York Times* article on jury behavior: "Bronx Juries: A Defense Dream, a Prosecution Nightmare."[33] Author Tom Wolfe, who spent a year observing Bronx courts for his novel *Bonfire of the Vanities*, is even more emphatic in the novel: "Bronx juries were difficult enough for a prosecutor ... [having been] drawn from the ranks of those who know that in fact the police are capable of lying. Bronx juries entertained a lot of doubts, both reasonable and unreasonable, and black and Puerto Rican defendants who were guilty, guilty as sin, did walk out of the fortress free as birds" [34]

Our data strongly suggest that it is, indeed, the presence of black and Hispanic jurors that spells the difference in jury conviction rates from county to county. The Bronx is the epitome of the "inner city," and the greater inclination of Bronx juries to give the benefit of the doubt to defendants reflects points of view common to this milieu.

Staten Island, at the other extreme, is sometimes thought of as a suburb within a city. It is rather isolated from the rest of the city, reachable directly from Manhattan only by ferry and accessible by car only via a roundabout route through Brooklyn. It is ideologically conservative; it largely comprises owner-occupied, single-family homes; and its relatively small minority population sets it apart from the other four boroughs. Staten Island's "whiteness" appears to account for the greater tendency of its juries to convict.

We must be careful not to overstate these findings. Tables 12.1 and 12.2 also reveal considerable uniformity among counties. While demographic composition varies enormously from jurisdictions that are virtually all-white to those where blacks and Hispanics are in the majority, the range in acquittal rates is not nearly so stark. Twenty of the twenty-seven counties in the study have acquittal rates between 20 and 29 percent, and within New York City the range across the five boroughs is from 21.3 to 38.4 percent despite gross differences in the racial composition of the their populations. Even the Bronx convicts almost twice as many defendants as it acquits.

The relationship between county demography and jury verdicts is explored another way in Table 12.3 which looks at changes over time, comparing acquittal rates in the 1986–1990 period with rates from 1991 to 1995. New York City has continued to witness an exodus of its white population and a growth of nonwhites, a transformation that has occurred in the city as a whole and in each of the five boroughs. Jury acquittal rates have drifted upward accordingly—slightly in Manhattan, more noticeably in Brooklyn, the Bronx, and Queens, and rather sharply in Staten Island. The growing minority presence in Westchester County to the north of the city has also been accompanied by a somewhat elevated acquittal rate in recent years. The only inconsistency in this analysis is Nassau County, east of the city, where the acquittal rate dropped, while the number of blacks and Hispanics rose substantially. All told, however, demographic shifts foreshadow trends in jury decision making. (see Table 12.3)

But these longitudinal comparisons must also be treated cautiously. The shifts in juries' penchant for acquittal are very small except in Staten Island, where the relatively small number of jury trials heightens the possibility of random fluctuations. While changes move in the predicted direction throughout New York City and in Westchester County, the drop in acquittals in Nassau County is not readily explained.

Table 12.3
Changing Racial Demography[1] and Changing Jury Acquittal Rates[2] in the New York City Metropolitan Area, 1986–1995, by County

	Percent Increase of Nonwhite Population, 1980–1990	Jury Acquittal Rate, 1986-1990	Jury Acquittal Rate, 1991-1995
Bronx	51.0 %	37.8 %	39.0 %
Kings (Brooklyn)	40.3	30.2	32.4
Nassau (Long Island)	90.3	20.7	19.2
New York (Manhattan)	29.6	23.5	23.9
Queens	82.5	27.6	29.1
Richmond (Staten Island)	96.7	17.0	26.0
Westchester	71.3	20.5	21.3

1. Data on race and ethnicity were obtained from the 1980 and 1990 federal census as reported in Nelson A. Rockefeller Institute of Government, *New York State Statistical Yearbook 1995* 9 (1995).
2. Data on jury verdicts were provided by the New York State Office of Court Administration.

The findings in toto suggest that race of jurors is more significant in doubtful cases than in open-and-shut ones. It is only one factor of many affecting jury behavior, not the least of which is the strength of the evidence. The cold-blooded murderer caught red-handed is unlikely to be acquitted by all-black juries, all-Hispanic juries, all-white juries, or mixed juries in the absence of exceptional circumstances. Thus, a predominantly Hispanic and African American jury in the Bronx wasted no time in convicting Julio Gonzalez of 87 murders after witnessing a videotaped confession in which he admitted burning down a crowded social club in retaliation for having been ejected after a squabble with his girlfriend; it summarily rejected his temporary insanity defense after only four hours of deliberations.[35]

The facts will generally be dispositive when the facts are crystal clear, as in the Gonzales case; minority jurors are not indiscriminately lenient. But when the evidence is problematic or the law is ambiguous, the racial characteristics of jurors and the special points of view that they generate may make the difference in trial outcomes.

DISCUSSION

Why do juries with significant black and Hispanic representation acquit more? One possible answer is racially based jury nullification—the purposeful exoneration of those thought to be guilty as a protest by jurors from minority groups against a justice system considered racist, as a way of expressing solidarity with kindred people on trial, or as a way of resisting the steady expansion of the minority population being imprisoned. Acquittals can be seen as forms of civil disobedience, a refusal of jurors to follow the law as announced by the judge in their pursuit of what they believe are more compelling norms of justice.

This interpretation, however, is dubious. First, there is substantial evidence that juries en masse take very seriously the admonitions from judges that they base their verdicts on the law and the evidence.[36] Even when cases entail heart-wrenching mitigating circumstances or absurd laws, jurors are reluctant to acquit those whose guilt is indisputable; outright jury nullification is a rare phenomenon. There is no reason to believe that blacks and Hispanics are any more willing to defy judicial authority than anyone else.

Second, ex-jurors who acquitted defendants in racially tinged cases have consistently denied using race or any other extralegal factor as a criterion in their decision making. No matter how preposterous acquittals may appear, jurors will claim that *their* reading of the evidence left them with reasonable doubt about guilt. They virtually never admit engaging in jury nullification.

Two examples illustrate this point. Although the aforementioned acquittal of Lemrick Nelson for the murder of a Hasidic Jew during anti-Semitic riots in Brooklyn's Crown Heights prompted strong criticism and was followed by a federal prosecution for the same offense on the grounds that a truly guilty man had been exonerated, jurors in the first case steadfastly stuck to their contention that the verdict was based on factual inconsistencies and police dishonesty. Said one black juror, a college student: "Religion and race were never brought up the whole time we were in deliberations. Yankel Rosenbaum could have been black. Lemrick Nelson could have been white—it wouldn't have made a difference."[37]

The jurors who exonerated O. J. Simpson of criminal charges were equally vehement in ascribing the not-guilty verdict to weaknesses in the prosecution's case. One of them, a black computer technician, maintained that the verdict had nothing to do with Simpson's being a hero in the black community. Her words were emphatic: "I was brought up to love everyone. I'm not for anyone, yellow, black, blue, green. I'm just for justice . . . . We were fair. It wasn't a matter of sympathy; it wasn't a matter of favoritism. It was a matter of evidence."[38]

Just as emphatic in disavowing racially based interpretations of their decision making were the mostly white jurors who ruled against Simpson in the civil case. In a postverdict news conference they, too, pointed to the evidence, with several claiming that Simpson's culpability was demonstrated beyond a reasonable doubt. Said one juror: "I needed—for myself—to be *beyond a shadow of a doubt*, and I felt that was proven to me"(emphasis added). Another asserted she was "100 per cent" convinced and that the verdict had "nothing to do with the color of his skin.[39]

It is doubtful that these jurors are deliberately lying. Both those who exonerated him in the first case and those who reached the opposite conclusion in the second are probably sincere in justifying their judgments by allusions to the evidence. In an adversarial system there always are fragments of evidence and conceivable lines of inference that are exculpatory; the facts never speak unequivocally for themselves. Outsiders who closely followed Simpson's televised criminal trial might condemn the acquittal as groundless, but who is to say for certain that these critics are right and the jury was wrong? The key to understanding jury decision making is the recognition that *the jurors* think they got things right.

A more persuasive interpretation of the linkage between race and verdicts than blatant juror partiality is that white and nonwhite jurors view evidence through different lenses. Jurors are not tabula rasa, "blank slates" whose minds are waiting to be filled with details from trials. They come to cases with an array of preconceptions about the world that inform their processing of the evidence. Jury scholar Phoebe Ellsworth makes the point nicely: "It is well known among pschologists that much of what is perceived is a function of the perceiver; it is a particular *construct* of the events perceived, rather than a true reflection.[40]

Black and Hispanic experiences with racism and their distrust of police may well lead them to be more suspicious of the prosecution's case, especially when it involves police testimony, which is often a vital element in attempting to prove charges. Having firsthand knowledge of racially discriminatory law enforcement practices ranging from unwarranted traffic stops to the planting of drugs and weapons by police officers, they may well be more skeptical of the probative evidence amassed by the state than their white counterparts whose interactions with the criminal justice system have been more benign. Indeed, a nationwide interview study of 800 ex-jurors done by telephone reveals that black jurors are much less likely than white jurors to believe police officers when their testimony conflicts with that given by defendants.[41] The greater incredulity of nonwhite jurors, rightly or wrongly, may well make them less predisposed to convict.

Another important factor impinging on juror treatment of the evidence is stereotyping, the use of generalizations about members of a group that fail to take individual differences within the group into account. Experimental research has shown that such overgeneralizing or false generalizing retards receptivity to new information[42]; one's eyes and mind are closed to discordant data.

Jurors, like everyone else, may fall back on stereotyping when information about individuals is incomplete or ambiguous. A pervasive stereotype held by many whites is that of the black thug, a point of view cynically, but successfully, manipulated in the infamous Willie Horton political advertisements by candidate George Bush in the 1988 presidential election campaign. White jurors harboring such racial stereotypes may be more inclined to judge black defendants negatively. Black jurors, normally having dealt with the full gamut of people within their own race, are able to make more discerning judgments. Mock jury research confirms such race-stereotypic thinking. [43]

Greater faith in the criminal justice system, when coupled with reliance on racial stereotypes, may make whites more prone to convict than blacks. Subtle perceptual and attitudinal differences between the races that prompt minorities to give defendants the benefit of the doubt in situations where whites would be satisfied that there is sufficient incriminating evidence is a likely cause of inter county disparities in conviction rates. The dominance of one race or another in the jury room can tilt the balance as the evidence is weighed.

CONCLUSION

The findings, based on thousands of cases, shed light on many puzzling and controversial verdicts, such as the two cases involving Bernhard Goetz, widely dubbed the "subway vigilante." Goetz was charged in 1987 in Manhattan with attempted murder for shooting four black youths who he claimed were about to rob him on a crowded subway train. Goetz testified that the victims looked and sounded menacing despite brandishing no weapons when they asked him for five dollars. The jury of 10 white jurors and two black jurors acquitted him of all charges, except possession of an unlicensed gun, on the basis of self-defense.

Critics of the verdict said that the largely white jury had fallen prey to their racial stereotypes and prejudices. Such was the opinion of two distinguished law professors: George Fletcher, who studied the case in depth, concluded that the largely white jury had bought a legal defense based on racial fear [44]; Stephen Carter is in accord, claiming that the jury fell prey to the popular image of "innocent whiteness surrounded by threatening blackness."[45] Journalist Dorothy Gillian, writing in the Washington Post, was more acerbic: "If you doubt that racism was a factor, just try to imagine whether a pistol-toting black man would have had such a sweeping vindication [from the jury] had he shot four white teenagers because two of them approached him and one of them had a 'shine' in his eyes and a 'funny' smile. . . If you believe that, I have a cheap bridge I want to sell you."[46]

Contrast this verdict with the outcome of the civil suit brought by one of the four youths who suffered brain damage and permanent paralysis from the shooting. The trial took place in 1996 in the Bronx, where the plaintiff resided; a jury, including four blacks and two Hispanics rejected Goetz's claim of self-defense and ordered Goetz to pay $43 million in damages. While the evidence introduced at both trials may have been somewhat different, the quality of Goetz's legal representation was higher in the first case than the second, and the more relaxed burden of proof in civil cases altered the juridical decision facing the second jury, it seems likely that extralegal factors were responsible for the divergent verdicts.

Our findings suggest that the locus of the trial was indeed a telling factor. The Bronx is three-fourths black or Hispanic, so the seating of an exclusively nonwhite jury, whose judgment is less colored by negativity toward the wounded minority youths and probably more affected by Goetz's seemingly paranoiac fear of blacks, was not all that unusual. On the other hand, whites remain in the majority in Manhattan, permitting selection of a largely white jury who may have reconstructed the facts on the basis of some degree of empathy with Goetz as a besieged victim of urban crime and some degree of bias against young black males stereotyped as aggressive and dangerous.

The significant variations in jury behavior within New York state over a 10-year period reported earlier are the two contradictory Goetz verdicts writ large. Racially based perspectives, although normally hidden to the jurors themselves and generally unacknowledged by them, seem to be a hovering presence in the jury box and the jury room. Race is far from everything, but, to be sure, race matters.

The jury, as Alexis de Tocqueville sagely noted 160 years ago in his classic volume *Democracy in America,* is, "above all," a political institution [47]; it reflects the tenor of the times. Political scientist Jeffrey Abramson has expanded on this theme:

The direct and raw character of jury democracy makes it our most honest mirror, reflecting both the good and the bad that ordinary people are capable of when called upon to do justice. The reflection sometimes attracts us, and it sometimes repels us. But we are the jury, and the image we see is our own.[48]

So long as people's consciousness and experiences are seared by deep-seated sentiments about race, juror thinking will be informed by race. Continuing racial polarization will perpetuate differences in jury behavior based on venue. But should this racial gap separating Americans diminish, the impact of local demography demonstrated in our findings will also subside. As goes the public, so goes the jury: the future of racially based verdicts depends on us.

NOTES

I would like to thank Professors Gil Gels and Marvin Zalman for their useful criticisms of the earlier manuscript and Gail Miller of the New York State Office of Court Administration for providing the raw data on jury verdicts.

1. Maureen Dowd, "The Sound and the Jury," *New York Times* November 21, 1996, A29.

2. A. Cooley, *Madam Foreman: A Rush to Judgment?* (1995).

3. M. Gottleib, "Racial Split at the End as at the Start," *New York Times* October 4, 1995, A11.

4. T. Purdum, "Simpson Verdict Confronts a Public Seemingly Numbed," *New York Times* February 2, 1997.

5. J. Abramson, *Postmortem: The O. J. Simpson Case* (1996).

6. S. Walker, *Sense and Nonsense about Crime* 30 (1994).

7. J. Abramson, *supra note 4,* at 108–112; J. Levine, *Juries and Politics* (1992), 136–140.

8. S. Whitfield, *A Death in the Delta: The Story of Emmmett Till* (1988), 42.

9. R. Meredith, "Jurors Acquit White Officer in the Death of Black Driver," *New York Times* November 14, 1996, A20; Meredith, "In Pittsburgh, White Officer's Acquittal Brings Protest March," *New York Times* November 15, 1996, B8.

10. R. McFadden, "TeenAger Acquitted in Slaying during '91 Crown Heights Melee," *New York Times* October 30, 1992, A1.

11. J. Fried, "2 Guilty in Fatal Crown Heights Violence," *New York Times* February 11, 1997, A1.

12. C. McCoy, "If Hard Cases Make Bad Law, Easy Juries Make Bad Facts: A Response to Professor Levine," *Legal Studies Forum* (18): 497, 501.

13. B. Holden, L. Cohen, and E. de Lisser, "Race Seems to Play an Increasing Role in Many Jury Verdicts," *Wall Street Journal* October 4, 1995, A1, A5.

14. J. Kifner, "Bronx Juries: A Defense Dream, a Prosecutor's Nightmare," *New York Times* December 5, 1988, B1.

15. P. Butler, "Racially Based Jury Nullification: Black Power in the Criminal Justice System," *Yale Law Journal* 105(1995): 677.

16. H. Kalven, Jr. and H. Zeisel, *The American Jury* (1966), 163–167.

17. P. Devlin, *The Enforcement of Morals* (1959), 21.

18. W. Bennett and M. Feldman, *Reconstructing Reality in the Courtroom: Justice and Judgment in American Culture* (1981).

19. N. Pennington and R. Hastie, "Explanation-Based Decision-Making: Effects of Memory Structure on Judgment," *Journal of Experimental Psvchology: Learning. Memory. and Cognition* 14( ): 521.

20. Kalven, Jr., and Zeisel, *American Jury*, 163.

21. A. Hacker, *Two Nations: Black and White. Separate. Hostile. Unequal* (1992).

22. C. West, *Race Matters* (1993).

23. M. Ford, "The Role of Extralegal Factors in Jury Verdicts," *Justice System Journal* 11(1986): 16.

24. S. Johnson, "Black Innocence and the White Jury," *Michigan Law Review* 83(1985): 1611.

25. N. King, "Postconviction Review of Jury Discrimination: Measuring the Effects of Juror Race on Jury Decisions," *Michigan Law Review* 92(1993): 63, 99.

26. *Batson v. Kentucky*, 476 U.S. 79 (1986).

27. H. Fukurai, E. Butler, and R. Krooth, *Race and the Jury: Racial Disenfranchisement and the Search for Justice* (1993).

28. Ibid., 10.

29. Levine, *Juries and Politics*, 40-60.

30. New York State Unified Court System, Jury Reform in New York State: A Progress Report, *Continuing Initiative* 4(1996).

31. M. Tonry, *Malign Neglect: Race. Crime and Punishment in America* (1995).

32. M. Maxfield and E. Babble, *Research Methods for Criminal Justice and Criminology* (1995), 77–78.

33. Kifner, *"Bronx Juries."*

34. T. Wolfe, *Bonfire of the Vanities* (1987), 133.

35. E. Nieves, "Refugee Found Guilty of Killing 87 in Bronx Happy Land Fire," *New York Times* August 20, 1991, B1.

36. V. Hans and N. Vidmar, *Judging the Jury* (1986), 163; I. Horowitz, "The Effects of Jury Nullification Instructions on Verdicts and Jury Functioning in Criminal Trials," *Law and Human Behavior* 9(1985): 25; I. Horowitz, "The Impact of Judicial Instructions, Argument, and Challenges on Jury Decision Making," *Law and Human Behavior* 12(1988): 439; H. Kalven, Jr., and H. Zeisel, American Jury, 498; Levine, Juries and Politics, 182; Van Dyke, "The Jury as a Political Institution," *Catholic Lawyer* 16(1970): 224.

37. M. Gottlieb, " 'Beyond a Reasonable Doubt' Often Puts Jury on Trial" *New York Times* November 22, 1992, IV6.

38. L. Adams, "Simpson Jurors Cite Weak Case, Not Race," *Washington Post* October 5, 1995, A1, A26.

39. C. Goldberg, "Jury Believed Evidence, Not Simpson," *New York Times* February 11, 1997, A12.

40. Phoebe Ellsworth, "Are Twelve Heads Better than One?" *Law and Contemporary Problems* 52(1989): 205, 206.

41. "Racial Divide Affects Black, White Panelists," *National Law Journal* (February 22, 1993: S8, S9.

42. G. Bodenhausen, "Stereotypic Biases in Social Decision Making and Memory: Testing Process Models in Stereotape Use," *Journal of Personality and Social Psvchology* 55(1988): 726.

43. R. Gordon, "Attributions for Blue-Collar and White-Collar Crime: The Effects of Subject and Defendant Race on Simulated Juror Decisions," *Journal of Applied Social Psvchology* 20(1990): 971. See King, "Postconviction," 77–80 for more extended discussion and additional references dealing with stereotyping and ethnocentrism in jury decisionmaking.

44. G. Fletcher, *A Crime of SelfDefense: Bernhard Goetz and the Law on Trial* (1988), 206–208. Also see L. Rubin, Quiet Rage: Bernie Goetz in a Time of Madness (1986).

45. Stephen Carter, "When Victims Happen to Be Black," *Yale Law Journal* 97(1988): 420, 428.

46. Dorothy Gillian, "Law of the Monster," *Washington Post* June 18, 1987, D3.

47. A. de Tocqueville, *Democracy in America* vol. 1(1946), 282; P. Bradley, ed., H. Reeve, trans., Revised by F. Bowers.

48. J. Abramson, *We, the Jury: The Jury System and the Ideal of Democracy* (1994), 250.

Chapter 13

Race and Ethnic Bias in Sentencing Decisions: A Review and Critique of the Literature

Darren E. Warner

INTRODUCTION

Between 1980 and 1992, the percentage of black state and federal prisoners increased from 46.5 percent to 50 percent at a time when the percentage of blacks in the overall population increased from 11.8 percent to 12.4 percent (U.S. Department of Justice 1995). At year-end 1992, there were 4,094 black male inmates per 100,000 black adults in the U.S. population, compared to 502 white male inmates per 100,000 adult white residents. These statistics compel us to ask some very poignant questions. Is the law color-blind, or does it contravene the principle of equal treatment and punish individuals differently depending on their race ? Or are minorities disproportionately involved in crime, which accounts for their higher representation in correctional facilities? Such questions raise fundamental social and legal issues. Racial influences on processes within the criminal justice system threaten and contradict both the legitimacy of the justice system itself and the U. S. Constitution under which it was formed. Yet if minorities are involved in criminal activity more than whites, what can be done to alleviate this malevolent social problem? Indeed, studying such issues is paramount to ensuring fairness and equity within our legal system.

Various theories have been used to address the possibility of selective decision making and bias against minorities in the system (e.g., labeling and conflict). Although prior research remains equivocal regarding whether race/ethnicity influences adjudication proceedings, it does suggest that the strongest racial effects (racial discrimination) are manifested at the sentencing stage and that the inclusion of process variables in sentencing equations and/or models contributes little (if anything) to the explained variation in sentencing outcomes (see, e.g., Petersilia 1985). Other research examines the possibility that minorities are disproportionately involved in crime, which would then account for discrepant rates of incarceration among races. Therefore, this line of research is primarily limited to examining racial disparities in sentencing at the state and federal level.

For this exploration, discrimination is defined as an action (e.g., disparate sentencing). It is the denial of opportunities and equal rights to individuals because of their membership in a particular racial and/or ethnic group (Levin & Levin 1982). Discrimination that is attributable to individual prejudices (negative attitudes held by individuals toward entire groups of people) is called individual discrimination (Nelson 1992). Discrimination that is attributable to the "normal" operation of society's institutions is called institutional discrimination (Schaefer 1984).

More succinctly, disparities are measurable differences in how persons are processed that cannot be attributed to differences in control variables that are considered to legitimately affect case-processing decisions (Nelson 1992). It is important to note that disparities do not necessarily represent discriminatory actions. Only when such actions are based on some immutable characteristic (e.g., race, gender) do they represent a form of discrimination.

The following is an exploration into the literature examining the influence of race and/or ethnicity on sentencing decisions in the United States. It is argued not only that much of the previous research is equivocal, but that many of the studies that illustrate racial influences on sentencing can be discredited due to flawed methodologies used by investigators. Although we have accumulated over 35 years of research on sentencing disparities, scholars have failed to demonstrate a consistent pattern of racial bias, with the exception of capital sentencing. This chapter concludes with a call for scholars and policymakers alike to focus their efforts on further studying racial disparities in capital offenses, in order to alleviate this travesty of justice.

DISPARITIES IN SENTENCING DECISIONS: STUDIES AT THE STATE LEVEL

Social scientists have long been concerned with racial bias and judicial inconsistency in the criminal justice system. Many consider it axiomatic that racial minorities receive unequal treatment at the sentencing stage of criminal justice processing (Chambliss & Seidman 1971; Quinney 1970). But the data regarding sentencing decisions remain inconsistent and controversial. One of the first quantitative studies of sentencing decisions was conducted by Sellin (1928), in which he examined the differential likelihood of death sentences being imposed on blacks and whites convicted of homicide. After studying Detroit's criminal court, Sellin found that blacks were more likely to receive the death sentence than whites. He concluded that there existed "a decided discrimination against the negro."

Since Sellin's research, numerous empirical studies of sentencing decisions have focused on racial discrimination as a predictor of differential sentencing among races. Most research on unequal sentencing practices comes from analyses of state and local courts, not federal courts (McDonald & Carlson 1993). For instance, Johnson (1941) studied those convicted of homicide between 1933 and 1939 in North Carolina. He found that sentences varied not only with the race of the offender but with the race of the victim as well. Blacks who had killed whites received the most severe sentences. Similarly, after examining data on El Paso, Texas, and Tucson, Arizona, criminal courts, Holmes and Daudistel (1984) found that blacks and Hispanics in El Paso who were tried before juries were considerably more likely to receive a severe sentence than similar Anglo defendants. The sentencing practices in Tucson were found to be more uniform. Holmes and Daudistel conjectured, "Perhaps judges and juries are fairer in some areas than others" (274).

The central question posed by these and other early sentencing studies was whether the findings could be interpreted as evidence of judicial discrimination (McDonald & Carlson 1993: 21). Another possibility is that unequal sentencing may indicate institutionalized discrimination within the criminal justice system itself. In other words, minorities may be discriminated against at arrest and prosecution—different stages of the criminal justice process over which judges have little, if any, control. Alternatively, sentencing differences may result from legitimate factors that judges need to consider when passing sentence. For example, Bensing and Schroeder's (1960) study of homicides in Cleveland found a similar sentencing pattern to that of Johnson (1941) and Garfinkel (1949) but then showed that blacks who killed whites were more often charged with felony murder. Felony murder cases were more likely to involve aggravating circumstances and to result in first-degree murder convictions than other homicides, thus receiving more severe sentences.

In the last 15 years, empirical and statistically based research on racial discrimination within the criminal justice system at the sentencing stage has become increasingly advanced, although no compelling evidence of widespread racial disparity is documented. Such contradictory evidence led Farnworth et. al. (1991: 58) to summarize that evaluation research tended to "conclude an absence of 'overt' discrimination against blacks once controls for legal variables were included in the analysis."

Several explanations for these contradictions have been explored. Often, studies have data bases too small to allow for generalizations. Other studies failed to control for enough (or any) legally relevant factors that may account for apparent racial discrimination, such as the criminal history of the offender, aggravating circumstances of the offense, and so on (Kleck 1981). Such methodological shortcomings led Hagan (1975), Hindelang (1969), and Kleck (1981) to conclude that "racial discrimination [in sentencing] is a thing of the past." For example, of the 57 studies reviewed by Kleck (1981), only 15 showed evidence of bias; 26 contradicted the racial bias hypothesis, and 16 had mixed results. Kleck (1981) concluded that some studies failed to use even rudimentary controls for offense severity or defendant's prior record, while most studies used crude and imprecise measures or failed to simultaneously control for both variables.

As previously noted, many earlier studies focused only on sentencing decisions. They did not examine criminals' prearrest contact with the system—the point at which many believe the greatest racial differences in treatment exist. Petersilia (1985) attempted to overcome these shortcomings by controlling for arrest history and aggravating circumstances and by examining for evidence of discrimination throughout the criminal justice system. Using both official and self-report data, Petersilia found several notable findings. First, her analyses revealed that the California justice system appears to treat white offenders more severely than minority offenders at the front end of the system (e.g., arrest, decision to prosecute, bond setting). But at the back end (e.g., sentencing), the reverse was found to be true. This means that whites were more likely than minorities to be officially charged following arrest. But after charges were filed, blacks and Hispanics were sentenced to prison at a rate far exceeding that for whites. Moreover, Petersilia also found that of those sentenced to prison, blacks served longer terms than their white counterparts and that blacks and Hispanics were less likely to be granted probation than were Caucasians.

Thus, in one of the most advanced studies of the race-sentencing debate, Petersilia (1985) found strong racial differences in the type of sentence imposed and length of time served. She did not find evidence of discrimination throughout the system. Minorities were no more likely than whites to be arrested or convicted. Indeed, Petersilia concluded that such racial differences have developed because procedures were adopted without systematic attempts to study whether they may have a differential effect on certain races.

One comprehensive study in 1986 argued that prior research that documented little evidence of bias erred by speculating that proper controls for prior record indicate equal sentencing, when instead there was evidence of interaction effects. More specifically, it found that when urbanization is considered, an interaction effect is suggested. Upon examining 2,907 tried cases in Pennsylvania, they found an independent race effect unfavorable to blacks in urban areas only. Blacks with convictions for serious (violent) crimes were more likely to be incarcerated than their white counterparts, especially in urban jurisdictions. Kramer and Stoffensmeir (1993) also conducted an advanced statistical analysis that included controls for prior record and offense severity on 61,294 cases in Pennsylvania. Results showed that blacks were more likely to be incarcerated than whites but that race has no direction effect on length of sentence.

Although these studies are germane, a major disadvantage continues to be their nearly exclusive emphasis on defendants' characteristics. Relatively unstudied have been the characteristics of legal decision makers and how they may influence sentencing outcomes. Little empirical research has examined whether judges' ethnic identities affect their sentencing practices. Contrary to expectations, studies of state judges have generally shown little, if any, differences in the sentences handed down by black and white judges (Spohn 1990a, b). An exception was found by Holmes and his colleagues (1993), who studied the disposition of noncapital felony cases from 1987 to 1989 in the Texas District Courts of El Paso County. They found that Hispanic judges sentenced both Anglo and Hispanic defendants more severely than did white judges regarding white defendants, while white judges' sentences imposed on Hispanics were equal to those meted out by Hispanic judges. This suggests that Anglo judges are not so much discriminating against Hispanics as they are favoring members of their own ethnic group (502). However, due to small sample size, the findings should be viewed with caution.

Still another shortcoming of extant research at the state level is its nearly exclusive focus on sentencing decisions for persons convicted of serious crimes (e.g., see Hagan 1974; Hindelang 1969; Kleck 1981). Such an emphasis ignores biases in case-processing decisions that affect persons arrested for the most common types of offenses. Nelson (1992) sought to provide a more comprehensive study by examining whether minority status affects sentencing outcomes for offenders arrested for misdemeanor crimes. Nelson used data on all persons aged 16 and over arrested for misdemeanor charges (excluding prostitution and driving while intoxicated [DWI]) in the state of New York between 1985 and 1986. Nelson concluded that minorities with prior arrests were sanctioned more harshly than whites, while minorities without prior arrests were sanctioned less harshly. Among those arrested for the first time, minorities were sentenced to conditional discharge more often than whites, and whites were sentenced to pay fines more often than comparably situated minorities (197). Further analysis of fine amounts and sentence lengths showed that whites and minorities received similar sentences. Interestingly, in about half of the counties tested, minorities were sentenced to lower fines than comparably situated whites. Nelson infers from these findings that such patterns are indicative of institutionalized discrimination, although such patterns could have arisen from a lack (real or imagined) of alternative sentences for sanctioning poor offenders.

In summary, then, early empirical research at the state level has failed to document consistent selection bias at sentencing decisions. Nonetheless, public perception has held firm that such discrimination does, in fact, exist and continues to taint criminal justice systems throughout the United States. Such attitudes encouraged legislators at both state and federal levels to adopt sentencing guidelines during the 1980s. Thus, changes in sentencing policy that originally sought to eliminate or reduce racial discrimination were not based on any consistent research demonstrating the existence of such discrimination. I now turn to federal studies both prior to, and after, sentencing guidelines were implemented. Results show that with the exception of capital sentencing, analyses of sentences imposed by federal courts do not reveal any consistent pattern of racial discrimination.

STUDIES OF FEDERAL DECISIONS

Prior to the Imposition of Sentencing Guidelines

Only a handful of studies have examined federal sentencing decisions prior to the introduction of sentencing guidelines. Taken together, they show that sentencing was not significantly dependent on the judge whom one drew (McDonald & Carlson 1993). Instead, outcomes corresponded to differences in the cases and offenders' characteristics that were commonly seen as intervening factors in sentencing. For instance, Sutton (1978) examined sentences imposed in federal district courts during 1971 on offenders convicted of eight offenses: bank robbery, interstate transportation of a stolen vehicle, narcotics violations, Marijuana Tax Act violations, Selective Service Act violations, counterfeiting, bank embezzle-

ment, and larceny from interstate commerce. Sutton found that the most significant predictors of the sentencing decision included the length of prior record,
method of conviction (plea/trial), and type of offense at conviction. Race was not
found to be a significant predictive factor (37).

In another study, Wheeler , Weisburd and Bode (1982) examined federal white-
collar cases reaching conviction in fiscal years 1976–1978 in seven federal dis-
tricts. Again, the offender's race was found to have no independent effect.
Moreover, the work by Wheeler et al. has been replicated with consistent results.

Studies of Federal Sentencing under the Guidelines

One of the first studies to analyze sentencing disparities under the guidelines
came from federal judge Gerald Heaney (1991). Heaney conducted a study of
sentences imposed in four district courts in the Eighth Circuit during 1989 and
then a separate analysis of sentencing data for all males aged 18 to 35 who were
sentenced during 1989 in all federal district courts. Comparing data from the four
district courts, Heaney found that the proportion of offenders pleading guilty
went down, the "penalty" for going to trial increased, the length of time an offender could expect to serve in prison increased, the proportion of probation-only sentences declined dramatically, and there were significant interdistrict differences in
the average length of sentence imposed (quoted in McDonald & Carlson 1993:
27). Upon analyzing the sentences given to males 18 to 35 years old, Heaney also
found that a larger proportion of those sentenced to prison under the guidelines
were black or Hispanic, compared to the proportion sentenced in nonguideline
cases. Heaney concluded this was evidence of a "disparity."

However, other researchers challenged Heaney's conclusions on the grounds
that they are based on a comparison of guideline cases with nonguideline cases
sentenced during 1989 only and thus contain divergent populations.
Nonguideline cases and guideline cases do not represent comparable populations
of offenders. For example, Katzenelson and McDanal (1991) improved on
Heaney's study by selecting comparable populations of only guideline cases. For
the 23,000 guideline cases disposed during the fiscal year 1990, the researchers
examined the relationship between the sentence imposed and the guideline range
computed for each offender. The general emerging pattern was that the majority
of sentences were found to be either at the extremes of the range or outside the
range altogether. Violent offenses tended to be sentenced at the high end of the
range; economic crimes at the lower end. Moreover, despite the fact that the
guideline range is computed to reflect the offender's prior criminal record, judges
tended to sentence below, or near, the bottom of the range. Although the study
was not designed to study disparate sentencing per se, the researchers found little evidence of unwarranted disparities (Katzenelson & McDanal 1991).

In a similar vein, Johnson (1993) examined the sentencing patterns of blacks
and Hispanics during the fiscal year 1991. Johnson found that whites were more
often rewarded with reduced sentences when they gave prosecutors "substantial
assistance" in developing cases against other offenders. Johnson also found that
some of the sentencing differences between whites and minorities could be attrib-

uted to racial differences in the degree to which offenders were sentenced at the top of their guideline range, based on severity of crime committed and criminal history. These factors were found to account for all of the white/Hispanic sentencing disparities, but there still remained a statistically significant unexplained difference between sentences given to black and white defendants (41).

Building from the work of Katzenelson and McDanal (1991) and Johnson (1993), McDonald and Carlson (1993) examined the sentencing decisions throughout the 1986–90 period by selecting two distinct populations of offenders. The first included all offenders sentenced from January 20, 1989, to June 30, 1990. Offenders sentenced prior to this period were omitted in order to minimize any bias in the comparisons that may have resulted from uneven application of the guidelines prior to *Mistretta v. the United States.* Before that landmark case, not all judges were implementing the guidelines. The second population consisted of all those sentenced in federal district courts during 1986, 1987, and 1988 who were not subject to the provisions of the Sentencing Reform Act of 1984. The study's major findings were:

- Before full implementation of sentencing guidelines, white, black, and Hispanic offend ers received similar sentences, on average, in federal district courts.

- After implementing the guidelines, 85 percent of Hispanic offenders and 78 percent of black offenders were given prison sentences, compared to 72 percent of white offenders. On average, black offenders sentenced to prison received sentences 41 percent longer than whites (21 months longer). For Hispanics, the length of sentence did not differ signif cantly from the sentence imposed on whites (38).

The main reason for such disparate sentencing practices was found to be the changing proportions of blacks and Hispanics convicted of crimes that were more severely punished. For instance, 83 percent of all federal offenders convicted of trafficking in crack cocaine in guideline cases were black, and the average sentence imposed for crack trafficking was twice as long as that for trafficking in powdered cocaine (43). Under the Act of 1986, those convicted of trafficking 50 grams or more of crack would be subject to no less than 10 years in prison—20 if they had a prior drug crime conviction. These punishments are identical to the minimum term required of offenders convicted of selling 100 times that amount of powdered cocaine. Excluding offenders convicted of trafficking in crack, the remaining difference in length of prison sentences imposed on blacks and whites was 13 months. Further, excluding offenders convicted of trafficking in powdered or crack cocaine from the total of offenders sentenced under the guidelines reveals that the remaining difference in the length of incarceration sentences imposed on blacks and whites for all other offenses was seven months (51).

But while the literature remains inconclusive concerning the effects of race on overall criminal sentencing, it remains decidedly firm when examining capital sentencing. Historically, race has played a role in the imposition of the death penalty in the United States. In *Furman v. Georgia* (1972), some Supreme Court justices raised serious questions about discrimination and arbitrariness in the application of the death penalty. For example, Justice Douglas noted, "It would seem incontestable that the death penalty inflicted on one defendant is 'unusual' if it discriminates against him by reason of his race . . . or if it is imposed under a procedure that gives room for the play of such prejudices (*Furman v. Georgia* 1972).

At the time of the *Furman* decision, a significant body of research existed demonstrating that blacks were far more likely to receive a death sentence than whites (Garfinkle 1949; Johnson 1957). It was also found that whites were more likely to have their death sentence reduced to a lesser sentence (Wolfgang et al. 1962). Still other studies found that the race of the victim influences capital sentencing. In particular, Zimring et al. (1976) found that blacks charged with murdering whites in Philadelphia were more likely to receive a capital sentence than whites who killed blacks. Arkin (1980) found similar patterns of sentencing in the state of Florida. In addition, of 28 studies deemed methodologically sound by the U.S. General Accounting Office (1990), it was found that in 82 percent of the studies the race of the victim influenced the probability of being charged with capital murder and/or receiving the death penalty (Kentucky Department of Public Advocacy 1995: 6). Moreover, the race of the victim was found to influence every stage of the criminal justice process. Legally relevant variables such as aggravating circumstances and prior record did not fully explain the evidence of racial disparity in capital sentencing. In total, of all studies identifying the race of the defendant, more than three-fourths clearly showed blacks were more likely to be put to death (11). These results show a discernible, consistent pattern: blacks are more likely to receive a death sentence than whites, especially in cases where a black offender murders a white victim.

DISCUSSION AND CONCLUSION

This review of the literature has provided the reader with an evaluation of research examining the influence of race and ethnicity on decisions made in state and federal courts. It has focused on analyzing the influence of race on sentencing practices. Despite overwhelming public perception of racial bias, no consistent pattern could be discerned from research on sentencing practices in state and federal courts. The one exception remains in the area of capital sentencing. Studies show conclusively that blacks are more likely to receive a death sentence than white offenders, especially in cases involving a white victim. These results are irrespective of aggravating circumstances and prior criminal history.

In the final analysis, the social problem of disproportionate minority involvement in crime and racial disparities in capital sentencing continues to taint our justice system and our society. Scholars and policymakers would do well to focus their efforts on alleviating the unequal use of the death penalty. Although this investigation has not focused on the role that institutional discrimination may play in unequal sentencing, there exists a great need for further studies to examine the influence of race on a priori sentencing processes. That is, researchers should focus their efforts at ascertaining the influence of race on stages that occur before a defendant is brought before a judge or jury for sentencing, such as decision to prosecute, charge imposed, and the allotment of bail. A plethora of racial bias task forces and/or commissions has been established at the state level and has examined such practices. Many have found race to influence the decisions by authorities in our justice system prior to sentencing (e.g., see California Judicial Council Advisory Committee on Racial and Ethnic Bias in the Courts; New Jersey Supreme Court Task Force on Minority Concerns; Oregon Judicial Department Supreme Court Task Force on Racial/Ethnic Issues in the Judicial System). The work done by these organizations, along with early empirical studies, implore us to further examine the influence of race/ethnicity on state and federal justice systems.

Finally, it is hoped that this review has given the reader a fuller, more detailed sense of the importance of research into the relationship between race and criminal processing. Without such research, we fail to properly ensure true justice for all citizens of the United States.

REFERENCES

Arkin, S. D. (1980). "Discrimination and Arbitrariness in Capital Punishment: An Analysis of Post-Furman Murder Cases in Dade County, Florida, 1973–1976." *Stanford Law Review* 33: 75–101.

Bensing, R., and O. Schroeder. (1960). *Homicide in an Urban Community*. Springfield, IL: Charles C. Thomas Company.

California Judicial Council Advisory Committee on Racial and Ethnic Bias in the Courts. (1993). *Fairness in the California State Courts: A Survey of the Public, Attorneys, and Court Personnel*. Los Angeles: Author.

Chambliss, W. J. and R. B. Seidman. (1971). *Law, Order, and Power*. Reading, MA: Addison–Wesley.

Farnworth, M., et al. (1991). "Ethnic, Racial, and Minority Disparities in Felony Court Processing." In M. J. Lynch and E. B. Patterson, *Race and Criminal Justice* Chapter 4. New York: Harrow and Heston.

Garfinkel, H. (1949). "Research Note on Inter- and Intra-Racial Homicides." *Social Forces* 27: 369.

Hagan, J. (1975). "Extra-Legal Attributes and Criminal Sentencing: An Assessment of a Sociological Viewpoint." *The Aldine Crime and Justice Annual*. Chicago: Aldine.

Heaney, G. W. (1991). "The Reality of Guideline Sentencing: No End to Disparity." *American Criminal Law Review* 28: 161–233.

Hindelang, M. J. (1969). "Equality under the Law." *Journal of Criminal Law and Crime Police Science* 60: 306–333.

Holmes, M. D. and H. C. Daudistel. (1984). "Ethnicity and Justice in the Southwest: The Sentencing of Anglo, Black, and Mexican Origin Defendants." *Social Science Quarterly* 65: 266–277.

Holmes, M. D., et al. (1993). "Judges' Ethnicity and Minority Sentencing: Evidence concerning Hispanics." *Social Science Quarterly* 74: 496–506.

Johnson, C. (1993). *An Investigation of Differences in Sentences of White, Black, and Hispanic Offenders Under the Federal Sentencing Guidelines*. Draft submitted to the U.S. Sentencing Commission.

Johnson, E. H. (1957). "Selective Forces in Capital Punishment." *Social Forces* 36: 165–169.

Johnson, G. (1941). "The Negro and Crime." *Annals of the American Academy of Political and Social Sciences* 217: 93.

Katzenelson, S. and C. McDanal. (1991). "Sentencing Guidelines and Judicial Discretion in Sentencing." *Journal of Quantitative Criminology* 2: 29–48.

Kentucky Department of Public Advocacy. (1995). "Race and the Death Penalty in Kentucky Murder Trials: 1976–1991." *The Advocate* 17: 5–15.

Kleck, G. (1981). "Racial Discrimination in Criminal Sentencing: A Critical Evaluation of the Evidence with Additional Evidence." *American Sociological Review* 46: 783–805.

Kramer, J. and D. Stoffensmeir. (1993). "Race and Imprisonment Decisions." *Sociological Quarterly* 34: 357–376.

Levin, J. and W. Levin. (1982). *The Functions of Discrimination and Prejudice.* New York: Harper and Row.

McDonald, D. C. and K E. Carlson. (1993). *Sentencing in the Federal Courts: Does Race Matter? The Transition to Sentencing Guidelines 1986–90.* Washington, DC: U.S. Department of Justice.

———. (1992). *Federal Sentencing Transition, 1980–90.* Washington, DC: Bureau of Justice Statistics.

Nagel, S. (1969). *The Legal Process from a Behavioral Perspective.* Homewood, IL: Dorsey Press.

Nelson, J. F. (1992). "Hidden Disparities in Case Processing: New York State, 1985–1986." *Journal of Criminal Justice* 20: 182–200.

New Jersey Supreme Court Task Force on Minority Concerns. (1989). *Survey of Perceptions of Bias in the New Jersey Courts.*

Oregon Judicial Department. Office of the State Court Administrator. (1994). *Report of the Oregon Supreme Court Task Force on Racial/Ethnic Issues in the Judicial System.*

Petersilia, J. (1985). "Racial Disparities in the Criminal Justice System: A Summary." *Crime and Delinquency* 31:15–34.

Quinney, R. (1970). *The Social Reality of Crime.* Boston: Little, Brown.

Radelet, M. L. and G. L. Pierce. (1991). "Chasing Those Who Will Die: Race and the Death Penalty in Florida." *Florida Law Review* 43: 1–34.

Schaefer, R. T. (1984). *Racial and Ethnic Groups.* Boston: Little, Brown.

Sellin, T. (1928). "The Negro Criminal: A Statistical Note." *Annals of the American Academy of Political and Social Sciences* 140: 52–64.

Spohn, C. (1990a). "Decision Making in Sexual Assault Cases: Do Black and Female Judges Make a Difference? *Women and Criminal Justice* 2: 83–105.

———. (1990b). "The Sentencing Decisions of Black and White Judges. Expected and Unexpected Similarities." *Law and Society Review* 24: 1197–1216.

Sutton, L. P. (1978). *Variations in Federal Criminal Sentences.* Washington, DC: U.S. Government Printing Office.

U. S. General Accounting Office. (1990). *Death Penalty Sentencing Research Indicates a Pattern of Racial Disparities.* Washington, DC.

Wheeler, S., D. Weisburd, and N. Bode. (1982). "Sentencing the White-Collar Offender. Rhetoric or Reality?" *American Sociological Review* 47: 641–659.

Wilkins, L., et al. (1978). *Sentencing Guidelines: Structuring Judicial Discretion.* Washington, DC: U.S. Government Printing Office.

Wolfgang, M. E., A. Kelly, and H. C. Nolde. (1962). "Comparisons of Executed and the Commuted among Admissions to Death Row." *Journal of Criminal Law and Criminology* 53: 301–310.

Zimring, F. E., J. Eigen, and S. O'Malley. (1976). "Punishing Homicides in Philadelphia: Perspectives on the Death Penalty." *University of Chicago Law Review* 43: 227–252

Media Images and the Victimization of Black Women: Exploring the Impact of Sexual Stereotyping on Prosecutorial Decision Making

Norma Manatu-Rupert

Within the criminal justice system, rape reform measures designed to provide legal correctives for all victims of rape than previously recognized have had ambiguous results (Caringella–McDonald 1988; Spohn & Horney 1992; Spears & Spohn 1997). While some acquaintance and date rape cases have been prosecuted, only those rapes considered "real rapes" (i.e., stranger-with-weapon rapes) have generally resulted in convictions (Estrich 1987; Fairstein 1993). Thus, though the recent decrease in the nation's crime rate is seen as a boon for criminal justice agencies (Bratton 1995), rape crimes and sexual abuse of women remain virtually constant.

The Uniform Crime Reports (UCR)(1996) note that in 1996 forcible rapes accounted for only 6 percent of all violent crimes. In that year, 95,769 forcible rapes were reported to law enforcement agencies nationwide, which represented a 2 percent decrease from the 1995 levels and a 12 percent decline below 1992 levels. When compared with figures from the previous decade, however, the 1996 rape rate actually increased 5 percent above the 1987 volume (UCR: 24). Thus, while the "official" numbers boast a decrease from the 1992 and 1995 levels, they also show a regression from levels nearly a decade old.

Indeed, the "official" number of forcible rapes may not be reflective of actual rapes (Williams & Holmes 1981; Lizotte 1985; Howard 1988). In her study of battered women, for example, Richie (1996) found that, despite forcible rapes against two subgroups of women in their intimate relationships, African American female victims were far less likely than their white counterparts to "use criminal justice agencies or other public services," primarily because of a "general mistrust" of the police (95–97). This suggests that, at least some of the time, more rapes occur than are reported. Stanko (1985), in fact, argues that "official" numbers may be misleading because the publicizing of only certain high-profile rape cases sends an erroneous message that rape is sporadic, not endemic.

A major reason for the ambiguity in the nation's rape rates may lie in UCR's very definition of rape: "the carnal knowledge of a female forcibly and against her will," which includes assaults or attempts to commit rape by force or threat of force but which excludes "statutory rape (without force) and other sexual offenses" (23). That "statutory rape" is exclusionary in the definition is equivocal, given that a 15-year-old may or may not be psychologically mature enough to grant consent; that "other sexual offenses" are also excluded is downright problematic, because the definition fails to account for those situations in which women, whose dates may have "doctored" the women's drinks, for example, would be in no position either to consent or to protest. In this and other such situations, "against her will" and "threat of force" become moot terms and, therefore, meaningless.

Feminists have argued that criminal justice officials base decisions to prosecute on "stereotypes of rape," where only "real rapes" are taken seriously (Estrich 1987; Caringella–McDonald 1988). Not only do stereotypes of real rapes appear to determine prosecution and conviction, but apparently, stereotypes of "genuine victims," preferably in sensational cases, also determine prosecution (Stanko 1985; LaFree 1989; Douglas 1995; Fairstein 1993), leading Loh (1980) to conclude that "discretionary decisions are more susceptible in rape than in other types of crimes to the interjection of personal attitudes toward women, sexuality, race, and class" (581).

Theoretical and empirical studies on rape consistently support Loh's (1980) view that "official" reactions to sexual assaults are influenced primarily by victim characteristics (Happerle 1985; Albonetti 1987; Estrich 1987; Stanko 1988; LaFree 1989; Kerstetter 1990; Frohmann 1991; Spears & Spohn 1997). Writers indicate that criminal justice personnel use stereotypes concerning "real victims" and victims' "appropriate behaviors" to determine victims' credibility. Accordingly, rape victims who do not fit the stereotype with respect to background, reputation, race, and behavior are perceived as less credible. Spears and Spohn (1997) argue that "victims' character and credibility may play an especially important role in charging decisions in sexual assault cases" (503). This, in fact, may be the case, for in their study of Detroit prosecutors' charging decisions in rape cases, Spears and Spohn (1997) found that the only significant predictor of prosecution was "victims' moral character" (513), despite the strength of the evidence.

This finding is important in light of the fact that within the purview of Spears and Spohn's study (1997), the majority of the sexual assaults involved "black victims" (521). Moreover, the finding of their study is especially significant given that blacks in general and black women in particular have been assumed to be driven primarily by their sexuality in U.S. culture (Stampp 1953; Jordan 1968; Pinkney 1969; Brownmiller 1975; Hooks 1981), and in the mass media especially (Hooks 1992, 1995; Jewell 1992; Jones 1992; Painter 1992) and, as a consequence, cannot then be seen as "real" rape victims. Yet, such assumptions not only negate the idea of black women as victims of sexual assaults but serve to undermine the probity of black female complainants and, more importantly, may work to perpetuate sexual assaults against these women.

Gilkes (1983) notes that the image of the black female as "prostitute" has been so widely communicated in the mass media that, in turn, the image has influenced the way black female victims are treated by the criminal justice system. One Pennsylvania Law Review study (1968), for instance, found that police classified nearly twice as many rape cases involving black female victims as "unfounded," as those involving whites and other groups. The researchers concluded that the differential in police decisions resulted "primarily from a lack of confidence in the veracity of black complainants and a belief in the myth of black promiscuity" (304).

Not only are police influenced by the myth of black female promiscuity but citizens who ultimately serve as jurors are also influenced. LaFree, et al. (1985) interviewed 331 jurors who served in 38 forcible rape cases in Indiana and found that jurors were more likely to render a "not guilty" verdict when the victim was a black woman (389–407). LaFree et al. suggest that such biased treatment against black female victims might be influenced by "stereotypes" of black females, who are viewed as more consenting in sexual matters and, thus, less harmed by any sexual assaults.

Stereotypes the police hold about those they serve have serious consequences, since most individuals who enter the criminal justice system encounter the police as the first representatives of that system. Police officers, especially, make up a great space in the daily lives of most Americans vis-a-vis protection. This space, while primarily a function of the time police spend in protecting victims and arresting offenders, is also a dynamic of the perceptions held by police about those they are entrusted to serve and protect. That is, based on their perceptions of the situation and the complainant, the police can use their "discretion" (Cooper 1980) to decide those cases they deem meritorious for investigation, which, in turn, will determine what cases are actually prosecuted. It is reasonable to assume that this "discretionary processing" stems, in part, from personal beliefs of whatever kind that the police hold about a given victim or group.

Due to their double membership in society, the police are simultaneously representatives of the dominant group that wields central authority and social subjects as well. As representatives, the police are expected to be unbiased protector of the citizenry; as social subjects, however, they are consumers of filmic images who, like other viewers, may be susceptible to the subtlety and power of filmic representations of the diverse groups the police serve. There is a delicate balance, then, a built-in tension, if you will, between the need of the police for impartiality as professionals and the ambivalence of being social subjects with potential human prejudices. The process is further accentuated by the fact that the majority of police officers are white (Cooper 1980), and most do not typically interact socially (outside the job) with large numbers of blacks over long periods of time. How the police view black women, thus, becomes of paramount importance because, in large part, their perceptions determine whether black women receive due protection under the law.

Gilkes' (1983) and LaFree et al.'s (1985) observation of the link between media stereotypes of black women as oversexed and biased treatment against black female rape victims within the criminal justice system is compelling. But neither writer goes far enough to fully investigate the media's role. Yet, the media's influence on prosecutorial decisions is pivotal in any discussions regarding rape reform laws, because those laws concern legal correctives for all victims of rape. If true reform is to take place within the system, that system must reexamine the built-in assumptions that preclude genuine change in the rape laws and that render the problem systemic. Accordingly, the media's role in fostering the stereotype must be examined in light of the fact that stereotypes in the mass media help formulate conceptualizations both of rape and of rape victims.

It has been noted that a culture's dominant symbolic system reflects and communicates subliminal meanings about a variety of issues deemed important in the social domain (Jowett & Linton 1980; Wolfenstein & Leites 1950), of which rape and its handling within the criminal justice system are a part. The mass media, particularly film, construct, limit, direct, and shape the images that influence viewers' perceptions of the world, its people, and the racial and gendered roles viewers occupy and, thus, value in society. A number of writers have already illustrated the power of the mass media in controlling the form and direction of information within a given society (Boorstin 1977; Postman 1979, 1985; Jowett & Linton 1980; Meyrowitz 1985). Empirical studies have also shown how such control frames the way viewers perceive and create social reality, which demonstrate that viewers are, indeed, influenced by media images (Haskell 1973; Rosen 1973; Bandura 1977, 1986; Gerbner 1982; White 1983; DeLauretis 1984; Hooks 1992, 1995). Some research has even gone so far as to suggest that individuals form impressions of social "others" with whom they have no direct social contact, chiefly from the mass media (Erikson 1978; Bandura 1977, 1986; Gerbner et al. 1986). Others have concluded that media myths of social "others" continue to operate culturally long after the myths are shown to be false (Bogle 1973; Mapp 1972; Gilkes 1983; Hooks 1981, 1995; Tong 1984). If the preceding arguments hold, and if in rape cases, "victims' character" is a major factor in prosecutorial decisions, it may be that decisions in rape cases involving black female victims are influenced by stereotypes of "victims' characterizations" found in filmic images.

The present chapter, thus, has adopted Hall's (1988) model of "other" formation, which argues that how a group of people is represented in film can play a determining role in how those people are perceived and treated socially. Such a broad assumption is useful in that it allows for examination of the interrelationship of the filmic representation of the black female's sexual imagery, its cultural meanings, and its ramification for sexual violence against black women, as well as its implications for the treatment of black female rape victims within the criminal justice system. I posit that how these women are perceived in the culture, particularly by criminal justice officials, is directly linked largely to how black women are sexually positioned in film, which may well result in their becoming more vulnerable to sexual assaults and less likely to be believed when so victimized. The filmic coding of the black female subject as "oversexed" is so commonplace that when, in reality, they are sexually assaulted, these women are not taken seriously, since viewers' perceptions about black female sexuality as depicted on-screen become fused with viewers' perceptions of black women in reality. As Hooks (1995) so aptly puts it, "contemporary audiences . . . are socialized to believe... sexist representations of the black female . . . as authentic" (27).

Viewers, I argue, tend toward an unmediated, "real-world" belief, and because film is a major way that America looks at itself by reflecting the values and perceptions of the dominant culture (Jowett & Linton 1980), the media's role cannot summarily be dismissed. If we minimize the media's role in helping to shape criminal justice officials' perceptions of those they serve, we are neglecting an important part of the critical discourse about the meaning and influence of the film medium in contemporary American institutions, including the criminal justice system. The central concern of this chapter, then, is showing how, through a process of deductive reasoning, filmic images of black female sexuality contribute to their sexual victimization and influence the criminal justice system's handling of these women's cases as rape victims. My purpose is twofold: to locate the black female subject in film by examining some of the specific ways in which she is sexually constructed and to link her filmic sexual construction to her cultural status, while simultaneously interweaving discussions of the implications for the treatment of black female rape victims within the criminal justice system.

THE FILMIC BLACK FEMALE

Historically, a variety of filmic stereotypes have been attributed to the black female subject, among them the "mammy," "Aunt Jemima," "Sapphire," "welfare queen," "tragic mulatto," "promiscuous bad girl" (Bogle 1973; Mapp 1972; Davis 1981; Gilkes 1983; Hooks 1981; Tong 1984; Jewell 1992; Painter 1992). While a number of these stereotypes seem to have decreased, in large part because black women have joined the mainstream workforce, many as professionals, the image of the "promiscuous" black woman has persisted.

Critics have voiced much concern about the "use" of the black female's filmic sexual imagery, which some have characterized as "functional" (Jones 1992) and others as "routine" (Guerrero 1993). So routine, in fact, is the use of this extreme sexual imagery that it appears to have replaced the "mammy" image that was so pervasive prior to the 1960s and that was a powerful cultural stronghold for long afterward (Gates 1989).

This oversexed black female subject is blatantly depicted in the film *She's Gotta Have It*. The central character, the highly sexually charged Nola Darling, is presented as having consciously and deliberately chosen to have simultaneous, ongoing sexual friendships with three separate men, each of whom knows about the others. Nola's decision is made not because she is a prostitute or a drug addict; rather, her decision is based solely on the fact that, as she proudly tells viewers, she "loves sex." Accordingly, she sees nothing untoward about her promiscuous conduct.

Nola's filmic coding quickly becomes "functional," working to cement the idea that black women are "sexually depraved and permissive," as Hooks (1981) argues, and "chronic[ally] promiscu[ous]," as Davis (1981) claims. Thus, when the lovesick Jamie (one of Nola's lovers) brutally rapes Nola for refusing to marry him, viewers are seduced into blaming Nola for the rape. Blame functions on several levels: first, Nola's symbolic representation as morally bankrupt adds to the "realism" of the film by assigning what Jones (1992: 96) calls "an accusatory space" to the female subject; second, Nola's refusal to conform to mainstream social mores by submitting to marriage is, on the emotional level, felt to be inimical to the institution of marriage and thus to family values; third, Nola's response to the rape further solidifies belief in the myth of the strong, "oversexed" black woman, for Nola seems unmoved and unharmed by the act of the rape; fourth, Nola's response to her rapist makes her doubly complicit in the assault because her casual response sends the message that black women are prone to such "sexual excess" that even rape is innocuous to them, and, as a result, seeking police intervention is never a consideration. Because Nola is coded as promiscuous, is positioned as treating the rape lightly, and is never seen in the act of seeking help, viewers are left with the sense that Nola deserves her fate. For given her conduct, to cry rape would be oxymoronic. By extension, all such women who behave in this manner are then felt to be deserving of a similar fate. Nola's characterizations seem to lend support to LaFree et al.'s (1985) contention that "stereotypes" influence biased attitude and treatment against black female victims of rape. *She's Gotta Have It*, thus, portrays black female sexuality as out of control, which carries a price, for rape and its attending blame become by-products of the plot's resolution.

Seemingly a subtler version of Nola's construct is reproduced in another film, *Lethal Weapon*. Its subtlety, in fact, makes it most appealing and, therefore, equally damaging. Here, the daughter of the black costar, Glover, develops a crush on the white protagonist, Gibson. Visual strategies used are close-ups of the daughter's eye movements and various facial expressions—dilated eyes that speak of lust and that follow Gibson's every move, intermittent biting of her lower lip while lowering her eyelids, and broad grins directed at him. But differences abound, for police detective Gibson is her father's partner and nearly 20 years her senior. Were it not for a historically potent memory, viewers might simply satisfy themselves with the whimsical fact that a young woman has experienced an unrequited crush on a male nearly twice her age. Instead, we are reminded of an even greater difference. The film mirrors the racial issue and its cultural meanings. Laplanche (1976) suggests that race is memory that, helps shape who we are. Thus, Jones (1993: 253) points to the daughter's positioning in *Lethal Weapon* to argue that there is a subtext to the crush: "The rationalization of the historic sexual abuse and exploitation of the black woman in America by white men, which has . . . controlled the imaging of black women in American film from its inception. By initiating sexual contact with the white male, the black temptress relinquishes all rights to, or claims for protection."

The subtext is twofold: it parallels the way middle-class America views black women, and it reinforces the view that these women are responsible for their own victimization. So when the daughter is kidnapped by a murderous group, the sudden, inexplicable, near-pornographic context within which her body is framed strikes a chord, and we wonder if this positioning is not the daughter's punishment for having earlier tried to initiate sexual contact with the white male (Gibson), indeed, with white males, generally. Viewers recall that not only is the daughter positioned as having been the sexual aggressor with the white male, but that she is also coded as dating the blond, blue-eyed suitor who is killed later in the film. At the very least, her choices are suspect. Why is such a young black girl coded as being interested only in white men, and, at least in one case, why so sexually aggressive?

Framed, thus, the daughter's seemingly innocuous imaging in *Lethal Weapon* is used, in a subtle manner, to sell the prevailing idea that black women are endowed with heightened sexuality, an idea that must be reinforced, because black women have gained ground in negating the "mammy" image by becoming educated. The negative sexual image, however, has had more currency because education does not exclude one from being a slut, and because negative sexual conduct (or the appearance thereof) is more difficult to disprove, so that even educated black women who file claims of rape are likely not to be believed by police because of the pervasiveness of the stereotype. When combined with the film's relentless depiction of black women as "sexual gratifiers," we see how this negative image has become seared in the minds of the collective unconscious.

Culturally, then, black women seem caught in an intractable position where two disparate types of black women emerge generally: the prude and the slut. On one hand, many black women, in an attempt to counter the negative sexual image, lead lives of strict morality or, worse, repressed sexuality (Hooks 1995). Neither option leads to fulfilled lives, and both deny the self. On the other hand, some black women attempt to defy the negative sexual image by engaging in exaggerated, harmful, and/or illegal sexual conduct, either by engaging in loose sex without emotional attachment (an immoral act) or by engaging in sex for profit (a criminal act).

Whether prude, slut, or in-between, black women appear to have little protection from the negative sexual image assigned to them. Jones' assertion that the daughter in *Lethal Weapon* has ceded claims for protection is no small point, because the film positions the daughter as having willfully surrendered and unabashedly forfeited rights to any protection. It is obvious that if one is highly sexually charged, and if one initiates sexual contact with one's historic oppressor, one can hardly expect to be protected from that oppressor's negative perception of one. The merging of "real life" and film then occasions a small leap on viewers' part to continue to devalue black women on grounds of moral inadequacy.

But before I proceed too far, it would be wise to note here that the foregoing discussion in no way suggests that white female subjects are not likewise coded in film as sex objects. Indeed, there are enough examples to which one can point, Sharon Stone being not the least of these. Rather, white female subjects are afforded a wider range of characterizations to which they can be culturally linked. But surely the most patently clear fact about black women's present situation, given their minuscule percentage of the population—about 6 1/2 percent—and their limited filmic roles, is that their persistent coding in film as sign of the whore (Guerrero 1993) does not allow them to be culturally linked with much else. Never mind that, in reality, this "sexually loose" black female is in the minority. Film's preoccupation with, and depiction of, this negative sexual image to the near exclusion of other images is speciously unrelenting.

What I want to stress here is that it is in the coalescence of two major cultural factors that images about black women are almost always denigrating. First is the sociosexual iconography in American culture, where the black woman has traditionally been cast as "whore" to the white woman's "madonna" (Painter 1992), itself a powerful cultural stronghold; second is the nature of film itself, with its allegorical potential for persuasiveness (Boyum 1985), which has worked to cement the madonna/whore duality. Precisely because film is a visual medium, which demands that viewers respond only to what is seen, film's ability to enunciate beliefs, even erroneous beliefs, feeds into, and perpetuates, the stereotype.

But audiences do not view images in a vacuum. Indeed, White (1983: 282) suggests that audiences assign meanings to images out of the reservoir of their own experiences. Presumably, those experiences are, in large part, culture-specific, so that, whatever the racial or ethnic group to which one belongs (e.g., black and white), Americans are organized around a broad cultural experience, media viewing being only one contributor. When we add to the cultural mix the myth, starting in slavery, that black women are sexually promiscuous (Stampp 1953; Jordan 1968), we see how deeply the social reservoir of beliefs can run. Viewers need not even give voice to their belief in the negative myth, because they have been so saturated with images of this myth and have grown so comfortable with it that the belief seems almost as natural as breathing. Filmic visuals stimulate acceptance, not contemplative thinking.

If we look again at the images in *Lethal Weapon* of the daughter and Gibson, we see a subtext that could easily be overlooked. Why, for example, is the daughter not coded as a romantic subject? The film seduces viewers on the visual level into wanting Gibson and the daughter to sleep together, while simultaneously dismissing the possibility of the two ever exploring a serious relationship. Bogle (1973) and Leab (1975) have already pointed to the connection between race and sex in film, the case being reiterated by Hooks (1981: 65) for the hundredth time when she writes that "whites condone interracial relationships between black women and white men only in the context of degrading sex." The positioning of the daughter in an aggressively explicit, sexual role, rather than in a soft, romantic one, precludes their developing a loving union. Thus framed, the daughter becomes sexually suspect and, like Nola in *She's Gotta Have It,* must be punished.

FILM'S SOCIAL IMPACT ON BLACK WOMEN

Applying Hall's (1988) model (discussed earlier) to how viewers interpret filmic images of the black female subject, I surveyed 88 of my criminal justice students, all of whom aspire to be police officers, lawyers, corrections officers, and so on , to see their responses to the female in the film, *She's Gotta Have It.*

The students' career interests are important because their views of black women could eventually determine how the students, in their professions, respond to these women. No student had seen the film, so I presented them with a still shot from the film. The still depicts a black female subject who is sitting up in bed, wearing a shirt that is buttoned up past her breast area. The bedsheet snugly hugs her lower half. Lying propped up on one shoulder and facing her is a black male, whose chest area is uncovered. They appear to be engaged in conversation.

I asked the students to speculate on the female's role in the film. Most thought she was his lover; others believed her to be his sex toy, that is, that, the two had no relationship outside sex. Interestingly, not one student thought that the female was his wife. Another question asked, "Does the female in this image suggest anything to you about her?" Sixty-three students felt that she had just had sex with the male but was dissatisfied with his performance; 20 students felt she was denying him sex to get what she wanted; while only 5 students felt that he wanted sex but she did not, so they were fighting, and not one suggested that he had been dissatisfied with her sexual performance.

In discussing the responses, I wanted to learn why most students had felt that the female had *had* sex with the male, since, presumably, two people could be in bed without benefit of sexual contact. The most telling responses concerned the "black woman as oversexed" image so prominent in films. One black male said: "Sisters are always gettin' down. In MTV, whew! I mean, all you see is black girls' butts in yo' face." Boisterous laughter followed this. "Getting down?" I asked. A Latino young man chimed in: "I don' mean to be disrespec'ful or nothin' professor (apparently he was mindful of my being a black woman), but, you know, gettin' down, kickin' it, you know? That's the way it is! Black girls be doin' it or talkin' 'bout it. It's all you see in the movies, on TV—Like the brother said, hey! It's all over. They be gettin' down! Know what I'm sayin'?" Again, much laughter accompanied by a slapping of hands and general fanfare.

Some female students defended women, arguing that sex is what sells, and it is really the media that are at fault. Other females retorted that women should refuse the roles, while not recognizing that they themselves, had, viewed the female subject in sexual terms. I finally asked the male students the following: "Do you then see black girls as sexually loose?" Vehemently denying that they did, many betrayed their denials by saying, "nah, but in the clubs—well, black girls are just, you know—hot!!" Again, hysterical laughter followed.

Now, admittedly, this was not a scientific survey. Still, it was clear to me that the survey and discussion by these criminal justice students who would someday become society's protector suggested that films influence viewers' negative attitudes about black women as extreme sexual beings. Arguably, even without film's input, black women's sexual history in the United States during and since slavery is a potent part of the mix creating the image. Yet, given the powerful medium that is film, it is dubious that American culture would persist in holding negative attitudes about these women as "oversexed" if that image was not reinforced in film. Let us not minimize the fact that films feature black female characters not only as "hypersexed" but also as bringing on their own victimization, as seen in such films as *She's Gotta Have It, The Bodyguard, New Jack City*, and a host of other such films.

One of the cultural impacts resulting from belief in these filmic portrayals of black women might be seen in actual sexual assaults against these women culturally. Painter (1992: 209–210) asserts that the oversexed black woman is "still taken at face value . . .She not only connotes sex . . . but . . . is assumed to be the instigator of sex . . . and appears nearly as often as black women are to be found in . . . movies of the 1980s and 1990s. Painter observes, further, that the idea of black women as victims of rape "hasn't yet penetrated the American mind, [since] the belief persists that black women are always ready for sex and as a consequence, cannot be raped" (211–212).

Yet, the evidence points to just the opposite, for the overall statistics on rape for black and white women are virtually equal. The United States Bureau of Justice Statistics (1994a: 232–233) reports that black women are raped at a rate of 4.7 per 1,000 compared to a rate of 4.0 per 1,000 for white women; a rate of 2.1 per 1,000 for Hispanics; and a rate of 2.3 per 1,000 for non-Hispanics. When broken down by age, however, black females between the ages of 12 and 15 are almost twice as likely to be victims of rape than whites of the same age. Here, black females are raped at a rate of 7.3 per 1,000 versus a rate of 3.8 per 1,000 for white females. The numbers equalize as both groups get older: 20–24-year-old black females are raped at a rate of 6.1 per 1,000, while white females of the same age are raped at a rate of 5.8 per 1,000; 35–49-year-old black females are raped at a rate of 2.5 per 1,000, with a rate of 1.6 per 1,000 for white females in the same age group. However, the decrease in rape rates is slower among black women than among white women (234).

The most recent data from the Bureau of Justice Statistics (1996) report even greater differentials for black female rape victims over the 1994 reports. Here, these females are raped at a rate of 4.5 per 1,000 versus a rate of 3.5 per 1,000 for white women (212), which represents a .3 percent increase in rapes for black women above the 1994 reports. When broken down by age, again, black females were more than likely to be victims of rape than their white counterparts: black women 16–19 were raped at a rate of 7.8 per 1,000 compared to a rate of 4.8 per 1,000 for white females of the same age; 20–24-year-old black females were raped at a rate of 8.8 per 1,000 while white females in the same age group were raped at a rate of 4.0 per 1,000. As with the 1994 reports, the numbers tended to equalize as both groups got older, with white females maintaining a slight edge in the 25–34 age group: 3.0 per 1,000 versus 2.6 per 1,000 (213).

While overall, black women's risk of being raped appears almost equal to that of white women's, more black women report being afraid of becoming victims of rape. A 1993 National Gallop poll measured women's fear of being raped or sexually assaulted and found that while 13 percent of white females reported worrying "very frequently," the number of black females who reported worrying "very frequently" was 22 percent (BJS 1994b: 166).

What the numbers suggest is that black women are victims of rape just as often as are white women and, in some cases, more frequently than other groups, yet rarely do we hear news reports of black women's sexual victimization. Similarly, more black women seem to fear becoming victims of rape. Still the cultural perception persists that these women are "oversexed" and, thus, not "susceptible to rape."

As a result, many black women suffer silently as victims of sexual abuse. Henriques (1995: 76–77) notes that black women know that they "cannot depend on the criminal justice system to protect them" or to dispense justice on their behalf since those who do report their victimization to police find that they are "judged by a different standard of conduct." It seems that the police and other criminal justice officials share the view of the culture, and, indeed, why would they not, since they belong to the culture? Bohmer (1974), for example, in her study, found, that among judges, there was a differential with respect to race in how these judges perceived and, therefore, judged the credibility of black female rape victims. In his study, LaFree (1980), too, reports that black women are less likely to have their rape cases pleaded or to have their cases result in guilty verdicts, suggesting that, like judges, prosecutors and jurors also lack confidence in the veracity of black female rape victims. LaFree (1980) attributes bias in rape cases to typification in the processing decisions of criminal justice officials about race.

These findings suggest that lack of confidence in black women's credibility regarding claims of rape appears to be a common theme throughout the criminal justice system. What seems to affirm this lack of confidence is belief in the myth of black female promiscuity. The image of the promiscuous black woman, both culturally and in film, has so permeated the cultural unconscious that, in turn, it has polluted the very institution that was designed to protect victims of rape crimes. As a result, the unspoken, yet "official," attitudes work against protection of black female rape victims to the point that Howard (1988), Richie (1996), and others have argued that black women are far less likely than other women to seek or receive help from criminal justice officials. It seems that, in matters of rape, "officials" have different behavioral expectations of black females than they have for other women (LaFave 1965; Smart 1976; Black 1980; Karmen 1982; Visher 1983), and less official protection is the consequence for black women.

Should the reader retain skepticism about film's influence in shaping viewers' perceptions or its contribution to sexual violence against women generally, he or she might take note of the results of a 1994 Harris Poll in which Americans were asked whether they thought movies contributed "a lot," "a little," or "not at all" to crimes of rape and sexual assaults. (1994c) Sixty-one percent of whites, 55 percent of blacks, and 58 percent of Hispanics said they thought that movies, more so than television, contributed "a lot" to these crimes. (160) This is not to suggest that films cause rape; but their depiction of women, particularly black women, as routine, easily accessible commodities clearly may encourage sexual violence against women generally. Minimally, films set a cultural tone about how women and their sexuality ought to be viewed, which then filters down to the viewing audience, where a certain legitimacy is achieved. Black women, it seems, reap the sting of this cultural tone, both in terms of not being believed by criminal justice officials when these women are sexually assaulted and in terms of being vulnerable to sexual assaults.

Another cultural impact that can be linked to film's negative portrayals of black women as "oversexed" is to be found in the language used to refer to these women in certain pockets of American society. As part of the aesthetics of films since the 1980s, rap music's lyrics use graphic language, such as "gang-bangin' 'ho" and "ghetto-bitch" to refer to black women, which then becomes part of the acceptable social jargon among certain groups. Much public debate has centered around the impact of rap's lyrics on the black female. Williams (1992: 168) notes that rap music: "feeds into, and intensifies the syndrome of early and promiscuous sex that has resulted in more than a 1/4 of all babies born in the black community being born to unwed mothers, most of whom are under the age of 18." It becomes clear that these women are being exploited sexually and then abandoned. The cost to the black community includes, among other factors, fractured families. The U.S. Department of Commerce (1992) reports that in 78 percent of poor black families, women head those households. Dr. H. Foster (1996), former adviser to the Clinton administration on teen pregnancy reduction, estimated that approximately 30 percent of the $25 billion spent on teen pregnancies in 1996 was spent on pregnancies in the inner cities. Foster contends that the media titillate teens with sexual images that contribute to these pregnancies. What of the cost to the girls personally? Most can expect to lead shattered lives of poverty, hopelessness, and degradation (Rothenberg 1988; Wallace 1992; Staples & Johnson 1993).

We have come to the uncomfortable stage of this discussion where we might be inclined to wish it away. We can pretend that negative attitudes about black women and sex in both film and the culture do not exist, or we can confront the issue head-on in our own lives and in our classrooms. To be sure, the problem is complex, yet we can begin to chip away at the negative attitudes by becoming critical viewers of the films we watch, by becoming critical of how we watch, and by teaching our students to be critical media consumers. More significantly, we can begin to adopt an ideology of "other valuation." For my purposes here, an ideology of "other valuation" involves our attempt consciously to generate a sense of agency where affirmation of our humanity, that is, self-love, leads to love of others through a process of empathy. When we place ourselves in another's situation, we come to "see" and feel as that other might. Where lack of empathy strips us of our humanity, embracing empathy moves us back toward that humanity.

Henriques (1995: 78) cautions us, however, that blacks and whites engage in "a charade of empathy" that limits and distorts communication, yet this charade does not minimize the fact that race is an issue that intrudes into every level of relationship between blacks and whites in America.

Such intrusion can be found in our cultural products, and, regrettably, the confluence of passive-viewer receptivity and the charade of empathy have contributed to undermining the triumph of an ideology of "other valuation." Yet all we need do to arrive at a place of empathy is to live consciously to "see" consciously. If criminal justice educators want to increase their students' sense of social justice and if educators want to help re-create students' occupational lives so students can honor the social contract guaranteed to all citizens, then educators must help students understand how media images control the form and direction of information and how such control impacts learners' cognitive behaviors, personal beliefs, and social relations regarding those they serve.

Toward that end, criminal justice educators can teach their students that when students are confronted with sexual images of a black female subject in a film, they might ask themselves, Is that black female subject's sexual coding central to the plot? If not, why is she coded in that manner? Does my passive acceptance of that coding contribute in any way to the perpetuation of the negative image and, by extension, to *how* I then subconsciously view and treat black women in reality, both professionally and personally? These are tough questions and, uncomfortable ones. But they are important questions to criminal justice students because their attitudes toward black women clearly may influence how they handle cases of sexual abuse among these women. Therefore, we must begin to challenge the way we "see," if we are ever to make any inroad.

It was both interesting and telling to note that the white male students in the class discussion about the black female in the still picture from the film, *She's Gotta Have It* had very little to say. But their joining in, the slapping of hands and in the boisterous laughter that erupted when negative attitudes were voiced about black women may have spoken volumes about *their* attitudes as well.

Do films help shape viewers' attitudes about black women as oversexed? Do these attitudes then influence how the criminal justice system views and treats these women culturally? If the answers to both questions are important to criminal justice officials and educators alike, do they have any options but to help students "see" films—and black women—through lenses set on justice occasioned by "empathy" rather than blame? Or is the consensus that the "ghetto bitches," the Nolas, deserve to be judged by a different standard of conduct?

REFERENCES

Albonetti, C. (1987). "Prosecutorial Discretion: The Effects of Uncertainty." *Law and Society Review* 21: 291–313.

Baker, Jr., H. (1993). "Spike Lee and the Commerce of Culture." In M. Diawara (ed.), *Black American Cinema* 154–176. New York: Routledge.

Bandura, A. (1986). *Social Foundations of Thought and Action: A Social Cognition Theory.* Englewood Cliffs, NJ: Prentice-Hall.

———. (1977). *Social Learning Theory.* Englewood Cliffs, NJ: Prentice-Hall.

Black, D. (1980). *The Manners and Customs of the Police.* New York: Academic Press.

Bogle, D. (1973). *Toms, Coons, Mulattoes, Mammies, and Bucks.* New York: Viking Press.

Bohmer, C. (1974). "Judicial Attitudes toward Rape Victims." *Judicature* 57: 303–307.

Boorstin, D. J. (1977). *The Image: A Guide to Pseudo-Events in America.* New York: Atheneum.

Boyum, J. (1985). *Double Exposure: Fiction into Film.* New York: New American Library.

Bratton, W. (1995). "Great Expectations: How Increasing Expectations for Police Departments Can Lead to a Decrease in Crime." Paper presented to the *National Institute of Justice Policing Institute,* "Measuring What Matters" Conference,

Washington, DC.

Brownmiller, S. (1975). *Against Our Will: Women & Rape.* New York: Simon & Schuster.

Bureau of Justice Statistics. (1996). Personal Victimization in the United States. Washington, DC: U.S. Department of Justice.

———. (1994a). *Criminal Victimization in the United States,* 1993. Washington, DC: U.S. Department of Justice, 1995, 232–234.

———. (1994b). *Respondents' Fear of Being Victimized,* December, 1993. Office of Justice Programs.

———. (1994c). *Attitudes Toward Whether Selected Influences Contribute to Violence.* Washington, DC: U.S. Department of Justice.

Caringella-McDonald, S. (1988). "Marxist and Feminist Interpretations on the Aftermath of Rape Reform." *Contemporary Crises* 12: 125–144.

Cooper, J. L. (1980). *The Police and the Ghetto.* Port Washington: Associated Faculty Press.

Davis, A. Y. (1981). "Rape, Racism, and the Myth of the Black Rapist." *Women, Race and Class* 172–201. New York: Vintage Books-A Division of Random House.

DeLauretis, T. (1984). *Alice Doesn't: Feminism, Semiotics, Cinema.* Bloomington: Indiana University Press.

Douglas, S. (1995). "Violence in TV News Promotes Violence against Women." In D. Bender, B. Leone, K. DeKoster, S. Barbour, and C. Wekesser (eds.), *Violence in the Media: Current Controversies* 28–30. San Diego: Greenhaven.

Erikson, E. H. (1978). Childhood and Society. 2d ed. New York: W. W. Norton.

Estrich, S. (1987). *Real Rape.* Cambridge: Harvard University Press.

Fairstein, L. (1993). Sexual Violence: Our War against Rape. New York: Morrow.

Foster, H. (1996). "Teen Pregnancies." In *Montel Williams Show.* New York:Fox Network.

Frohmann, L. (1991). "Discrediting Victims' Allegations of Sexual Assault: Prosecutorial Accounts of Case Rejections." *Social Problems* 38: 213–226.

Gates, H. L., Jr. (1989). "TV's Black World Turns—but Stays Unreal." *New York Times,* November 12, II (1).

Gerbner, G. (1982). "Television and Role Socializations: An Overview." In D. Pearl et al. (eds.), *Television and Behavior: Ten Years of Scientific Progress and Implications for the Eighties* 1. Washington, DC: U.S. Government Printing Office.

Gerbner, G., L. Gross, M. Morgan, and N. Signorielli. (1986). "Living with Television: The Dynamics of the Cultivation Process." In J. Bryant and D. Zillman (eds.), *Perspectives on Media Effects* 17–40. Hillsdale, NJ: Lawrence Erlbaum Associates.

Gilkes, C. T. (1983). "From Slavery to Social Welfare: Racism and the Control of Black Women (1981)." In A. Swerdlow and H. Leesinger (eds.), *Class, Race and Sex: The Dynamics of Control* 288–300. Bernard College Women's Center, Boston: G. K. Hall.

Guerrero, E. (1993). "The Black Image in Protective Custody: Hollywood's Biracial Buddy Films of the Eighties." In M. Diawara (ed.), *Black American Cinema* 237–246. New York: Routledge.

Hall, S. (1988). "New Ethnicities." In K. Mercer (ed.), *Black Film/British Cinema,* ICA Document 7 27–3). London: Institute of Contemporary Arts.

Happerle, W. (1985). "Women Victims in the Criminal Justice System." In I. Moyer (ed.), *The Changing Role of Women in the Criminal Justice System* 165–79. Prospect Heights, IL: Waveland.

Haskell, M. (1973). *From Reverence to Rape: The Treatment of Women in the Movies.*

2d ed. Chicago: University of Chicago Press.

Henriques, Z. W. (1995). "African-American Women: The Oppressive Intersection of Gender, Race and Class." *Women and Criminal Justice* 7(1): 67–78.

Hooks, B. (1995). "Beyond a Politics of Shape." *Z Magazine* 26–28.

———. (1992). *Black Looks: Race and Representation. Boston*: South End Press.

———. (1981). *Ain't I a Woman: Black Women and Feminism. Boston*, MA: South End Press.

Howard, J. (1988). "A Structural Approach to Sexual Attitudes: Interracial Patterns in Adolescents' Judgments about Sexual Intimacy." *Sociological Perspectives* 31(1): 88–121.

Jewell, K. S. (1992). *From Mammy to Ms. America and Beyond: Cultural Images and the Shaping of US Social Policy*. New York: Routledge.

Jones, J. (1993). "The Construction of Black Sexuality: Towards Normalizing the Black Cinematic Experience." In M. Diawara (ed.), *Black American Cinema* 247–256. New York: Routledge.

———. (1992). "The Accusatory Space." In G. Dent (ed.), *Black Popular Culture* [A project by Michele Wallace] 95–98. Seattle: Bay Press.

Jordan, W. D. (1968). *White Over Black: American Attitudes Towards the Negro* (1950-1812). Chapel Hill, NC: University of North Carolina Press.

Jowett, G. and J. M. Linton. (1980). *Movies as Mass Communication. Beverly Hills*: Sage.

Karmen, A. (1982). "Introduction, Women Victims of Crime." In B. R. Price and N. J. Sokoloff (eds.), *The Criminal Justice System and Women* 185–201. New York: Clark Boardman.

Kennedy, L. (1992). The Body in Question." In G. Dent (ed.), *Black Popular Culture* [A project by Michele Wallace] 106–111. Seattle: Bay Press.

Kerstetter, W. (1990). Gateway to justice: Police and Prosecutorial Response to Sexual Assaults against Women." *Criminology* 81: 267–313.

LaFave, W. (1965). *Arrest: The Decision to Take a Suspect into Custody*. Boston: Little, Brown.

LaFree, G. (1989). *Rape and Criminal Justice: The Social Construction of Sexual Assault*. Belmont, CA: Wadsworth.

———. (1980b). "Variables Affecting Guilty Pleas and Convictions in Rape Cases: Toward a Social Theory of Rape Processing." *Social Forces* 58(3): 833–850.

LaFree, G., B. Reskin, and C. Visher. (1985). "Jurors' Responses to Victims' Behavior and Legal Issues in Sexual Assault Trials." *Social Problems* 32(4): 389–407.

Laplanche, J. (1976). *Life and Death in Psychoanalysis*. Baltimore: John Hopkins University Press.

Leab, D. J. (1975). *From Sambo to Superspade: The Black Experience in Motion Pictures*. Boston: Houghton Mifflin.

Lizotte, A. J. (1985). "The Uniqueness of Rape: Reporting Assaultive Violence to the Police." *Crime and Delinquency* 31: 169–190.

Loh, W. (1980). "The Impact of Common Law and Reform Rape Statutes on Prosecution: An Empirical Study." *Washington Law Review* 55: 543–625.

McLuhan, M. (1964). *Understanding Media*. 2d ed. New York: New American Library.

Mead, G. H. (1934). *Mind, Self and Society*. Chicago: University of Chicago Press.

Meyrowitz, J. (1985). *No Sense of Place*. New York: Oxford University Press.

Painter, N. I. (1992). "*Hill, Thomas, and the Use of Racial Stereotype*." In T. Morrison (ed.), *Race-ing Justice, En-gendering Power* 201–214. New York: Pantheon Books.

Parks, S. (1995). "Seeing through Our Own Eyes." *Black Film Review* 8(2): 14–15.

Pinkney, A. (1969). *Black Americans.* Englewood Cliffs, NJ: Prentice-Hall.

Postman, N. (1979). *Teaching as a Conserving Activity.* New York: Delacorte Press.

———. (1985). *Amusing Ourselves to Death.* New York: Viking.

Richie, B. E. (1996). *Compelled to Crime: The Gender Entrapment of Battered Black Women.* New York: Routledge.

Rosen, M. (1973). *Popcorn Venus: Movies and the American Dream.* New York: Coward, McCann, and Geoghigan.

Rothenberg, P. S. (1988). "The Feminization of Poverty." In the Women's Agenda Working Group for the Institute of Policy Studies, *Racism and Sexism: Integrated Study* 80–84. New York: St. Martin's Press.

Smart, C. (1976). *Women, Crime & Criminology.* Boston: Rutledge & Kegan Paul.

Spears, J. W. and C. C. Spohn. (1997). "The Effect of Evidence Factors and Victim Characteristics on Prosecutors' Charging Decisions in Sexual Assault Cases." *Justice Quarterly* 14(3): 501–524.

Spohn, C. and J. Horney. (1992). *Rape Law Reform: A Grassroots Revolution and Its Impact.* New York: Plenum.

Stampp, K. M. (1953). *The Peculiar Institution.* New York: Knopf.

Stanko, E. (1988). "The Impact of Victim Assessment on Prosecutors' Screening Decisions: The Case of the New York County District Attorney's Office." In G. Cole (ed.), *Criminal Justice: Law and Politics* 169–180. Pacific Grove, CA: Brooks/Cole.

———. (1985). *Intimate Intrusions.* London: Routledge.

Staples, R. and L. B. Johnson. (1993). *Black Families at the Crossroads.* San Francisco, CA: Jossey-Bass.

Tong, R. (1984). *Women, Sex and the Law.* New Jersey: Rowman and Allenheld.

Uniform Crime Reports. (1996). *Crime Index Total, 1996.* Washington, DC: U.S. Government Printing Office.

University of Pennsylvania. (1968) "Police Discretion and the Judgment That a Crime Has Been Committed: Rape in Philadelphia." *University of Pennsylvania Law Review* 117: 227–238.

U.S. Department of Commerce. (1992). *Money, Income of Household, Family and Persons in the United States, 1991.* Washington, DC: U.S. Government Printing Office.

Visher, C. (1983). "Gender, Police Arrest Decisions, and Notions of Chivalry." *Criminology* 21: 5–28.

Wallace, M. (1992). "Boyz N the Hood and Jungle Fever." In G. Dent (ed.), *Black Popular Culture* [A project by M. Wallace] 123–131. Seattle: Bay Press.

White, R. A. (1983). "Mass Communication and Culture: Transition to a New Paradigm." *Journal of Communications* 33: 279–301.

Williams, J. F. and K. A. Holmes. (1981). *The Second Assault: Rape and Public Attitudes.* Westport, CT: Greenwood.

Williams, L. S. (1985). "The Classic Rape: When Do Victims Report?" *Social Problems* 31: 459–467.

Williams, S. A. (1992). "Two Words on Music: Black Community." In G. Dent (ed.), *Black Popular Culture* [A project by Michele Wallace] 164–172. Seattle: Bay Press.

Willis, E. (1994). "Villains and Victims." *Salmagundi* 101–102, 68–78.

Wolfenstein, M. and N. Leites. (1950). *Movies: A Psychological Study.* Glencoe, IL: Free Press.

Part IV

Racial Dimensions of Punishment and Delinquency

Chapter 15

The Significance of Race in the Use of Restitution

Evelyn Gilbert

INTRODUCTION

Compensating the victim of a crime is an ancient concept found in the Code of Hammurabi, which dates back to 1700 B.C. requiring an offender to pay the victim for an injury sustained rests on the biblical authority of lex talionis. Reparation was the manifest objective of punishment under these systems of justice. The reparation established proportionality between the offender's punishment and the victim's losses. That is, the punishment was made analogous to the harm inflicted. Under a reparative system, harm and injury were quantified, and punishment was measured in cash amounts. The main tenets of reparative justice are victim restoration and offender accountability. Restitution is the modern-day incarnation of these tenets (McCarthy & McCarthy 1991). However, the objective intended and the objective achieved with restitution are less evident today than in ancient times. Under the ancient systems, the victim was the central focus. Making the victim whole was the goal of punishment, and imposing economic sanctions established "proportionality between the offender's punishment and the victim's losses" (Klein 1997). Over time, however, the administration of justice and punishment changed so that the state replaced the victim as the injured party. Offender responsibility for victim harm was overshadowed and replaced with state responsibility for offender punishment. The justice system bestowed new punishments upon the offender—incapacitation, incarceration, and, finally, rehabilitation.

With each new punishment and objective, the "real" victim became more obscure, and the offender became more prominent in the administration of justice. No longer were punishments designed to restore the victim. Offender accountability to the victim disappeared. Each new punishment and goal also redefined the role of the offender. The offender was cast as a beneficiary of punishment. The central question in sentencing became, and continues to be, what can be done to and for the offender?

Beginning in the 1970s, restoration and reparation (Klein 1997) were reintroduced in the justice system. The introduction of victim compensation programs brought the "real" victim back to the administration of justice. Similarly, the reintroduction of restitution reestablished offender accountability to the victim. However, the existence of both victim compensation and restitution programs camouflages the goal of this punishment. It does not beg the question to ask the necessity of two different methods of repaying the victim for harm or injury sustained. Victim compensation programs are reparative and restorative in nature and fairly straightforward. In compensation programs crime victims receive payment from a pool of money maintained by the state. Offender accountability is less apparent in victim compensation programs. On the other hand, restitution programs are based on offender accountability, which is realized through the imposition of economic sanctions. Offender fulfillment of economic sanctions is necessary to compensate crime victims.

Victim reparation is guaranteed under compensation programs; it is not guaranteed under restitution programs. Compensation programs are funded by taxpayers and administered by the state. Under restitution, the offender pays the victim under court-administered arrangements. The willingness and ability of the offender to pay determine whether or not the victim receives reparation. Therefore, restitution seems superfluous and redundant, given the existence of victim compensation programs. Yet, the widespread use of restitution by state courts appears to have made restitution a permanent alternative sentence in the administration of justice.[1] Perhaps restitution's appeal does not lie in its manifest objective of victim reparation but in a latent objective yet to be identified.

Early research in this area is both descriptive (Hudson & Galaway 1974; Schneider, Reiter & Cleary 1977; Newton 1979; Read 1977, Schneider & Schneider 1979, 1980) and empirical (Landis, Mercer & Wolff 1969; Fogel, Galaway & Hudson 1972; Heinz, Galaway & Hudson 1976; Heide & Voorhis 1981). The findings from these early efforts suggest that victim reparation is the objective of restitution sentences. However, the victims in these early studies were business organizations. Typically, offenders were white and middle-class and were required to complete some form of symbolic service or community work. Monetary restitution was the exception, compelling an examination of why the court imposes monetary restitution as a sentence for offenders.

While the deterrent effect of severe punishment has been demonstrated for criminal offenders (Gibbs 1968; Gray & Martin 1969; Logan 1972), the literature is less forthcoming in supporting a deterrence goal of restitution. In fact, it is suggested that a morally acceptable use of economic sanctions is to deter. Unlawful behavior is diminished to the degree that costs levied upon the offender exceed the benefits of the criminal behavior. If the reduction is sufficiently high, unlawful conduct is diminished to an "efficient level."

Although economic sanctions impose costs on offenders, benefits may also accrue to the offender. Colson (1989) believes that "the deterrent potential of restitution lies in its benefit to the victim, offender, and community." For

McCarthy and McCarthy (1991), restitution is an official recognition of the victim's injury and right to equity. The victim's anticipation of recompense may induce a healing process and lessen the desire for retaliation. Restitution brings a degree of satisfaction and closure that is missing with the mere imprisonment of the offender (144). Similarly, restitution may have a self-healing effect on the offender. An offender who must work to pay a victim is forced to confront the consequences of the crime in a financial way. In so doing, the anxiety and rationalizations that sustain offending behavior are channeled into personal responsibility. Personal responsibility engendered in this manner may transfer discipline and performance standards to other aspects of the offender's lifestyle (143). The community benefits the most from restitution because of the decreased need to expend large sums of money to provide prison bed space (145).

The beneficiaries of the Restitution Pilot Project of Mississippi[2] are clearly identifiable, as is the objective of restitution. Offenders participating in the restitution project are required to work at a job to pay their victims for the value of property damaged or stolen. Half of the money earned by project participants went to satisfy restitution assessments. Consequently, victims and the community benefited from the economic sanctions imposed on offenders. The project participants retained 47 percent of their earnings, thus becoming beneficiaries of their own labor. Since two-thirds of the participants did not recidivate within one year of project completion, it is reasonable to conclude that deterrence is the objective achieved by the developers of the restitution project in Mississippi. Similarly, in the Minnesota program that operated between 1972 and 1976, the beneficiary was the community. Half the offenders completing the program fulfilled their restitution orders. Recidivism (6 percent) was uncommon among the offenders completing the program. Again, deterrence appears to be the objective of the restitution project in Minnesota.

The literature supports retribution (Eglash 1958; Newton 1976; Mueller 1955; Schafer 1974) or what Schafer (1970) refers to as punitive restitution. The imposition of monetary obligations beyond the cost of the crime is vindictive. States and the federal systems permit the addition of multiple expenses (e.g., medical, burial, loss-of-work, treatment) to restitution orders.[3] Mills (1992) has identified at least 26 penalty assessments, including attorney fees, supervision fees, court costs, fines and surcharges, child support, charitable donations, cash or surety bonds, and forfeitures. These add-on monetary sanctions do not go to the victim. Other monetary assessments usually benefit the agency supervising the offender (Parent 1990; Finn & Parent 1992) and as such may be considered punitive. Restitution comprising primarily add-on costs does not repay victims for injuries incurred. Add-on costs represent economic liens assessed by the criminal justice system. These costs literally tax the offender. The Georgia program is an example of punitive retribution. The residential program for probationers and parolees began in 1975 (Read 1977; Flowers 1977). Offenders remained in residence at the Restitution Center until restitution was made. Upon full payment of the restitution order, participants were discharged from the program and transferred to the probation/parole authority. Under the supervision of the probation/parole authority, offenders completed the remainder of their sentence. After one year of operation, the program had collected a little more than $1 million from program participants. Only 6 percent of this money was disbursed to victims. Almost 80 percent of the offenders' earnings was returned to the correctional authority as supervision fees and program costs; offenders kept less than 20 percent of their earnings. Clearly, this type of restitution is retributive.

While monetary payments from the offender to the victim is a form of restitution that restores the victim (McCarthy & McCarthy 1991), monetary payments to agents of the state exact just deserts from the offender. This just deserts or punitive objective is most evident when restitution programs exist alongside victim compensation programs and in restitution programs that impose economic sanctions and require offenders to reside in special facilities until the sanction is discharged. Using the programs in Georgia, Minnesota, and Mississippi as representative restitution programs, several observations may be made about the underlying objective. First, property offenders predominate in restitution programs (McCarty & McCarthy 1991). It appears that type of crime is a determinant of whether just deserts, victim restoration, or deterrence is the goal. While there are indications that punitive restitution is reserved for property offenders, it does not follow that reparative restitution is the domain of violent offenders. Second, restitution may be symbolic, that is, community work, service, or economic sanctions. Courts have at their disposal a cadre of non economic sanctions. A tendency to impose economic sanctions beyond that required to restore the victim (i.e., add-on) suggests that restitution is used against the offender.

Finally, the philosophy of restitution is that "crime is a violation of one person by another, rather than against the state" (Galaway & Hudson 1996). Yet, the majority of money paid in restitution by property offenders does not go to the owners of the lost property, nor do offenders retain most of the income they earn while participating in restitution programs. Rather, the correctional authority receives the lion's share of the money paid by restitution offenders. These observations support retribution as a latent objective of restitution and raise a very important question, Are offense or offender factors predictive of punitive restitution? This study addresses this question by examining data from a residential restitution program. The add-on monetary sanctions imposed on participants suggest a punitive objective of restitution programs.

METHODOLOGY

Site

Alabama's first restitution program opened May 1980 in Montgomery County. Authorized to provide probation supervision to male offenders referred from the criminal court, the restitution center began housing and supervising family court referrals four months after opening its doors (family court referrals were released from the restitution center when they paid the amount of money ordered by the court). Probationers were either ordered by the court to reside at the restitution center for a specific period of time as a condition of probation or as a prerequisite to a suspended sentence. In those cases in which the court did not indicate a specific length of residence for probationers, the center director determined when the offender was transferred to regular probation. In placing offenders in the restitution program, the criminal court imposed monetary obligations consisting of the actual cost of damages caused by the crime, fines, preexisting personal debts, court costs, and indigent attorney fees. To be eligible for the restitution program, offenders were required (by the program director) to have a job and (by the court) to spend a short period of time in jail prior to admission into residence. Failure to maintain gainful employment while in residence was sufficient grounds for the offender to be returned to jail.

The residential facility is staffed 24 hours a day by four houseparents assisted by volunteers and student interns. The nighttime houseparent and the director of the restitution are probation officers employed by the Board of Pardons and Parole. In addition to preparing meals, assigning chores,[4] and imposing restrictions, houseparents conduct individual and group counseling with the residents. Program participants' restitution includes reimbursement to the correctional authority for room and board[5] (25 percent subsistence fee per pay period) and cost of supervision ($15/month for probationers). Approximately $122,000 was expended to operate the restitution program during its first year; residents remitted a little more than $107,000 in restitution during this same time period (see Table 15.1).

Table 15.1
Financial Obligations of Residents (N=118)

TYPE	AVERAGE $	
	White	African American
Subsistence	$300	$ 242
Supervision Fee	47	29
Court Costs	139	125
Attorney Fees	69	64
Restitution	158	345
Fines	81	57
Money Owed	815	876
Money Earned	1,300	1,200
Earnings Paid	604	506

During its first year of operation, the restitution center housed 118 male residents (see Table 15.2) and released 109. The majority of residents were property offenders. African Americans constituted 70 percent of this population. Residents ranged in age from 18 to 57, with 54 percent in the 22–29 age category. While most of the men were single, one-fifth were married. The average amount of restitution imposed was just over $950; and the average amount paid was $621. Residents stayed an average of 70 days at the restitution center.

Table 15.2
Characteristics of Residents (N = 118)

VARIABLE	PERCENT	VARIABLE	PERCENT
1. Age		6. Release Type	
18 – 21	28.0	Court	25.0
22 – 29	54.2	Probation	46.0
30 – 39	12.7	Abscond	9.4
40 – 57	3.4	Detention	11.0
		Revocation	7.6
2. Race			
African American	70.3	7. Income Earned	
White	29.7	Up to $500	31.7
		501- 999	18.8
3. Marital Status		1,000 - 2,000	32.7
Single/Never Married	28.0	2,001 - 3,000	11.8
Separated/Divorced	8.4	3,001 +	4.9
Married/Common Law	22.9		
		8. Restitution Owed	
4. Offense		Up to $500	29.7
Felony	64.0	501 - 1000	29.8
Misdemeanor	36.0	1,001 - 2,000	29.7
		2001 - 3000	10.8
5. Sentence			
1 - 12 months	39.8	9. Restitution Paid	
13 - 36 months	52.5	Up to $250	29.7
37 - 60 months	5.1	250 - 500	20.8
60+ months	2.5	501 - 999	28.7
		1,000 - 2,000	18.8
		2,001 +	2.0

Sample

The study group consists of all probationers in residence at the restitution center between May 29, 1980, and May 31, 1981. Table 15.3 presents a description of this study group of 88 probationers. A youthful group, over half of the men were between the ages of 22 and 29. The majority of offenders had committed felony property crimes (64 percent), but many had prior histories of nonviolent felony charges. Two-thirds of the residents were African Americans. The average length of residence at the restitution center was 78 days. All but seven of the probationers were released from the restitution center during the study period.[6] The majority (71 percent) of the releases were successful. Rates of success were 61 percent and 73 percent for African Americans and whites respectively.

Table 15.3
Description of Sample (N=88)

VARIABLE	MEAN	STANDARD DEVIATION
Age	24	5.78
Days at Center	88.19	62.58
Sentence in Months	23.63	20.42
Money Owed	885.81	651.82
Income	1340.17	917.68
Restitution Paid	630.48	485.86
Prior Misdemeanor(s)	1.19	.99
Number of Priors	1.10	1.15

Variables

Preliminary analysis of a dozen demographic, offense, and financial variables revealed two outcome measures and six predictors. The outcome variables are length of time in residence at the restitution center and type of release from the restitution center. Length of residence refers to the number of days spent at the restitution center prior to release. Type of release indicates how the offender was removed from the restitution center: successfully or unsuccessfully. Successful release is a composite measure of release from probation and transfer to straight probation. Unsuccessful release is a composite measure of abscond, probation revocation, and detention in jail. Age, race, or type of offense (misdemeanor or felony), length of sentence, amount owed, and amount paid are independent variables. The variables used in the analyses are shown in Table 15.4. Multiple regression techniques were used to determine the statistical significance of the predictors to the outcome variables.

Table 15.4
Variables Used in the Analyses

NAME	LABEL
RACE	African American
	White
AGE	Years
CURRENT OFFENSE	Felony
	Misdemeanor
SENTENCE LENGTH	Months
TOTAL AMOUNT OWED	Dollars
TOTAL AMOUNT PAID	Dollars
RELEASE TYPE	Successful
	Unsuccessful
TIME AT CENTER	Days

RESULTS

Table 15.5 reports summary regression statistics. The outcome variables have two correlates in common, demographic and financial variable. Race is a significant predictor of length of residence (B=-.245) and type of release (B=-.228); however, the stronger relationship is with length of residence (r=-.341). The financial variable of dollar amount paid is significantly related to length of residence (B=.363) and type of release (B=-.664). The relationship with length of residence is a strong one (r=.604), whereas there is an inverse relationship with type of release. While race and amount of money paid were the only significant predictors of length of residence, the two variables explained 41 percent of the variance. There were variables predictive of type of release. The variables showed weak relationships and accounted for only 14 percent of the variance in type of release. In addition to race and amount of money paid, the variable amount owed is related to type of release (B=.486). Amount of money owed is a measure of the add-on costs and reveals that type of release is determined by the amount of add-on costs.

The offense variables (type of crime and sentence) were not significantly correlated with either of the outcome variables. While none of the variables demonstrated strong relationships with type of release, the financial variables and race reported the highest correlations with length of residence. Stepwise multiple regression was used to determine how race influences the statistical significance of the predictors to length of residence and type of release. The outcome variables emerged as unique factors in the preliminary analysis. The variables are assumed unique to the study site because the imposition of restitution by the court did not include a time limit. Further, offenders released from the restitution program were released from remaining restitution obligations.

Table 15.5
Correlation and Regression Statistics (N=80)

Predictor	r	B	SE BETA	F	p <
			(LENGTH of RESIDENCE)		
Race	-.341	-.245	.092	10.210	.0021
Age	-.060	-.114	.089	1.630	.2057
Offense Type	.184	.064	.093	.467	.4964
Sentence	.055	-.037	.089	.167	.6836
Amount Owed	.509	.239	.140	2.904	.0926
Amount Paid	.604	.363	.144	6.335	.0140
	Adjusted R Square		.414		
	F		10.294		
	Significance		.000		

Table 15.5 continues

Table 15.5 Continued

Predictor	r	B	SE BETA	F	p <
			(TYPE of RELEASE)		
Race	.119	-.228	.112	5.844	.0181
Age	-.109	-.166	.108	2.362	.1287
Offense Type	.024	.040	.113	.128	.7220
Sentence	.114	.149	.109	1.856	.1773
Amount Owed	-.004	.486	.167	8.485	.0047
Amount Paid	-.208	-.665	.175	14.434	.0003

Adjusted R Square	.139
F	3.123
Significance	.009

White Offenders

Of the 88 probationers in residence at the restitution center, 34 were white. The average age of these men was 22 years. Sixty-one percent were single and stayed an average of 61 days at the restitution center. While a majority of the men had one or no prior offense, the prior offense was just as likely to be a felony as a misdemeanor. The average prison sentence was 27 months for the current felony. Over 60 percent of the offenders were released to regular probation from the restitution center. The average amount of money owed was $876 (with $158 for restitution), although they paid only an average of $506 while in residence at the restitution center.

Table 15.6 shows the summary statistics for white residents. Although age is not a significant predictor of either outcome variable, it shows a slight negative correlation with length of residence. While type of offense is a correlate of length of residence (r=.356), and sentence is a correlate of type of release (r=.441), only the latter is a predictor. The financial variables of amount owed (r=.66) and dollar amount paid (r=.71) are highly correlated with, and predictive of, length of residence. Neither of the financial variables is a significant predictor of type of release, but amount paid (r=-. 197) has an inverse relationship with type of release. Of the five variables analyzed, amount of money owed (B=-.419) and amount of money paid (B=.321) explained 29 percent of the variance in length of residence. For type of release, only one of the five variables analyzed was a significant predictor. Sentence length (B=.441), explained 19 percent of the variance in type of release.

The evidence regarding offenders is that restitution is less punitive. It appears that the size of economic sanctions is not as important as the actual payment of money to fulfill the economic sanctions. The higher the amount of money owed, the less the offender was required to pay to be discharged from the restitution obligation and the shorter the period of time in residence at the restitution center.

On average, offenders paid 57 percent of the economic sanctions and stayed two months at the center. Further, offenders with longer sentences were more likely to be transferred to regular probation. Summarily, while white offenders are ordered to pay a lot of money in restitution, the amount they pay in a short period of time is accepted as fulfillment of the entire economic sanction.

Table 15.6
Correlation and Regression Summary for White Residents (N=32)

Predictor	r	B	SE BETA	F
	(LENGTH of RESIDENCE)			
Age	-.108	.063	.144	.191
Offense Type	.356*	.223	.115	3.770
Sentence	.130	-.169	.129	1.704
Amount Owed	.657*	-.419*	.590	.504
Amount Paid	.709*	.321*	.164	3.842
Adjusted R Square		.286		
F		8.565		
Significance		.000		
	(TYPE OF RELEASE)			
Age	.062	-.754	.209	.005
Offense Type	-.049	-.192	.194	.138
Sentence	.441*	.441*	.180	6.038
Amount Owed	.031	.539	.855	.397
Amount Paid	-.197	-.285	.164	3.003
Adjusted R Square		.193		
F		4.698		
Significance		.000		

*denotes significance at the .05 level

African American Offenders

There were almost twice as many African American probationers as white probationers in residence at the restitution center. The average age of these men was 25 years. Fifty-three percent were single and were in residence an average of 96 days. While a majority of the men had one or no prior offense, the prior was more likely to be a felony. The average prison sentence was 23 months for the current felony. Sixty-one percent of the offenders were transferred to regular probation when released from the restitution center. On average, the offenders paid $626 toward the restitution obligation of $815.

Table 15.7 shows the summary regression results for African American offenders. For this group of offenders, the demographic variable of age is moderately correlated with both dependent variables but is not predictive of either. Similarly, the offense variables are not correlated with either outcome variable. Only financial variables are significantly correlated with length of residence and type of release. While amount of money owed (r=.503) and amount of money paid (r=.554) show a significant positive relationship with length of residence, only amount of money owed (B=.286) is predictive. This variable accounts for 25 percent of the variance in length of residence. In the case of type of release, age (r=-.226) and amount of money paid (r=-.254) are significant correlates. However, only amount of money paid (B=-.213) is a predictor of type of release, explaining 20percent of the variance.

The results of the analysis for African American probationers demonstrate that race influences the nature of punitive restitution. Economic sanctions alone determine when monetary obligations are fulfilled and under what conditions an offender is released. Unlike white offenders who owe a lot of money and are released in a short period of time, black offenders must reside a long period of time no matter how much (or less) money they owe. In fact, the less money paid, the greater the likelihood of transfer to regular probation. On average, offenders paid 87 percent of the monetary obligations (mean=$814) and stayed three months at the restitution center. The evidence for African Americans is that the size of economic sanctions is more important than the actual amount of money paid to fulfill the restitution order. In other words, while offenders are ordered to pay a less amount of money in restitution, the amount paid over a long period of time is accepted as fulfillment of the entire economic sanction.

Table 15.7
Correlation and Regression Summary for African American Residents (N=48)

Predictor	r	B	SE BETA	F
	(LENGTH of RESIDENCE)			
Age	-.145	-.170	.127	1.781
Offense Type	.059	-.137	.059	.018
Sentence	.050	-.004	.135	.001
Amount Owed	.503*	.286*	.773	.137
Amount Paid	.554*	.483	.263	3.375
Adjusted R Square		.200		
F		2.964		
Significance		.000		

*denotes significance at the .05 level

Support for punitive restitution was most evident for African Americans. The program described herein not only imposed add-on economic sanctions but also required close supervision until the monetary obligations were paid. This feature of the program points to the net-widening dimension of punitive restitution. Offenders who otherwise would not be under close supervision were the primary participants. This observation is credible given the time frame of this study. The time frame is significant because a monetary sanction was the exception, not the rule, in restitution programs extant in the 1980s.

While selection for program participation appears to be based on objective criteria (e.g., financial resources of the offender, victim characteristics and injury, and actual costs of the crime), the race differential in the amount of money the court accepted in fulfillment of the restitution sanction repudiates this observation. The evidence supporting this contention is compelling when one considers the fate of offenders who paid the entire amount of the restitution sanction. In several instances, offenders who had paid all of their monetary obligations were retained in residence, subsequently committed an infraction (e.g., house rule), and ended up with a probation revocation. African Americans were more likely to be retained in residence beyond the time at which they had fulfilled the economic sanctions imposed by the court. This study clearly indicates that there is a racial difference in the use of restitution.

CONCLUSION

This inquiry attempted to uncover the intended objective of restitution. In this era of restorative justice, reparation and offender accountability are touted as the objectives of restitution (Umbreit 1994). The reparation objective of restitution makes it acceptable to the public and the criminal justice system because the focus is on the victim. While fines and victim compensation are widely used to bring about accountability, true offender accountability is achieved only with the certainty of restitution (Colson 1989). Accountability attaches responsibility for the crime and its victim directly to the offender. Accountability has very long historical roots, extending to the biblical dictum "an eye for an eye." The modern-day corollary of this *lex talionis* appears to be restitution (McCarthy & McCarthy 1991). Although some jurisdictions utilize restitution to divert offenders, the assumption in this inquiry is that retribution is the goal of restitution. Perhaps a closer examination of other programs may reveal that there are differential objectives based on race. The argument may be made that the results reported here are consistent with restitution as an incapacitative objective for white offenders and a punitive objective for African American offenders. Whereas punitive restitution was the underlying assumption in this study, subsequent inquiries must demonstrate the retributive dimensions of nonresidential and post-incarceration programs.

NOTES

1. The states include Alabama, Alaska, Arizona, Arkansas, California, Colorado, Connecticut, Florida, Georgia, Hawaii, Illinois, Kentucky, Louisiana, Maryland, Maine, Michigan, Minnesota, Mississippi, Missouri, New Jersey, New York, Ohio, Oregon, South

Dakota, Texas, Vermont, Virginia, Wisconsin.

2. Mississippi House Bill 2 (1977).

3. Comprehensive Crime Control Act of 1984, Pub. L. No. 98-473,1984 U.S. Code Cong. & Ad. News (98 Stat.) 1837, 2170 (to be codified at 42 U.S.C. §1401).

4. Chores include washing dishes, making beds, and grounds upkeep.

5. Residents receive a hot breakfast and dinner, and sandwiches for lunch.

6. Release from the restitution program may be successful or unsuccessful. Successful release occurs when the probationer is transferred to regular probation or released from all probation supervision. An unsuccessful release means the probationer absconded from the Center, was jailed for violating house rules, or had probation revoked.

REFERENCES

Colson, Charles. (1989). "Crime and Restitution." In William Dudley (ed.) *Crime and Criminals: Opposing Viewpoints*. San Diego, CA: Greenhaven Press.

Eglash, A. (1958). "Creative Restitution : Some Suggestions for Prison Rehabilitation Programs." *American Journal of Corrections* 20: 20.

Finn, P. and D. Parent. (1992). Making the Offender Foot the Bill, a Texas Program. Washington, DC: National Institute of Justice.

Flowers, G. (1977), "The Georgia Restitution Shelter Program." *Evaluation Report No. 1-150*. Georgia Department of Offender Rehabilitation. September 30.

Fogel, G., B. Galaway, and J. Hudson. (1972). "Restitution in Criminal Justice: A Minnesota Experiment." *Criminal Law Bulletin* 9: 681–691.

Galaway, B. and J. Hudson (eds.). (1996). *Restorative Justice: International Perspective*. NY: Criminal Justice Press

Gibbs, J. (1968). "Crime, Punishment, and Deterrence." *Southwestern Social Science Quarterly* 48: 515–530.

Gray, L. and J. Martin. (1969). "Punishment and Deterrence: Another Analysis of Gibbs' Data." *Social Science Quarterly* 50: 389–395.

Heide, K. and P. Voorhis. (1981). "Highlights of an Empirical Assessment of the Relationship of I-level and Moral Judgment to Restitution Outcome." Paper presented at annual meeting of the American Society of Criminology, Washington, DC.

Heinz, J., B. Galaway, and J. Hudson. (1976). "Restitution or Parole: A Follow-Up Study of Adult Offenders." *Social Service Review* 50: 148–156.

Hudson, J. and Burt Galaway. (1974). "Undoing the Wrong." Social Work 19: 313–318.

Klein, Andrew R. (1997). *Alternative Sentencing. Intermediate Sanctions and Probation*. 2d ed. Cincinnati, OH: Anderson.

Landis, J., J. Mercer, and C. Wolff. (1969). "Success and Failure of Adult Probationers in California." *Journal of Research in Crime and Delinquency* 6: 34–41.

Logan, C. (1972). "General Deterrent Effects of Imprisonment." *Social Forces* 51: 64–73.

McCarthy, Belinda and Bernard McCarthy (1991). *Community-Based Corrections*. 2d ed. Belmont, CA: Wadsworth.

Mills, J. (1992). "Supervision Fees: APPA Issues Committee Report." *Perspectives* 16(Fall): 4.

Mueller, G.O.W. (1955). "Tort, Crime and the Primitive." *Journal of Criminal Law, Criminology, and Police Science* 46: 303–332.

Newton, A. (1979). "Sentencing to Community Service and Restitution." *Criminal Justice Abstracts* 9: 435–468.

_____. (1976). "Alternatives to Imprisonment—Day Fines, Community Service Orders, and Restitution." *Crime and Delinquency Literature* 8: 109–125.

Parent, D. (1990). *Recovering Correctional Costs Through Offender Fees*. Washington, DC: National Institute of Justice.

Read, B. (1977). "How Restitution Works in Georgia." *Judicature* 60: 323–331.

Schafer, Stephen. (1974). "Compensation of Victims of Criminal Offenses." *Criminal Law Bulletin* 10: 605–636.

_____. (1970). *Compensation and Restitution to Crime Victims*. 2d ed.

Schneider, A. and P. Schneider. (1980). "An Overview of Restitution Program Models in the Juvenile Justice System." *Juvenile and Family Court Journal* 31: 3–22.

Schneider, P. and A. Schneider. (1979). "Monthly Report of the National Juvenile Restitution Evaluation Project." *Criminal Justice Abstracts* 12: 500–502.

Schneider, P., A. Schneider, P. Reiter, and C. Cleary. (1977). "Restitution Requirements for Juvenile Offenders: A Survey of the Practices in American Juvenile Courts." *Juvenile Justice* 11: 43–56.

Umbreit, M. (1994). *Victim Meets Offender: The Impact of Restorative Justice and Mediation*. NY: Criminal Justice Press.

CASES

18 U.S.C. §3556, 366–364 (Supp. 1984).
18 U.S.C. §2248(b)(3–4)(B,C,E) (1994).
18 U.S.C. §2327 (1994).

Chapter 16

Diversity in a Jail Work Setting: Evaluating the Impact of Racial Intolerance

Annette M. Girondi and Michael W. Markowitz

INTRODUCTION — DIVERSITY ACCEPTANCE

Diversity awareness is the knowledge that people are different from each other and can include a broad range of individual differences, among them race, culture, gender, age, personality, and social history. An understanding of such diversity allows for both the recognition that people behave and think differently, and for an enhancement of interpersonal interactions. An appreciation of "difference" can be particularly helpful in the employment setting.

When diversity awareness grows into diversity acceptance, the result can be an increase in effective team performance. Effective team performance is most important in occupations in which employees depend on each other to ensure the safety of others and themselves. This chapter focuses on the acceptance of diversity among correctional officers in the jail environment and how acceptance of differences among themselves (i.e., diversity) has served to help or hinder their performance. To emphasize this point, we present examples from our research in the jail environment and the research of others conducted in other environments that demonstrate how the lack of diversity awareness and acceptance can interfere with effective work performance.

Correctional officers are more than simply a collection of employees who begin their shifts together and go home at the same time. In daily situations, correctional officers as team members are on duty together, offering each other support and safety and sharing joint responsibility for what goes on at the jail (Gardenswartz & Rowe 1994). Correctional officers can also find themselves in special situations in which they must rely on each other for their personal safety. For example, if the officer is outnumbered in a confrontation with several inmates or is not the same sex as the inmates causing the disturbance, the officer will require backup from one or more colleagues. In both daily interactions as well as special situations, correctional officers offer a clear example of how teams operate and the importance of building these teams to ensure that they can count on each other on a daily basis.

TEAM BUILDING

Team building is an activity that allows members to progress to the point of viewing their particular group as simply individuals who work together (Gardenswartz & Rowe 1994). All work teams, including correctional officers, must progress from being a subset of employees who work the same shift together to really believing in their joint responsibility and accountability as a team. Katzenbach and Smith (1994) discuss the stages that a team must go through to evolve from individuals into a team. Groups of individuals become a team when they take risks to engage in team behavior.

In the beginning of a team, a team is simply individuals, and while it may perform adequately, it's performance will not truly be effective until it goes through the painful stages of development. When a team is going through the early stages of team development, it's performance may actually suffer. When employees go through the first stage of being a "pseudoteam," they are still functioning as individuals. These individuals become a "potential team," the second stage, once they commit to a common goal. Individuals operating in teams at this stage are still trying to determine who they are and how they work together as a team.

Individuals evolve into the third stage by becoming a "real team," a group of individuals who "are equally committed to a common purpose, goals, and working approach for which they hold themselves mutually accountable" (Katzenbach & Smith 1994). At this stage, they are truly operating as a team, and their performance will reflect this change. The fourth and highest level of team performance is the "high-performance team." These teams are similar to "real teams" but have "members who are also deeply committed to one another's personal growth and success"; a true concern exists for those with whom they work. Not every group of individuals is a team, however, and not every team can progress into being a high- performance team, but the goal of team building is to bring work groups as close as they can be to a high-performance team.

For a team to progress into a highly productive team, it's members must do the work of the team as well as direct some focus on who they are as a team. But focusing on who the team is falls outside the work of the group and may not be valued as much as the daily activities that the team is required to perform. This is the difference between doing the job (work of the team) and focusing on who is doing the job (who makes up the team). Diversity is one area of self-focus for a team. We believe that it has not received much focus because it is not what the team "does"; however, without a focus on the diversity of the team and how it affects the team's performance, we believe that team performance will suffer.

RESPONSES TO DIVERSITY

Diversity awareness is not a new concept. Its literal meaning has already been established as the awareness that people are different from each other in many and varied ways. Employees in all types of occupations, including corrections, have always been aware that there are differences among them. What has changed dramatically is how people deal with these differences at work. Responses to diversity among employees may vary (Thomas 1996). One extreme might be the denial of obvious differences or total denial that differences do exist. At the other extreme are total acceptance and encouragement of differences that have the potential to enhance individual and team performance. The most effective option for team performance actually depends on the task as well as the members of the team (Elsass & Graves 1997; Thomas 1996).

Denial or sublimation of differences for a specific team member must be avoided. Ignoring the differences of this individual will make that team member feel as if he or she is simply going along with the team to get along with other team members (Gardenswartz & Rowe 1994). This member will not feel like a true team member, and this team will not be a real team. But employees sometimes question the purpose of focusing on their differences. We propose that in the corrections setting, to achieve true team performance, team members must become aware of their diversity and learn to use this diversity to enhance group performance. We are thus focusing our discussion on racial diversity and its impact on jail corrections.

IMPORTANCE OF AWARENESS OF RACIAL DIVERSITY

Awareness and understanding of racial diversity are important for two key reasons. First, awareness of racial differences is important because it is an obvious area in which employees are different. It is similar to other characteristics like sex, physical ability, and age (Gardenswartz & Rowe 1994). These differences are important to understand primarily because they are salient to the contemporary work environment; employees cannot help but notice such differences when they are interacting. These differences are also important to understand because employees make assumptions about how these differences affect work performance. For example, research suggests that whites do not perceive racial minorities with whom they work to be as qualified as the racial minorities perceive themselves (Gardenswartz & Rowe 1994). As discussed later, these perceptions interfere with effective team interaction and subsequent performance of the team.

The second reason that awareness of racial differences is important is the changing demographics of the workforce, including corrections. Racial minorities are entering the workforce in increasing numbers, and estimates suggest that the increase in the African American workforce will increase by approximately 30 percent, the Hispanic workforce by 74 percent, and other races by 70 percent as we approach the year 2000 (Curry 1993). Since changes in demographics are already occurring and not expected to stop, addressing this issue will go far toward understanding any biases that employees have about this change that could interfere with their positive interaction at work and consequently interfere with their productivity.

IMPORTANT ASPECTS OF DIVERSITY

The concept of diversity is often conceptualized as a double-edged sword. To promote diversity among people is to recognize that people are different from each other. Taking a sociological view, individuals adopt an identity based on the culture with which they identify, and they share this with other members of their culture (Hostager, Al-Khatib, Swyer, & Close, 1995). However, evidence suggests that, typically, there are more differences within groups than there are between groups, a phenomenon found to be constant across cultural groups. Therefore, people from the same culture may actually be more different than they are alike. Part of diversity acceptance is to recognize that while there may be cultural similarities between people, there are differences among individuals that are based on social groups with which individuals identify. With this psychological approach, a person is unique because he or she can choose the social groups with whom to identify, making that person a unique individual despite membership in a specific cultural group (Hostager et al. 1995). The reality of individual diversity probably lies somewhere between the two approaches.

In an effort to discover this "reality," however, researchers must elicit perceptions of employees about diverse colleagues that help them draw on their differences to make their work teams more productive, without imposing unfounded stereotypes on these same employees (Lindsay 1993). The challenge such a goal presents to correctional analyses is that existing research has presented two very different pictures of the dynamics of diversity in the correctional workplace. The differences in question emanate from the type of research being conducted and the types of questions being asked.

THE EMPIRICAL PARADOX

Efforts to assess the dimensions of difference existing between diverse racial groups of correctional workers have been made primarily through empirical studies of prison employee populations. This research has used interviews as well as questionnaires to attempt to determine if any meaningful differences exist.

Do differences exist? The short answer is yes. However, the answers drawn from different empirical examinations are not always consistent. For example, research using questionnaires does not always use the same questionnaires; the use of different questions, even if the questions are designed to tap the same construct, does not always yield similar findings. In addition, different modes of data collection may also yield different results, such as the differences found when interview and questionnaire methodologies are used to tap the same constructs.

The *empirical paradox* (Britton 1997) is a term used to conceptualize the contrasts that arise when interview and questionnaire data are compared with regard to assessments of diversity in the correctional workplace. When interviewed by researchers, correctional officers may refer to certain work-related attitudes or events. However, when these same correctional officers are asked to complete a questionnaire that is designed to assess the same information, results from the questionnaire are different from the data collected from the interviews. Occurrence of this inconsistency has led researchers to question the true nature of differences among correctional officers in the work environment (Britton 1997). An alternative explanation is to conclude that the researcher's quantitative measures are not asking the "right" questions. Using an interview methodology, employees may have a greater opportunity to interpret questions and to answer these questions in a manner with which they are comfortable. Being able to discuss answers with a researcher is in sharp contrast to requiring participants to answer questions on a Likert-type scale. However, answering questions on a five- or a seven-point scale is less time- consuming and costly than interviewing a large number of employees.

ALLEVIATING THE EMPIRICAL PARADOX

A compromise exists between questionnaire and interview research: a combination of interview and questionnaire methodology. Many different types of questionnaires exist to assess job-related attitudes. Questionnaires on job satisfaction, commitment, and motivation can be found, and respondents' answers can be compared based on group membership (such as race). But their usefulness in assessing these constructs in a given setting, including the corrections setting, may be limited to how well the questions included assess the true nature of the setting.

A way to alleviate the imprecision of any given questionnaire for a particular setting is to interview the population and to use the results of the interview to prepare the questionnaire for administration (Fine, Johnson, & Ryan, 1990). A methodology of this type allows for cost-effectiveness and ease of administration while tailoring the questions to a specific setting.

Another alternative to alleviating the empirical paradox is to use a questionnaire that has been constructed for a particular work environment and validated many times in that environment with many employees. For the correctional environment, one such questionnaire is the Prison Social Climate Survey. Use of this measure has yielded some interesting findings relevant to the examination of race-related differences (e.g., Britton 1997) in the prison setting.

THE JAIL SETTING

Armed with the knowledge that different perceptions exist for employees of different races both inside and outside the corrections setting, we were interested in determining if these differences also exist for correctional officers in the jail setting. Since very little research has been conducted examining racial differences in attitudes of correctional officers in jails, our efforts to assess the extent of effective teamwork among diverse employees in such an environment seemed particularly relevant.

JAIL SOCIAL CLIMATE SURVEY

Based on interviews with approximately 10 percent of the correctional officers in a suburban New Jersey jail, we were able to modify the PSCS to reflect more of the dynamics of the jail work environment. Entitled the "Jail Social Climate Survey" (JSCS; Markowitz & Girondi 1997), this revised instrument comprises sixty multiple-response questions that are broken down into eight subscales: communication, general opportunities, training (two subscales), staffing, diversity, leadership, and emotional stress. We also included two open-ended questions about the work environment and about cultural and gender diversity. Full details of these interviews and the creation of the items can be obtained from the authors.

In addition to the 60 attitude questions, we asked respondents to tell us their race, gender, education, and length of service at the county jail. One hundred and nine correctional officers were employed at the men's and women's facilities we studied, with 34 percent of the employees responding to our survey. At the time of this research, only whites (non-Hispanics) and African Americans were employed by the jail. Our sample consisted of 92 percent white and 8 percent African American respondents.

LEADERSHIP

Minority males in leadership positions are a relatively rare phenomenon. *The Glass Ceiling Report*, issued in 1995, reported that the 43 percent of the work-force made up of white males holds 95 percent of the senior management positions; black women and black men hold 5 percent and 4 percent of middle management jobs, respectively (Wicker 1996). Therefore, most minorities who are entering any field (including corrections) are entering a work environment that is run predominantly by white males. While we cannot generalize and say that this would bother all employees, research suggests that perceptions of a dominant culture not their own is perceived by minority employees as an obstacle to promotion (Fine et al. 1990) and as a factor that lessens work group commitment (Riordan & Shore 1997).

A factor that compounds the problem of a white male leadership is the political nature of the selection of leadership in the jail; the employees are dependent on public elections and not necessarily performance as the determinant of their leadership. To illustrate the effect that the political nature of the leadership may have, one of our questionnaire respondents told us in an open-ended question response that "the county jail is run by politicians; as such no one will make important decisions for fear of losing a vote." In this type of environment, the employees are powerless to determine their supervisors or the dominant race of the leadership, a factor not likely to change even if the jail is located in a district dominated by the minority race (Wicker 1996).

During the interviews with correctional officers in our research setting, we found significant dissatisfaction with the current leadership, a fact that led us to include questions about the leadership at the jail in the JSCS. Two questions were included on how comfortable the correctional officers felt about going to their immediate supervisor with suggestions or concerns about institutional operations and how comfortable they felt going to their supervisor's supervisor with the suggestions or concerns.

In the jail used in our research, the leadership is predominantly white. Thus, we were interested in determining if a racial difference existed in the comfort levels expressed by correctional officers in approaching their supervisors (and their supervisor's supervisor) with suggestions and concerns. This issue had been similarly explored through data collected using the PSCS which showed non-white males to evaluate their supervision less satisfactorily than did white males (Britton 1997).

Our findings suggest that the African Americans in our jail setting were no more comfortable than other minority research populations with approaching their supervisors. Controlling for sex, education, and tenure, race was a significant contributor to comfort levels for approaching supervisors with suggestions or concerns. White correctional officers had a more favorable view about approaching their own supervisor as well as their supervisor's supervisor with suggestions or concerns, whereas minorities (African Americans) were clearly less comfortable engaging in this behavior.

While we did not offer a follow-up question to explain the possible reason(s) for this attitude, it is possible that the all-white leadership of the jail may contribute to the attitude of African American officers. We also found that race and sex were able to account for 19 percent of the variance in the responses to these two questions. When we added tenure into the analysis, we found that officers who had been at the jail between 10 and 30 years were more comfortable than new officers (5 years or less) with approaching their supervisor or their supervisor's supervisor. The effect of tenure was significant over and above that of race, together accounting for 51 percent of the variance. Although this finding is consistent with other research in correlating length of tenure with work attitudes (viz., Riordan & Shore 1997), its interpretation must be cautiously made in light of the fact that only white correctional officers fell into the tenured group. Research of this kind on correctional populations with a more even distribution of races would provide further corroboration. Perceptions of "comfort" could be based on the fact that the longer individuals work within a given group (or setting), the more they are defined by that group (or setting) (Lindsay 1993). If this finding were significant for both races, it would suggest a factor that has an equal effect on attitudes across races, demonstrating a commonality not yet explored.

This attitude difference between whites and African Americans has additional importance in terms of the effective functioning of work teams. For a team to be effective, it is important that the team "take risks involving conflict, trust, interdependence, and hard work" (Katzenbach & Smith 1994:132). The ability to engage in these behaviors will help a group of correctional officers to move from a "potential team" into the realm of being a "real team," thus causing an increase in team effectiveness. The result would be an increase in the performance of jail employees. Unfortunately, the findings from the group under study suggest that race plays a significant role in limiting the trust and sense of belonging felt by minority officers, a fact that serves to inhibit team building potential among this group.

Also important in this process is the team leader. While the team may be mostly autonomous, there are times when it must rely on a leader for guidance. If some team members do not feel comfortable relying on the team leader to provide guidance when it is necessary or to approach these leaders with suggestions or concerns, the performance of the team may suffer. A decline in performance could be hard to detect. While external appearance may suggest that daily activities are being performed, and everything is going along well, a crisis situation can reveal significant distrust that can negatively impact problem-solving potential. Unless performance is charted over time, or the correctional officers are asked about their feelings (as we did in our interviews), team members who are uncomfortable with the leadership and who feel unable to approach leaders with concerns may be unable to "be themselves" and may not feel like true members of the group. This could prevent the entire team from reaching its full, long-term potential as a team that functions efficiently in crisis as well as in everyday situations. Research from this group of employees suggests a significant level of distrust of leadership within the ranks of the jail hierarchy based on race, a fact that further corroborates the racial divide among these employees.

JOB SATISFACTION

Job satisfaction is a multifaceted concept (Locke 1976) suggesting that no one factor determines how satisfied a person is with his or her job. Satisfaction includes all aspects of the job such as satisfaction with the work performed, the workplace, supervisors, and coworkers. The determination of a person's overall level of satisfaction with his or her job is important because it has been found to predict a variety of work-related behaviors, including absenteeism and turnover.

Understanding people's cognitive processes has been shown to be a means through which job satisfaction can be measured and can be a significant factor in explaining patterns of workplace interaction and the opinions and expectations formed by employees. Sometimes opinions and expectations are formed with no more than physical features as the motivating factors (Elsass & Graves 1997). Could that person's opinions and expectations be incorrect? Yes. But their importance rests in the specific expectations about others that guide workplace attitudes, expectations, and behaviors (Elsass & Graves 1997).

Several factors have been identified through correctional research as having an impact on varying levels of job satisfaction based on race. One such factor has been called the racial identification hypothesis (Britton 1997). A disproportionate number of black inmates are incarcerated in the U.S. prison system, seven times as many as whites (Wicker 1996). According to the racial identification hypothesis, black correctional officers should feel a personal stake in the rehabilitation of, and feel more connected to, these inmates, raising their satisfaction with the work that they do.

The findings from our interviews suggest that this hypothesis should hold true. Due to the limited availability of African American officers on the shifts in which we interviewed, we were limited to interviewing only white officers (with the exception of one black female officer). Invariably, the white officers expressed certainty that the black officers were able to get away with disciplinary infractions without penalty. Moreover, white officers believed that the black officers received preferential treatment from the jail administration because the administration was afraid of them (in a legal way). Answers to our questionnaire also suggest support for this hypothesis. When asked about cultural and gender issues at the jail (open-ended question), officers repeated this sentiment, stating that the "administration needs to be more consistent in disciplinary matters with officers and stop being partial," and "the supervisors need to be more strict and enforce all rules concerning ...officers." White officers also expressed the feeling that "black officers are often friends with most inmates and leave officers [white] feeling uncomfortable."

From the comments we received on the open-ended questions and in the interviews from white officers, we were left with the initial impression that black officers in this institution possessed a distinct advantage. However, this was not supported by the responses to our questionnaire when we specifically assessed correction officers' job satisfaction. For this assessment, we included nine questions that assessed officers' general opinion of the jail, preference to remain at that facility, satisfaction with job assignment, sensitivity of supervisors to their personal needs, and job advancement opportunities.

We found that that when we controlled for sex, tenure, and education level, whites had a significantly higher level of satisfaction with their jobs at the jail than African Americans. This finding demonstrates that, similar to research on prison officers (Britton 1997), blacks and whites clearly have different attitudes about the work environment, thus precluding the assumption that correctional officers working at the same facility experience that facility the same way. Also interesting to note is that the findings based on these nine questions do not support the racial identification hypothesis, suggesting that this phenomenon may not occur simply due to correction officers' identification with the inmate population but instead may be due to more complex factors.

Whatever the reason for these differences in job satisfaction, they clearly have the potential to cause significant problems in team performance. Team members who have different perceptions about the workplace bring such differences to the work of the team. In the extreme, these differences affect uniformity in decision making and the overall performance of the team. In the jail setting that we surveyed, each group perceives the other to have the greater advantage; whites whom we interviewed believed the blacks had the advantage and expressed their related dissatisfaction with the jail, while blacks surveyed with the questionnaire expressed lower levels of satisfaction than whites. If the correctional officers at this jail are not forced to face these very real differences, the differences could interfere with successful group performance by causing the focus of the team to be on these differences rather than on good performance (Gardenswartz & Rowe 1994).

Attempts to erase illegal racial discrimination in the workplace are another factor that may contribute to differing levels of satisfaction between whites and African Americans at the jail. The most crucial piece of legislation in this area is the Civil Rights Act of 1964; however, perceptions of this legislation, specifically Title VII, have not always been favorable. Title VII of the Civil Rights Act was designed to protect specific groups of people, including those of different races, from discrimination. Settings in which discrimination was disallowed included private employers with 25 or more employees, labor unions, and employment agencies (Thernstrom & Thernstrom 1997). However, since its inception in 1964, some believe that Title VII has been transformed from a document that tries to prevent illegal discrimination, to one that actively promotes the preferential treatment of people based on their race (Thernstrom & Thernstrom 1997).

Attempts to promote preferential treatment, later known as affirmative action, have been met with mixed reviews by recipients and nonrecipients alike (Summers 1997). Efforts in recent years to encourage affirmative action have, unfortunately, been misnamed and promoted as "diversity initiatives" by some employers, causing employees to view the term "diversity" to mean "we are hiring more blacks." When employers use the term "diversity" as a code for affirmative action, employees are less likely to see the value of diversity acceptance and are more likely to feel threatened by lowered employment standards (Thernstrom & Thernstrom 1997) and the threat of changing power structure differentials (Kossek & Zonia 1993).

Nonminorities who understand diversity as a threat often claim that they are the victims of "reverse discrimination." Nonminority employees feel that they are excluded from receiving the opportunities that they have worked hard to achieve, causing them to resent the beneficiaries of diversity initiatives (Rowan 1996; Cose 1997). Responses to our open-ended question about cultural and gender diversity yielded comments that definitely suggest paranoia about diversity initiatives. For example, one officer wrote: "I am getting really tired of reverse discrimination in this operation. It seems anymore that if you're black (Afro-American) you can do or get anything with no consequences where as a White female I am ignored or patronized unless I do something wrong." Another officer wrote, "Affirmative action has given us a poor selection of officers based solely on cultural and gender differences." A third officer wrote that "cultural and gender diversity, that's bull___," clearly expressing his dislike of the concept.

A common misperception among nonminorities of affirmative action (and related diversity initiatives) is that qualifications are not important. However, affirmative action does not require employers to hire unqualified applicants. The qualifications of African Americans may be the same as the whites at this jail, but the white officers' perceptions could be affected by two specific factors. First, research suggests that white officers may be applying their own behavioral standard to the black officers. If the black officers don't mirror the white majority standard, white officers could evaluate the behavior of black officers as inferior (Elsass & Graves 1997).

Second, the white officers could also believe that the only reason the black officers are working alongside the white officers is due to preferential treatment. Evidence suggests that whites have a negative view of the benefits that minorities receive, suggesting that they receive a disproportionate amount of resources that are allocated among employees, and that Whites perceive minorities to be less qualified than the minorities perceive themselves (Kossek & Zonia, 1993). Again, these perceptions, real or imagined, will act as impediments to effective team performance. It is not possible for a team to capitalize on its diversity if the team members resent each other due to their diversity. As seen in this research setting, an inadequate or poorly executed effort toward diversity awareness can and does impede, rather than enhance, effective team performance.

CONCLUSIONS AND POLICY RECOMMENDATIONS

The results of this study illustrate several important aspects of the correctional work environment related to race that must be addressed if employees in these setting are to be effectively linked to their fellow workers as team members. First, racial diversity and gender diversity are institutionalized facts with regard to the correctional workplace. While significant research has established this point for prisons, this study suggests the same holds true for jails as well. Thus, effective performance and a team approach among workers will depend on the extent to which correctional administrators recognize this reality and engage in meaningful efforts to incorporate acceptance of diversity in the workplace.

The findings here indicate that reported levels of job satisfaction and confidence in the organizational hierarchy clearly vary by race, a fact attributable, at least in part, to the racial intolerance and mistrust in evidence among the workforce. This condition is further exacerbated by the fact that the institution in question has attempted to engender diversity acceptance without much success. While the finding that jail employees appear to experience and exhibit the same types of racial intolerance as found in prisons provides insight into the similarity of these institutions, it does little to address these problems in a way that fosters productivity and trust among workplace team members. To overcome this facet of the correctional work environment in a meaningful way, planners and policymakers must undertake several important problem-solving steps.

First, the organizational leadership must commit to the goal of *racial respect*. Avoiding trite notions of racial "harmony" that have failed in the past, the goal of mutual respect recognizes that deeply held beliefs regarding other races are not easily changed. If correctional organizations are to develop productive work teams, there must be a thorough and *ongoing* effort to educate all participants on the value of everyone who contributes to meeting organizational goals. By placing such training in an organizational, rather than a personal, context, the emphasis on respect for diversity becomes an incentive for productivity, rather than an effort to change individual beliefs. Financial and organizational incentives can be introduced as rewards for those teams that successfully meet criteria designed to reflect both increased diversity tolerance and institutional progress. An example of the latter could take the form of a reduction in "sicktime" call-outs by each team, a problem reported as significantly affecting the overall function of jail environments (Markowitz & Girondi 1997).

For such a program to succeed, there must also be a solid commitment to the allocation of resources for its development. Piecemeal efforts at diversity training have uniformly failed in the past (the present research site being no exception). In order to accomplish meaningful change in this regard, jails and prisons will need to allocate funds toward the establishment of a permanent team of professionals to develop an ongoing program for the building of diversity respect. This will involve research into needs assessment, program development/implementation, and evaluation and redesign. It will also require the hiring of qualified professionals with expertise in the fields of psychology, criminal justice, and organizational change to develop programs of this kind.

The preceding proposal highlights an additional challenge, namely, the limited resources allocated to most correctional systems. While state-run and federally-run prisons often experience financial shortfalls due to the social unpopularity of their function, the local administration of most jails makes this problem even more acute. It is realistic to recognize that financially meeting the safety needs of correctional workers takes precedence over the "softer" issue of mutual respect. Such decisions are made at the highest levels of jail and prison administration and clearly reflect what is seen as a "priority." Nevertheless, if disharmony and mistrust continue to significantly erode the productivity of correctional workteams, the need to address institutional intolerance may become equally compelling.

The overall conclusion from this discussion highlights the need for correctional administrators in jails, as well as prisons, to emphasize the development of racial respect among officers. The recommendations made before are necessarily general, as it will be the task of each institution to tailor these proposals to the unique qualities of their respective work environments. While additional jail research is needed to confirm the similarity of the workplace intolerance they share with prisons, the conclusions of this study highlight the compelling need for such intolerance to be addressed in a meaningful way. In the absence of such efforts, correctional institutions will not only continue to deal with racial hatred among inmates, but will also suffer its negative effects among those entrusted with inmate control—a fact that will inevitably perpetuate the current state of institutional crisis plaguing American corrections.

REFERENCES

Britton, D. M. (1997). "Perceptions of the Work Environment among Correctional Officer: Do Race and Sex Matter?" *Criminology* 35: 85–105.

Cose, E. (1997). *Color Blind: Seeing beyond Race in a Race-Obsessed World.* New York: HarperCollins.

Curry, T. H. (1993). "How to Prepare for Tomorrow's Workforce." *Corrections Today* August:168–172.

Elsass, P. M. and L. M. Graves. (1997). "Demographic Diversity in Decision-Making Groups: The Experiences of Women and People of Color." *The Academy of Management Review* 22: 946–973.

Fine, M. G., F. L. Johnson, and M. S. Ryan. (1990). "Cultural Diversity in the Workplace." *Public Personnel Management* 19: 305–319.

Gardenswartz, L. and A. Rowe. (1994). *Diverse Teams at Work: Capitalizing on the Power of Diversity.* Chicago: Irwin.

Katzenbach, J. R. and D. K. Smith. (1994). *The Wisdom of Teams: Creating the High-Performance Organization.* New York: Harper Business.

Kossek, E. E. and S. C. Zonia. (1993). "Assessing Diversity Climate: A Field Study of Reactions to Employer Efforts to Promote Diversity." *Journal of Organizational Behavior* 14: 61–81

Lindsay, C. P. (1993). "Paradoxes of Organizational Diversity." *Journal of Managerial Issues* 5: 547–566

Locke, E. A. (1976). Chapter 30. In M. Dunnette (ed.), *The Handbook of Industrial/Organizational Psychology.* Chicago: Rand-McNally.

Markowitz, M. W. and A. M. Girondi. (1997). "Studying the Dynamics of the Jail Work Environment: Methodology and Applications." Paper presented at the annual meeting of the American Society of Criminology, San Diego.

Parker, G. M. (1994). *Cross-Functional Work Teams: Working with Allies, Enemies, and Other Strangers.* San Francisco: Jossey-Bass.

Riordan, C. M. and L. M. Shore. (1997). "Demographic Diversity and Employee Attitudes: An Empirical Examination of Relational Demography within Work Units. *Journal of Applied Psychology* 82: 342–358.

Rowan, C. T. (1996). *The Coming Race War in America.* Boston: Little, Brown.

Summers, R. J. (1997). Affirmative Action. In P. J. Dubeck and K. Borman (eds.), *Women and Work: A Reader 257*–260 New Brunswick, N.J.: Rutgers University Press.

Thernstrom, S. and A. Thernstrom. (1997). *America in Black and White: One Nation, Indivisible.* New York: Simon and Schuster.

Thomas, R. R. T., Jr. (1996). *Redefining Diversity.* New York: AMACOM.

Wicker, T. (1996). *Tragic Failure: Racial Integration in America.* New York: William Morrow.

Chapter 17

Overrepresentation of Minority Youth in the Juvenile Justice System: Discrimination or Disproportionality of Delinquent Acts?

Janice Joseph

INTRODUCTION

Research indicates that minorities are overrepresented in the juvenile justice system. In 1988, Congress amended the Juvenile Justice and Delinquency Prevention Act to require states to investigate the overrepresentation of minority youths in institutions. The federal government made it clear to states that this was one of the issues they should address if they were to continue to receive federal funding. In addition, in 1988, the National Coalition of State Juvenile Justice Advocacy Groups focused on the issues of minority youths in the juvenile justice system. The disproportionate number of minorities in the juvenile justice system raises some critical issues about discrimination in the system. This chapter attempts to address the question, Does the juvenile justice system act in a discriminatory way, or do minority youths commit a disproportionate number of delinquent acts? The answer to this question will have implications for policymakers. The chapter, therefore, makes several policy recommendations.

EXTENT OF OVERREPRESENTATION OF MINORITIES

Over the past three decades, a body of literature has accumulated that indicates that minority youths are overrepresented at every stage in the juvenile justice system. For example, in 1995, official data showed that juvenile arrests disproportionately involved blacks. The racial composition of the juvenile population in 1995 was 80 percent white, 15 percent black, and 5 percent other races, with juveniles of Hispanic ethnicity being classified as white. However, black youths constituted 28 percent of all arrests for juvenile crimes in 1995 (Snyder 1997). Also in 1995, 49 percent of youths arrested for violent crimes and 27 percent of those arrested for property crimes were blacks. Black youths constituted 31 percent of all arrests for index crimes in 1995. While blacks were overrepresented in arrest rates for 1995, other minority groups, such as Asian and Pacific Islanders, were underrepresented (Federal Bureau of Investigation 1996).

In 1995, the Office of Juvenile Justice and Delinquency Prevention reported that the arrest rate of African American juveniles was two times that of white juveniles for property offenses, four times more than whites for person-oriented crimes, and five times more than whites for drug law violations (Synder & Sickmund 1995). The National Juvenile Corrections System Reporting Program selected six test states to study the admission and release of juveniles in those states. The results show that black youths had the highest rate of arrest of any racial or ethnic group in all six states (Krisberg & DeComo 1993).

Minority youths are detained more often than white youths. In 1994, 28 percent of black youths arrested were detained, 22 percent of other races were detained compared with only 17 percent of white youths (Butts 1996). Studies from New Jersey (Juvenile Delinquency Commission 1993), California (Austin et al. 1992), Florida (Tollett & Close 1991), Nebraska (Johnson & Secret 1990), and Pennsylvania (Leonard & Sontheimer 1995) indicate an overrepresentation of minority youth in detention.

Minority youths are also overrepresented in referrals to juvenile court. Leonard and Sontheimer (1995) argued that minority youths were overrepresented in referrals to juvenile court in 14 counties in Pennsylvania. In the juvenile court procedure in Florida between 1989 and 1990, black males were two and a half times more likely to be petitioned to the juvenile court, and black females were twice as likely as white females to be petitioned to juvenile court (Tollett & Close 1991). In New Jersey in 1992, 51 percent of youths referred to juvenile court were whites, 33 percent were blacks, 15 percent were Hispanic, and 1 percent were other minorities (Juvenile Delinquency Commission 1993).

Minority youth are more likely than whites to be adjudicated as delinquents. In 1993, 55 percent of whites, 59 percent of blacks, and 64 percent of other races of youths referred to juvenile court were formally adjudicated as delinquents (Butts 1995). The 1993 national data showed that 25 percent of white youths and 32 percent of black youths who were adjudicated as delinquent were placed out of the home; the rates for black and white youths placed on probation were 57 percent of white youths and 54 percent of black youths, and the rate for other races was 52 percent (Butts 1995). Other research indicates that minority youths, once adjudicated as delinquents, receive severe dispositions (Austin et al. 1992; Juvenile Delinquency Commission 1993).

Minority youths are institutionalized at a disproportionate rate in comparison to whites. Between 1987 and 1991, the proportion of blacks in juvenile facilities increased from 37 percent to 44 percent (Parent et al. 1994). In 1991, 57 percent of youths in private facilities were white, 32 percent were black, 9 percent Hispanic, and 2 percent others (Maguire & Pastore 1996). Krisberg, et al. (1987) found that minority youths are incarcerated at a rate three to four times that of white youths. Black youths are overrepresented in institutions in several states. In Georgia, for example, although blacks account for half of all delinquent acts, they represented 61 percent of those in institutions (Hansen 1988). In New York, young African American males are more than 23 times more likely than young white males to be locked up in prisons. The sad truth is that two times as many young black males are incarcerated in New York's institutions than are enrolled full-time in New York colleges (Gangi & Murphy 1990; Kaplan & Busner 1992). In Arizona, black juveniles are treated differently than are non black juveniles, and this results in overrepresentation of blacks in the juvenile institutions. Also, because of the lack of private residential facilities, blacks remain in institutional facilities for longer periods of time (Bortner et al. 1990). The typical juvenile in a public facility is most likely to be an African American male between the ages of 14 and 17 years (Siegel & Senna 1994).

LITERATURE REVIEW: DISCRIMINATION VERSUS DISPROPORTIONALITY OF DELINQUENT ACTS

The overrepresentation of minority youths in the juvenile justice system is indisputable. The preceding studies clearly indicate that minority youths are disproportionately involved in the juvenile justice system. The crucial question that arises is, What factors relate to the overrepresentation of minority youths in the juvenile justice system? The National Coalition of State Juvenile Advisory Groups (1993: 35) states:

One [view] urges that the problem rests with the system which employs, unintentionally or not, a "selection bias" that results in disproportionate number of minority youth in the system. In other words, minority youth do not commit more crimes than any other youth; they merely get treated differently and more harshly at various points in the system. The other view point posits that the nature and volume of offenses committed by minority youth are the real issue. In other words, minority youth commit more offenses, and more serious offenses, than other youth because of the social and economic conditions in which they are forced to live.

The issue here, therefore, is, To what extent is the overrepresentation of minority youths in the juvenile justice system related to discrimination on the part of the system or to the involvement of minority youths in delinquent acts?

Issue of Discrimination

A review of the literature regarding discrimination in the juvenile justice system indicates that several studies report that race and ethnicity have both direct (Conley 1994; Eigen 1981; Kempf 1992; Pope & Feyerherm 1992; Wordes & Bynum 1995) and indirect effects (Fagan, Forst et al. 1987; Frazier & Bishop 1995; Pope & Feyerherm 1992) on how minority juveniles are processed through the system.

Specifically, a number of studies have confirmed that regardless of the seriousness of the crime, racial and ethnic minorities, especially African Americans and Hispanics, are more likely to be arrested than their white counterparts (Bishop & Frazier 1988; Bortner & Reed 1985; Dannefer & Schutt 1982; Fagan, Slaughter, et al. 1987; Goldman 1963; Huizinga & Elliott 1987; Marshall & Thomas 1983; McCarthy & Smith 1986; Reed 1984; Smith, et al. 1980; Thornberry 1973).

Other studies have identified race and ethnicity as predictors of juvenile court dispositions, even after controlling for prior record, offense seriousness, type, and level of injury or damage (Bishop & Frazier 1988; Bortner, et al. 1986; Marshall & Thomas 1983). Research also found that disproportional treatment occurred at each stage of the juvenile justice process, and, in some instances, the racial and ethnic differences become more pronounced as minority youth proceed further into the system (Bishop & Frazier 1988; Leiber 1994; Pope & Feyerherm 1992). Other researchers have found racial effects in some circumstances and jurisdictions but not in others (Dannefer & Schutt 1982; Peterson, 1988; Tittle & Curran 1988).

Elsewhere, evidence tends to suggest the opposite to the preceding findings. Some researchers have reported little or no discrimination against minorities (Bailey & Peterson 1981; Bortner & Reed 1985; Cohen & Kluegel 1978; Kowalski & Rickicki 1982), discrimination against minorities conditional on decision stage (Dannefer & Schutt 1982; Peterson 1988), and discrimination favoring minorities and against whites (Bishop & Frazier 1988; Dannefer & Schutt 1982; Thomas & Cage 1977).

Kurtz, et al. (1993) (b) tracked youths through four decision points (police apprehension, court intake, adjudication, and disposition) in the juvenile justice system in eight communities in Georgia and concluded that socioeconomic factors of the offenders were more important than race in those four decision points. Moreover, the extralegal factors of race and social class have been found to have limited importance in determining police actions.

Nine interviews with juvenile justice professionals, conducted by the author specifically for this chapter, revealed that some officials view discrimination as a major problem in the system, while others believe that it is a minor problem. Still others report that it does not exist at all and is only a fabrication in some people's minds.

Issue of Disproportionate Involvement in Delinquent Acts

Minority youths are often from neighborhoods plagued with poverty, high unemployment and underemployment, family dysfunction, low education, and crime. The minority youth is, therefore, marginalized, and such marginalization engenders delinquent acts. These delinquent acts create and reinforce stereotypes of the marginalized minority youth as highly "delinquent." Consequently, some people believe that minority youths commit a greater number and more serious delinquent acts than white youths, thus, their overrepresentation in the juvenile justice system. Several research studies support the proposition that the high arrest rates of minority youths are strongly influenced by the seriousness of the offenses (Black & Reiss 1970; Dannefer & Schutt 1982; Fagan, Slaughter et al. 1987; Gaines, et al. 1994; Krisberg & Austin 1978; Lundman, et al. 1978; Piliavin & Briar 1964; Staples 1987; Walker, et al. 1996).

Other self-report studies indicate that African American females were more likely than white females to admit to more delinquent acts than white females (Jensen & Eve 1976; Joseph 1995) or engage in more serious acts than white females (Cernknovich & Giordano, 1979; Joseph, 1995).

Some researchers consider race and ethnicity to be important only because they are incidentally related to seriousness of an offense (Black 1970; Wilbanks 1987). Some experts argue that if minority groups commit a disproportionate number of delinquent acts as reflected in the official data, then this is a consequence of their socioeconomic status and the racism that they face in American society (Duster 1987; Georges-Abeyie 1989; Joe 1987; McCord & Ensminger 1995).

On the other hand, some studies argue that racial differences in delinquency are either nonexistent or marginal (Bachman, et al. 1996; Bridges et al. 1995; Gould 1969; Huizinga & Elliot 1987; Tracy 1987). These studies suggest that differences in official responses, rather than differences in delinquent acts, explain the differences in arrest, conviction, and incarceration rates between white and minority youths. This literature implies that racial and ethnic differences in official delinquency data are artifacts of the juvenile justice system. However, some critics warned that self-report studies cannot accurately measure racial differences in delinquent acts because minority youths may underreport their involvement in serious delinquent acts (Walter et al. 1996).

In sum, the literature on discrimination in the juvenile justice system is contradictory and inconclusive. Some studies report discrimination against minorities in certain circumstances, in some types of cases, with some types of crimes, and in some jurisdictions while others find no discrimination. Likewise, some studies find that minority youths commit a disproportionate number of delinquent acts, while other studies find no such disproportionality. These findings are further complicated by major shortcomings in the studies. Some of these shortcomings are discussed in the following.

Criticisms of Research on Minority Youths and Juvenile Justice

Studies that attempt to evaluate the extent of discrimination in the juvenile justice system or to determine the extent to which minority youths engage in a disproportionate number of delinquent acts have been fraught with problems. One major problem with the studies is their methodological weaknesses. First, there are problems with the samples used in these studies. Many of the studies used samples that are too small to control for legal and nonlegal factors. In addition, many samples are not representative of either minority youths or white youths to make any meaningful comparisons between the two groups. Researchers also use samples primarily from metropolitan areas. Although most African Americans and Hispanics reside in urban areas, this may not be true for other minority groups, such as Native Americans. There is inconsistency in the type of samples used by researchers. Some use random sampling, while others use total population or large aggregate of jurisdictions. Second, the studies utilize different methods. Some studies, for example, use surveys, while others use observation. Third, some studies fail to use multivariate designs that could measure direct, as well as indirect, race effects. For example, very few studies examine the combined effects of race and class on the processing of delinquents in the juvenile justice system. Because of these methodological problems, it is difficult to use the findings in the various studies as a body, since the conclusions drawn do not all point in the same direction.

Another major problem with these studies is that they focus primarily on African Americans and whites and, to a lesser extent, Hispanics, while virtually ignoring Asian and Native American populations. The characteristics of minority groups differ from those of whites, but they also differ from each other in the sense that some minority groups are more similar to whites than they are to other minority groups. Moreover, minority groups are stratified internally by class, gender, age, language, and even religion. Given the range of different and overlapping divisions among minority groups, studies should include additional minority groups in any analysis on race and ethnicity, rather than focusing exclusively on African Americans and Hispanics. There is also the issue of whether Hispanics should be categorized as a separate group since Hispanics are from several racial groups.

The research on discrimination in the juvenile justice system tends to focus on specific stages, such as arrest, judicial process, or disposition, rather than examining the relationships between these stages. This narrow focus fails to assess the extent to which minority youths are propelled through the system as a whole in relation to whites.

A multistage analysis of the juvenile justice process is essential to determine whether there is less discrimination at the "front end" (police) than at subsequent points in the juvenile justice system, such as adjudication or disposition. Frazier and Bishop (1995) argue that one advantage of focusing on multistages of the processing of minority youths through the juvenile justice system is that it highlights cumulative effects of race and ethnicity on case processing. A second advantage for using multistage analyses of the juvenile justice process is that they allow researchers to consider direct and indirect effects of race and ethnicity on case processing.

The difficulty in determining the role played by a defendant's racial or ethnic background apart from a whole host of other factors, such as prior delinquent record, nature of the offense, socioeconomic status, and age, stems from the fact that many studies treat race and ethnicity as residual variables in analyzing decisions in the juvenile justice process. It would appear that the tendency is for some researchers to view racial and ethnic differences in the juvenile justice system as a consequence of discrimination when they cannot be explained by other factors. Conversely, when the overrepresentation of minorities in the juvenile justice system appears to be explained by other factors, some researchers tend to assume that discrimination does not exist. The problem, however, is that such conclusions ignore the effects of discrimination on other social factors at various stages of the process. For example, Bortner and Reed (1985) argue that the issue of race and disposition is complicated by the fact that the discrimination that occurs in earlier processing decisions may mask later discrimination. To illustrate this point, they argue that there is considerable evidence that detained juveniles are more likely than nondetained juveniles to receive severe dispositions. Since detention affects the severity of dispositions (because judges often give longer sentences to detained juveniles), race can have an indirect effect on dispositions. To the extent that detention decisions are biased against minority youngsters, dispositions will be discriminatory even if juvenile court judges do not take race into account in deciding the dispositions of cases.

Although the research on overrepresentation of minority youth in the juvenile justice system is inconclusive and subject to various interpretations, the broad picture that emerges is that the juvenile justice system acts in a discriminatory manner against minority youth. Of equal importance is the evidence that some minority youths are disproportionately involved in delinquency. In general, however, there appears to be stronger empirical evidence for discrimination than for the disproportionate involvement of minority youths in delinquency.

The fact remains that minority youths are overrepresented in the juvenile justice system. Unless there is a reversal of this, the system will continue to socialize minority youths. Once a minority enters the system, he or she becomes trapped in the mechanism of the system. When the minority youth develops a prior record, this becomes a liability in the future. The presence of a prior record increases the likelihood that the minority youth will become entrenched in the system if he or she reoffends. Thus, the initial involvement in the system has a "snowball" effect that can lead to later criminal behavior. For many minority youth, involvement in the juvenile justice system is the first step toward a criminal lifestyle. It is, therefore, imperative that the overrepresentation of minority youths in the juvenile justice system be prevented. There is no one solution, because this is a multiple and complex problem. However, the goals should be to reduce the racial and ethnic inequities in the system and to prevent minority youths from engaging in delinquency.

POLICY IMPLICATIONS

Reducing Discrimination

A "racially biased juvenile justice system is not only indefensible, it is potentially self defeating in every function the juvenile justice system is designed to perform. Moreover, such a system undermines the legitimacy of the system" (Johnson & Secret 1990: 181). Following are some recommendations intended to reduce inequality in the juvenile justice system.

1. *States should develop comprehensive, culturally sensitive training programs for all juvenile justice personnel.* Too often, minority youths are subjected to the decisions, views, and perceptions of officials in the juvenile justice system who lack cultural understanding of minority youths. Cultural insensitivity has the potential to contribute to misunderstandings and, ultimately, discrimination in the system. Training programs should focus on racial and ethnic differences and how insensitivity to these differences can impact juvenile justice decisions. They should be designed to dispel myths about racial and ethnic minorities and should be conducted on a regular basis; the completion of such training should be a requirement for employment in the juvenile justice system. Training programs could take the form of workshops, seminars, and conferences focusing on the needs of minority youths. Frazier and Bishop (1995) have suggested that state

legislatures mandate the development of a cultural diversity curriculum that personnel at every level of the juvenile justice system should be required to complete through state university continuing education credits. Although this suggestion appears ideal, it may be difficult to implement given the fact that some officials in the juvenile justice system have no college education or may not be able to meet the college requirements in their respective states. Moreover, some colleges may not offer courses in cultural diversity. Training programs on cultural diversity and sensitivity seem a more realistic alternative than college education courses. Whatever the approach, training that desensitizes officials to racial and ethnic stereotypes is critical for equality in a justice system that appears to be unjust.

2. *States should increase the number of minorities employed at all levels of the juvenile justice system.* Greater representation of minority personnel is needed in the critical decision-making processes in the juvenile justice system, so states need to employ more minority police officers, attorneys, and judges. The recruitment of minorities in juvenile justice agencies will not in itself ensure complete sensitivity to racial and ethnic differences, but this can create a better understanding of minority youths. Such officials can make more appropriate decisions for the minority youth. This can also restore confidence of minorities in the juvenile justice system.

3. *States should mandate that all agents of the juvenile justice system thoroughly monitor, evaluate, and review decisions for discrimination.* From arrest to institutionalization, all stages of the juvenile justice system should be monitored. To accomplish this, the states should provide clear and specific guidelines as to the criteria on which decisions by juvenile justice personnel are to be based. Monitoring the system will be of enormous value to the individual agency concerned because each will be able to review its own policy and procedures. It will also allow assessment of the cumulative effects of decisions made by several agencies. Comprehensive monitoring will provide a better understanding of where discrimination and inequality are occurring in the system as a whole. This will provide a basis for determining where changes are needed and what the changes should be. A tracking system could be implemented to monitor the system.

4. *States should establish procedures for reporting, recording, and investigating discrimination in the system.* States need to establish reporting procedures, similar to those regarding sexual harassment, of professionals who engage in discrimination in the juvenile justice system. These procedures may allow for self-monitoring as well. Formal action should be taken against individuals found guilty of discrimination. These procedures will increase awareness and sensitivity about cultural bias (Leonard & Sontheimer 1995).

Reducing Involvement in Delinquency

Whether minority youths are disproportionately involved in delinquency is debatable. What is clear is that they engage in delinquent acts, and what is necessary is to prevent them from being involved in delinquency in the first place. Therefore:

5. *States should provide more economic and social opportunities for minority youths.* When minority youths are denied access to vital economic and social opportunities, they are unable to compete with others in the real world. They become victims of a system of oppression that is debilitating and dehumanizing. As a result, minority youths often engage in self-defeating and self-destructive activities. This trend can be reversed if they are given opportunities to make them feel like worthwhile members of society. States need to provide better education, job training, more jobs, and better living conditions for minority groups. Minority communities should assume collective responsibility for the socialization of their youths.

The family is the foundation for the child's development, but the task of socializing the minority youth in today's society is too complex for many minority families to achieve alone. All minority families are at risk in a system plagued with racism and discrimination. The responsibility for the socialization of minority youth has been left to other institutions, such as the school and even the juvenile justice system. To ensure that all minority youths are socialized in the values of society, the minority community should be involved in the process. This may take the form of mentoring, Big Brother/Big Sister, rite of passage, and cultural values programs. Unless minority communities take responsibility for the socialization of the youths, the future for many minority youths will be indisputably bleak. The struggle to save minority youths from the juvenile justice system cannot be overstated. It must be a priority of minority communities.

SUMMARY

Minority youths are overrepresented at every point in the judicial process. While some studies have shown that discrimination accounts for the overrepresentation of minority youths, others indicate that the disproportionate involvement in delinquency plays a major role in that overrepresentation. Despite the claims of some researchers that the juvenile justice system is not discriminatory, there is clear evidence that, in some cases, discrimination is a factor in the juvenile justice decision-making process. Equal justice dictates that every delinquent in the system be treated fairly irrespective of his or her racial or ethnic background. This fact calls for significant changes in the juvenile justice process.

Policy changes are usually slow to be implemented, but discrimination in the juvenile justice system should no longer be tolerated. Of equal importance is the prevention of delinquency among minority youths. It is, therefore, imperative that policymakers, juvenile justice officials, and the minority communities work together to reduce overrepresentation of minority youths in the system.

REFERENCES

Austin, J., J. Dimas, and D. Steinhart. (1992). *The Over-Representation of Minority Youth in the California Juvenile Justice System: Report Summary.* San Francisco: National Council on Crime and Delinquency.

Bachman, J., L. Johnsone, and P. O'Malley. (1996). *Monitoring the Future: Questionnaire Responses from Nation's High School Seniors*. Ann Arbor, MI: Institute of Social Research.

Bailey, W. and R. Peterson. (1981). "Legal versus Extralegal Determinants of Juvenile Court Dispositions." *Juvenile and Family Court Journal* 32: 41–59.

Bishop, D. M. and C. E. Frazier. (1988). "The Influence of Race in Juvenile Justice Processing." *Journal of Research in Crime and Delinquency* 25: 242–263.

Black, D. J. (1970). "The Production of Crime Rates." *American Sociological Review* 35: 733–48.

Black, D. J. and A. J. Reiss. (1970). "Police Control of Juvenile Delinquents." *American Sociological Review* 35: 63–77.

Bortner, M. A. and W. L. Reed. (1985). "The Preeminence of Process: An Example of Refocused Research. *Social Science Quarterly* 66: 413–425.

Bortner, M. A., A. L. Schneider, R. Hermann, L. C. Miller, and M. Cech-Soucy. (1990). *Black Adolescents and Juvenile Justice: Background Report to Arizona Black Town Hall*. Tempe, AZ.

Bridges, G. S., D. J. Conley, R. L. Engen, and T. Price-Spratlen,. (1995). "Racial Disparity in the Confinement of Juveniles: Effects of Crime and Community Social Structure on Punishment." In K. K. Leonard, C. Pope, and W. H. Feyerherm (eds.), *Minorities in Juvenile Justice* 128–152. Thousands Oaks, CA: Sage.

Butts, J. (1996). *Offenders in Juvenile Court, 1994*. Washington, DC: U.S. Government Printing Office.

———— (1995). *Offenders in Juvenile Court, 1993*. Washington, DC: U.S. Government Printing Office.

Cernknovich, S. A. and P. C. Giordano. (1979). "A Comparative Analysis of Male and Female Delinquency." *Sociological Quarterly* 20: 136–137.

Cohen, L. E. and J. R. Kluegel. (1978). "Determinants of Juvenile Court Dispositions: Ascriptive and Achieved Factors in Two Metropolitan Courts." *American Sociological Review* 43: 162–176.

Conley, D. J. (1994). "Adding Color to Black and White Picture: Using Qualitative Data to Explain Racial Disproportionality in the Juvenile Justice System." *Journal of Research in Crime and Delinquency* 31: 135–148,

Dannefer, D. and R. Schutt. (1982). "Race and Juvenile Justice Processing in Court and Police Agencies." *American Journal of Sociology* 87: 1113–1132.

Duster, T. (1987). "Crime, Youth, Unemployment, and the Black Underclass." *Crime and Delinquency* 33: 300–317.

Eigen, S. (1981). "The Determinants and Impacts of Jurisdictional Transfer in Philadelphia." In J. Hall et al. (eds.), *Major Issues in Juvenile Information and Training: Readings in Public Policy*. Columbus, OH: Academy of Contemporary Problems.

————., E. Slaughter, and E. Hartstone. (1987). "Blind Justice?: The Impact of Race on the Juvenile Justice Process." *Crime and Delinquency* 33: 224–258.

Fagan, J., M. Forst, and T.S. Vivona. (1987). "Racial Determinants of Judicial Transfer Decisions: Prosecuting Violent Youth in Criminal Court." *Crime and Delinquency* 33: 259–286.

Federal Bureau of Investigation. (1996). *Crime in United States 1995*. Washington, DC: U.S. Government Printing Office.

Frazier, C. E., and D. M. Bishop. (1995). "Reflections on Race Effects in Juvenile Justice." In K. K. Leonard, C. Pope, and W. H. Feyerherm (eds.), *Minorities in Juvenile*

Justice 16–46. Thousands Oaks, CA: Sage.

Gaines, L. K., V. E. Kappler, and J. B. Vaughn. (1994). *Policing in America*. Cincinnati, OH: Anderson.

Gangi, R. and J. Murphy. (1990). *Imprisoned Generation: Young Men under the Criminal Justice Custody in New York State*. New York: Correctional Association of New York.

Georges-Abeyie, G. (1989). "Review of William Wilbanks: The Myth of a Racist Criminal Justice System." *The Critical Criminologist* 1: 5–6.

Goldman, N. (1963). The Differential Selection of Juvenile Offenders for Court Appearance." New York: National Council on Crime and Delinquency.

Gould, L. (1969). "Who Defines Delinquency? A Comparison of Self-Report and Officially Reported Indices of Delinquency for Three Racial Groups." *Social Problems* 16: 325–336.

Hansen, J. O. (1988). "A New Report on Georgia's Juvenile Justice System." *Atlantic Journal of Constitution* 1.

Huizinga, D. and D. S. Elliott. (1987). "Juvenile Offenders: Prevalence, Offender Incidence, and Arrest Rate by Race." *Crime and Delinquency* 33: 206–223.

Jensen, G. and R. Eve. (1976). "Sex Differences in Delinquency: An Examination of Popular Sociological Explanations." *Criminology* 13: 427–448.

Joe, T. (1987). "Economic Inequality: The Picture in Black and White." *Crime and Delinquency* 33: 287–299.

Johnson, J. B. and P. E. Secret. (1990). "Race and Juvenile Court Decision Making Revisited." *Criminal Justice Policy Review* 4: 159–187.

Joseph, J. (1995). *Female Delinquency: Racial Differences*. Paper presented at the American Society of Criminology meeting, Boston, November.

Juvenile Delinquency Commission. (1993). *Profile 93: A Sourcebook of Juvenile Justice Data and Trends in New Jersey*. Trenton: State of New Jersey.

Kaplan, S. L. and J. Busner. (1992). "Note on Racial Bias in the Admission of Children and Adolescents to State Mental Health Facilities versus Correctional Facilities in New York." *American Journal of Psychiatry* 149: 768–772.

Kempf, K. L. (1992). *Role of Race in Juvenile Justice Processing in Pennsylvania*. Shippenburg, PA: Shippenburg University, Center for Juvenile Justice Training and Research.

Kowalski, G. and J. Rickicki. (1982). "Determinants of Juvenile Postadjudication Dispositions." *Journal of Research in Crime and Delinquency* 19: 66–83.

Krisberg, B. and J. Austin. (1978). *The Children of Ishmael*. Palo Alto: Mayfield.

_____. , and R. DeComo. (1993). *Juveniles Taken Into Custody: Fiscal Year 1991*. Washington, DC: Office of Juvenile Justice and Delinquency Prevention.

_____. , I. Schwartz, G. Fishman, Z. Eisikovits, E. Guttman, and K. Joe. (1987). The Incarceration of Minority Youth." *Crime and Delinquency* 33: 173–205.

Kurtz, F. D., M. M. Giddings, and R. Sutphen. (1993). "Prospective Investigations of Racial Disparity in the Juvenile Justice System." *Juvenile and Family Court Journal* 44: 43–59.

Kurtz, F. D., M. M. Giddings, and R. Sutphen. (1993). "Influence of Juveniles' Race on Police Decision-Making: An Exploratory Study." *Juvenile and Family Court Journal* 44: 69–78.

Leiber, R. (1994). "A Comparison of Juvenile Court Outcomes for Native Americans, African Americans, and Whites." *Justice Quarterly* 11: 257–279.

Leonard, K. K. and H. Sontheimer. (1995). "The Role of Race in Juvenile Justice in

Pennsylvania." In K. K. Leonard, C. Pope, and W. H. Feyerherm (eds.), *Minorities in Juvenile Justice* 98–127. Thousands Oaks, CA: Sage.

Lundman, R. J., R. E. Sykes, and J. P. Clark. (1978). "Police Control of Juveniles: A Replication." *Journal of Research in Crime and Delinquency* 15(January): 74–91.

Maguire, K. and A. L. Pastore. (1996). *Sourcebook of Criminal Justice Statistics 1995.* Washington, DC: U.S. Department of Justice, Bureau of Justice Statistics.

Marshall, I. H. and C. W. Thomas. (1983). "Discretionary Decision-Making and the Juvenile Court." *Juvenile and Family Court Journal* 34: 47–59.

McCarthy, B. R. and B. L. Smith. (1986). "The Conceptualization of Discrimination in the Juvenile Justice Process: The Impact of Administrative Factors and Screening Decisions on Juvenile Court Dispositions." *Criminology* 24: 41–64.

McCord, J. and M. Ensminger. (1995). "Pathways from Aggressive Childhood to Criminality." Paper presented at the American Society of Criminology meeting, Boston, November.

National Coalition of State Juvenile Advisory Groups. (1993). *Myths and Realities: Meeting the Challenge of Serious, Violent, and Chronic Juvenile Offenders,* 1992 Annual Report. Washington, DC: Office of Juvenile Justice and Delinquency Prevention.

Parent, D. G., V. Leiter., S. Kennedy, L. Livens, D. Wentworth, and S. Wilcox. (1994). *Conditions of Confinement: Juvenile Detention and Corrections Facilities.* Washington, DC: Office of Juvenile Justice and Delinquency Prevention.

Peterson, R. D. (1988). "Youthful Offender Designations and Sentencing in New York Criminal Courts." *Social Problems* 32: 111–130.

Piliavin, I. and S. Briar. (1964). "Police Encounters with Juveniles." American Journal of *Sociology* 70: 206–14.

Pope, C. E. and W. Feyerherm. (1992). *Minorities and the Juvenile Justice System.* Washington, DC: U.S. Department of Justice Office of Juvenile Justice and Delinquency Prevention.

Reed, W. L. (1984). *Racial Differentials in Juvenile Court Decision-Making: Final Report.* Washington, DC: U.S. Department of Justice, National Institute of Juvenile Justice and Delinquency.

Siegel, L. J. and J. J. Senna. (1994). *Juvenile Delinquency: Theory, Practice and Law.* St. Paul, MN: West.

Smith, C. P., T. V. Alexander, and C. F. Roberts. (1980). *A National Assessment of Serious Juvenile Crime and the Juvenile Justice System: Final Report.* Sacramento, CA: American Justice Institute.

Staples, W. G. (1987). "Law and Social Control in Juvenile Justice Dispositions." *Journal of Research in Crime and Delinquency* 24: 7–22.

Synder, H. and M. Sickmund. (1995). *Juvenile Offenders and Victims: A National Report.* Washington, DC: Office of Juvenile Justice and Delinquency Prevention.

Synder, N. (1997). Juvenile Arrests 1995. Washington, DC: U.S. Department of Justice.

Thomas, C. W. and R. Cage. (1977). "The Effects of Social Characteristics on Juvenile Court Dispositions." *Sociological Quarterly* 18: 237–252.

Thornberry, T. P. (1973). "Race, Socioeconomic Status and Sentencing in the Juvenile Justice System." *Journal of Law and Criminology* 64: 90–98.

Tittle, C. R and D. A. Curran. (1988). "Contingencies for Dispositional Disparities in Juvenile Justice." *Social Forces* 67: 23–58.

Tollett, T. and B. R. Close. (1991). "The Over-Representation of Blacks in Florida's Juvenile Justice System." In M. J. Lynch and E. Britt Paterson (eds.), *Race and*

Criminal Justice 88–99. New York: Harrow and Heston.

Tracy, P. (1987). "Race and Class Differences in Official and Self-Reported Delinquency." In M.E. Wolgang, T. Thornberry, and R. Figlio (eds.), *From Boy to Man, from Delinquency to Crime* 87–121. Chicago: University of Chicago Press.

Walter, S., C. Spohn, and M. DeLone. (1996). "The Color of Justice." Belmont, CA: Wadsworth.

Wilbanks, W. (1987). *The Myth of a Racist Criminal Justice System.* Monterey, CA: Brooks/Cole.

Wordes, M. and T. S. Bynum. (1995). "Policing Juveniles: Is There Bias against Youths of Color?" In K. K. Leonard, C. Pope, and W. H. Feyerherm (eds.), *Minorities in Juvenile Justice* 47–65. Thousands Oaks, CA: Sage.

Chapter 18

Substance Abuse and Race in a Delinquent Population

Philip W. Harris, Peter R. Jones, and Jamie J. Fader

INTRODUCTION

Philadelphia's juvenile justice system is experiencing significant shifts in the population that it serves, alerting stakeholders that models of service delivery may need to be restructured to respond to these changes. Notably, the racial composition of juveniles entering delinquent placements is rapidly changing, with a steady decline in the proportion of African American youths and a sharp increase in the proportion of Latino youths (Jones, Harris, and Bachovchin, 1997), the fastest-growing racial/ ethnic segment of the U.S. population (Glick & Moore 1990).

At the same time that racial trends are shifting, other changes have been observed since the mid 1990s. The number of delinquents identified as having substance abuse problems has dramatically increased, expanding the need for placements that address drug and alcohol abuse. In addition, an increasing number of youths admitted to placements come from homes where parents themselves abuse drugs and alcohol. The extent of parental substance abuse, then, also has implications for treatment modalities, especially those involving family therapy.

Within the literature on delinquency, substance abuse has been treated largely as a companion behavior. Many of the factors that have been found to predict delinquency are also theorized as predictors of substance abuse, as well as dropping out of school and educational problems. Prominent among these predictors are gender (Hawkins & Catalano 1992), a delinquent peer group (Hawkins & Catalano 1992; Greenwood 1992), parental drug use (Greenwood 1992; Hawkins & Catalano 1992; Resnick et al. 1997), parental alcohol use (Hawkins & Catalano 1992), parental criminality (Greenwood 1992), family violence (Lehman et al. 1994), abuse or neglect (Hawkins & Catalano 1992), and poor family management (Hawkins & Catalano 1992). Counteracting these risk factors are what are termed protective factors. Among these protective factors are family bonding

(Hawkins & Catalano 1992; Resnick et al. 1997), school bonding (Greenwood 1992; Hawkins & Catalano 1992; Resnick et al. 1997), school commitment (Hawkins & Catalano 1992), a resilient personality (Hawkins & Catalano 1992), and prosocial values (Greenwood 1992; Hawkins & Catalano 1992). The relationship between race and substance abuse is quite different from the relationship between race and delinquency. Moreover, substance abuse has been identified as a problem in slightly less than half of all delinquent cases in Philadelphia. Within juvenile corrections, only a minority of delinquent youths are placed in programs that address substance abuse problems. It follows, then, that the causes of substance abuse among delinquent youths may be somewhat different from those found in the general youth population but that they are equally worth pursuing. As Fagan (Fagan, Weis & Cheng 1990) has argued, the stressors that shape drug use within a high-risk population may appear too infrequently in the general population to emerge as significant contributors. Moreover, because the etiology of drug use appears to differ by racial or ethnic group, we believe that race/ethnicity is worth considering when developing models of substance abuse.

This chapter explores the connections between race and substance abuse in a delinquent population. It compares national data on adolescents with the trends in Philadelphia's delinquent population, identifies key predictors of drug abuse among delinquent youths and within racial categories of delinquent youths, and identifies relevant research and policy issues for responding to substance abuse among high-risk adolescents.

RACIAL/ETHNIC DIFFERENCES IN RATES OF SUBSTANCE ABUSE

The bulk of the research focused on differences in rates of substance abuse between various racial/ethnic groups has occurred during the last decade. While many have focused on black/white differences (Ringwalt & Palmer 1990), some have included other groups in their analysis, including Native Americans and/or Asian Americans (Bachman et al., 1991; Oetting & Beauvais 1990; Rebach 1992; Swaim et al. 1997; Welte & Barnes 1986). In addition, there is a growing collection of literature dealing with Latino youth (Booth et al. 1990; Chavez & Swaim 1992a; Coombs et al. 1991; Farabee et al. 1995; Felix-Ortiz & Newcomb 1992, 1995; Flannery et al. 1994; Frauenglass et al. 1997; Gilbert & Alcocer 1988; Glick & Moore 1990; Hernandez & Lucero 1996; Johnson & Delgado 1989; Khoury et al. 1996; Schinke et al. 1988; Vega et al. 1993; Wallace et al. 1995).

Most of our knowledge of substance-abusing adolescents derives from two national surveys (Oetting & Beauvais 1990). The first is the Monitoring the Future study, provided annually since 1974. This self-report survey is administered in schools and provides continuous data about adolescent drug use from 8th to 12th grades (Bachman et al. 1991). The other is the National Household Survey, conducted every two to three years since 1971 (Kandel 1995; National Institute on Drug Abuse [NIDA] 1992). The National Household Survey is administered through interviews in homes, where respondents are asked to self-report levels of drug use. Both studies are funded by the National Institute on

Drug Abuse. Other data have been gathered from areas that serve as ethnic enclaves, allowing for a more substantial minority sample (e.g., Farabee et al. 1995; Frauenglass et al. 1997; Khoury et al. 1996; Vega et al. 1993).

Epidemiology

With few exceptions, the data suggest that black adolescents have significantly lower rates of general substance use than do whites or latinos[1] (Bachman et al. 1991; Khoury et al. 1996; Oetting & Beauvais 1990; Rebach 1992; Ringwalt & Palmer 1990; Vega et al. 1993; Wallace et al. 1995; Welte & Barnes 1986). This remains constant across grade levels surveyed, substance categories (e.g., alcohol, marijuana, cocaine), and definitions of prevalence (e.g., lifetime use, recent use, heavy use).[2] Comparisons between Anglos and Latinos generally show similar rates of prevalence, with differences that can likely be attributed to varying employment of Latino ethnic subgroups such as Mexican Americans, Cuban Americans, or Puerto Ricans across studies and/or sample selection from ethnic enclaves.

Results of National Surveys

Oetting and Beauvais (1990) compare several national surveys, two of which collect data on racial/ethnic differences in level of substance use. The National Senior Survey,[3] administered in 1986 to African American and white high school seniors, reports higher levels of lifetime use among Anglo adolescents for all drugs surveyed,[4] including alcohol, marijuana, cocaine, inhalants, stimulants, downers, quaaludes, tranquilizers, LSD, other narcotics, and cigarettes. The American Drug and Alcohol Survey, administered in 1988, reports comparisons between whites, Mexican Americans, and western Spanish Americans. Results from this study indicate lifetime prevalence over a range of drugs (those just mentioned, as well as legal stimulants and PCP) is generally highest among Anglos and western Spanish Americans, respectively (with the exception that both Latino subgroups are slightly more likely to use cocaine and crack than are whites). For all racial/ethnic groups, alcohol and marijuana are the drugs of choice. Bachman et al (1991) report similar data from their Monitoring the Future study for white, African American, Puerto Rican/ Latin American, and Mexican American males and females.

While the Monitoring the Future study is often criticized for its underrepresentation of minority youth (Oetting & Beauvais 1990), the American Drug and Alcohol Survey randomly samples U.S. communities of populations 2,500 or more, at least 10 percent of which is Mexican American. Chavez and Swaim (1992a) explore these data and make Anglo-Latino comparisons for 8th and 12th graders. For the 8th grade sample, Mexican Americans have generally higher rates of lifetime substance use, significantly so for marijuana, cocaine or crack, crack, steroids, and cigarettes. However, when examining the 12th grade sample, the opposite trend is apparent. Generally, white seniors have higher lifetime prevalence and rates of current usage than do Latinos. By their senior year, the only drug that Mexican Americans use significantly more than do whites is diet pills.

Other studies drawing from national samples focus on racial/ethnic differences in alcohol use only (Gilbert & Alcocer 1988; Ringwalt & Palmer 1990). Gilbert and Alcocer (1988) use data from 1987 on adolescents from grades 7–12, concurring with previous studies that find higher rates of alcohol use among white than black adolescents. Significantly, they conclude that white youths are also more likely to drink heavily when they do drink.

Results From State, Regional, and Local Surveys

The vast majority of nonnational surveys are those attempting to target Latinos, either in states in which they are heavily represented (e.g., those formerly belonging to Mexico) or in ethnic enclaves, such as those found in south Florida (Farabee et al. 1995; Flannery et al. 1994; Khoury et al. 1996; Vega et al. 1993). These authors tend to underscore the importance of distinguishing among Latino subgroups, since Mexican Americans, Puerto Ricans, Cuban Americans, South/Central Americans and other Latinos have important differences in terms of history, culture, and socioeconomic status that may impact on their rates of, and reasons for, using/abusing drugs and alcohol (Farabee et al. 1995; Gilbert & Alcocer 1988; Swaim et al. 1997).[5]

Vega et al. (1993) examine a sample of preadolescents in the greater Miami area, comparing whites', African Americans', and Cuban Americans' rates of lifetime prevalence of cigarette and alcohol use. Even among a sample of sixth and seventh graders, the authors conclude that the general pattern holds true: Anglo adolescents report the highest levels of alcohol and cigarette usage, while African Americans report the least. In addition, Welte and Barnes (1986) find that, among a large sample of 7th to 12th graders in New York state ($n = 27,335$), whites and Latinos have the highest rates of alcohol use, while blacks have the lowest rates. Finally, Farabee et al.'s (1995) study of adults in Texas indicates that Anglos are likely to begin drinking alcohol and using drugs an average of one year younger than Latinos (primarily Mexican Americans).

In sum, it seems that samples of varying sizes, and age groups and from both national and local surveys are in general agreement about the relationship of race/ethnicity to substance use. These findings support data from Philadelphia's delinquent population, which report the highest rates of substance abuse among White adolescents, the lowest among blacks, and intermediate (and rising) rates among Latino youth (Jones, et al. 1997).

Etiology

That there are racial/ethnic differences in rates of substance use is no surprise. Blacks, Anglos, and Latinos of all backgrounds have distinct experiences, histories, and cultural attitudes toward drug and alcohol use and distinct levels of economic disadvantage. While there are myriad explanations for why Latinos and African Americans might abuse drugs and alcohol (see Welte & Barnes 1986), researchers almost unfailingly register a level of surprise that white adolescents' rates of substance use are consistently higher than those for persons of color. It may be helpful, then, to briefly explore the sources of the commonly held assumption that minorities are more likely to use and abuse drugs and alcohol.

The most obvious culprits in this conception are morbidity and mortality reports and data from public health centers (Bachman et al. 1991; Kandel 1995). Since minorities (specifically, African Americans) are disproportionately represented in these statistics, the public easily concludes that substance abuse is primarily a problem for persons of color.   Some authors argue that African Americans and Latinos, while less likely to drink alcohol, are more likely to drink to excess and incur "problems" as a result of alcohol abuse (Gilbert & Alcocer 1988; Wallace et al. 1995; Welte & Barnes 1986).   Bachman et al. (1991) point out that there may be "two worlds" of drug use (especially alcohol use) within the black community.   At one end, there is abstinence, while at the other extreme, there are heavy use and abuse. Welte and Barnes (1986) conclude that, when controlling for the amount of alcohol consumed, minority groups tend to experience more "problems" than whites.   Finally, some of this paradox can be explained by the "precocious initiation" of drug and alcohol use by Anglos and Latinos, as compared to blacks (Wallace et al. 1995). Though African American adolescents have lower rates of substance use than do Anglos, this trend reverses itself when looking at those aged 35 and over (Kandel 1995).

It does seem apparent that there are "two worlds" of data on adolescent substance use, one from surveys (predominantly administered in schools) and one from public health reports (Bachman et al. 1991).   While public health facilities are more likely to capture statistics on low-income blacks and Latinos, they are unable to account for the number of whites receiving treatment from private physicians.

At the same time, there are considerable shortcomings involved in surveys and selfreporting of drug and/or alcohol use. Most significant is the effect that the dropout rate has on differential rates of substance use. This is a critical issue to examine, since dropouts tend to have a higher incidence of drug and alcohol use than do students who remain in school. Swaim et al. (1997) report that dropouts in their sample were 1.2 to 6.4 times more likely than students to use drugs and alcohol.   In addition, African Americans and Latinos are significantly more likely to drop out of school than are Anglos. In short, a possible explanation for minority students' lower rates of substance use is that the most frequent black and Latino users are underrepresented in school samples, significantly so by their senior year.

There is conflicting evidence, however, as to the extent of influence that dropout rates have on data regarding adolescent drug and alcohol use. Chavez and Swaim (1992a), for instance, attribute increased levels of white students' substance use from 8th to 12th grade entirely to the effects of Latino sample attrition due to dropping out (though they do not take measures to test for this). Bachman et al. (1991) defend the validity of their data by noting that, while Latino–white comparisons may be affected by the unusually high rate of Latino dropouts, black-white comparisons are not likely to be as affected, since African Americans and Anglos have similar rates of dropping out.[6] They also argue that household surveys, which do not omit dropouts, report similar findings to those of their schoolbased survey. In their 1995 Monitoring the Future report, they conclude from estimates of absentees (adolescents who were absent during survey administration) and from household surveys that dropouts differ from participating seniors at a rate of about 1.5 times the difference between absentees and seniors. Using this estimate, they assert that corrections based on dropouts would be very small.

In addition to the dropout question, some scholars concerned with the validity of self-report surveys have examined the prevalence of inconsistent responses (e.g., denial, underreporting) occurring when adolescents are asked to report on a sensitive topic such as substance use (Bachman et al. 1991; Fendrich & Vaughn 1994; Johnston & O'Malley 1997; Kandel 1995; Wallace et al. 1995). These scholars agree that racial/ethnic minorities are more likely to give inconsistent responses than are white adolescents, especially so for African Americans. In fact, black respondents are as least twice at likely to underreport than Anglo/other respondents (Fendrich & Vaughn 1994). Johnston and O'Malley's (1997) report using the Monitoring the Future study finds similar results.

Oetting and Beauvais (1990) suggest that the most important factor in the lower rates of minority substance use could be a consequence of using national surveys that are representative of the U.S. population as a whole. As a result, the residents of ethnic enclaves, where there is the greatest prevalence of drug and alcohol involvement, are rarely captured. Ghettos, barrios, and Indian reservations, they argue, are areas of concentrated racial/ethnic prejudice, social isolation, poverty, unemployment, deviant role models, and gang influence. Therefore, geographic "pockets" where drug-using minorities reside are not likely to be reflected in national statistics.[7]

Interestingly, the discussion of higher white rates seems to center around statistical and methodological shortcomings, while explanations for minority substance use tend to focus on cultural and structural factors. While this may be partly a reflection of the tendency to see whites as lacking both color and culture (Frankenberg 1993), it probably stems from a genuine sense of surprise that minority youth do not abuse drug and alcohol at a greater rate than is reported, considering the influences of racism, poverty, stress of acculturation, and so on that many blacks and Latinos experience. The following explores these and other factors as they relate to minority substance use.

Cultural/Structural Factors in Latino Youths' Substance Use

In the last five years, several studies have been published that establish level of acculturation as a significant and positive indicator of substance use (Booth et al. 1990; Farabee et al. 1995; Khoury et al. 1996; Vega et al. 1993).[8] This research suggests that, for whatever reason, as Latinos become more aligned with U.S. culture, they begin to use drugs and alcohol at a similar rate to that of Anglos. Farabee et al. (1995) classify their Texas sample as high-, medium-, and low-acculturated based on nativity (born in Mexico or the United States), the language in which the interview was conducted, primary language spoken at home, and importance of ethnic identity to the respondent. They find that lifetime and current alcohol and drug use is significantly and positively related to level of acculturation. U.S.-born respondents report higher rates of substance use than those born in Mexico, and those U.S.-born respondents with higher levels of acculturation have higher drug and alcohol use rates than those who speak Spanish primarily and believe ethnic identity to be important.

Farabee et al. (1995) suggest two models for explaining increased prevalence of substance use with increased exposure to U.S. culture. The acculturative stress model suggests that the acculturation process is stress-inducing; therefore, the stress of adapting to U.S. culture is responsible for Latino drug and alcohol use. The acculturation model, however, argues that substance use is a characteristic engrained in U.S. society and that Latino immigrants are simply assimilating that norm. Little research has been done to test these hypotheses; such exploration could provide insight into the best prevention/ intervention efforts for Latino youth.[9]

Schinke et al. (1988) expand upon the notion of stress as a factor in adolescent substance use. Aside from the stress of acculturation, the authors argue that Latinos in particular are exposed to environmental, social milieu, and cognitive stressors. Latinos (especially those in New York City, on whom Schinke et al. focus) experience environmental stressors through noise, substandard and crowded housing, and safety hazards; social milieu stressors through poverty, unemployment and underemployment, and racial discrimination; and cognitive stressors such as helplessness perceptions, fatalism, and low self-esteem. As a result, Latino youths turn to drugs and alcohol as a means to cope with these pressures.

Finally, some scholars reject cultural explanations as stereotypical and advocate the use of a model that incorporates risk and protective factors for adolescent substance use (Felix-Ortiz & Newcomb 1992). Risk factors for Latino substance abuse include substance use by parents and/or older siblings, family disintegration, low social selfconcept, poverty, drug availability, poor school performance, and peer drug use. Protective factors that serve to buffer the youth from risk factors include frequent church attendance and religious affiliation. The authors select 14 factors empirically and theoretically related to risk or protection and condense them into risk and protective indexes. They examine each index separately as well as combined in a risk protection interaction variable; each index is regressed on the frequency of use over the last six months for male and female whites and Latinos. Felix-Ortiz and Newcomb conclude that the risk and protective factors (as well as their interaction term) are significant predictors of most types of substance use. In addition, they find few differences between Latinos and Anglos, suggesting a cultural approach to explaining adolescent drug and alcohol use may not be the most parsimonious model.

Other studies focusing on peer and family influence as risk and protective factors also fail to find significant differences between these two racial/ethnic groups (Booth et al. 1990; Coombs et al. 1991; Flannery et al. 1994). This research concludes that substance users, regardless of gender and race/ethnicity, are more likely than abstainers to be influenced by their peers. In Flannery et al.'s (1994) study, having a friend who drinks alcohol and perceived susceptibility to peer pressure are the two best predictors of substance use for both whites and Latinos. Similarly, Coombs et al. (1991) report that level of marijuana use by youths' friends is the most significant factor in substance use. However, it appears that parental involvement can mediate peer influence, at least for Latinos (Frauenglass et al. 1997).

Factors Involved in Black Youths' Substance Use

Much less is apparently written that discusses the etiology of African American adolescents' substance use. Bachman et al. (1991) note that analyses of the Monitoring the Future data indicate that blacks are more likely than Anglos to perceive high risk involved in drug use. African Americans are also less likely to report smoking, alcohol use, and drunkenness by friends. Another study (Ringwalt & Palmer 1990) finds that black youths are significantly more likely to rate high the importance of adults' disapproval, while white adolescents report their friends' approval as being the most important. African American youth are apparently greatly affected by the degree to which parents, teachers and counselors, and adults in their neighborhoods disapprove of substance use.[10] In addition, they are more likely than Anglos to report that there is a good chance that someone their age will develop health problems if they get drunk once or twice or have one or two drinks occasionally.

Studies of black adolescents leave a glaring hole in the literature on racial/ethnic differences in substance use. Instead of focusing so much energy on the factors that are responsible for Latinos' higher rates of drug and alcohol use (as compared to blacks), it may be more useful to look at the reasons for blacks' lower rates of use. Despite cultural and structural stressors that would normally lead to increased substance use, what is the key that prevents African American youths from doing so? If these stressors are significant factors in substance use, why are whites and Latinos more similar than Latinos and blacks? Finally, if adults are more influential in the decision making of African American adolescents, why? The answers to these questions and many others unanswered by the extant literature are critical to developing and supporting the most appropriate prevention and intervention programs for adolescents. However, while there are many gaps in our knowledge of this topic, policymakers and service providers can draw several clues from this literature that deserve to be reviewed.

Research Questions

This study represents a departure from previous research in that it examines substance abuse in a delinquent population. As in the studies of the general population, however, African American delinquent youths abuse drugs and alcohol at lower rates than their white and Hispanic counterparts. Moreover, many of the same risk factors identified in the literature review are present in the lives of delinquent youths, but the weight of their impact may differ as the result of selecting out nondelinquent youths. We recognize that the implications of this study will be most relevant to programs that serve a delinquent population.

In designing this study we addressed three questions. First, before embarking on a study of predictors of substance abuse, we found it important to test the validity of the racial differences in levels of drug use that we found. Because the dependent variable used for this study was drawn from court records, the potential for bias could not be discounted easily.

Second, since less than half of all of the youths in the sample were known to use illegal drugs, we wanted to know what factors explained differences in drug use among the delinquent population generally. Our hypothesis was that family characteristics would play a major role in any causal model produced. We noted, however, that few substance abuse programs used by Philadelphia's Family Court focus on the dynamics of family systems. More typical in juvenile corrections are therapeutic communities or other interventions that focus on changes in the individual.

Lastly, our intent was to test the hypothesis that the predictors of adolescent drug abuse differ depending on race/ethnicity. If differences exist, then programs designed to address drug abuse may need to address the different dynamics of different racial groups of youths.

METHODS

The purpose of this study was to further our knowledge regarding the interaction between race and adolescent substance abuse by analyzing a variety of factors demonstrated by past research to be predictors of drug and alcohol abuse. Unlike most studies on this topic, this study focuses on a sample of delinquent youths who reside in one large metropolitan area. Our aim was to develop knowledge that could be translated into recommendations for program design within a juvenile justice system.

There has been previous discussion about potential biases resulting from studies of this nature that use high-risk or delinquent samples. Clearly, those factors that predict drug abuse in the general population may be different from those that predict drug abuse among a delinquent sample. At the same time, researchers have noted the absence of stressors in the general population and the potential irrelevance of findings based on the general population to the behaviors of high-risk populations (Dembo, et al. 1998; Fagan, et al. 1990). In addition, many recent attempts to develop explanations of both delinquency and drug abuse have produced findings that may not be relevant to differentiating among delinquent youths (Elliot, et al. 1985).

Our sample included all delinquency cases committed by Philadelphia's Family Court to any program during the years 1994–1996. This sample of 7,806 delinquency cases excluded only youths who were committed to ordinary probation. The data were drawn from the ProDES database. ProDES, an outcome-based information system designed and operated by the authors for the city of Philadelphia, gathers data from four sources: Family Court records, standardized program staff assessments conducted shortly after admission to the program and again at discharge, self-reported scale data obtained from standardized instruments administered shortly after program admission and again at discharge, and follow-up telephone interviews conducted with the youths and their parents by

ProDES staff.

Because self-report data were missing on a large proportion of the sample, we were able to study only a subset of the entire sample. This smaller subsample, numbering 3,980, was found not to differ significantly from sample members not included in the study on our measures of age, gender, race, offense type, prior offenses, court record of drug abuse, and court record of parental drug abuse.

The sample subjected to analysis, then, consisted of 3,980 juvenile delinquency cases that were adjudicated and disposed by Philadelphia's Family Court during the period January 1994 through December 1996. The characteristics of these youths are listed in Table 18.1.

Table 18.1
Sample Characteristics

Characteristic	Description
Age	15.8 years, s.d.=1.55
Gender	9.3 percent female
Race	76% black, 12 % Hispanic, 10% white
Most Serious Current Charge	37% personal, 35% property, 19% drugs
Has At Least One Prior Offense	56%
History of Drug Abuse	54%
History of Dependency Services	12%
Parent Has History of Drug Abuse	14% father, 18% mother
Youth Living With Parent at Time of Arrest	62%

Source: Juvenile Court Record.
Sampling Frame: All Committed Cases, 1994–1996, *n*=7,806

This study made use of court record data and self-report data from the intake data tables. Specifically, the following categories of data were extracted from the database for analysis: demographic characteristics, offense characteristics, prior delinquency record, probation record data on juvenile and parental substance abuse, probation record data on the criminal behavior of other family members, risk and needs scores derived from program staff ratings, self-reported standardized scales (measuring self-esteem, values, family bonding, and school bonding), and self-reports of substance abuse.

The analysis was conducted using CHAID (the chi-squared automatic interaction detector). The principal aim of a segmentation device like CHAID is to divide the population into two or more distinct groups based on categories of the best predictor of a dependent variable. The analysis continues splitting based on other predictors until no more significant predictors can be found (or some other stopping rule is met). The method attempts to explain as much variation as possible in the dependent variable. Technically, CHAID proceeds by successive applications of a one-way analysis of variance. At each step an attempt is made to obtain the largest possible reduction in the unexplained sum of squares by first examining the groups to see which has the largest internal sum of squares (TSSi). CHAID replicates this approach using chi-squared as the criterion. Predictor variables and all possible divisions of each predictor are scanned to find the one that maximizes the between-group sum of squares (BSSi) when the group is divided into two or more categories. Therefore, maximum explanatory power of a split is achieved by maximizing the ratio BSSi / TSSi.   Segments derived through CHAID are always mutually exclusive and exhaustive.

FINDINGS

The Validity of Racial Differences

Figure 18.1 illustrates two findings from the official Philadelphia data: (1) drug abuse is rising among youths committed by the Family Court, and (2) black youths are less likely to use drugs than white and Hispanic youths. In addition to probation records, two sources of data were examined in order to test the validity of the race-specific patterns of substance abuse found in probation records: program staff reports and self-reports. As part of every program admission, a program staff member completes an assessment. Within this assessment is the item, "Drug/Chemical Abuse". The staff person rates this item for each youth with one of the following responses: no known use or no interference with functioning, some disruption to functioning, or chronic abuse or dependency.

Figure 18.1
Drug Abuse ("J" File) by Race/Ethnicity 1994–1996

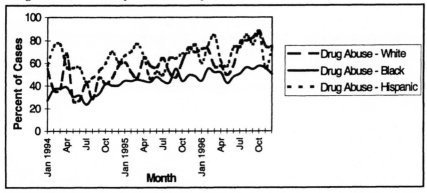

Another source of drug abuse is self-reported information. As part of the program intake process, each youth responds to several questions pertaining to alcohol and drug use. These questions include:

- On how many occasions, if any, have you had (marijuana, cocaine, crack, inhalants, speed, depressants, hallucinogens) in the past 12 months?

- Do you feel that you have a drug use problem?

- Do you feel that you ever have had a drug abuse problem in the past?

- In the past 12 months have you ever sold marijuana, cocaine, or any other drugs?

- Does either of your natural parents now have a drug use problem?

- Does either of your current caregivers now have a drug use problem?

While the levels of substance abuse derived from the self-reports are substantially lower than those found in the record data and staff reports, the patterns of differences, shown in Table 18.2, are identical: Hispanic youths are the heaviest abusers; abuse by black youths is substantially lower than that of either Hispanic or white youths.

Table 18.2
Race and Drug Abuse: Three Measures (in percent)

Data Source	White	Black	Hispanic	p	n
Probation Records	59	45	67	<.001	7806
Staff Report	53	35	60	<.001	4481
Self Report	19	7	21	<.001	3980

In contrast to these patterns in substance abuse, Hispanic youths, relative to white and black youths, are more often charged with drug-related offenses. White youths, however, have the lowest rates of petitions in juvenile court for this category of offenses, As can be seen in Table 18.3, a drug offense was the most serious charge in more than half of all cases involving a Hispanic juvenile. In contrast, less than 1 in 5 black juveniles and less than 1 in 12 white juveniles had a drug offense as his or her most serious charge. Rather than pertaining to drug use, all of these charges involved the manufacture or possession of drugs. We can see ,then, that Hispanic youths have high rates of both abuse and trafficking in drugs. In contrast, white youths have high rates of drug abuse but low rates of drug trafficking. Black juveniles exhibit still another pattern: relatively low rates of drug abuse but moderate levels of drug trafficking. Undoubtedly, these offense patterns have shaped the expectations noted in our literature review about usage levels.

Table 18.3
Sample Characteristics

CONSTRUCT	MEASURE	SOURCE
RISK FACTORS	RISK FACTORS	RISK FACTORS
Delinquent peer group	Negative peers	Staff (Risk Scale)
Parental drug use	Mother has drug problem	Court Record
	Father has drug problem	Court Record
Parental alcohol use	Mother has alcohol problem	Court Record
	Father has alcohol problem	Court Record
Parental criminality	Mother has criminal record	Court Record
	Father has criminal record	Court Record

Table 18.3 continues

Table 18.3 Continued

RISK FACTORS	RISK FACTORS	RISK FACTORS
Sibling Criminality	Sibling has been arrested	Court Record
Family violence	History of family violence	Court Record
Abuse or neglect	History of abuse or neglect	Court Record
Poor family management	Family stability	Staff (Needs Scale)
Poverty	Family income	Record
Academic failure	Reading level, grade in school	Record

PROTECTIVE FACTORS	PROTECTIVE FACTORS	PROTECTIVE FACTORS*
Family bonding	Family bonding Instrumental communication Intimate communication Caring and trust	
School bonding	School bonding School attachment	*All such links have been established through various research studies.
School commitment	School commitment Perceived opportunities	
Resilient personality	Self-esteem	
Prosocial value orientation	Values (prosocial to antisocial)	

Because of the expected low rate of self-reported drug abuse in this population, we selected the probation record rating for our analysis. This measure asks the coder to rate, based on all the information in the file, whether or not the youth has a history of occasional or chronic drug abuse. The level of reported use and the pattern of drug use were identical for the probation record and staff-reported measures. Moreover, we became aware of the fact that program staff completing the risk and needs instruments drew heavily on probation records and typically had very little firsthand knowledge of youths' substance-abusing behavior. Additionally, we found that the data collection methods employed by probation staff were more consistent than were those used by the 64 programs participating in the ProDES information system.

Drug trafficking is, indeed, a problem behavior that has spawned its own set of interventions. Drug sellers' programs are often distinguished from programs that target drug use. In this study, however, our interest is in the consumption side of the problem. Why do some delinquent youths abuse drugs and not others? In order to address this question, we drew on the constructs developed in previous research on this question, employing the structural framework promulgated by Hawkins and Catalano (1992), namely, the identification of risk and protective factors.

This body of research suggests several factors that put a youth at risk of becoming involved in drug-abusing behavior as well as other factors that serve to protect youths from involvement in this behavior (Hawkins & Catalano 1992; Greenwood 1992; Felix-Ortiz & Newcomb 1992). In Table 18.3, we summarize these constructs and identify the measures that we have used to operationalize them. We have elected to treat some constructs as protective factors when the literature suggests that their opposite is a risk factor. For example, Hawkins and Catalano classify "lack of commitment to school" as a risk factor, while we have defined "commitment to school" as a protective factor. The analysis provides for both interpretations in that the entire scale, from low to high commitment, is included.

It may be, however, that the demographic characteristics of age, gender, and race explain a large proportion of the variance in drug-abusing behavior. As can be seen in Figure 18.1, where these three demographic characteristics are analyzed, age is the first predictor selected by the CHAID, and the second is race. In each age group, the percentage of white and Hispanic youths abusing drugs was greater than the percentage for black youths. Gender did not play an important role in differentiating between drug-abusing delinquent youths and those who had no history of drug abuse. Using the three demographic variables, the proportion of drug abusers (occasional and chronic combined) varies from 20 percent (youths under the age of 13 of any race) to 83 percent (white and Hispanic youths aged 18 or higher), against a base rate of 50 percent. We conclude, then, that gender is less important than age and race in predicting drug abuse among delinquent youths. Race appears to be a more critical predictor of drug abuse among older adolescents than among younger adolescents.

Predicting Substance Abuse

Before examining differences by racial group, we analyzed the effect of the protective and risk factors on the entire sample. Restricting our analysis to protective factors, we find that school commitment is the first predictor: drug abuse, especially chronic abuse, is slightly higher for juveniles with lower school commitment (see Figure 18.2). For juveniles with low school commitment, the next predictor is intimacy and communication, a family bonding scale, but, surprisingly, the relationship is in a positive direction. Juveniles with low levels of school commitment and moderate to high levels of intimacy and communication are most likely to abuse drugs. For youths with high levels of school commitment, those with negative self esteem are most likely to be abusing drugs. Finally, youths with lower intimate communication scores and lower levels of instrumental communication (another family bonding scale) are more likely to be abusing drugs. Using these four predictors, the model identifies groups of juveniles within which the percent with drug abuse problems ranges from 44 percent (youths with high school commitment and high self esteem) to 73 percent (youths reporting low school commitment, high levels of intimate communication within the family, but low levels of instrumental communication) against a base rate of 47 percent.

Figure 18.2
Predicting Drug Abuse: Protective Factors Only

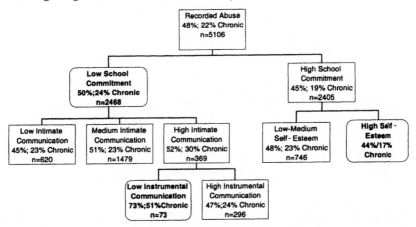

Next we turn our attention to risk factors (see Figure 18.3). Here we find that the first predictor of a juvenile's drug abuse is paternal drug use. Juvenile drug abuse is significantly higher when there is evidence of paternal drug use. The second-tier predictors are maternal alcohol abuse for juveniles with no paternal drug abuse and, for juveniles with evidence of paternal drug use, prior referral to Children and Youth Services (these are cases of abuse or neglect). Juveniles whose mothers have a history of abuse are significantly more likely to abuse drugs. Additionally, prior referrals to Children and Youths Services are associated with more juvenile drug abuse.

There is one third-tier predictor for juveniles with no evidence of paternal substance abuse and no evidence of maternal substance abuse: history of family violence. History of family violence is a single item indicating a history of domestic violence in the home, as opposed to referral to Children and Youth Services, which measures the history of reports of abuse and neglect. The relationship is positive—juveniles with a history of family violence are more likely to abuse drugs. There are two fourth-tier predictors—staff-assessed primary family relations and history of prior paternal alcohol abuse. Both apply to specific groups of juveniles. In both cases the association is, as expected, positive—more family disorganization, more juvenile drug abuse, more paternal alcohol abuse and more juvenile drug abuse. Using these predictors, the model identifies groups of juveniles within which the percent with drug abuse problems ranges from 38 percent (youths with no parental substance abuse and no history of family violence, whose family relations are rated by staff as stable) to 72 percent (youths whose fathers abuse drugs and who have been referred to Children and Youth Services as victims of abuse or neglect). These figures can be compared to the sample base rate of 47 percent.

Figure 18.3
Predicting Drug Abuse: Risk Factors Only

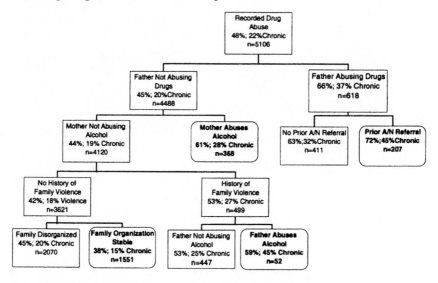

At this point in the analysis, we can see that parental substance abuse and family conflict are factors that increase the likelihood of substance abuse in this population, while commitment to school, high levels of instrumental communication within the family, and high self-esteem serve to reduce the chances of substance abuse. When we combine protective and risk factors into a single model, however, we find that the risk factors dominate the model.

None of the protective factors entered the model until the fifth tier. (see Figure 18.4). In fact, the combined risk/protective factor model is the same as the prior risk-factor-only model (Figure 18.3) until the fifth tier. For juveniles with no evidence of parental drug abuse, there are several fifth-tier predictors— intimate communication, siblings arrested, and values orientation. The association between intimate communication (with parents) and drug abuse is associated with more juvenile drug abuse. In other words, youths who report that they can discuss with their parents romantic relationships or actions that make them feel guilty are more likely to use drugs. Moreover, the variable siblings arrested produced an unexpected outcome: arrests of siblings make no difference, but not having a sibling is associated with a lower rate of drug abuse. Finally, for this group of youths whose parents do not abuse drugs, having very antisocial values is associated with drug abuse.   Using these predictors, the model identifies groups of juveniles within which the percent with drug abuse problems ranges from 29 percent (youths whose parents do not abuse drugs, who are from families with no record of family violence, who are from stable family environments, and who report low levels of intimate communication with parents), to 72 percent (youths with substance-abusing fathers who have been referred in the past to Children and Youth Services as victims of abuse and neglect), against a base rate of 47 percent.

Figure 18.4
Predicting Drug Abuse: Protective and Risk Factors

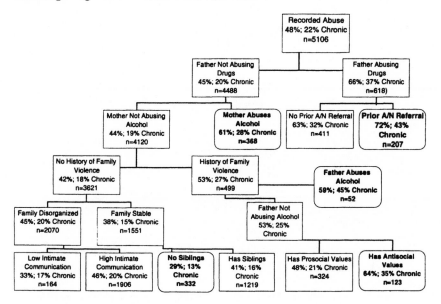

Race and Substance Abuse

Our next question is whether the effects of risk and protective factors operate differently for different racial groups. The literature discussed earlier points to different usage patterns as well as different causal explanations for drug abuse among black, hispanic, and white youths. Since these groups are not equally represented in the sample, it is likely that the more highly represented groups have shaped the overall pattern of relationships reported in the previous section.

As can be seen in Figure 18.5, the first predictor of drug abuse among white youths is family organization (assessed by staff as part of the needs assessment). Youths from disorganized families are far more likely to abuse drugs. The second-tier predictors for white youths are family income and the juvenile's statement that father has an alcohol abuse problem. Among stable families, youths from low-income families less often abuse drugs. Among disorganized families, youths who report that their fathers abuse alcohol are more likely to abuse drugs.

Among white juveniles who report that their fathers do not abuse alcohol, a record of father's alcohol abuse is the next predictor of drug abuse. Youths whose fathers are known to abuse alcohol are also more likely to abuse drugs. For white youths, none of the protective factors enter the final model.

Figure 18.5
Predicting Drug Abuse by Race: Protective and Risk Factors

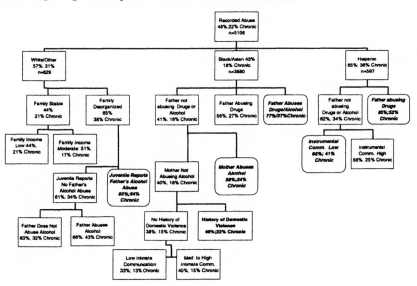

Among black and Hispanic youths, the first predictor of drug abuse is a record of father's drug abuse. Youths whose fathers abuse drugs are more likely to abuse drugs themselves and those whose fathers abuse both alcohol and drugs are even more likely to abuse drugs. Among black youths, the percentage reaches 68 percent, while among Hispanic youths, 85 percent of those whose fathers abuse drugs abuse drugs themselves, and 52 percent are chronic abusers. Among black youths whose fathers have no record of substance abuse, 41 percent abuse drugs themselves.

Mother's alcohol abuse was the next predictor for black youths whose fathers do not abuse alcohol. For those whose mothers abuse alcohol, the percentage who also abused drugs was substantially greater. Among black youths whose fathers did not abuse drugs and whose mothers did not abuse alcohol, a history of domestic violence was the next predictor. Domestic violence alone was almost as strongly associated with a youth's drug abuse as a mother who abused alcohol.

Using these seven risk predictors alone, the model identifies groups of juveniles within which the percent with drug abuse problems ranges from 36 percent (white youths from stable families who are also from the poorest of families), to 85 percent (Hispanic youths whose fathers abuse drugs) against a base rate of 47 percent. Combining the protective and risk variables shows the risk variables to be the more important—no protective variable enters the model until the fourth tier.

For black youths whose fathers do not abuse drugs, whose mothers do not abuse alcohol, and whose families have no histories of domestic violence, the next predictor is intimate communication. Higher scores on intimate communication within the family are again associated with greater drug abuse. On the other hand, for Hispanic youths, whose fathers do not abuse drugs, higher levels of instrumental communication within the family are associated with reduced levels of drug abuse.

The highest level of chronic drug abuse (83 percent) was found for white juveniles who are from disorganized families and who report that their fathers have an alcohol abuse problem.

DISCUSSION

Although levels of drug abuse differ depending on source of data, patterns of abuse across racial groups are valid: abuse levels by black youths are substantially lower than those of white and Hispanic youths. This finding leads to the question of why these usage levels differ by race.

Overall, risk factors are more powerful than protective factors in predicting drug abuse among delinquent youths. This finding may be partly due to the self-report measures of protective factors used for this study. That is, our source of information for level of drug abuse and for many of the risk factors was probation records, while our source of data for protective factors was self-reported scales. This difference in data source my have produced differences in the relative prevalence of risk and protective factors. We do find, however, that self-reports of parental substance abuse were similar to those reported in probation records.

Among delinquent youths, school commitment is the strongest protective factor, followed by intimacy and communication for the low school commitment group and self-esteem for those youths whose school commitment scores are high. Of the potential risk factors, father's drug abuse, mother's alcohol abuse, history of family violence, and prior referral for abuse or neglect are the strongest predictors of drug abuse. Drug abuse is greatest among youths whose fathers abuse drugs and who have been previously referred to the Department of Human Services for Abuse or Neglect (72 percent abuse drugs; 45 percent abuse chronically). Running a close second are two groups of juveniles: (1) youths whose fathers are not known to use drugs but whose mothers abuse alcohol (61 percent abuse; 28 percent abuse chronically) and (2) youths whose fathers and mothers are not known to be substance abusers but whose families have histories of domestic violence (59 percent abuse; 45 percent abuse chronically).

Racial differences exist in the manner in which protective and risk factors are associated with juvenile drug abuse:

• Among white youths, family disorganization and father's alcohol abuse are the strongest predictors of drug abuse. Instrumental communication appears to be an effective protective factor.

- Among black youths, father's drug abuse, mother's alcohol abuse and family (domestic) violence are the strongest predictors. None of the protective factors identified appear to reduce drug abuse. In fact, low levels of school attachment, intimate communication, and self-esteem are associated with lower levels of drug abuse.
- Among Hispanic youths, father's drug abuse and instrumental communication within the family are the strongest predictors, with drug abuse decreasing as instrumental comunication improves.

CONCLUSION

Examining substance abuse within a delinquent population has two advantages over studies of the general population: (1) such studies detach the etiology of substance abuse from causes of delinquency, and (2) delinquent populations are more likely to contain high levels of those stressors associated with substance abuse. Furthermore, an examination of substance abuse by race exposes causal dynamics that are unique to youths whose relevant life experiences are associated with race. That this perspective is important is underscored by the frequent observation that drug usage rates are associated with race.

Previous research on risk and protective factors has implied that these factors play equal roles in shaping problem behavior. The research reported here demonstrates otherwise: risk factors are more powerful predictors of substance abuse than are protective factors. In some cases, however, the lack of a protective factor is interpreted as a risk factor. For example, low self-esteem is viewed as a problem both in studies of delinquency and in our culture generally. Positive self-esteem, on the other hand, is thought to act as a safeguard against negative peer influence and the stresses of everyday life. Nonetheless, this study has demonstrated the power of specific, family-based risk factors in increasing the likelihood of adolescent substance abuse.

We find support for the conclusions of Felix-Ortiz and Newcomb (1992) regarding drug use among Latino and white youths. Usage by parents and family disorganization clearly dominate our final model. Differences in the nature of these relationships by race were also found, however. For Latino youths, a drug-using father increases the likelihood of a youth's drug use. For white youths, however, the substance abuse problem is with alcohol. Both the youths themselves and the probation records identify alcohol abuse as the problem substance of white fathers.

Among families of Latino youths, low levels of instrumental communication increase the likelihood of adolescent drug use. Among the families of white youths, however, the behavioral issues pertain to family disorganization combined with relatively high family incomes.

Black youths share with Latino youths the impact of drug-abusing fathers. This fact seems at odds with the finding that a high proportion of black youths lives with single mothers. It may be that these youths are very aware of their fathers and their substance abuse, in spite of their absence in the home. Their exposure to domestic violence appears, too, to contribute to an increase in substance abuse. Domestic violence alone was almost as strongly associated with a youth's drug abuse as a mother who abused alcohol. What is most puzzling among black youths is the way in which the self-report scale "Intimate Communication (with parents)" was associated with drug abuse. For those black youths whose fathers do not abuse drugs, whose mothers do not abuse alcohol, and whose families have no histories of domestic violence, higher scores on intimate communication within the family are associated with greater drug abuse. In fact, when we isolated the protective factors for analysis, a low level of school attachment, a high intimate communication score and a high self-esteem score were a pattern associated with higher levels of drug abuse, but only for black youths. The discontinuity between self-esteem and personal efficacy among blacks that has been noted in the literature would indicate that for some of these youths, alienation from the rules of the larger society may explain a comfort with behaviors generally seen as deviant (Hughes & Denno 1989).

The paramount importance of parental drug use in shaping the drug-using behavior of adolescents has been greatly underestimated in previous research. Those treatment programs serving Philadelphia's delinquent youths and directed at drug-abusing delinquents focus on the individual youths; few program activities are directed at family issues, and none are directed at substance abuse by parents. This seems rather odd to us, in light of the impact of social learning theories on our understanding of child and adolescent behavior. Rather than build more therapeutic communities that isolate juveniles from the environments that helped to mold the behavior patterns with which we are concerned, family systems approaches may hold more promise. Granted, substance-abusing parents may not be amenable to treatment, but ignoring the impact of their values, attitudes, and actions with respect to drug use seems naive.

Implications for Further Research

It is apparent that, taken as a whole, research into racial/ethnic differences in substance use has barely stepped outside the realm of epidemiology, or simply making cross-group comparisons of rates. Scholars are still at the point of working out the best, most accurate ways to collect, analyze, and report these data. While most recognize that the disproportionate rate of dropping out is likely to affect group comparisons, the development of correction formulas is in the nascent stages. Some are beginning to address issues of underreporting. More researchers are recognizing the importance of disaggregating rates by gender and racial/ethnic subgroup. In short, while there is nearly across-the-board concurrence regarding the relative frequency of drug and alcohol use among African American, Latino, and Anglo youth, scholars are far from agreeing that these results reflect reality.

ProDES is unusual in that it collects information on substance use/abuse from a number of sources, including self-report and assessment by staff professionals. Triangulation of methods such as this can improve confidence that racial trends in substance use/abuse are not simply a statistical artifact. This is an important first step toward moving to issues of etiology, or explaining these differences.

Future theory testing needs to address issues of acculturation, stress, family and peer influences, and other structural and/or cultural factors that may better enable us to predict substance use across racial/ethnic groups. Issues of social class or socioeconomic status need to be addressed (Booth et al. 1990; Gilbert & Alcocer 1988; Negy & Woods 1992b). Perhaps most importantly, more research needs to be carried out on African American youths and their reasons for abstaining (Tyre 1998). This approach could hold the key to preventing and intervening with white and Latino substance users.

Finally, the relative impact of specific risk and protective factors that impact drug abuse among adolescents needs further investigation. Prevention strategies based on lists of such factors may be misdirected if the relative potency of these different factors is not taken into account. We have found, in particular, that the impact of parental substance abuse and chaotic, conflict-filled families is much greater than any other risk and protective factors. New intervention strategies are needed that target these problems.

NOTES

1. Studies including rates for other racial/ethnic groups indicate that Native Americans have the highest prevalence of substance use and Asian Americans have the lowest (Oetting & Beauvais, 1990). Etiology of substance use and further discussion of rates will not be included here, as the racial/ethnic groups of interest in this review are African Americans, Latinos, and Whites.

2. In addition, race remains a significant predictor of substance use after controls are provided for sociodemographic characteristics and lifestyle variables (Kandel, 1995).

3. The National Senior Survey is part of the Monitoring the Future project (Bachman et al., 1991).

4. One percent of both White and Black seniors reported ever using heroin.

5. Indeed, rates of substance use vary between Latino subgroups. For instance, Puerto Ricans are more likely than Cubans to use drugs and alcohol (Booth et al., 1990).

6. It should be noted that accurate assessments of dropout rates are very difficult to obtain (Oetting & Beauvais, 1990).

7. Note that, while previously mentioned studies do focus on ethnic enclaves (e.g., Miami and areas of the Southwest), these are not necessarily the areas of concentrated social and economic disadvantage to which Oetting and Beauvais (1990) are referring.

8. For a discussion of issues relating to measuring acculturation, see Negy and Woods (1992a) and Felix-Ortiz and Newcomb (1992).

9. Some research suggests that socioeconomic status (SES) and acculturation are strongly correlated and that SES has an even stronger effect on some outcomes than acculturation (Negy & Woods, 1992b). SES is rarely controlled for in these studies, however.

10. Family members can also negatively influence Black adolescents. Parker and Sussman (1993) report that African American youths frequently begin tobacco use because their parents and relatives provide them with access to it.

REFERENCES

Bachman, Jerald G., J. M. Wallace Jr., P. M. O'Malley, L. D. Johnston, C.L. Kurth, and H. W. Neighbors. (1991). "Racial/Ethnic Differences in Smoking, Drinking, and Illicit Drug Use among American High School Seniors, 1976–89." *American Journal of Public Health* 81: 372–377.University Press.

Booth, Mary W., F. G. Castro, and M. D. Anglin. (1990). "What Do We Know About Hispanic Substance Abuse? A Review of the Literature." In Ronald Glick and J. Moore, *Drugs in Hispanic Communities*. New Brunswick, NJ: Rutgers University Press.

Chavez, E. L. and R. C. Swaim. (1992a). "An Epidemiological Comparison of Mexican American and White Non-Hispanic 8th- and 12th-Grade Students' Substance Use." *American Journal of Public Health* 82: 445–447.

———. (1992b). "Hispanic Substance Use: Problems in Epidemiology." In Trimble, Bolek, and Niemcryk (eds.), *Ethnic and Multicultural Drug Abuse: Perspectives on Current Research*.

Coombs, R. H., M. J. Paulson, and M. A. Richardson. (1991). "Peer vs. Parental Influence in Substance Use among Hispanic and Anglo Children and Adolescents." *Journal of Youth and Adolescence* 20: 73–88.

Dembo, R., L. Williams, and J. Schmeidler. (1998). "A Theory of Drug Use and Delinquency among High-Risk Youths." In A. R. Roberts (ed.), *Juvenile Justice: Policies, Programs and Services* 273–311. Chicago: Nelson-Hall.

Elliot, D. S., D. Huizinga, and S. S. Ageton. (1985). *Explaining Delinquency and Drug Use*. Beverly Hills, CA: Sage.

Fagan, J., J. G. Weis, and Y. Cheng. (1990). "Delinquency and Substance Use among Inner-City Students." *Journal of Drug Issues* 20: 351–402.

Farabee, David, L. Wallisch, and J. C. Maxwell. (1995). "Substance Use among Texas Hispanics and Non-Hispanics: Who's Using, Who's Not, and Why." *Hispanic Journal of Behavioral Sciences* 17: 523–536.

Felix-Ortiz, M. and M. D. Newcomb. (1995). "Cultural Identity and Drug Use among Latino and Latina Adolescents." In G. J. Botvin, G. P. Schinke, and Orlandi, (eds.), *Drug Abuse Prevention With Multiethnic Youth*.

———. (1992). "Risk and Protective Factors for Drug Use among Latino and White Adolescents." Hispanic Journal of Behavioral Sciences 14: 291–309.

Fendrich, M. and C. M. Vaughn. (1994). "Diminished Lifetime Substance Use over Time: An Inquiry into Differential Underreporting." *Public Opinion Quarterly* 58: 96–123.

Flannery, D. J., A. T. Vazsonyi, J. Torquati, and A. Fridrich. (1994). "Ethnic and Gender Differences in Risk for Early Adolescent Substance Abuse." *Journal of Youth and Adolescence* 23: 195–213.

Frankenberg, R. (1993). *White Women, Race Matters*. St. Paul: University of Minnesota Press.

Frauenglass, S., D. K. Routh, H. M. Pantin, and C. A. Mason. (1997). "Family Support Decreases Influence of Deviant Peers on Hispanic Adolescents' Substance Use." *Journal of Clinical Child Psychology* 26: 15–23.

Gilbert, M. J. and A. M. Alcocer. (1988). "Alcohol Use and Hispanic Youth: An Overview." *Journal of Drug Issues* 18: 33–48.

Glick, R. and J. Moore. (1990). *Drugs in Hispanic Communities*. New Brunswick, NJ: Rutgers University Press.

Greenwood, P. W. (1992). "Substance Abuse Problems among High-Risk Youth and Potential Interventions." *Crime and Delinquency* 38: 444–458.

Hawkins, J. D. and R. F. Catalano. (1992). *Communities That Care*. San Francisco: Jossey-Bass.

Hernandez, L. P. and E. Lucero. (1996). "DAYS La Familia Community Drug and Alcohol Prevention Program: Family-Centered Model for Working with Inner-City

Hispanic Families." *The Journal of Primary Prevention* 16: 255–272.

Hughes, M. and D. H. Denno. (1989). "Self-Perceptions of Black Americans: Self-Esteem and Personal Efficacy." *American Journal of Sociology* 16: 132–159.

Johnson, E. M. and J. L. Delgado. (1989). "Reaching Hispanics with Messages to Prevent Alcohol and Other Drug Abuse." *Public Health Reports* 104: 588–594.

Jones, P. R., P. W. Harris, and M. W. Bachovchin. (1997). *ProDES System Trends Report, 1994–1996.* Philadelphia: Crime and Justice Research Institute.

Kandel, D. B. (1995). "Ethnic Differences in Drug Use: Patterns and Paradoxes." In Botvin, Schinke, and Orlandi (eds.), *Drug Abuse Prevention with Multiethnic Youth.*

Khoury, E. L., G. J. Warheit, R. S. Zimmerman, W. A. Vega, and A. G. Gil. (1996). "Gender and Ethnic Differences in the Prevalence of Alcohol, Cigarette, and Illicit Drug Use over Time in a Cohort of Young Hispanic Adolescents in South Florida." *Women and Health* 24: 21–40.

Lehman, J. D., J. D. Hawkins, and R. F. Catalano. (1994). "Reducing Risks and Protecting Our Youths: A Community Mission." *Corrections Today* 56(5): 92–100.

National Institute on Drug Abuse. (1992) *National Household Survey on Drug Abuse: Population Estimates 1991.* Rockville, MD: Denise B. Kandel.

Negy, C. and D. J. Woods. (1992a). "The Importance of Acculturation in Understanding Research with Hispanic-Americans." *Hispanic Journal of Behavioral Sciences* 14: 224–247.

———. (1992b). "A Note on the Relationship between Acculturation and Socioeconomic Status." *Hispanic Journal of Behavioral Sciences* 14: 248–251.

Oetting, E. R., and F. Beauvais. (1990). "Adolescent Drug Use: Findings of National and Local Surveys." *Journal of Consulting and Clinical Psychology* 58: 385–394.

Parker, V. and S. Sussman. (1993). "Socioenvironmental Influences on the Introduction of African American Youth to Cigarettes." Paper presented at the 121st annual meeting of the American Public Health Association, San Francisco.

Rebach, H. (1992). "Alcohol and Drug Use among American Minorities." In Trimble, Bolek, and Niemcryk (eds.), *Ethnic and Multicultural Drug Abuse: Perspectives on Current Research.*

Resnick, M. D., P. S. Bearman, R. W. Blum, K. E. Bauman, K. M. Harris, J. Jones, J. Tabor, T. Beuhring, R. E. Sieving, M. Shew, M. Irelan, L. H. Bearinger, and R. Udry. (1997). *Journal of the American Medical Association* 278(September 10): 823–832.

Ringwalt, Christopher L. and J. H. Palmer. (1990). "Differences between White and Black Youth Who Drink Heavily." *Addictive Behaviors* 15: 455–460.

Schinke, S. P., M. S. Moncher, J. Palleja, L. H. Zayas, and R. F. Schilling. (1988). "Hispanic Youth, Substance Abuse, and Stress: Implications for Prevention Research." *The International Journal of the Addictions* 23: 809–826.

Swaim, R. C., F. Beauvais, E. L. Chavez, and E. R. Oetting. (1997). "The Effect of Dropout Rates on Estimates of Adolescent Substance Use among Three Racial/Ethnic Groups." *American Journal of Public Health* 87: 51–55.

Tyre, Peg. (1998). "African American Teens in NYC Stop Using Heroin." *CNN interactive.* http://cnn.com/US9805/19/heroin.unchic/index.html? (May 19).

Vega, W. A., A. G. Gil, and R. S. Zimmerman. (1993). "Patterns of Drug Use among Cuban-American, African American, and White Non-Hispanic Boys." *American Journal of Public Health* 83: 257–259.

Wallace, J. M., Jr., J. G. Bachman, P. M. O'Malley, and L. D. Johnston. (1995). "Racial/

Ethnic Differences in Adolescent Drug Use: Exploring Possible Explanations. In Botvin, Schinke, and Orlandi (eds.), *Drug Abuse Prevention with Multiethnic Youth.*

Welte, J. W. and Grace M. Barnes. (1986). "Alcohol Use among Minority Groups." *Journal of Studies on Alcohol* 48: 329–336.

Chapter 19

Prisons as "Safe Havens" for African-American Women

Zelma Weston-Henriques and
Delores D. Jones-Brown

INTRODUCTION

While men continue to return to prison after their release, and with more women now being incarcerated, they, too, are returning to prison in increasing numbers. While conventional society views prisons as places of punishment and terror, there is a mounting body of evidence that, for some, prisons are, in fact, viewed as safe havens—places of relative comfort and stability (in comparison to the threat of hunger and homelessness), places where the government is mandated to protect the individual (in comparison to neighborhoods where the police and ambulance services never arrive or never arrive in time), and places of employment (in comparison to neighborhoods where hopes of legitimate gainful employment have long departed like white and middle-class black neighbors). Not surprisingly, therefore, minorities, especially African Americans and Hispanics, are among those most likely to describe prison as a safe haven.

However, the following quote from a judge in reference to a female offender reflects a consensus of sorts. He notes:

I've put her in programs and she's violated probation three times. She's out there in the street hurting herself and doesn't have any place to stay or any people to go to. So I give her six months at the House of Correction. There aren't any other alternatives. And I'm sending her there only because there's nothing for her in the community. At least in there she's safe, at least being there gives her a chance to dry out and a safe place to sleep. (Watterson 1996: 29).

Based on this scenario, it is clear not only that some offenders regard prison as a safe haven but that those who administer the system also consider it such. Consequently, it appears that the notion of prisons as safe havens warrants further examination, especially within a society that intends its prisons to have a punitive and deterrent effect. While prison appears to be considered a safe haven by men and women confined there, the focus of this chapter is on African American women.

AFRICAN AMERICAN WOMEN AND PENAL CONFINEMENT

Like African American men, African American women make up a disproportionate share of the population of people in state and federal prisons. Drug laws have significantly increased the rate of African American women's incarceration, with more than 80 percent of imprisoned female crack cocaine offenders falling within that group. Compared to white women in prison, incarcerated African American women are less likely to be high school graduates, more likely to be single mothers, less likely to have ever had a (legitimate) job, more likely to be on welfare, and more likely to have been raised in a father-absent family. Prior to incarceration, the majority of such women were the single-parent provider for more than one child, which for most means that they lived at or near the poverty level. Given this combination of circumstances, a significant number of African American women who find themselves behind bars have been raised in neighborhoods of concentrated poverty and subjected to both childhood and adulthood physical, emotional, and often sexual abuse (Richie 1996). Given this state of affairs, there is little wonder that such women view prison as a safe haven.

As noted in the statements of women offenders included later in this chapter, being confined does, in fact, provide such women an opportunity to be free from the overwhelming responsibilities of parenthood; to attempt drug addiction treatment without as much temptation as presented by "free" life; to avoid the pressures of "free" life that may have led to drug addiction; and to avoid the fists and influences of lovers who may have entrapped them into crime (Richie 1996).

In a sense, the safe haven of prison for these women is much like the Quakers' penitentiary. It provides the women with an opportunity to reflect and repent, but it also provides food, shelter, employment, and medical, psychological, and other treatment not available in the outside world without a welfare or Medicaid card. According to Shelden (1998) it is especially ironic that we are experiencing what politicians are calling "the end of welfare as we know it. The irony is that we are experiencing a new form of welfare and it's called the prison system." (7)

BEYOND THE PENITENTIARY

Beyond perhaps having contributed to the recent and, in most places, rather small national drop in crime, Watterson (1996) notes that the expansion of our prison system over the past two decades has had no impact on crime rates, except, perhaps, to destroy lives and to create more crime by producing more hardened criminals. He notes additionally that prisons strip prisoners of their dignity, their health, and whatever self-esteem they once might have had. Prisons also punish the children and families of prisoners (21).

However, for those already feeling a sense of social disfranchisement (the have-nots), while producing all of the negatives that Watterson suggests, prison simultaneously provides many of the comforts regularly accruing to the haves. While the goods and services received inside prison may not be comparable in quality to those received by the haves on the outside, at least for this group of disfranchised individuals the goods and services do exist.

Beyond the walls of the prison, many of these individuals live in neighborhoods we call communities, but are they really? Perhaps it is the lack of community on the outside that makes the prison community seem attractive. While some would argue that imprisonment destroys the fiber of a community, perhaps the more pertinent question is whether these individuals ever felt a part of their communities. McCold and Wachtel (1998: 72) note: "Where there is no perception of connectedness among a group of people, there is no community." They note further, "Although we may live in the same neighborhood, municipality, county, state or nation, be governed and served by the same institutions, we may have no sense that we are part of a unified group. As such, we are not a community."

For reasons outlined in Chapter 11, African Americans may have cause to feel isolated from community more so than do other groups. For reasons related to existence within a male-dominant, paternalistic society, African American women may be more susceptible to feeling isolated from a sense of community, especially when they must raise their children alone. Braithwaite (1989) explains how offenders who have been stigmatized by the justice system often are drawn together to form their own subcultures. These become communities in themselves, unsympathetic to the norms of conduct and the morality of the larger society. Weiss (1987) notes that the influence any community has on individuals belonging to that community (community as a perception of connectedness to an individual or a group) is an important source of informal control. Especially within the confines of the prison environment, where there is less external stimulus, women may feel a greater sense of personal control.

For example, they may get a prison job despite the fact that evidence suggests that, for the most part, the people who populate our prisons are people who have few marketable skills and are not good at making money (Watterson 1996: 23). The fact that the prison job pays only a few dollars a week is inconsequential, given the fact that evidence from the Bureau of Justice Statistics indicates that in 1989, 55.7 percent of the women in jail reported that prior to being arrested, they had earned less than $500 a month, and their mostly petty economic crimes produce equally insubstantial sums (23). On the outside, the women still had to care for children and pay for rent, clothing, and food with that $500. In the safe haven of prison the demands on meager earnings are much less stringent. Also, the lack of complexity of most prison jobs makes irrelevant the fact that the vast number of those in prison lack legitimate, marketable skills.

THE FALLOUT

According to Carnegie-Mellon University criminologist Alfred Blumstein, we are weakening the role of the criminal justice system by locking up as many people as we do. Incarceration totals in 1996 reached almost 1.7 million (Butterfield 1997). In California, where the number of prisoners grew from 19,000 two decades ago to 150,000 in 1997, the state now faces a crisis because it is caught between voters' refusal to approve more money for prison construction and an unexpectedly huge influx of inmates over the next few years as more and more tough sentencing laws take effect (Butterfield 1997).

To avoid this dilemma, the North Carolina legislature recently adopted sentencing guidelines for judges based on a computer model showing how much bed space is available in the state's prisons, much like a hotel reservation system. While the huge increase in the number of inmates has helped to slightly lower the crime rate by incapacitating more criminals behind bars, this increase has had an impact in other areas. For example, in 1990 alone, the number of prison and jail guards nationwide increased by about 30 percent, to more than 60,000. Consequently, there are now communities vigorously competing to become the site of future prisons. Recently, this became the case in Tupper Lake, New York. Jack Dewyea, a lifetime resident of Tupper Lake and a strong supporter of the location of a supermaximum prison in Tupper Lake, argued that if the location of the prison is moved farther north, Tupper Lake would be denied an opportunity for the community to build an economic future. "I've never heard of the state closing down a prison," said Dean Lefebvre, supervisor of the town of Atamont, population 6,200, which includes Tupper Lake. "They'll be here long after I'm gone. It's a stable industry (Hughes 1997: 24A). (The prison represents the biggest investment in Tupper Lake, where the median income is 28 percent below state average.)

Hence, much as the economic base of the country was built upon the backs of both male and female African American slaves, the economic future of numerous business-deprived areas depends on the continued imprisonment of a substantial portion of people. A significant portion, probably the majority, of those people will be African American, and, given current sentencing patterns, a substantial subset of that portion will be African American women.

Acknowledging that incarceration/imprisonment was meant to deter crime by stigmatizing people with the threat of imprisonment, Blumstein argues that we have locked up so many people that imprisonment has lost its stigmatizing effect (Butterfield 1997). Evidence that both inmates and the judges who send them to prison have come to view the prison as a safe haven confirms Blumstein's claim. The fact that those for whom this view is likely to be espoused and those offenders from whom the view is likely to be recounted are African American (and, to a lesser degree, Hispanic) is evidence of a surrender of sorts. Society, having failed to provide adequate opportunities for such individuals to gain socioeconomic well-being within the larger structure, has settled for providing what is necessary through institutionalization. Individuals, having failed to achieve the elusive trappings of the American Dream, have settled for safety in institutionalization. This is so despite the fact that being locked up hastens the breakdown of their relationships with their families and communities, further damages the fragile balance of their lives, removes them from their responsibility for their behavior, and then returns them illequipped to live normal, crime-free lives (Watterson 1996: 23). As a result, a growing number of those released after being imprisoned return to the institution before very long.

While recidivism and the concept of becoming "institutionalized" are not new, the fact that these phenomena are occurring after only short prison terms and among relatively young offenders is a matter for great concern.

The following quotes from African American women involved in a prison therapeutic community support the notion that prison is, indeed, a safe haven from poverty, drug addiction, and homelessness:

For me prison hasn't been the end of the world. It's been a beginning—a chance to stand aside and look. When I tell you I've grown in the seven months I've been here, I mean it. Not because of any programs—there aren't any. But because of the people I've lived with and the bed I've slept on. And I'm beginning to live with myself and accept myself. I know I'm more of a woman, a valuable soul, than I ever would have been if I hadn't come here. (Watterson 1996: 5)

If you can't stop me from coming, do something with me once you have me confined. (Thomie Harper in her presentation "The Trilogy", December 2, 1997, at John Jay College.)

WHY HAVE PRISONS BECOME SAFE HAVENS?

Offenders' experiences following their release have a powerful influence on their adjustment to life in the community. The new releasee faces three harsh realities: the strangeness of reentry, unmet personal needs, and barriers to success (Clear & Cole 1997: 460). For the most part, humans crave familiarity and fear the unknown. One reason that prison has become a safe haven is that women, over time, due to their repeated incarcerations become familiar with the staff and with other women.

To use one prison as an example, the environment at Bedford Hills Correctional Facility in New York provides more than a period of "removal" from society. Its many programs and services provide opportunities for women to reinvent and redefine themselves. Prisons provide for some offenders alternative cognitive frameworks that women can use to understand themselves and their lives. For example, in the Family Violence Program at Bedford Hills, women are encouraged to draw connections between their experience in childhood abuse and their destructive and self-destructive behaviors as adults (Clark 1995: 310). Watterson (1996) notes that in prison, some friendships give women a chance to address old issues, make connections, and get comfort that helps to heal some of the abuse, emptiness, loneliness, and lack of support they've experienced in the past.

Choices and Changes, another program at Bedford Hills Correctional Facility, encourages women to look at their lives not solely as events that happened to them but as a series of choices determined by circumstances and relationships that they can analyze and change (Clark 1995: 310). A therapist in the Family Violence Program noted that prison life was like a second adolescence (313). This conceptualization, however, raises an old area of concern about women's prisons and their programs. Traditionally, women's prisons have also infantilized and encouraged dependency within women. This enables women to experience/live their childhood, some for the first time. The prison—represented by officers, staff, and administration—acts as a "parent" imposing rules and sanctions, much like the model of a punitive parent who seeks to control the child through sanctions and punishments (315). In fact, prison for many is a substitute for early family life, something they missed or did not have. In that sense it represents something that was taken away and is now being given back, especially among women whose lives have been controlled by abuse and drugs. This, however, may be viewed as simply providing women with an alternative mode of dependency.

For some women, however, the total freedom to administer their own lives may seem too much. Why do so many women refer to prison as a safe haven? Is it that being in prison saved them from destruction, death, and possible mental breakdown? Many women feel that before prison they were out of control (Clark 1995: 309). Prison forces them to take a break and provides time out from the pressures and problems that they faced outside: drugs, violence, finances, housing, child care. It provides time to reevaluate.

For many women, it is an opportunity to live drug-free. It enables the women to focus and think about themselves, sometimes for the first time in their lives. Some of these women did not have the time or the will to think when they were on the outside. In the words of one woman, " I am glad I came back to prison. It gave me time to review." (309).

CONCLUSION

In Richie's (1996) view , even before African American women's official detention, they are imprisoned at different points in their lives in other, more symbolic ways. "They are confined by social conditions in their communities, restrained by their families' circumstances, severely limited by abuse in their intimate relationships, and forced to make hard choices with very few options." The notion, then, of imprisonment is not new and may not require significant adjustment mentally or physically.

It appears, then, that a primary goal for the community adjustment of such women should be mobilizing informal social control mechanisms by strengthening, creating, or restoring healthy interdependence in the outside world and by encouraging the development of a mature sense of internalized control or conscience (McCold & Wachtel (1998: 74). However, this suggestion may be more of an ideal than a real solution, given the numerous obstacles that these women will face. Unless society is willing to make available, in the neighborhoods where these women live, real economic opportunities and real opportunities for social enrichment, rather than menial jobs and poor-quality handouts, the prospect of the prison as a safe, available, and "free" haven looms ever large.

REFERENCES

Braithwaite,J. (1989).*Crime, Shame and Reintegration*. New York: Cambridge University Press.

Butterfield, F. (1997). Crime Keeps On Falling, but Prisons Keep On Filling. *New York Times*, Week in Review Section, September 28, 1, 4.

Clark, J. (1995). The Impact of the Prison Environment on Mothers. *The Prison Journal* 75(3)(September): 306-329.

Clear, T. and G. Cole. (1997). *American Corrections*. 4th ed. Belmont, CA: Wadsworth.

Hughes, K. (1997) "Proposed Prison Splits Adirondack Community." *Gannett Newspaper*, November 16, 24A.

McCold, Paul and Benjamin Wachtel. (1998). "Community Is Not a Place: A New Look at Community Justice Initiatives." *Contemporary Justice Review Issues in Criminal, Social and Restorative Justice, Special Issue* 1(1).

Richie, B. E. (1996). *Compelled to Crime: The Gender Entrapment of Battered Black Women*. New York: Routledge.

Shelden, Randall G. (1998). "The New American Apartheid: The Incarceration of African-Americans." Paper presented at the Annual Meeting of the North Eastern Association of Criminal Justice Sciences, Bristol, Rhode Island, June 11-14.

Watterson, K. (1996). *Women in Prison*. Rev. ed. Boston: Northeastern University Press.

Weiss, R. P. (1987). "The Community and Prevention." In E. H. Johnson (ed.), *Handbook on Crime and Delinquency Prevention* 113-135. Westport, CT: Greenwood Press.

Index

About the Editors and Contributors

ANTHONY TROY ADAMS is Associate Professor of Sociology at Eastern Michigan University. He regularly teaches courses in introductory sociology, statistics, research methodology, and sociology of education. Adams' research interests include school discipline and policy, violence, and the impact of race and class on educational attainment. He is currently at work on the effects of class size and other organizational variables on punishment in public secondary schools.

RAMONA BROCKETT is Assistant Professor of Criminal Justice at Kent State University in Kent, Ohio. Her research and publishing focus primarily concerns civil liberties issues affected by the U. S. Supreme Court, police, race, and class. Her 1995 publication *The Role of the JD in Criminal Justice Education,* coauthored by Delores Jones-Brown, focuses on her "Coca-Cola bottle theory," which analyzes the twentieth-century Supreme Court. Presently, she is developing this theory and working on a book that will elaborate her theory and focus on Supreme Court outcomes for the twenty-first century.

LIQUN CAO is Associate Professor of Sociology, Anthropology and Criminology at Eastern Michigan University. Currently, his research interests are in the areas of community-oriented policing, police brutality, juvenile delinquency, criminological theory, and comparative criminology.

STEVEN R. CURETON was the recipient of the 1996 American Society of Criminology Minority Fellowship Award. His interests are primarily in gang formation, development, and activity, the effects of race on formal social control, and the effects of family processes on crime/deviance. He is currently Assistant Professor at the University of North Carolina at Greensboro.

JAMIE J. FADER is Research Associate at the Crime and Justice Research Institute in Philadelphia, Pennsylvania.

EVELYN GILBERT is a criminologist whose research interests include criminal justice education, minorities and criminal justice, elderly homicide, and the military justice system.

ANNETTE M. GIRONDI has been a member of the psychology faculty at Widener University in Chester, Pennsylvania, since 1995. She has published articles on topics related to social interaction, perceptions, and work-related attitudes. She has worked as a consultant to develop selection and promotion tests and has developed and presented a seminar on team building and diversity. She is a member of various professional organizations, including the Society for Human Resource Management, the Association for Quality and Participation, and the Society for Industrial and Organizational Psychologists. She is also a board member for the Delaware Valley Chapter of the Association for Quality and Participation.

HELEN TAYLOR GREENE is Associate Professor in the Department of Sociology and Criminal Justice at Old Dominion University, Norfolk, Virginia. Her primary research area is blacks, crime, and justice. She is also involved in efforts to integrate contributions by black scholars into criminology and criminal justice courses. She coauthored with Vernetta Young an article entitled "Pedagogical Reconstruction: Incorporating African American Perspectives into the Curriculum." She has also published articles on black female delinquency, community policing in Florida and Virginia, police brutality, and teaching delinquency. She is currently completing a book on African American criminological thought, coauthored by Shaun Gabbidon.

PHILIP W. HARRIS is Associate Professor of Criminal Justice in Philadelphia, Pennsylvania. His areas of research include ongoing studies of the effectiveness of programs for delinquent youths in Philadelphia.

VICKIE J. JENSEN is Assistant Professor in the Department of Sociology, California State University–Northridge. Her research interests are women in crime, violence, homelessness, and the social organization of prisons and other institutions. Her research has included social types in a women's prison, conversation analysis of homeless women, and prejudice against ex-offenders.

SCOTT L. JOHNSON is Assistant Professor of Criminal Justice at Buffalo State College in Buffalo, New York. His research interests include minority perspectives in criminal justice, theories of crime and justice, and criminal justice ethics. He is currently researching applications of Christian ethics to policy and institutional racism in the administration of the death penalty.

PETER R. JONES is Associate Professor of Criminal Justice at Temple University in Philadelphia, Pennsylvania. His current research agenda focuses on issues dealing with juvenile justice, law enforcement, and program development.

DELORES D. JONES-BROWN is Assistant Professor in the department of Law, Police Science, and Criminal Justice Administration at John Jay College, City University of New York. She has also taught at Temple University, the Newark Campus of Rutgers University, and Rowan College of New Jersey (formerly Glassboro State College). She is currently a fellow at the National Development and Research Institutes, Inc. Her practical experience in criminal justice includes having spent 3 years as an assistant prosecutor and more than 15 years working with institutional and community-based corrections programs for adult offenders. She has spent the last 5 years conducting research and developing programs for at-risk and delinquent youth.

JANICE JOSEPH is a member of the faculty at Richard Stockton College in Pomona, New Jersey.

PAUL KNEPPER is Associate Professor, East Carolina University School of Social Work, where he teaches in the criminal justice program. His articles on judicial definitions of race, the politics of race/crime statistics, and imprisonment of ethnic minority populations have appeared in diverse journals, including *Criminal Justice Review, Southeast Review of Asian Studies, Social Justice,* and *Southern University Law Review.*

DANIEL KOLODZIEJSKI is a 1998 criminal justice graduate of Widener University in Chester, Pennsylvania.

JAMES P. LEVINE is Executive Officer of the Doctoral Program in Criminal Justice of the City University of New York and Professor of Government at John Jay College of Criminal Justice.

NORMA MANATU-RUPERT is presently Assistant Professor of Speech, Communication and Media Studies at John Jay College of Criminal Justice (CUNY). Her ongoing research interests include ideologies of race and gender as they are represented in film and in the popular culture.

MICHAEL W. MARKOWITZ is Associate Professor and Coordinator of Criminal Justice at Widener University in Chester, Pennsylvania. His areas of research interest and publication include criminology theory, correctional issues, and the nexus between race, crime, and justice.

H. BRUCE PIERCE is currently Associate Professor of Criminal Justice at North Carolina Central University. He was formerly Associate Professor of Criminal

Justice and Police Science at John Jay College of Criminal Justice. His practitioner background includes service as a member of the New York City Transit Police Department and the New York City Police Department's elite Tactical Patrol Force. He has taught psychology at Rikers Island and Brooklyn House of Detention and has chaired the Westchester County Justice Advisory Board and been a member of the county's conditional release commission. He served on the New York State Governor's Law Enforcement Advisory Group and been a consultant-lecturer for the New York City Police Department's Executive Development Program, the New York–New Jersey Port Authority Police, the New York City Housing Police, and the New York City Department of Corrections.

JOHN STILWELL is a 1998 criminal justice graduate of Widener University in Chester, Pennsylvania.

BECKY L. TATUM is Assistant Professor of Criminal Justice at Southern University at New Orleans. Her primary research interests include the etiology of juvenile violence and minority perspectives on crime. She is currently completing a two-year study that examines the utility of African American perspectives on crime and violence for mainstream theorizing and in helping to frame testable hypotheses of crime causation.

KIMBERLY TORCHIANA is a 1998 criminal justice graduate of Widener University in Chester, Pennsylvania.

DARREN E. WARNER has worked for the Kentucky Administrative Office of the Courts as a Research Analyst, where he conducted a statewide study to measure racial bias in the Kentucky courts. He has served as a consultant in developing a telephone survey research center and conducted marketing research for a major marketing firm. He currently serves as Research Associate for the Michigan Public Health Institute, coordinating community health improvement research and evaluation projects. He also teaches at Lansing Community College in Lansing, Michigan.

ZELMA WESTON-HENRIQUES is Professor in the Department of Law, Police Science, and Criminal Justice Administration at John Jay College, City University of New York. Her major research interests are imprisoned mothers and their children; women in prison; race, class, and gender issues; and cross-cultural studies of crime. She is the author of *Imprisoned Mothers and Their Children*.